THE SUPREME COURT

Recent Titles in
Contributions in American Studies
Series Editor: Robert H. Walker

The Modern Corporate State: Private Governments and the
American Constitution
Arthur Selwyn Miller

American Studies: Topics and Sources
Robert H. Walker, editor and compiler

In the Driver's Seat: The Automobile in American Literature
and Popular Culture
Cynthia Golomb Dettelbach

The United States in Norwegian History
Sigmund Skard

Milestones in American Literary History
Robert E. Spiller

A Divided People
Kenneth S. Lynn

The American Dream in the Great Depression
Charles R. Hearn

Several More Lives to Live: Thoreau's Political Reputation
in America
Michael Meyer

The Indians and Their Captives
James Levernier and Hennig Cohen, editors and compilers

Concerned About the Planet: *The Reporter* Magazine and
American Liberalism, 1949–1968
Martin K. Doudna

New World Journeys: Contemporary Italian Writers and
the Experience of America
Angela M. Jeannet and Louise K. Barnett, editors and translators

Family, Drama, and American Dreams
Tom Scanlan

Hemispheric Perspectives on the United States: Papers from
the New World Conference
Joseph S. Tulchin, editor, with the assistance of Maria A. Leal

"Ezra Pound Speaking": Radio Speeches of World War II
Leonard W. Doob, editor

THE SUPREME COURT

COURT
Myth
and
Reality

ARTHUR SELWYN MILLER

CONTRIBUTIONS IN AMERICAN STUDIES, NUMBER 38

GREENWOOD PRESS

WESTPORT, CONNECTICUT • LONDON, ENGLAND

Library of Congress Cataloging in Publication Data

Miller, Arthur Selwyn, 1917-
    The Supreme Court.

    (Contributions in American studies ; no. 38
ISSN 0084-9227)
    Bibliography: p.
    Includes index.
    1. United States.   Supreme Court.   I. Title.
KF8742.M54   347'.73'26   77-91106
ISBN 0-313-20046-7

Library of Congress Catalog Card Number: 77-91106
ISBN: 0-313-20046-7
ISSN: 0084-9227

First published in 1978

Greenwood Press, Inc.
51 Riverside Avenue, Westport, Connecticut 06880

Printed in the United States of America

10 9 8 7 6 5 4 3 2 1

. . . for Dagmar
con amor . . . siempre . . .

CONTENTS

FOREWORD

WE ARE so accustomed to thinking of the Constitution as law that we forget that first and foremost it is a political document. The creation of a government is a political act. The Constitution specifies the structure, organization, and many of the processes of the various branches of the government, and it sets forth the powers of the national government and limitations on the powers of both national and state governments. A critical question before the framers in 1787 was how to enforce the Constitution, both its powers and its limitations. Most governments throughout history have enforced their powers through a police state, which means that there are no limitations on power. Such an alternative was never considered by the framers. James Madison thought the greatest threat to the Constitution would come from the state governments. (He was right.) Accordingly, he advocated that national supremacy be protected by a device called the congressional negative, which meant that all state laws would routinely be subject to approval or veto by Congress—a breathtaking conception, then and now. The method finally chosen by the framers was judicial enforcement through the normal processes of litigation and adjudication. Hence the intentional parallelism between Article VI, which states that the Constitution, laws, and treaties of the United States are the supreme law of the land, and Article III, which grants judicial power over all cases that arise under the Constitution, laws, and treaties.

This was something new in history: a government whose powers were specifically limited in writing, and the enforcement of a political system through legal processes instead of military force, placing government itself under the rule of law as declared by one branch of the government, the judiciary.

Even a first reading of the Constitution reveals that it speaks in different levels of language. The provisions dealing with the qualifications for office, structure, organization, and the like are written in relatively specific and definite terms. However, when we look at the Constitution's great substantive clauses, those dealing with powers and limitations, we find highly general language which on its face does not define its content and scope. Obvious examples are "commerce among the several states"; "necessary and proper"; "unreasonable searches and seizures";—and that most important phrase of all—"due process of law." These ambiguous provisions demand interpretation and application to a host of specific contexts. Since our society is not static but dynamic, endlessly changing and evolving, the problem situations to which the broad language of the Constitution must be applied are always contemporary and novel. As early as the 1830s, de Tocqueville noted the phenomenon that American social and economic controversies tend to become constitutional issues resolved by the courts and ultimately the Supreme Court. He could never have imagined the extent to which that process would be carried by the 1970s.

Through the rendition of thousands of constitutional decisions over the years, the Supreme Court has created a vast reservoir of doctrines, principles, tests, techniques, and case precedents, and it continues to create new ones. The results of the cases and the opinions that are written (usually several) are, to put it mildly, conflicting and confusing, and one can always find language somewhere in some opinion to support just about any point of view. Hence, any case can be disposed of in several ways, all of which are legally justifiable. It seems altogether clear that in its constitutional decisions the Supreme Court is not bound, but merely guided, by the text of the document, the historical intention of the framers, its own doctrines, or its own case precedents. The Court exercises what Holmes called the "sovereign prerogative of choice" and, in the final analysis, the decision is a policy judgment that reflects the legal, political, social, and economic philosophies of the members of the Court. The disclaimer of one Justice was unintentionally revealing: "It is not we who speak, but the Constitution which speaks through us." Two other variables should be mentioned—the changing composition of the Court, which alters the philosophic mix, and the Court's power to decide what cases it will decide.

In short, constitutional law is not like other law and the Supreme Court is not like other courts. Constitutional law is public policy and the Supreme Court is a policy-making instrument of government.

Many years ago, Charles Evans Hughes (the only Justice in history to be appointed to the Supreme Court twice, once as an Associate Justice and later as Chief) said that "We live under a Constitution, but the Constitution is what the Supreme Court says it is." As one would guess, he was not on the Court when he said it. Another much-quoted phrase describes the Court as a standing constitutional convention. A famous constitutional law professor at Harvard used to tell his students: "Don't read the Constitution. It will only confuse you. Read the Supreme Court's decisions." I cannot understand how he thought that would dispel the confusion.

Do not misunderstand. No one believes that the Court's decisions are quixotic or capricious. To the contrary, they are reasoned and principled, but—and this is the point—they are discretionary within a wide range of available legal guidelines that can be manipulated to produce an opinion, supporting any one of several different results, a result based partially, and perhaps ultimately, on nonlegal factors. This is what it means to be a court of last resort, a court which in the past has frequently, but not recently, been called the conscience of the country. No doubt, the Court's unreviewable discretionary power can be squared with the proposition that we have a government of laws and not of men. But the proposition would have to be interpreted, and, in any event, the argument should be made by someone who feels more strongly about it than I do.

The Court's authority as the final and authoritative interpreter of the Constitution has not always been accepted with docility and respect; sometimes it has been defied with success. I think it fair to say, however, that today the Court's authority is unchallenged and is accepted as binding at all levels—state and federal, public and private—even when disagreement with a particular decision is most intense. On the state level, in the 1950s, an editor in Richmond sought to resurrect the long dormant doctrine of state interposition, but the effort was aborted without even getting into the first trimester. The school segregation, criminal justice, and legislative apportionment cases, among others, dramatically demonstrate the Supreme Court's dominance of the most essential of state powers. On the congressional level, Congress has long acquiesced in the Court's power to invalidate statutes, but more recently has accepted the Court's authority in such peculiarly legislative matters as Congress's power to determine the seating of its own members and the reach of the Speech and Debate Clause. Both President Truman, in the steel seizure case, and

President Nixon, in the Watergate subpoena case, bowed to the Court's definition of presidential power. Obviously, the lower federal and the state courts are bound by the Court's mandates, and certainly they are recognized by the American people as the law. This unanimous national acquiescence in the Court's authority is the prime example at the highest level of what we mean by the rule of law.

Perhaps it would be best to stop there. But if we proceed to ask in what sense the Court itself is bound by the rule of law, we realize at once that the answer is neither simple nor easy. The external controls over the Court's authority—impeachment, curtailment of jurisdiction, or constitutional amendment—are either illusory or impractical. Forty years ago, Justice Stone stated the fact of the matter: "While unconstitutional exercise of power by the executive and legislative branches of the government is subject to judicial restraint, the only check upon our exercise of power is our own sense of self-restraint." That, of course, was written in a dissenting opinion.

Indeed, some of the most devastating and scathing attacks on the Supreme Court's performance in the last twenty years have come from members of the Court themselves in dissenting opinions. At one time or another, I venture to say, every member of the Court has accused the majority of an unwarranted usurpation of the power of Congress, the President, or the states, or of having distorted or ignored the Constitution. Perhaps some enterprising law review student could do a doctrinal analysis of the differences between sheer power, naked power and raw power as those terms are used in dissenting opinions. I would add only that each member of the Court has been not only an accuser but also an accused.

Again, do not misunderstand. I am not being critical, but only descriptive. I have no doubt that the Court's present exalted status is thoroughly legitimate, the logical and natural culmination of the power first exercised in 1803 in *Marbury* and gradually developed and extended through our whole history and experience as a nation. I do believe the country at large does not fully understand the Court's power. Nor do I have much doubt that, on net balance, the Court's exercise of power over the years merits more approval than censure. The point is that the Court's decisions are not predestinate or inevitable.

The facility with which men can find in the amorphous language of the Constitution approval and sanction of their own political, social, and economic philosophies prompted John Adams, at an early date in our history, to call the Constitution "a game at leap frog." As historic examples, the Court has alternately expanded and contracted national powers and the limitations on state power, and has changed course, veered, and trimmed on other questions countless numbers of times. The years of the

Warren Court were characterized by a substantial expansion of the constitutional rights and freedoms of individuals against government at all
levels. Today a Court with a more statist philosophy takes a much narrower and more restrictive view of those rights and freedoms. Justice
Black used to liken the process to an accordion.

It was my good fortune, when I began teaching law twenty-five years
ago, to inherit the course in constitutional law. Since I started on short
notice, I used the casebook which had been used by my predecessor, and
that was another piece of luck. The book was *Cases and Materials in Constitutional Law* by John P. Frank, then an associate professor at the Yale
Law School. Originally published in 1950, it went out of print after its
1952 revision when Frank traded law teaching for law practice. My per-
ceptions of the Constitution and the Supreme Court, and the way I have
taught constitutional law through the years, are directly traceable to that
casebook. In large part, it treated constitutional development in historical
chronology and contained excerpts describing the contemporary setting
in which the cases and the decisions emerged. This led me to spend considerable time reading constitutional histories instead of concentrating
exclusively on the analysis of current Court decisions. Thus, I early learned
the truth of Professor Miller's observation that constitutional law is determined to a great extent by the *zeitgeist.*

The Frank casebook also contained biographical sketches of leading
Supreme Court Justices, most of which were taken from the *Dictionary of
American Biography.* I found these sketches so interesting that I turned to
the available full-length biographies of the Justices. I can still remember
the excitement of Mason's 1956 biography of Stone with its fascinating
revelation of the inside maneuverings on the Court and the personalized
nature of the decisional process. I am still a devotee of judicial biographies, the quantity of which, happily, has increased substantially in the
last twenty years.

In short, in my formative years as a teacher I became convinced that
the "what" of constitutional law depends principally on the "when" and
the "who." Thus, I never was victimized by many of the myths about the
Court that are so ably exposed by Professor Miller. (I say "many" because
I happen to believe in two of his myths—that the Supreme Court is un-
democratic and that the Court sometimes encroaches on the legislature.)
The best piece of advice I could give anyone seeking to understand the
Constitution and the Court is to read, in addition to the Court's opinions,
constitutional histories and biographies of Supreme Court Justices.

Unfortunately, most lawyers and law professors never get beyond the
staple diet of the Court's own opinions and the periodical commentary
on those opinions. The opinions themselves are too often no more than

argumentative rationalizations justifying the result which is reached. In accordance with Professor Miller's principle of doctrinal polarity, they demonstrate that, using existing precedents, doctrines, and standard techniques of legal reasoning, most cases at the Supreme Court level can plausibly be decided in many different ways with varying results. While the rationalization may display great or little technical skill, it usually fails to tell us precisely why the opinion-writer chose one result and avenue to reach it rather than another. The opinions which candidly reveal that the choice was dictated by policy considerations are the exceptions rather than the rule.

Most of the law review commentary is similarly unenlightening. It consists largely of doctrinal analysis of the various opinions, in which the commentator seeks to demonstrate the correlation between the "better" reasoning and the result he prefers. Another kind of writing seeks to synthesize a series of decisions dealing with a common problem into a harmonious whole in which a larger consistency explains away smaller ones. This assumes naively that the Court has a higher wisdom which can be found in all its opinions if we only work hard enough to discern it. The most tedious kind of all is the exhaustive over-analysis of a point far beyond its doctrinal or practical importance. Much/some of this writing is well done, and in small doses it is interesting mental exercise. But it reveals little about how well or how poorly the Court is fulfilling its unique function in the American system. I feel free to disparage this kind of writing about the Court because I have done my own fair share of it.

Professor Miller's body of published commentary on the Court, of which the essays in this book are a representative sampling, is of an entirely different order. I feel pretty confident that he would agree with virtually everything I have written so far in this Foreword, but what I have said is in the nature of conclusions. Miller's essays supply the intellectual and analytical foundation upon which those conclusions can solidly rest. More importantly, they should persuade all but the most determined myopics that the myths and realities are truly as he depicts them. My particular favorite among the essays, "The Myth of Neutrality in Constitutional Adjudication," was written in response to Professor Herbert Wechsler's "Toward Neutral Principles of Constitutional Law." My initial reaction to the Wechsler piece was that it showed how misguided even a Holmes lecture at Harvard by a renowned scholar could be. Even so, because it was so highly touted, I felt obliged to require my seminar students to read it, and I provided my own critique. How I welcomed Miller's devastating refutation of Wechsler. Seminars thereafter read the articles back to back, and Miller was always the winner going away.

Miller is not willing to accept the proposition that the Court's constitutional adjudication is just a continuous judicial shell game. He is not content, as the title of the book might suggest, with exposing the myths and revealing the realities. His thinking goes forward to the problem of improving the system in light of its realities. Thus, he does not stop with demonstrating the inadequacy of the adversary system to provide the Court with the information it needs to perform its functions responsibly and well. In addition, he makes several suggestions for improving the flow of information to the Justices. One may believe that it is probably better to leave it to the Justices to develop their own ways of overcoming the deficiencies of the adversary process, or one may disagree with one or more of Miller's suggestions. It must be recognized, however, that Miller's identification of the problem and tentatively proposed solutions constitute perceptive and innovative scholarship at its best.

Miller's call for more impact analysis of Supreme Court decisions is one of the truly seminal articles in recent years. Since the purpose of law is to serve society, it surely is more important to study what the social impact of Court decisions is and ought to be than to parse them internally for flaws in legal reasoning and writing. I think the courts (at least the federal courts) are far ahead of the academic commentators in their appreciation of the consequences of their decisions. In academic circles, the term *result-oriented* has come to be used more to denigrate the judicial process than to praise it. Many professional critics apparently equate Supreme Court decisions with law student examinations—sterile exercises, divorced from reality, to be graded on how well they are written in terms of assumed professional skill standards. Of course, clear thinking and good writing are prime desiderata in judicial decisions and may have an influence on the acceptability of the decision. But the Court's decisions presumably have a significant impact on millions of Americans who never read them. It is that transcendent importance of the decisions which Miller so correctly urges should be the subject of more critical inquiry.

Two components of the Supreme Court's role in our system are not examined in these essays. I mention them in this Foreword in the hope that Miller may bring his impressive talents to bear upon them.

One is the matter of selecting those persons who will exercise the extraordinary judicial power possessed by Supreme Court Justices. The Constitution prescribes only the formal provision that the President appoints subject to the approval of the Senate. The President's discretion is unlimited, and the factors that determine the choice are not usually knowable in entirety. It is clear, however, that throughout our history political and personal considerations have been predominant and that more mediocrities than towering intellects have been ensconced on the High Bench. Senate confirmation hearings usually amount to no more than polite fencing matches over the nominee's political philosophy. Senate refusals to approve nominations have frequently been for questionable reasons and clearly have failed to produce any durable qualification standards. In recent years, persons under consideration by the White House have been submitted to the American Bar Association for grading as to professional qualification. Obviously, this is much too narrow a gauge by which to measure a possible Supreme Court Justice. President Carter has instituted a novel practice for Court of Appeals positions, whereby merit selection committees consisting in part of representatives of nonlegal groups recommend a panel to the President for consideration. I hope that President Carter will use this technique for any future Supreme Court vacancy. For just as war is too important to leave to generals, the appointment of a Supreme Court Justice is too important to be determined solely on the basis of purely professional credentials. At this point, it should be asked whether it is desirable or possible to develop better procedures for screening and selecting those persons who wield the awesome power of Supreme Court Justices.

A second area that needs further inquiry is the selection of cases the Court hears and decides. Each term the Court renders opinions in only 150 to 200 cases out of 4,000 requests for review. The Court's certiorari jurisdiction is, by statute, discretionary. Its jurisdiction of appeals, in which review is theoretically a right of the litigants, has come to be equally discretionary under the Court's "substantial" federal question test. In short, the Court has the power to decide what cases it will decide. But the Court never discloses the reasons for its choices. It is a source of perennial puzzlement why the Court each year denies review of many cases which, to an outsider, seem to pose issues of much greater importance to the nation than the narrow, nitpicking issues that form a substantial portion of the Court's work product each term. Some years back, a Yale law professor compared grants and denials of review over a series of Court terms and finally confessed his inability to make sense out of what the Court was doing. As it stands now, the Court can and does, for its own undisclosed reasons, select critical areas of public policy in American life; bring them before its bar in litigated cases of its own choosing; and then shape and direct them through the medium of constitutional decisions. Recent proposals for a National Court of Appeals and similar suggestions are directed more toward reducing the work load of the Court than influencing the content of its docket. We should ask whether it is desirable or possible to develop mechanisms, other than the Court's private judgment, for choosing the constitutional and statutory problem areas (or at least influencing the choice of such areas) to which the Court's limited resources should be directed. The Office of the Solicitor-General is such a mechanism, but the nature and bases of its screening function—what its criteria for recommending cases for full review are and how they are applied—are virtually free of professional awareness and evaluation.

These essays by my good friend Arthur Miller are a stimulating current of fresh air in the musty corridors where the higher legal learning is presumably researched and expounded. In my judgment, they constitute a significant body of commentary such as can be claimed by few constitutional scholars in America. Whatever future topics he may choose for attention, we can be sure that Professor Miller will be in the legal-intellectual vanguard, exposing myth, coming to grips with reality, and opening up new avenues of constructive thought. Would that the breadth and perception reflected in these essays were found more often in the legal worlds of teaching, advocacy, and judging. I wish I could be more optimistic that it will come to pass.

William P. Murphy
PROFESSOR OF LAW
University of North Carolina
Chapel Hill, North Carolina

ACKNOWLEDGMENTS

THE ESSAYS in this volume were first published in eight different legal periodicals over a period of fifteen years—1960 to 1975. I had the pleasure of working with colleagues on three of them. I wish at the outset to express formally my deep appreciation for all they added to the intrinsic merit of Chapters 3, 6, and 8. Their names are noted in the Table of Contents and at the beginning of these essays.

I am grateful to my friend Bill Murphy for taking the time to write the Foreword. A man of insight and of great courage (during the 1950s, he taught constitutional law in Mississippi in ways not approved by the local power structure), Murphy's basic agreement with what is said in this volume means much to me. I should also like to thank my friend and colleague Robert Walker, the series editor, for his help and guidance. Miss LaMona Rivers has been of indispensable help in the preparation of the manuscript—all of it done with characteristic skill, dispatch, and good nature. Finally, Associate Law Librarian Robert Bidwell provided substantial aid in the compilation of the bibliography.

THE SUPREME COURT

1
INTRODUCTION: THE SUPREME COURT IN AMERICAN SOCIETY

TO UNDERSTAND the Supreme Court is a task that forces lawyers to become philosophers, for the Constitution, as Woodrow Wilson said, is not a mere lawyers' document. It is much more: it is an arcane theological instrument that at once establishes a framework of government and serves as a symbolic, unifying force around which Americans can and do rally. As its most authoritative interpreter, the Supreme Court is vested with some of the awe and mystery of the Constitution.

The Court deliberately, even sedulously, cultivates this aura of mystery. Throughout American history the Justices have realized that their powers were limited mainly to persuasion, to convincing others that the lawyers (only 101 since 1789) who sit upon the High Bench should speak the ultimate word in giving meaning to the delphic clauses of the Document of 1787 (and its twenty-six amendments). The imposing building in which they are ensconced; the courtroom itself, with its high ceilings and the red curtain from behind which the nine Justices, robed in funereal black, silently emerge; the reverential respect with which they and the Court generally are treated, both on and off the bench—all these, and more, coalesce to spin webs of self-esteem around those who are appointed to the bench. It is an attitude carefully nurtured by the priesthood of the organized bar.

As Chief Justice John Marshall asserted in 1803 and Chief Justice Warren

Burger repeated in 1974, the Justices have by and large been able "to say what the law is." Thus, they have been able to prevail in constitutional questions over the Congress, state governments, and the President. That success has come at the price of carefully husbanding resources and powers, and using them, speaking broadly, only when the times were propitious. In its long history, the Supreme Court has suffered some self-inflicted wounds, but remarkably few considering the great number and range of problems cast before them for decision. Almost 150 years ago, Alexis de Tocqueville observed in *Democracy in America* that *political* questions in the United States tend to become *legal* and to be brought to the judiciary (mainly the Supreme Court) for decision.

De Tocqueville was partially correct, for the questions the judges decide do indeed have an enormous range. He did not go on to say, however, that this judicialization of politics plunged the courts deeply and irretrievably into the political process. Thus, the Supreme Court should be studied as one of the policy-making organs of government and also as a target of pressure-group tactics, not dissimilar in the final analysis from the avowedly political branches. Furthermore, de Tocqueville did not note what Mr. Dooley well knew, and others should know, that the Court tends to follow the election returns. In other words, it is not long out of phase with the dominant themes of the American experience. The *zeitgeist*, not the law, rules. The Justices are able to "say what the law is," but generally their statements must, and do, reflect what Lord Bryce called "the will of the people." Put another way, the law, in Emerson's phrase, is "only a memorandum."

At times the rule, not of law, but of the *zeitgeist* is candidly admitted. Witness, for example, Justice Felix Frankfurter's statement in the famous *Francis* case of 1947. The question was whether Louisiana could send a person to the electric chair a second time and kill him, after the first effort had failed because the electricity was not powerful enough. The prisoner, one Willie Francis, had merely sizzled the first time. His lawyers promptly maintained that to strap him in the chair a second time would be cruel and unusual punishment proscribed by the Eighth and Fourteenth Amendments. Frankfurter's key vote in a 5 to 4 decision sent Francis to his death. The Justice warned that the Court should not enforce its private view, but "the consensus of society's opinion which, for purposes of due process, is the standard enjoined by the Constitution." That would be a noble sentiment, were it accurate—but it is not. As is the rule in such situations, Frankfurter did not enlighten us as to how he determined "the consensus of society's opinion" in a case for which there was no precedent. We are left to infer that he and his four colleagues in the majority had their personal radar finely tuned to society's wavelength and thus were able to pick up signals that the dissenting Justices could not.

Witness also Chief Justice Earl Warren's affirmation in 1958 that the

Eighth Amendment (and inferentially other limitations on government) "must draw its meaning from the evolving standards of decency that mark the progress of a maturing society." Again, he did nothing to enlighten anyone as to how he determined those "standards of decency" — standards which, in this instance, were not evident to the dissenting Justice Frankfurter. What Frankfurter and Warren ultimately meant is that the Justices may determine for themselves what is decent or what is society's opinion. Moreover, they and their colleagues take an anthropomorphic view of society, making it an entity and endowing it with human characteristics. That organismic conception of the nation is a theme that runs through hundreds of Supreme Court decisions; it is one of the major unexplored areas of scholarship. No one really knows what Supreme Court Justices mean when they speak of society. One result of this ambiguity of meaning (as is said in Chapter 5), is that the opinions of the Justices that supposedly explain their decisions are in fact rationalizations couched in lawyers' language.

In their task of putting current meaning in ancient constitutional words, the Justices have insufficient help from the bar, as the essay from the *Virginia Law Review* suggests (see Chapter 8). The point, however, is to criticize neither the specific Supreme Court decisions nor the language used to explain them. Rather, it is to suggest that the Frankfurter and Warren statements are typical tacit acknowledgments that Mr. Dooley was indeed correct. Further evidence that it is the *zeitgeist* that controls may be found in the collected papers of Judge Learned Hand: "In response to a message of congratulations from Judge Learned Hand, Charles E. Wyzanski, Jr., who had argued on behalf of the Labor Board, wrote: 'I . . . tell my friends that it was not really Mr. Wyzanski who won the Wagner cases, but Mr. Zeitgeist.'" The cases involved the constitutionality of the Wagner Act—the National Labor Relations Act of 1935—as an exercise of the power of Congress to regulate interstate commerce. Much evidence of the *zeitgeist* as controlling is readily available. For example, the Justices bowed to pent-up hydraulic forces of social discontent when they began abdicating their role as final policymaker in economic matters in 1937. The *Abortion Cases* of 1973 can be explained only as an example of the recognition of the spirit of the times by a Court dominated by so-called strict constructionists. Cases during the Civil War and World War II upheld governmental actions, such as the internment of citizens of Japanese ancestry, that surely would have been invalidated in the absence of wartime emergency. In recent years, the Court under Chief Justice Burger has steadily chipped away at the protections once accorded criminal defendants. The list of cases demonstrating the *zeitgeist's* control need not be expanded.

Because it is indeed the *zeitgeist* and not the law that greatly influences, and even controls, Supreme Court decisions, some basic changes must be made in the belief-system of Americans. The orthodox view is that ours is "a government of laws and not of men" — or so we were told ad nauseam during the bicentennial celebrations of 1976. But that is at least an impossible, and probably an absurd, dream. The reality is otherwise, at least at the highest levels of all branches of government. Law generally, including the explosion of new laws that has occurred in recent years, does little to circumscribe the activities of those in the highest rungs of the governmental hierarchies, however much it has intervened and intruded into the daily lives of the citizenry and of those artificial constitutional persons, the corporations. Individuals, natural and corporate, may feel ever more tightly bound by the chains of an expanding government, but that does not apply to the officials, elected and appointed, who sit atop the troika of bureaucracies that is the government of the United States. What those officials do is determined less by law (in an interdictory sense) than by politics (using that term in its noninvidious sense). For the Supreme Court, this means that the Justices in constitutional decisions (and elsewhere) create the law as they go along. Justice Byron White said exactly that when dissenting in *Miranda v. Arizona* in 1966:

> The Court has not discovered or found the law in making today's decision, nor has it derived it from some irrefutable sources; what it has done is to make new law and new public policy in much the same way that it has in the course of interpreting other great clauses of the Constitution. This is what the Court historically has done. Indeed, it is what we must do and will continue to do until and unless there is some fundamental change in the constitutional division of governmental powers.

The meaning is clear: historically, the principal function of the Supreme Court has been to validate constitutional change, to update the Document of 1787 in order to make it fit the exigencies of succeeding generations of Americans. Each generation writes its own constitution, principally (but far from always) through the decisions of the Court. The President and Congress also make decisions of constitutional dimension. Ready examples are the war powers the Chief Executive exercises, such as was used by President Gerald Ford in the Mayaguez incident in 1975; for Congress, the Budget and Impoundment Control Act of 1974 is an attempt to alter the balance of power within government, and thus is constitutional in nature. Quite obviously, therefore, the meanings given the cryptic provisions of the Constitution have changed through time. The late Justice Hugo Black often asserted that the Constitution could change only by amendment, but no thoughtful observer accepts that position.

The Supreme Court (even including Justice Black) has always been in the business of making new constitutional law, of changing the meanings of some of the specific clauses (for example, interstate commerce) and of some of the silences (for example, federalism and separation of powers). (A person has a good legal mind if he understands that although words remain the same, their content changes through time. A constitutional provision is not a crystal, transparent and unchanging; it can and does change with the social milieu.) Only rarely does the Court invalidate an act of Congress, although it rather more frequently invalidates state and local governmental actions. Since 1789, as new problems faced the American people the Justices have found new meanings lurking in the majestic generalities of the fundamental law. This has had a spinoff effect: the rare invalidations of statutes tend to further the belief that all other statutes are both constitutional *and* wise.

The position whereby constitutionality is equated with social wisdom does not wash. The two should never be confused; they *may* be synonymous, but not necessarily so. Justice Frankfurter made the point in *Dennis v. United States* (1952): "Much that should be rejected as illegal, because repressive and envenoming, may well not be unconstitutional." Constitutionality deals with *power,* with the question of whether a given governmental act squares with the Justices' current reading of the delphic language of the document. Justices have often stated that their function is not to inquire into the wisdom of a governmental act. That they are not always true to that credo is beside the point. Furthermore, they have no way of determining their own power—the social impact of given decisions (see Chapter 7).

Several themes dominate the essays reprinted in this volume. Most fundamental is the goal of furthering an understanding of that peculiarly American institution, the Supreme Court, with self-assumed power to rule on the validity of the actions of other governmental officers. No other nation, in the past or present, has had such an institution. As is often pointed out, the Court is this nation's unique contribution to the art of governance, what Woodrow Wilson once called a constitutional assembly in continuous session.

The Supreme Court epitomizes the idea of government under law, the basic myth of American constitutionalism. An understanding of both the Court and Constitution requires an inquiry analogous to that which Walter Bagehot accomplished in his classic study, *The English Constitution.* The myth or myths must be pierced, and the underlying reality exposed; only then can there be a full understanding of Court and Constitution. This is not to talk lightly of the dignity of the Court, but to provide a more accurate way of thinking about it. To do so means that the symbolism of Court and Constitution must be penetrated (see Chapter 6).

"We live by symbols," Justice Oliver Wendell Holmes once said. One of the most pervasive is that of an impartial tribunal, above the passions of ordinary man, deciding questions of fundamental import. (That this is not and cannot be accurate is discussed in Chapter 3.)

The Constitution of the United States, inscribed on its original parchment, is enshrined in the National Archives. Each year it is visited by thousands of tourists, who scrutinize it much as religious fundamentalists seek out and revere ancient artifacts from their particular sects. For Americans, that makes the Constitution a theological instrument. In a secular society, it and the Supreme Court serve as substitutes, if not for God, then at least for a personified king. A century ago, Gladstone in a moment of hyperbole asserted that "the American Constitution is, so far as I can see, the most wonderful work ever struck off at a given time by the brain and purpose of man." Such effusiveness is more appropriate to the pulpit than to the political arena, save for the fact that Americans (and others) seem to need some symbol of certainty, some compass by which their lives may be steered. Americans (and others) yearn, as Dostoevsky's Grand Inquisitor knew, for miracle, mystery, and authority. In some obscure way, for reasons we do not fully comprehend, that is precisely what our eighteenth-century Constitution provides, together with its most authoritative interpreter, the Supreme Court of the United States. The Founding Fathers were thought to have created a miracle. They, and the Court, are wrapped in mystery and secrecy, and the eighteenth-century words, as interpreted by the Justices, are accorded authority.

Gladstone's praise surely was excessive: The United States has prospered, has waxed strong and wealthy, has survived, not because of the Constitution but in spite of it. Macauley was probably more accurate when he maintained in 1857: "Your Constitution, sir, is all sail and no anchor." Whatever the case, there is something peculiarly American about the Supreme Court and the men who have sat upon the High Bench since the beginning of the republic. No other nation permits a transient majority of nine lawyer-judges so much ostensible power. In 1934, to cite only one example, a 5 to 4 decision of the Court in the *Gold Clause Cases* decided American monetary policy — in a lawsuit between private parties involving the sum of $15.60 — a fact that astonished Europeans.

The deeper meaning involves the question of elitism in a nation that both calls itself a democracy and seeks to achieve it. That is, how can a small group of men who are appointed for life and responsible, as Chief Justice Warren once said, only to the Constitution and their own consciences be accorded so much power? That question has been unresolved since at least 1803. Although all lawyers know it as a matter of course, many who have not been exposed to legal education or to university courses in constitutional law fail to realize that nothing in the Constitution expressly permits the Supreme Court to make final determinations on the meaning of the fundamental law. Only by a bold, bald, and still controversial decision rendered by Chief Justice Marshall in 1803 did the Justices assert that it was "emphatically the province and duty of the judicial department to say what the law is" — and in so doing declared an act of Congress unconstitutional. Not until the 1820s did decisions of state supreme courts become reviewable — again, in decisions that were then controversial. Thomas Jefferson was incensed by Marshall's grab for power in 1803; and Judge Spencer Roane of Virginia called the 1821 decision that state criminal convictions were reviewable by the Court in Washington "monstrous."

But that settled the pattern: The nation was to have a small group of what Judge Learned Hand in 1958 called "Platonic Guardians." The power of the Court rests somewhat uneasily in the Marble Palace; it is seldom used, despite headlines suggesting the contrary. The Court did not again invalidate an act of Congress until 1857, in the infamous case involving a freed slave, Dred Scott. In 1940, Attorney General Robert H. Jackson (who himself later became a Court Justice) wrote that once having asserted the power of judicial review, the Court has a philosophy of not using it. The Justices know that their powers are more apparent than real. That was true historically and remains true today, even though some recent noteworthy cases may give a contrary impression. One such decision was *United States v. Nixon,* decided in July 1974, in which the President was ordered to turn over tape recordings of his office conversations to a court. Lost in the intense interest of the Watergate episode, of which the *Nixon* decision was a major part, was the fact that it marked the first time in American history that the writ of the Court ran against the President. Before then, it had been assumed that the Chief Executive was immune from legal process.

The legitimacy in a democratic system of a group of lawyers appointed for life making public policy has never been settled. Arguments over what the Supreme Court decides are routine, while in scholarly circles the main focus of attention is upon how the Justices go about their duties. Each of the essays reprinted here stands on its own, so that each can be read by itself. Nevertheless, the thread that unifies them all is that of a perspective on a very special court basically different from most other scholarship on the Supreme Court. The Justices' reasoning is examined, as is the power of the Court to alter behavior patterns and attitudes of Americans. The final two papers probe two relevant but different themes — the question of public confidence in the judiciary and the Court's treatment of the interest in personal privacy.

As noted earlier, the essays that follow were first printed between 1960 and 1975. Their texts have been reprinted without alteration, but each is preceded by a headnote that updates the comments and relates them to the central themes of this collection.

2
SOME PERVASIVE MYTHS ABOUT THE UNITED STATES SUPREME COURT

The conventional wisdom about the Supreme Court substantially varies from reality. For example, to consider the Court — any court, for that matter — solely from the perspective of a legal institution clouds the actuality that it and other courts are significant segments in the American political system. Americans have never been completely willing to accept the fact that the Supreme Court is a political institution. The knowledgeable observer, however, has long known it, but often seeks to deny it. The meaning is clear: Americans are able, in this as well as other instances, to adhere to two mutually inconsistent ideas at the same time. This would have amused F. Scott Fitzgerald, who once said one has a mature mind when he can hold two inconsistent ideas at the same time and still operate. But it is confusing to those who believe that human knowledge can and should be placed in separate categories; and it perplexes Europeans who cannot understand how judges can be "political."

As part of the belief that the court is a "legal" institution pure and simple are a number of other beliefs that must be called myths. Myths, it is appropriate to note, are to be distinguished from lies and legal fictions. A lie is a falsehood knowingly used, often for improper purposes, while a legal fiction is a statement known to be untrue but used for benign reasons. (One of the most important of all legal fictions is that which makes the

"Some Pervasive Myths About the United States Supreme Court" was originally published in 10 *St. Louis University Law Journal* 153 (1965). Reprinted with permission.

corporation a person—the same as a natural person—in the eyes of the law.) A myth, however, is a belief not in consonance with reality, but not known as such; it is believed to be true. Myths serve some deep human need, one that is not fully known.

In Chapter 2, ten of the more widespread myths that eddy around the Supreme Court are discussed. Some, but not all, of these myths are treated in greater detail in subsequent chapters. The need at the outset is to perceive that the Court is much more than simply another law court—even the highest law court. Supreme Court Justices, and others called upon to decide constitutional questions, should have a special type of mind. Judge Learned Hand, one of our wisest jurists, put it this way in 1930:

> I venture to believe that it is as important to a judge called upon to pass on a question of constitutional law, to have at least a bowing acquaintance with Acton and Maitland, with Thucydides, Gibbon and Carlyle, with Homer, Dante, Shakespeare and Milton, with Machiavelli, Montaigne and Rabelais, with Plato, Bacon, Hume and Kant, as with the books which have been specifically written on the subject. For in such matters everything turns upon the spirit in which he approaches the questions before him. The words he must construe are empty vessels into which he can pour nearly anything he will. Men do not gather figs of thistles, nor supple institutions from judges whose outlook is limited by parish or class. They must be aware that there are before them more than verbal problems; more than final solutions cast in generalizations of universal applicability. They must be aware of the changing social tensions in every society which make it an organism; which demand new schemata of adaptation; which will disrupt it, if rigidly confined.

As with judges, so with those who would understand the Constitution of the United States and the Supreme Court. Chapter 2 sets forth some of the needs for a greater understanding of the Court and Constitution.

> "The law is not a homeless, wandering ghost. It is a phase of human life located in time and space."
>
> —M. R. Cohen[1]

INTRODUCTION

As any anthropologist will testify, one of the more interesting aspects of a culture is its myth structure. Europeans and Americans are wont to travel to far-off lands to study primitive societies and to determine, among other things, what the beliefs of the people are and how much consonance those beliefs have with reality. Thus Margaret Mead has studied *Coming of Age in Samoa*, Malinowski the Trobriand Islanders, Gluckman the Barotse, and Sir James Frazer's *The Golden Bough* is a systematic delineation of primitive myths. Within the United States the Indian has been singled out for concentrated study; Llewellyn and Hoebel's *The Cheyenne Way* inquires into the Cheyenne culture from the legal perspective.[2] But anthropologists have not seen fit to scrutinize their own societies in a similar manner, perhaps because they are culture-bound and cannot see myths as myths. Rather they may well perceive them as belief patterns or philosophies or theologies or eternal verities, all of which have some degree of credibility and thus are not to be considered mythical. Myths, in other words, are an interesting segment of other, allegedly primitive societies to study, but it goes against the grain to find parallels in American society.[3]

Nonetheless, myths there are in this country, myths which are ripe for analysis. One set concerns the government and its role in social affairs, and particularly the Constitution and its most authoritative interpreter, the United States Supreme Court. The purpose of this brief paper is to outline some of those myths which concern the Supreme Court and the manner in which the Court operates in the American polity. Since myths are kin to the supernatural, some mention will also be made to the theological character of the Supreme Court and the Constitution.

What, first, is a myth? The dictionary defines it as "a purely fictitious narrative usually involving supernatural persons, actions, or events,

---

1. REASON AND LAW 4 (1950).
2. LLEWELLYN & HOEBEL, THE CHEYENNE WAY (1953).
3. See, however, ARNOLD, THE SYMBOLS OF GOVERNMENT (1935); ARNOLD, THE FOLKLORE OF CAPITALISM (1937); ARNOLD, FAIR FIGHTS AND FOUL (1965), all of which delineate some of the myths of American society. The legal realists of the 1920's and 1930's readily saw myths as myths. See, *e.g.*, FRANK, LAW AND MODERN MIND (1930). See also Riesman, *Toward an Anthropological Science of the Law and the Legal Profession*, 57 AM. J. SOCIOLOGY 121 (1951).

and embodying some popular idea concerning natural or historical phenomena. Often used vaguely to include any narrative having fictitious elements." Myths are beliefs not in consonance with reality, but not known as such; they are believed to be true. They are to be distinguished from liês, which are falsehoods knowingly used for improper purposes, and fictions, which in law are suppositions known to be in variance with fact but nonetheless accepted because they are believed to help attain beneficial ends. Myths, lies, and (legal) fictions, in other words, are all forms of statements or beliefs that are erroneous or false; the distinction between them is that the latter two are known to be false, but still are used, while myths are both false and not known as such.[4]

When speaking of the United States Supreme Court, one may readily see a congeries of beliefs widely held among the American populace. Some attain general acceptance, at least among lawyers, while others are tenaciously adhered to by smaller numbers. All of them, however, have vocal and even shrill adherents. There is an element of the supernatural or the irrational about the Constitution and the Court, as Max Lerner pointed out three decades ago.[5] To some extent, Americans are a nation of Constitution-worshippers, with the Supreme Court acting as a high priesthood administering to the faithful. Because the Constitution seems to be or is considered to be the rock upon which the nation was built and because the Justices have the task of exegesis of the sacred text, it is not surprising that attacks on the Court by some critics bear a marked similarity to the attacks by the faithful upon heresies and heretics. "Economics," Thurman Arnold is fond of saying, "is theology";[6] so, too, with Court and Constitution.

Further evidence of the theological nature of Court and Constitution may be seen in the fact that both bear, similarly to the Supreme Being, capitalized word symbols—the Supreme Court is the only court which lawyers and legal periodicals habitually give the dignity of a capital *C*. So, too, with the Constitution: When one is speaking of the 1787 document, it receives the same reverential treatment. Perhaps it is not surprising then to note a school of fundamentalist interpreters of the document.[7] One recent example is Mr. Reed Benson, son of a

---

4. See FRANK, COURTS ON TRIAL (1949); VAIHINGER, THE PHILOSOPHY OF "AS IF" (1925).
5. Lerner, *Constitution and Court as Symbols*, 46 YALE L.J. 1290 (1937). Thomas Jefferson put it this way:
Some men look at constitutions with sanctimonious reverence, and deem them like the ark of the covenant, too sacred to be touched. They ascribe to the men of the preceding age a wisdom more than human, and suppose what they did to be beyond amendment. I knew this age well; I belonged to it, and labored with it. It deserved well of its country. It was very like the present, but without the experience of the present; and forty years of experience in government is worth a century of book-reading; and this they would say themselves, were they to rise from the dead. Quoted in DOUGLAS, STARE DECISIS 31 (1949).
6. ARNOLD, THE SYMBOLS OF GOVERNMENT 72 (1935).
7. *Cf.* Griswold, *Absolute is in the Dark—A Discussion of the Approach of the Supreme Court to Constitutional Questions*, 8 UTAH L. REV. 167 (1963).

former Secretary of Agriculture and prominent Mormon layman, who in May 1965 was quoted as saying: "It's a part of my religious training that the Constitution is an inspired document, that the time will come when it will hang by a thread and it will be our task to save it . . . . We believe that the Lord helped raise up the Founding Fathers to establish the Constitution so there could be the opportunity for religious freedom."[8]

If the Supreme Court Justices are the high priesthood of the Constitution, then the Founding Fathers (capital letters again) are the saints in America's hagiology. We worship our ancestors as well as the Document. The analogy can be pressed further. The law clerks of the Justices are the altar boys; the lawyers the acolytes. Law professors (and some political scientists) are the Pharisees. The high priests, aided by the altar boys, produce exegesis on the sacred text. The acolytes pay respectful court (though sometimes not so respectful), while the Pharisees grind out heavily footnoted critiques of what the high priests have said. All of this is conducted with ceremony and ritual, particularly within the architecturally monstrous and acoustically impossible courtroom, the Temple within the Marble Palace. Dialogues are conducted with the high priests in the form of oral argument. Newsmen pay close attention, hanging on the words of the Justices and scurrying to get their opinions—the Revealed Word—when they are released. The press sends The Word to the populace, which, as to most sermons, reacts with varying degrees of boredom or indifference. Not so with the acolytes and the Pharisees; here is the very stuff of their existence; here is the latest interpretation; here is something to be gnawed over and worried in scholarly disputations of The Word. Finally, there is the dogma of Supreme Court infallibility, once stated by the late Justice Robert H. Jackson in this manner: "We are not final because we are infallible, but we are infallible only because we are final."[9]

To the extent that the foregoing is valid, there is added reason for

---

8. Quoted in The New Republic, May 8, 1965, p. 8. Dean Don K. Price attributes some of this attitude to the scientific revolution. See PRICE, THE SCIENTIFIC ESTATE 163 (1965):

Science by helping technology to increase prosperity, has weakened the kind of radicalism that comes from a lack of economic security. But science has helped to produce other kinds of insecurity: the fear of a new kind of war that science has made possible, the fear of rapid social and economic change and the fear that we no longer have a fixed and stable constitutional system by which to cope without political problems. And these fears are breeding a new type of radicalism.

The new radicalism is ostensibly conservative. It springs in part from the resentment men feel when their basic view of life is unsettled—as medieval man must have felt when he was asked to think of a universe that did not revolve around the earth, or as some physicists felt a generation or two ago when their colleagues began to talk about relativity and indeterminacy. The new conservative radicalism had a fundamentalist faith in the written Constitution, and the high priests of that faith seem to have desecrated it. The Supreme Court has applied relative policy standards in place of fixed rules of precedent; but worse still it has admitted into its system of thinking not only the moral law as revealed in tradition, but arguments from the sciences, even the behavioral sciences.

9. Brown v. Allen, 344 U.S. 443, 540 (1953).

the violent verbal battles that rage around the Marble Palace. The irrational element that is present makes those conflicts over Court decisions resemble theological disputations. "We are very quiet there," Justice Holmes once remarked, "but it is the quiet of a storm center. . . ."[10] Controversy swirls around the Temple. The other major reason for contention is that the Court's pronouncements can and do have some impact upon American society; as is well known, the decisions of the Justices are "political" as well as "legal." De Tocqueville noted long ago that scarcely an important question of public policy presents itself which does not sooner or later become a judicial question. His observation was accurate for the time that he wrote, and remained so for another several decades. But it is now no more than a half-truth, the advent of the "Positive State" having transferred the locus of power to the Executive.[11] Now it may be said with complete accuracy that there are few important questions of public policy which arise in the United States today that do not find the Executive at or close to the center of the decisional process. Often, indeed perhaps usually, the Executive is the prime mover of new public policy. The nation and government have been so transformed since de Tocqueville's day that his observation, once valid, no longer reflects reality. Even so, judicial pronouncements are not without importance. What the Justices say at least *articulates* public policy in certain areas, whatever may have been the motivations or influences leading to such statements.

SUPREME COURT MYTHS

Some of the myths which eddy around the Supreme Court are unique to that body, while others are shared with other segments of the judicial system. Some are attributable to the special position the highest bench has in the value hierarchy of Americans (pollsters note that the most prestigeful position in the United States is that of a Supreme Court Justice); others derive from the heritage of superstition that has come down through history from the dim beginnings of governmental adjudication as a way of settling disputes and of setting public policy. We are far from a rational analysis and explication of the Supreme Court and its role in the American polity. There are many roads to the truth about this peculiarly American institution.[12] One of them would seem to be a close and hard look at the myth structure that revolves around it. As Justice Frankfurter once said, we are not likely to get correct answers about law and government

10. HOLMES, COLLECTED LEGAL PAPERS 292 (1920).

11. In other words, the "constitutional revolution" of the 1930's has diminished the power of the Supreme Court in many important fields of public policy. *Cf.* Miller, *An Affirmative Thrust to Due Process of Law?*, 30 GEO. WASH. L. REV. 399 (1962); ROSTOW, PLANNING FOR FREEDOM: THE PUBLIC LAW OF AMERICAN CAPITALISM (1959). See text at notes 119-26, *infra.*

12. See the several essays in SCHUBERT, JUDICIAL BEHAVIOR: A READER IN THEORY AND RESEARCH (1964).

unless correct questions are first posed and analyzed.[13] One of those questions is that which is under discussion here. The listing below is not intended to be exhaustive; rather, it is illustrative of a situation which exists concerning the Supreme Court (and concerning, for that matter, other organs of government and, indeed, the role of government in society).

1. *The Myth of Usurpation of Power*

This is one of the hoariest; it dates back to the seminal decision of *Marbury v. Madison*,[14] when Chief Justice Marshall in an opinion noteworthy for its result but not for its reasoning at once struck down an attempt by Congress to enlarge upon the Court's original jurisdiction and asserted the power of judicial review of acts of the national legislature. When *Marbury* was followed by *Martin v. Hunter's Lessee*[15] and *Cohens v. Virginia*,[16] the pattern was set and since that time the Supreme Court has putative, albeit usually unused, power to review acts of other governmental organs, both state and federal. The familiar history of that development and that controversy need not be retraced now. For that matter, it would scarcely merit mention were it not for the fact that the respected, even revered, late Judge Learned Hand challenged, in 1958, the Marshallian assumption of judicial power and maintained that it should be limited to determining the "frontiers of another 'Department's' authority and the propriety of its choices within these frontiers." Judge Hand found a "necessity in such a system as ours of some authority whose word should be final as to when another 'Department' had overstepped the borders of its authority"; but lent his prestigious name to the usurpation myth by maintaining that "within its prescribed borders each 'Department' and the states [should] be free from [judicial] interference."[17] In other words, the task of the Court is that of determining the "competence" under the Constitution of a given governmental organ to deal with a problem; once competence is found, then the Court is not authorized to reweigh what already has been weighed by a competent authority.

The Hand thesis is untenable, for at least three reasons. First, as Charles E. Wyzanski, Jr., himself an outstanding federal judge, has said, "[it has] not yet been supported by a single eminent judge or pro-

---

13. See Estate of Rogers v. Commissioner, 320 U.S. 410, 413 (1943) ("In law also the right answer usually depends on putting the right question") and Priebe & Sons v. United States, 332 U.S. 407, 420 (1947) ("but answers are not obtained by putting the wrong question and thereby begging the real one").
14. 5 U.S. (1 Cranch) 137 (1803). See COHEN, AMERICAN THOUGHT: A CRITICAL SKETCH 146 (1954) and FREUND, STANDARDS OF AMERICAN LEGISLATION 276-77 (1917) for criticism of Chief Justice Marshall's opinion in the *Marbury* case.
15. 14 U.S. (1 Wheat.) 304 (1816).
16. 19 U.S. (6 Wheat.) 264 (1821).
17. HAND, THE BILL OF RIGHTS 29, 31 (1958). See Mendelson, *Learned Hand: Patient Democrat*, 76 HARV. L. REV. 322 (1962), effectively criticized in Hyman & Newhouse, *Standards for Preferred Freedoms: Beyond the First*, 60 Nw. U.L. REV. 1, 43 n.149 (1965).

fessor." The overwhelming scholarly view is that the "Eighteenth
Century consensus was that the Constitution did give the Court a
power to invalidate action which transcended the substantive limitations of the document."[18] Although Judge Wyzanski's conclusion may
well be valid, it nonetheless is meet to ask why the Court was not
expressly vested with that power. On this question Judge Hand seems
to have the better of the argument—that is, that the "consensus" of
1787 may have been something different from what Wyzanski says.
Even so, the idea of judicial review was not unknown at that time, as
historians have demonstrated,[19] and that review was not limited to the
jurisdictional question as Judge Hand would have us believe. In the
second place, even if a case could be made for charging the "Marshall
Court" with usurpation, what might be called "constitutional adverse
possession" over the ensuing sixteen-plus decades has effectively given
it "title" to the power. More than 160 years of history cannot lightly
be swept aside. Whatever the intention of the fifty-five men in America's hagiology now called the Founding Fathers, acceptance by the
American people of judicial review both of governmental competences
and of substantive actions, has now put the matter beyond question.
The Civil War amendments add further testimony buttressing that
conclusion. What Dean Ray Forrester calls the "third Constitution"
sealed the title of the Supreme Court.[20] Finally, the failure of Congress
to act, save in relatively rare instances, to "overrule" the Supreme
Court[21] or (once) to remove a case from the Court's jurisdiction,[22] may
be taken as a silent testimony that the American people at large feel
that judicial review, as it has been handled, is by and large proper. The
upper hand still lies with the people and the political branches of the
government. If Chief Justice Marshall and the Supreme Court had
acted improperly in 1803, then it should have been easy to get an
amendment promulgated denying the judicial power. That it was not
is itself significant.

However approached, accordingly, the notion that the Supreme
Court has usurped power may be said to be mythical. To the extent
that it is believed, it is not in consonance with reality. However, the
usurpation myth is seldom stated today in its bald form; rather, it at
times is directed to certain specific alleged usurpations, principally
upon the fabric of federalism and upon the legislative prerogative.
Perhaps it is the "basic myth," to employ Jerome Franks' label in a
different context,[23] variations upon which crop up in a number of

---

18. Wyzanski's views may be found in his introduction to the paperbound edition of
HAND, THE BILL OF RIGHTS ix (Atheneum ed. 1963).
19. See, e.g., DOWLING, CASES ON CONSTITUTIONAL LAW (6th ed. 1959).
20. FORRESTER, CASES ON CONSTITUTIONAL LAW (1959).
21. See Congressional Reversal of Supreme Court Decisions, 1945–1957, 71 HARV. L.
REV. 1324 (1958).
22. Ex parte McCardle, 74 U.S. (7 Wall.) 506 (1868).
23. See FRANK, op. cit. supra note 3. As recently as June 1965, however, Justice Black

contexts. Moreover, some overlap; this may be seen in the second in this listing of mythical beliefs.

2. *The Myth that the Supreme Court is Undemocratic*

This is a hardy perennial, seen in various contexts and articulated by a variety of commentators. In essence, it is predicated upon the fact that the Court is composed of Justices who are appointed for life and who thus are not "accountable" or "responsible" to the electorate. Justice Frankfurter once called the Court "oligarchic,"[24] and apparently it was this belief that helped motivate him into becoming the great apostle of judicial self-restraint. Possibly he was influenced in the position by James Bradley Thayer, who, at the Harvard Law School, "taught that it would discourage the citizenry from bearing its fair share of political responsibility if courts, except in the plainest cases, exercised a jurisdiction to invalidate a legislative choice."[25] He sat, too, in the seat of Justice Holmes, a Justice who in different circumstances and in different times also preached the gospel of self-restraint. Judge Hand also raised the question of the democratic nature of judicial review in his lectures mentioned above. Believing that "it would be most irksome to be ruled by a bevy of Platonic Guardians,"[26] Hand would accord a high degree of deference to legislative majorities.

How can judicial vetoes be reconciled with democratic theory? The question asks much. The answer, it is submitted, must be derived not only by according attention to the *procedure* by which governmental decisions are made—which is the Frankfurter-Hand position—but also to the *content* of the decisions themselves. Whether or not an institution is "democratic," in other words, depends as much as or more upon *what* is decided than upon the manner in which it is decided. The difference is one between substance and procedure, and the history of the concept of due process of law provides apt analogy.[27] Is the decision made by the Supreme Court one which furthers the dignity and integrity of the individual person, which is the core of a free and democratic society? If the answer is yes, than it is difficult indeed to see how the fact that it was made by an appointed Court can vary the conclusion that democracy is in action.

Judge Hand, with his mentor Thayer, probably would counter, however, with the proposition that even admitting the conclusion as stated, still the procedural forms so necessary to the proper functioning of

thought it necessary to reaffirm his adherence to *Marbury v. Madison*, in the course of a dissenting opinion in which he accused his brethren of acting as a "superlegislature." Griswold v. Connecticut, 381 U.S. 479, 511 (1965).

24. AFL v. American Sash & Door Co., 335 U.S. 538, 555 (1949). See CAHILL, JUDICIAL LEGISLATION 9 (1952). Asseverations that the Court is democratic may be found in BLACK, THE OCCASIONS OF JUSTICE (1963); BICKEL, THE LEAST DANGEROUS BRANCH (1962); ROSTOW, THE SOVEREIGN PREROGATIVE (1962).

25. WYZANSKI, *op. cit. supra* note 18, at v, vii.

26. HAND, *op. cit. supra* note 17, at 72-73.

27. Traced in Miller, *supra* note 11.

democracy are subtly eroded by the process. But is this so? Certainly it is not a self-evident proposition. For one thing, judicial decisions are always subject in the American system to "recall." One need only advert to the eleventh and sixteenth amendments to illustrate the point. Even more importantly, however, is the fact that the Court cannot long impose its will upon militant legislative majorities which are bent upon furthering the "common good" through social and economic legislation; so much the "Court-packing" imbroglio of 1937 teaches.[28] The history of that familiar encounter between public opinion and judicial decision need not be restated at this time. Suffice it only to say that the Supreme Court, as that episode lent impressive evidence, has never long stood in fundamental opposition to what the American people have determined to have. Certainly it has not long stood in the way of what both the President and Congress wanted.[29]

There is, furthermore, a valid public educational function in the manner in which the Court has operated. Public understanding of political issues has been enhanced by judicial opinions. Acting as a "national conscience" of the American people, the Court has in a number of instances erected standards toward which public and private behavior could aspire. The clear instance here is the manner in which the Justices grasped the nettle of racial segregation in 1954[30] and struck a blow for human dignity, the reverberations of which still echo and re-echo throughout the land. So, too, in the administration of the criminal law; here, since *Powell v. Alabama*,[31] the Court has been engaged in an effort the net result of which is greatly to improve the overall way crimes and criminals are handled. The educational function of the Court, particularly when the Justices insist upon the protection of the disadvantaged minorities or of individuals in adverse circumstances, can surely be said to be in accordance with the finest traditions of democratic polity.

Another factor, suggested by *Baker v. Carr* and its progeny,[32] bears mention. What happens to a constitutional order when the very process of democracy and its representative character become so distorted that in fact the government is under the control of those who represent only a minority of the population? This was the essential condition at

---

28. *Cf.* McCloskey, *Economic Due Process and the Supreme Court; An Exhumation and Reburial*, 1962 Sup. Ct. Rev. 34; Dahl, *Decision-Making in a Democracy: The Supreme Court as a National Policy-Maker*, 6 J. Pub. L. 275 (1957).

29. In this connection, it is instructive to compare what happened in 1952 when President Truman seized the steel mills (see Youngstown Sheet & Tube Co. v. Sawyer, 343 U.S. 579 (1952)) and in 1962 when President Kennedy forced a rescission of a price increase by the steel industry. An account of the latter may be found in Reich, *Another Such Victory: The President's Short War Against Steel*, The New Republic, April 30, 1962, p. 8. What Truman could not do, purportedly because Congress had not authorized it, Kennedy did accomplish through the use of existing statutory and constitutional authority.

30. Brown v. Board of Educ., 347 U.S. 483 (1954).

31. 287 U.S. 45 (1932).

32. Baker v. Carr, 369 U.S. 186 (1962); Reynolds v. Sims, 377 U.S. 533 (1964); Wesberry v. Sanders, 376 U.S. 1 (1964).

issue in *Baker*. Justices Frankfurter and Harlan held fast to the position that legislative apportionment was a "political thicket" and would have told the complainants to go back to the same people they were complaining about and, in effect, ask those people to vote themselves out of office. Such an obviously inadequate "solution" hardly comports with democracy. There are times when the democratic process has broken down or has become stymied. In such cases—and they are exceedingly rare—it is difficult indeed to maintain that by breaking logjams, which were preventing full participation in the political process, the Court has acted contrary to democratic theory. Moreover, decisions in legislative apportionment subsequent to *Baker*, such as the "one-man, one-vote" decision in *Reynolds v. Sims*[33] contribute substantially to public enlightenment. In effect, they provide the impetus to make the American people think through their beliefs as to representative government and, if after such deliberation it is considered desirable, then, to amend the Constitution. Whatever the final outcome of the "Dirksen Amendment" to overturn *Reynolds v. Sims*, surely the public debate has clarified and ventilated, perhaps even greased, the operation of American state governments.[34]

It may well be that the lesson of *Baker v. Carr* will have a wider application. Even earlier, the use by the Negro of the judicial process had pointed the way to disadvantaged urban voters. One specific area seems ripe for further judicial application of the principle, enunciated in *Baker*, that the Court may intervene when social conditions have outrun the constitutional structure and the call for change becomes insistent but unheeded politically. Reference is made here to the fundamental alteration in American society that is the consequence of the growth of organizations, principally corporations and labor unions but also farmers' leagues, veterans' legions, churches, and even the large foundations. Already some judicial harbingers have been decided, so that it is not fanciful to suggest that the place of the organization in the constitutional order will be an important focus of interest in the future.[35] In other words, while the Constitution "runs against governments only," we may be on the verge of greater judicial recognition of "private" governments. The first suggestion along these lines seems to have been made by Alexander Pekelis about twenty years ago;[36] A. A. Berle agrees,[37] at least in part, and others have proffered similar suggestions.[38]

---

33. 377 U.S. 533.
34. An effort to have the Senate pass the "Dirksen Amendment" failed by 7 votes on August 4, 1965. See N.Y. Times, Aug. 5, 1965, p. 1.
35. *Cf.* HORN, GROUPS AND THE CONSTITUTION (1956).
36. PEKELIS, LAW AND SOCIAL ACTION 91-127 (Konvitz ed. 1950).
37. BERLE, 20TH CENTURY CAPITALIST REVOLUTION (1954); BERLE, POWER WITHOUT PROPERTY (1959); BERLE, ECONOMIC POWER AND THE FREE SOCIETY (Fund for the Republic Pamphlet 1957).
38. The relevant citations may be found in Miller, *The Corporation as a Private Government in the World Community*, 46 VA. L. REV. 1539 (1960).

The courts have not hesitated to apply the Constitution to purportedly private institutions when the deprivation complained of was sufficiently severe. The *White Primary Cases*, in which the Constitution was applied to those private entities called political parties are the clearest illustration.[39] In at least one case, *Marsh v. Alabama*,[40] the Supreme Court imposed constitutional limitations on a private corporation, and there are some dicta in other cases with respect to labor unions.[41] Some state courts, furthermore, have gone along.[42] The *Sit-In Cases*, culminating in 1964, as well as other decisions in the area of ethnic relations, have in addition so chipped away the concept of "state action" that the line between public and private has become increasingly blurred in recent years.[43] The lesson here is that judicial recognition is being accorded the "organizational revolution"[44] (which has resulted in a diminution of the individual qua individual in the "private" sector of the American polity). If the trickle becomes a stream, then another example of the Court stepping in to attempt to rectify an imbalance will become evident. The suggestion is that this, too, would comport with democracy in that it would result in protection of the individual against deprivations of his liberty from improper actions by private governments. (Whether the Court will do it depends in large part on whether Congress acts.)[45]

3. *The Myth that the Supreme Court is to be Equated with a Court of Law*

In a recent article discussing the principles of judicial decision-making, Professors Jacob D. Hyman and Wade D. Newhouse assert that the judicial process in constitutional litigation "is but a specific instance of the judicial process" and that the Supreme Court is not different from other courts.[46] This at best is a dubious proposition. While it is indubitably true, as Karl Llewellyn put it, Supreme Court Justices have been raised in the "common law and case law system,"[47]

---

39. *E.g.*, Terry v. Adams, 345 U.S. 461 (1953).
40. 326 U.S. 501 (1946).
41. See Steele v. Louisville & Nashville R.R., 323 U.S. 192 (1944); Syres v. Oil Workers Int'l Union, 350 U.S. 892 (1955); 54 MICH. L. REV. 567 (1956).
42. *E.g.*, Betts v. Easley, 161 Kan. 459, 169 P.2d 831 (1946); James v. Marinship Corp., 25 Cal. 2d 721, 155 P.2d 329 (1944).
43. See Williams, *The Twilight of State Action*, 41 TEXAS L. REV. 347 (1963).
44. See BOULDING, THE ORGANIZATIONAL REVOLUTION (1953); SEIDENBERG, POST-HISTORIC MAN (1950); Miller, *The Constitutional Law of the "Security State,"* 10 STAN. L. REV. 620 (1958).
45. The Civil Rights Act of 1964, 78 Stat. 252, may be said to be such a congressional intervention, particularly titles II & VII. In this respect, the statute is sufficiently important to be considered to be a "constitutional" decision or change. For brief discussion of this point, see Miller, *Presidential Power to Impound Appropriated Funds: An Exercise in Constitutional Decision-Making*, 43 N.C.L. REV. 502, 539 (1965).
46. Hyman & Newhouse, *supra* note 17, at 41-44.
47. LLEWELLYN, THE COMMON LAW TRADITION 385 (1960). See Henkin, *Some Reflections on Current Constitutional Controversy*, 109 U. PA. L. REV. 637, 653-55 (1961).
Judges, including Supreme Court Justices, are indubitably raised and nurtured in a private-law tradition. See COHEN, REASON AND LAW (1950). But that tradition, as Justice Frankfurter maintained in asserting that Cardozo's lectures on THE NATURE OF THE JUDI-

it is also true that the cases they decide concern far more than the routine disputes of *meum* and *tuum*, as are handled by, say, the Supreme Court of Minnesota. In discussing the Supreme Court we should never forget that it is a Constitution the Justices are expounding, a Constitution designed to endure for the ages to come, a Constitution which, in Woodrow Wilson's language, is not "a mere lawyer's document" but the "vehicle of the nation's life."[48]

The pretence (myth) that the Supreme Court can and may be equated with an ordinary court of law derives from the failure of lawyers and political theorists to assign to the Court its real role in the American system. By pretending that the Court is simply a court of law, it becomes easier to parse decisions and easier to ignore the part that the high bench plays in the decisional structure of the government. But Morris R. Cohen, no lawyer but as keen a student of the judiciary as this country has produced, appears to be much closer to the mark when he stated some years ago: "[W]e cannot pretend that the United States Supreme Court is simply a court of law. Actually, the issues before it generally depend on the determination of all sorts of facts, their consequences, and the values we attach to these consequences. These are questions of economics, politics, and social policy which legal training cannot solve unless law includes all social knowledge."[49] This statement may provide at least a partial key to an understanding of why lawyers persist in equating the Supreme Court with any other appellate bench; namely, that once one goes beyond the orthodox parsing of judicial opinions and looks to the facts, their consequences, and the values attached to those conseqences, it becomes necessary to have much more than the usual tools of the lawyer. In other words, legal education has not yet developed a way of thinking about the Supreme Court and its governmental role. Until such a conceptualization is produced, it is easier to proceed on the myth that a court is a court is a court—and, hence, that the high priests of the Marble Palace are the same and that they act in the same manner, as their brethren on state courts.

A moment's reflection should show the contrary. What court deals with political theory in the way the Supreme Court has in, say, the *Reapportionment Cases*?[50] What court has attempted to realign the

---

CIAL PROCESS (1921) did not help him (Frankfurter) in his task on the Court, merely defines the perimeter of the Supreme Court's task; it does not set out the details. See FRANKFURTER, SOME OBSERVATIONS ON SUPREME COURT LITIGATION AND LEGAL EDUCATION (1954). See also, FRANK, *op. cit. supra* note 4, at ch. XXII.

48. WILSON, CONSTITUTIONAL GOVERNMENT IN THE UNITED STATES 157 (1908) (pagination from Columbia paper edition 1961). See Miller, *Notes on the Concept of the "Living" Constitution*, 31 GEO. WASH. L. REV. 881 (1963).

49. COHEN, *op. cit. supra* note 47, at 73-74. As Cardozo said: "The New York Court of Appeals is a great common law court; its problems are lawyers' problems. But the Supreme Court is occupied chiefly with statutory construction . . . and with politics." Quoted in JACKSON, THE SUPREME COURT IN THE AMERICAN SYSTEM OF GOVERNMENT 54 (1954).

50. Baker v. Carr, 369 U.S. 186 (1962) and its aftermath.

position of ethnic groups within American society as the high bench has in the racial segregation decisions? What court deals in a definitive way with the troublous question of the relationship of church and state, as did the Supreme Court in the *Prayer Cases*?[51] What court has had an impact upon the manner in which the criminal law is administered? The list may be extended, not ad infinitum, but certainly to cover a full range of socioeconomic questions of fundamental importance to America.

But even so, even if the Supreme Court is not to be equated with an ordinary court of law in its constitutional determinations, still the Court *is* a court—and cannot escape the institutional norms within which courts have operated and continue to operate. Thus Justice Frankfurter's appellation of "a very special kind of court"[52] perhaps is close to the mark. The distinction may become important when the question of the type of person who should be appointed to the Supreme Court is posed. Some commentators advocate that only those with prior judicial experience should be named. These may be numbered among those who believe in the myth. However, a political scientist who has studied the backgrounds of Court appointees has concluded that "it is not at all clear that experience on an inferior federal court or a state court is necessary to or intimately related to the sort of service performed on the nation's highest court."[53] That conclusion coincides with Justice Frankfurter's (who, it may be noted, did not have prior judicial experience): " 'Judicial service' as such has no significant relation to the kinds of litigation that come before the Supreme Court, to the types of issues they raise, to qualities that these actualities require for wise decision."[54]

A submyth to the main myth of equating the Supreme Court with other appellate courts may, accordingly, be noted: that prior judicial experience would improve the quality of Supreme Court decision-making. The studies which have been made on the social and political background factors of the Justices simply do not support this conclusion. Members of the present Court may be used as coarse examples to illustrate the point: Justice Brennan, an "activist," a liberal, had the most judicial experience before coming to the Court (on the Supreme Court of New Jersey). Justice Harlan, a "self-restrainer" had less judicial experience (on the United States Court of Appeals). Justice Black came from the Senate, never went to law school, and had only

---

51. Engel v. Vitale, 370 U.S. 421 (1962); School District v. Schempp, 374 U.S. 203 (1963).

52. Frankfurter, *The Supreme Court in the Mirror of Justices*, 105 U. PA. L. REV. 781 (1957).

53. Schmidhauser, *The Background Characteristics of United States Supreme Court Justices*, in JUDICIAL BEHAVIOR 206, 229 (Schubert ed. 1964). See SCHMIDHAUSER, THE SUPREME COURT: ITS POLITICS, PERSONALITIES, AND PROCEDURES 58 (1960): "Actually the data indicate that a higher proportion of the justices possessing significant prior judicial experience showed a stronger propensity to abandon stare decisis than did the justices lacking such experience."

54. Frankfurter, *supra* note 52, at 785.

a modicum of experience as a police court judge. Justice Frankfurter, on the other hand, was a Harvard law graduate, a professor, without any prior judicial experience. The latter two are assigned diametrically opposed points of view, with Justice Frankfurter being the angel of the "Society of Jobbists"[55] and Justice Black the devil. The list could be expanded, but need not be, for the point seems clear: There is no necessary correlation between prior judicial experience and work on the Supreme Court. It is a submyth of the larger myth that the Supreme Court is to be equated with any other appellate court.

In maintaining that the Supreme Court is a very special sort of court, it is not asserted that other courts do not also deal with questions of "policy." Every case concerns an aspect of public policy, even an action to replevy a dog—for in such an action the concept of private property is in the background, and that concept is a fundamental tenet of the American polity. But there is more than a difference of degree between, say, the Supreme Court of Alabama and the United States Supreme Court. This difference is so great that it is close to a difference in type. Only if it could be demonstrated that state appellate courts deal mostly with large questions of public law and public policy could it be maintained that the federal supreme bench should be equated with other appellate courts. It is doubtful that this can be shown.

4. *The Myth that the Intention of the Founding Fathers Can Guide Present Decisions*

Having canonized the fifty-five men who drafted the Document in 1787, reference must be made, according to this hardy myth, to what they said, both in the convention and outside. Some care must be taken in describing it because the shades of the Founding Fathers—note, again, the capital *F*'s and note also the use of the term "Father," a word not without some parallel use in theological discourse and institutions —are invoked at times by Supreme Court Justices in the course of their opinions. This is not to say that the Justices are taken in by such references; the office of judicial opinion is such that at times it becomes convenient, even useful, to remember the Fathers. *Engel v. Vitale*,[56] the Regents' Prayer Case, is instructive on the point. In the opinion of Justice Black may be found citations to statements made contemporaneously with the formation of the new government. So also may similar citations be found with Justice Stewart, who dissents in the same case. It is not unfair to say that both Justices used history to buttress an already conceived conclusion. The use and abuse of history

---

55. The Society of Jobbists is "that strange cult . . . which 'undertakes only those jobs which the members can do in proper workmanlike fashion' . . . . It demands right quality, better than the market will pass." Kurland, *Equal in Origin and Equal in Title to the Legislative and Executive Branches of the Government*, 78 HARV. L. REV. 143, 144-45 (citing HAND, THE SPIRIT OF LIBERTY 57, 62 (2d ed. Dilliard 1963)). Their patron saint is Holmes, their membership small; presumably Frankfurter belonged and I suppose that Professor Kurland is a candidate for membership.

56. 370 U.S. 421 (1962).

may be seen in many decisions, so much so that it becomes a rationalization rather than a scheme of analysis.

Whether the filio-pietistic notion that the intention of the Framers can be the basis for the determination of present cases is a question that raises at least two others: (a) To what extent can such an intention be determined with respect to any important question of the day? (b) Even if such an intention is ascertainable, is it relevant? Both questions pose basic issues in adjudication, constitutional or otherwise, for the same sort of problem arises whenever any written instrument (contract, will, conveyance, statute, or whatever) must be construed or interpreted by a judge. For writings other than constitutions, it apparently is generally accepted that a search will be made for intent—of the parties to a contract, of a testator, of the parties to a conveyance, of the legislature. But whether intent is ascertainable in those instances is dubious at best, even though judicial opinions are written making reference to the frame of mind of such parties.

If, however, intention is at the very best quite difficult and usually impossible to find in these examples of legal writings, the situation is magnified in the case of the Constitution. The sparse amount of contemporary documentation and the inconsistency—often with one person uttering inconsistent statements himself, as Jefferson does—make the use of the intention of the Framers and of other community leaders of the time questionable. In other words, on most questions—perhaps *all* questions—"the history," in the words of Chief Justice Warren in the *School Segregation Cases*, is "inconclusive."[57] The question, then, of whether the intention of the Founding Fathers is ascertainable must, speaking generally, be answered in the negative.

The second question—whether that intention, assuming it is ascertainable, is relevant to present-day decision-making?—cannot be disposed of so easily. Involved is the more basic question: What are the proper ingredients of a constitutional decision? I know of no one who has satisfactorily answered that question. For if intention is ruled out, what does become relevant? Precedent? The answer here must be "no" if one considers almost any question accepted by the Court and ruled on the merits. In many or most respects, each constitutional case is unique, sui generis. So much can be derived from reflection upon the nature of constitutional precepts, such as due process or freedom of speech, and the manner in which the Court handles cases. The "interests" are balanced, it is said, or some other evaluation is made which does not involve the application of known rules. In other words, the precepts are at such a high level of abstraction, having been deliberately left so by the Court, that they of course cannot decide specific cases. As Justice Holmes observed, "general propositions do not decide concrete

---

57. Brown v. Board of Educ., 347 U.S. 483, 489 (1954).

cases."[58] (Nor can they be decided without them, it should be noted.)[59] The point here is that general propositions (precepts) in the Constitution do not provide the precision which will enable the resolution of a given case. Further searches and additional thought must be made. (The matter will be further discussed in Myth Number Five, below.)

The essential question is one of interpretation. It arises whenever an authoritative text exists over a period of time. In smallest form, perhaps, it may be seen in the routine legal instruments like contracts and wills and conveyances. Of broader and more general importance are statutes[60] and other rules of generalized application (*e.g.*, some administrative rules). Constitutions are even broader and more abstract. The legal problem in each instance tends to differ, although judges have not been careful in distinguishing the problems. Much loose language may be observed concerning such matters as effectuating the intentions of the parties and so on. The language is just that—loose—and nothing more. For it seems obvious that if intention must be searched for, it is likely the parties did not have a specific intention in the first place. The same may be said for statutes and for constitutions. Language about intention then may be said to be either a cloak for other, unstated, reasons, or it is added to an opinion because lawyers are familiar with it and accordingly would feel more comfortable with it.[61]

What may be said about legal documents is also true of any other written instrument or text which exists over a period of time and which must be applied in differing situations. The most obvious is the sacred literature of the various religions of the world—the Bible, the Talmud, the Koran come immediately to mind. Here, too, the "intention of the Framer" is of paramount importance; but here, too, that intention may be obscure and unascertainable. Finally, the idea of intention as a determinant of present-day decisions rests upon the fallacy that words have a single, undeviating meaning good for all times and places. The context in which a statement is made or words are used is important. As for constitutions, the words remain the same but their content changes—as is quite evident from a glance at the evolution of "due process" and of "state action." The Constitution as an evolving document—a living instrument of governance—has been discussed elsewhere, so that no need exists to expand upon the concept of the "living" Constitution.[62] Suffice it to say that since the Document is a living

58. Lochner v. New York, 198 U.S. 45, 76 (1905).
59. COHEN, *op. cit. supra* note 47, at 63:
[W]ithout the use of concepts and general principles we can have no science, or intelligible systematic account, of the law or of any other field. And the demand for system in the law is urgent not only on theoretical but also on practical grounds. Without general ideas, human experience is dumb as well as blind.
60. See Frankfurter, *Some Reflections of the Reading of Statutes*, 47 COLUM. L. REV. 527 (1947); Friendly, *Mr. Justice Frankfurter and the Reading of Statutes*, in FELIX FRANKFURTER: THE JUDGE 30 (Mendelson ed. 1964).
61. *Cf.* Wofford, *The Blinding Light: The Uses of History in Constitutional Interpretation*, 31 U. CHI. L. REV. 502 (1964).
62. Miller, *supra* note 48. Mr. Justice Black—of all people—appears to deny the va-

instrument, then a search for intention is a mere academic (and boot-less) exercise. Justice Holmes put it effectively in *Missouri v. Holland*: "[W]hen we are dealing with words that also are a constituent act, like the Constitution of the United States, we must realize that they have called into life a being the development of which could not have been foreseen completely by the most gifted of its begetters. It was enough for them to realize or to hope that they had created an organism; it has taken a century and has cost their successors much sweat and blood to prove that they created a nation. The case before us must be con-sidered in the light of our whole experience and not merely in that of what we said a hundred years ago."[63]

5. *The Myth that Decisions May Be Deduced from the Constitution*

A corollary to the previous proposition that intention can and should guide present decision is the notion that "every decision follows logi-cally from the Constitution"; as Morris R. Cohen maintained three decades ago, this idea is a "pretence" and a "superstition." He went on to assert: "No rational argument can prove that when the people adopted the Constitution they actually intended all the fine distinctions which the courts have introduced into its interpretation."[64] The myth that decisions may be logically deduced from the Constitution inheres particularly in those who take a simplistic view of the Document. Only by employing the most transparent of fictions can, say, the relationships between the units of the federal system be determined from the divi-sion of powers between central and local governments. So, too, with the separation of powers—and with any of the great generalities of the Constitution.

The frame of government, the generalized statement of powers and limitations, provides at best a point of departure—not irrelevant, to

---

lidity of the concept of the living Constitution in his dissenting opinion in Griswold v. Connecticut, 381 U.S. 479 (1965). But his statement can hardly be taken seriously.

63.   252 U.S. 416, 433 (1920). *Cf.* Wofford, *supra* note 61, at 532: "[H]istory makes no judgments; only individuals do. History should be merely one aid in helping that indi-vidual come to a sensible—but necessarily personal-judgment." And see Baldwin & Mc-Laughlin, *The Reapportionment Cases: A Study in the Constitutional Adjudicative Proc-ess*, 17 U. FLA. L. REV. 301, 322 (1964): "The framers apparently did not 'intend' that later generations look for their 'intent.'"

The conventional wisdom is restated in Merrill, *Constitutional Interpretation: The Obligation to Respect the Text*, in PERSPECTIVES OF THE LAW: ESSAYS FOR AUSTIN WAKEMAN SCOTT 260 (Pound, Griswold & Sutherland ed. 1964). Professor Merrill's attempt to resur-rect mechanical jurisprudence is both unconvincing (in that he takes a far too simplistic view of the problem of interpretation) and surprising (in cavalierly sweeping aside all that the legal realists taught).

64.   COHEN, *op. cit. supra* note 47, at 84.

Human society keeps changing. Needs emerge, first vaguely felt and unexpressed im-perceptibly gathering strength steadily becoming more and more exigent, generating a force which, if left unheeded and denied response so as to satisfy the impulse be-hind it at least in part, may burst forth with an intensity that exacts more than a reasonable satisfaction. Law as the response to these needs is not merely a system of logical deduction, though considerations of logic are far from irrelevant. Law pre-supposes sociological wisdom as well as logical unfolding. Frankfurter, J., in AN AUTO-BIOGRAPHY OF THE SUPREME COURT (Westin ed. 1963).

be sure, for one must not fall into the trap of what Cohen called "nihilistic absolutism,"[65] but merely a datum from which reasoning to a conclusion may proceed. The difficult problem, as noted above, is how that process of reasoning should proceed. No satisfactory answer, except in the vaguest of abstract admonitions, has as yet been given to that problem.[66] For if intention is at best but one of the factors of decision and if conclusions cannot logically be deduced from the Constitution itself, the actual and preferred methodology of the Justices becomes of crucial importance. With respect to that methodology, it may well be that the problem differs depending upon the nature of the question. For instance, if the issue is one involving separation of powers or federalism, then the Supreme Court faces an essentially political question. What Morris R. Cohen said about federalism is equally applicable to separation of powers: "In a changing society the relations between the states and the nation are essentially political, *i.e.*, determined on grounds of social policy, and . . . it is only by an intellectually indefensible fiction that they can be deduced from a written document such as our Federal Constitution."[67]

If the issue, however, is one of government deprivations upon the individual—that is, if it involves the question of limitations upon government vis-à-vis individuals—can it be said that the relations are otherwise determined? Are they not equally "political," *i.e.*, decided upon the grounds of good social policy? One would think so after a perusal of any number of Supreme Court opinions. For it seems obvious that it is only by an "intellectually indefensible fiction" that the vagueness of the constitution proscriptions can be used as a major premise from which to deduce specific conclusions.[68] This writer has elsewhere asserted that the adjudicative process is "either mechanistic or teleological" and that there is no halfway-house between the two.[69] On reflection, I should like to reaffirm that conclusion—that the judicial decision-making process in constitutional questions is inescapably and principally teleological in nature. By this is meant that the ends or purposes of the Constitution are at the center of the judicial scrutiny and that the inquiry unavoidably is forward or purposive, rather than retrospective. One of those "ends," of course, is continuity with the past, for, as Justice Holmes has said, "we cannot escape history." But

65. *Ibid.* COHEN, *op. cit. supra* note 47, at 84.

66. The complexities of the decisional process in adjudication are discussed in Mayo & Jones, *Legal-Policy Decision Process: Alternative Thinking and the Predictive Function*, 33 GEO. WASH. L. REV. 318 (1964). Justice Douglas has said that the problems with which the Supreme Court deals are "delicate and imponderable, complex and tangled. They require at times the economist's understanding, the poet's insight, the executive's experience, the political scientist's understanding, the historian's perspective." Douglas, *The Supreme Court and Its Case Load*, 45 CORNELL L.Q. 401, 414 (1960).

67. COHEN, AMERICAN THOUGHT: A CRITICAL SKETCH 169 (1964).

68. See Miller, *On the Choice of Major Premises in Supreme Court Opinions*, 14 J. PUB. L. — (1965); Miller, *supra* note 45, at 527-32.

69. Miller, *A Note on the Criticism of Supreme Court Decisions*, 10 J. Pub. L. 139, 150 (1961).

reference to the past is merely a necessity, not a duty; and the past (as precedent, as antecedent principle, as a body of received norms) is merely one of the factors of relevance in constitutional decision-making. The very nature of the vague precepts of the Constitution and the lines of decisional doctrine thereunder indicate that Justice Douglas's observation that "matters of constitutional interpretation are always open"[70] is a statement of the discretion the Justices have, if they wish to employ it.

The continuing debate over "principled decision-making," initiated by the late Judge Learned Hand and by Professor Herbert Wechsler, involves an attempt to reconcile the conflicting demands of adherence to "principle" or pre-existing rule and the pull of the impact that given decisions make upon the value positions of designated Americans. It would serve no useful purpose to review the details of this debate, but some of the principal papers may be found cited in the footnotes.[71] One lesson to be derived from the debate is important, however; it is this: There is, after more than 1000 years of Anglo-American legal history, no accepted conception of the nature of the judicial process.

In this connection, another submyth may be noted (as a corollary to the main myth that decisions may be logically deduced from the Constitution): that the Justices look only antecedently to an existing corpus of principle which has been produced since 1789, as exegesis upon the text of the Constitution, to find the standards by which given cases are decided. At most, that states a half-truth. The contrary seems to be nearer the mark: that Justices look prospectively as well as retrospectively when making decisions; in other words, there is a judicial concern for the consequences of alternative decisions as great as (or perhaps greater than) the concern for pre-existing principles or rules which may be applied in the decisional process.[72] As two astute legal scholars recently said, "American jurisprudential thought, certainly since the famous lectures of Holmes on the common law, has reflected an ever-increasing tendency to look forward to the consequences of decision rather than backward to first principles."[73] They spoke of the judicial process generally, but the conclusion seems apposite beyond peradventure for constitutional adjudication. It is the *effects* of alternative

---

70. Glidden Co. v. Zdanok, 370 U.S. 530, 592 (1962).

71. Wechsler, *Toward Neutral Principles of Constitutional Law*, 73 HARV. L. REV. 1 (1959); Pollak, *Racial Discrimination and Judicial Integrity: A Reply to Professor Wechsler*, 108 U. PA. L. REV. 1 (1959); Mueller & Schwartz, *The Principle of Neutral Principles*, 7 U.C.L.A.L. REV. 571 (1960); Miller & Howell, *The Myth of Neutrality in Constitutional Adjudication*, 27 U. CHI. L. REV. 661 (1960); Hart, *The Time Chart of the Justices*, 73 HARV. L. REV. 84 (1959); Arnold, *Professor Hart's Theology*, 73 HARV. L. REV. 1298 (1960); Griswold, *Of Time and Attitudes—Professor Hart and Judge Arnold*, 74 HARV. L. REV. 81 (1960); Hyman & Newhouse, *supra* note 17; Henkin, *supra* note 47; Golding, *Principled Decision-Making and Supreme Court*, 63 COLUM. L. REV. 35 (1963).

72. See Miller, *On the Need for "Impact Analysis" of Supreme Court Decisions*, 53 GEO. L.J. 365 (1965).

73. Mayo & Jones, *supra* note 66, at 318. See ROSTOW, THE SOVEREIGN PREROGATIVE (1962).

decisions which concern the Court quite as much as any other factor. The proper discharge of the judicial function thus depends less on conceptualized formulae, however derived, than on "correct appreciation of social conditions and a true appraisal of the actual effects of conduct."[74] The Supreme Court, accordingly, is as much "result oriented" as it is "concept oriented," perhaps more so; it is interested in what difference its decisions make in the institutional practices within the United States, although the myth is to the contrary.[75] This has direct bearing upon the next of this listing of Supreme Court myths.

6. The Myth that the Justices Can Be Passionless Vehicles for Discovering and Applying "The Law"

This is a conception of the judicial process which appears to be generally accepted by most laymen and which still has some adherents among lawyers, even though it has long been exploded. It may be found in many forms and contexts. The ancient notion of a "government of laws and not of men" embodies the assumption that the "law" can rule without the intervention of a human hand.[76] In its starkest form, perhaps, the myth took the form of what Dean Roscoe Pound castigated fifty years ago as "mechanical jurisprudence" and what Morris R. Cohen derided as the "phonograph" theory of justice.[77] Under this view, the task of the appellate judge is to be a human automaton rigidly applying known rules of law, which are found or discovered and never created, to the facts of the case before the court. Jerome Frank put this in the form of an equation—$R(\text{rule}) \times F(\text{facts}) = D(\text{decision})$.[78] The mere statement of the $R \times F = D$ equation is its own refutation, as the legal realists convincingly demonstrated years ago.

But having smashed the facade of classical jurisprudence, the legal realists were content to leave the place in shambles. They did nothing to construct a viable jurisprudence to replace the classical belief. The result is that we still do not have a viable conception of the adjudicative process, in the sense of a jurisprudence that will comprehensively analyze and explicate all aspects of the judicial decision. This much was

---

74. JACKSON, THE STRUGGLE FOR JUDICIAL SUPREMACY 44 (1941). See MASON, THE SUPREME COURT FROM TAFT TO WARREN (1958).

75. See Mason, *Myth and Reality in Supreme Court Decisions*, 48 VA. L. REV. 1385 (1962) for discussion.

76. Charles Horsky said in 1952 that this is a government of men and not of law. HORSKY, THE WASHINGTON LAWYER (1952). *But see*, HYNEMAN, THE SUPREME COURT ON TRIAL (1963) for a statement of the conventional wisdom. A general discussion of the problem may be found in SAWER, LAW IN SOCIETY Ch. II (1965).

77. Pound, *Mechanical Jurisprudence*, 8 COLUM. L. REV. 605 (1908); COHEN, LAW AND THE SOCIAL ORDER 380-81 n.86 (1933). See MASON, *op. cit. supra* note 74, at 95: Discussing "the myth that in constitutional cases judges discover the law, merely placing the controverted statute beside the relevant clause of the Constitution. Overnight, Supreme Court Justices were once again pictured as demigods far above the sweaty crowd, abstractly weighing public policy in the delicate scales of the law."

78. FRANK, COURTS ON TRIAL 14 (1949); See LEVI, AN INTRODUCTION TO LEGAL REASONING (1949); CORBIN, CONTRACTS (1950-51) (particularly Professor Corbin's remarks on "working rules").

noted above; it is repeated here because of its relevance to the present discussion.

The starting point, it seems, for any construction of a new jurisprudence must be a recognition of the nature of human thought and the limitations of the human mind. For judicial thought processes are a segment of human thought, and probably not dissimilar from other modes of thinking or of reaching decisions. If this is taken as the point of departure, then the first thing to be recognized is that very little is known about how decisions are reached in any situation, let alone the judiciary. At best, some tentative hypotheses are available, mainly from preliminary forays by behavioral scientists and others who have sought to probe the mysteries of judicial behavior.[79] The predilections, the inarticulate major premises, which everyone carries with him, inevitably color the manner in which he views any given problem. This much can be learned from the behavioral scientists, although they cannot state in detail and with precision what the decision of a given judge might be. The law, and particularly constitutional law, is more a tool for manipulation than a set of interdictory commands.

This, it may be noted, is not a crude attempt at what was once called "gastronomical jurisprudence." It is not suggested that the state of a man's digestion determines the decisions he reaches. But what is suggested is that there is a myth of neutrality about judges and others concerned with the legal process, a myth in the sense that a judge cannot escape his background and heredity. A recognition must be made, accordingly, of this factor as being of as much importance as "The Law" in the resolution of any given case. This question has been discussed at length in a previous paper by this writer, and the reasons for such a conclusion will not now be expanded upon.[80]

If it is granted that a judge carries with him his biases and prejudices —his "can't helps," in Justice Holmes' terms—and that he cannot entirely eliminate them no matter how hard he tries, the problem then becomes one of how to deal with the situation. The late Justice Frankfurter, who gave as much thought as any to the problem, stated his conclusions in this manner:

> It is important to appreciate the qualifications requisite for those who exercise this extraordinary authority (of judicial review), demanding as it does a breadth of outlook and an invincible disinterestedness rooted in temperament and confirmed by discipline. Of course, individual judgment and feeling cannot be wholly shut out of the judicial process. But if they dominate, the judicial process becomes a dangerous sham. The conception by a judge of the scope and limits of his function may exert an intellectual and moral force as much as responsiveness to a particular audience or congenial environment.[81]

---

79. See SCHUBERT, *op. cit. supra* note 12.
80. Miller & Howell, *supra* note 71. See Powell, *The Logic and Rhetoric of Constitutional Law*, in ESSAYS IN CONSTITUTIONAL LAW 85 (McCloskey ed. 1957).
81. Frankfurter, *John Marshall and the Judicial Function*, in GOVERNMENT UNDER LAW 6, 21 (Sutherland ed. 1956). *But see*, FRANKFURTER, LAW AND POLITICS 13 (1939).

And in *Rochin v. California*,[82] in a celebrated exchange with Justice Black who accused his brethren of reading their ideas of good social policy (which he called "natural law") into the fourteenth amendment, Justice Frankfurter said:

> We may not draw on our merely personal and private notions and dis-regard the limits that bind judges in their judicial function. . . . To practice the requisite detachment and to achieve sufficient objectivity no doubt demands of judges the habit of self-discipline and self-criticism, incertitude that one's own views are incontestable and alert tolerance toward views not shared. . . . [T]hese are precisely the presuppositions of our judicial process. They are precisely the qualities society has a right to expect from those entrusted with ultimate judicial power.[83]

That does not tell us very much, particularly since the language is that of high-level abstraction, but perhaps it is as much as can be gotten from judges, as much as we are entitled to. One other alternative exists, however: It is possible to posit that there should be a conscious facing up to one's valuations and stating them with as much precision as possible.[84] No doubt this would help clarify the decisional process as it is seen from the outside. Even so, two problems would still remain. In the first place, it is not at all certain that one can transcend or even state his personal valuations with any degree of precision and completeness. Short of psychoanalysis of judges, which has been suggested[85] but which most observers shy from, it is doubtful at best that a judge could state what his "real" motivations might be. That problem is difficult enough, but the second objection may be even more so: the idea that the Supreme Court (and all courts) might lose their high position in the value hierarchy of the American people if it ever became widely known that judges were not passionless vehicles for the enunciation of "The

---

82. 342 U.S. 165 (1952).

83. 342 U.S. at 170-72. The problem of informing the judicial mind is particularly acute. Compare these statements: "Can we not take judicial notice of writing by people who competently deal with these problems? Can I not take judicial notice of Myrdal's book without having him called as a witness? . . . How to inform the judicial mind, as you know, is one of the most complicated problems. It is better to have witnesses, but I did not know that we could not read the works of competent writers." Frankfurter, J., quoted from oral argument in MURPHY & PRITCHETT, COURTS, JUDGES, AND POLITICS (1961). "The briefs of counsel are always helpful, but each of us is better satisfied when he not only checks but also supplements those materials with independent research." Brennan, J., quoted in AN AUTOBIOGRAPHY OF THE SUPREME COURT 303 (Westin ed. 1963). See Wormuth, *The Impact of Economic Legislation upon the Supreme Court*, 6 J. PUB. L. 296 (1957); Karst, *Legislative Facts in Constitutional Litigation*, 1960 SUP. CT. REV. 75; Massel, *Economic Analysis in Judicial Antitrust Decisions*, 20 A.B.A. SEC. ANTITRUST L. 46 (1962).

84. See Myrdal, *Value in Social Theory* 132 (Streeten ed. 1958): "There is no other device for excluding biases in the social sciences than to face the valuations and to introduce them as explicitly stated, specific, and sufficiently concretized, value premises." Myrdal was discussing methodology in the social sciences; the suggestion here is that his point may be—is—equally valid for constitutional adjudication.

85. LASSWELL, POWER AND PERSONALITY (1947).

Frankfurter, J., in an off-bench statement, asserted: "The fact is that pitifully little of significance has been contributed by judges regarding the nature of their endeavor, and I might add, that which is written by those who are not judges is too often a confident caricature rather than a seer's version of the judicial process of the Supreme Court." FRANKFURTER, OF LAW AND MEN 32 (Elman ed. 1956).

Law." As Max Lerner put it in 1941: "Talk to the men on the street, the men in the mines and factories and steel mills and real-estate offices and filling stations, dig into their minds and even below the threshold of their consciousness, and you will find in the main that the Constitution and the Supreme Court are symbols of ancient sureness and comforting stability."[86] Forsaking the mythology of an infallible finder of truth and getting involved in "politics" and value judgments may, accordingly, result in a substantial diminution of Court prestige. For some, this argues for retaining the myth and keeping the truth from the laity, who in the view of those who espouse the notion do not have the moral and intellectual stamina to withstand knowing that Supreme Court Justices are human. But as will be argued below, it is better to know the truth and adjust to it than to be kept in the dark.

In any event, it is important to note a submyth to the main myth, namely, that in making decisions the Justices do not decide upon the wisdom of the governmental act under consideration. The submyth is particularly to be seen in the older economic due process decisions of the Court, but may also be perceived in such more recent decisions as *Griswold v. Connecticut*[87] (invalidating a state anti-contraceptive statute). Compare, in this connection, Justice Frankfurter's opinion in *Bridges v. California:* "We are not invested with jurisdiction to pass upon the expediency, wisdom, or justice of the laws of the states as declared by their courts but only to determine their conformity to the federal constitution and the paramount laws enacted pursuant to it,"[88] with Chief Justice Taft's dissent in *Adkins v. Children's Hospital:* "But it is not the function of this Court to hold congressional acts invalid simply because they are passed to carry out economic views which the Court believes unwise or unsound,"[89] and with Justice Douglas's opinion in *Griswold:* "We do not sit as a super-legislature to determine the wisdom, need, and propriety of laws that touch economic problems, business affairs, or social conditions."[90]

True it is that the Supreme Court of course has no mandate to roam at will and to strike down state statutes or federal governmental actions willy-nilly. Within the area of their competence, however, which after all is largely self-determined, it is difficult not to say that at times the Court in fact does rule on the wisdom of what other governmental organs wish to do. *Griswold* provides illustration. There the Court struck down Connecticut's anti-contraceptive statute because it invaded a "penumbral" right of privacy which Justice Douglas found as an "emanation" from the Bill of Rights (a most remarkable example of purposive, forward-looking adjudication), and which Justice Goldberg,

---

86. LERNER, IDEAS FOR THE ICE AGE 232 (1941).
87. 381 U.S. 479 (1965).
88. 314 U.S. 252, 281 (1941).
89. 261 U.S. 525, 562 (1923).
90. 381 U.S. at 482.

in a concurring opinion, said was protected by the ninth amendment. This was too heady for Justices White and Harlan, however, both of whom concurred in the result but only because they found due process of law to be violated. Just why this formulation is any less judicial law-making the learned Justices did not say. Dissenting Justice Black was particularly miffed at the due process argument: "If these formulas . . . [to ascertain what is due process] are to prevail, they require judges to determine what is or is not constitutional on the basis of their own appraisal of what laws are unwise or unneccessary. . . . Surely it has to be admitted that no provision of the Constitution specifically gives such a blanket power to courts to exercise a supervisory veto over the wisdom and value of legislative policies and to hold unconstitutional those laws which they believe unwise or dangerous."[91] Justice Stewart echoed this in another dissenting opinion, calling it "the essence of judicial duty to subordinate our personal views, our own ideas of what legislation is wise and what is not."[92]

Griswold, thus, raised fundamental questions about the role and methodology of the Supreme Court. It is difficult to fault Justice Black in his view that his brethren are substituting their own notions of legislative wisdom for those of Connecticut's legislature. (Peripherally, Justice Black's position may confound those who consider him to be the great judicial activist of this era.)[93] In this instance at least, and surely in many others, the Court is substituting its notion of good public policy for that of a state legislature. The view that Supreme Court Justices do not, at times, so substitute may be said to be mythical, whatever the protestations of some Justices. But even so, even if it is granted that the social wisdom of some policies is reviewed, that is not the whole of the matter. It is not a new technique. Supreme Court members have been reading their ideas of good public policy into the Constitution since the Court was first constituted and began its mission of judicial review. Without going into the question of whether it is desirable or not,[94] it is indeed hard to see how judicial review could be conducted in any other way; if the Court is to do its assumed and his-torically validated task, it cannot escape getting from time to time into an evaluation of the wisdom of given policies enunciated by another organ of government. To Justice Black the touchstone of constitution-ality is some express statement in the document which can be inter-preted to cover (or not to cover) the case before the Court at a particular time. But this does not seem to be adequate, for, as the learned Justice knows very well, express language is not limited to a fixed meaning.

---

91. *Id.* at 511.
92. *Id.* at 530.
93. See, *e.g.,* MENDELSON, JUSTICES BLACK AND FRANKFURTER: CONFLICT ON THE COURT (1961).
94. *Compare* the many examples cited by Black, J., in his dissenting opinion in the *Griswold* case with his own statement of his judicial philosophy, Black, *The Bill of Rights,* 37 N.Y.U.L. REV. 549 (1962).

Accordingly, even in those parts which are stated expressly, such as the first amendment, interpretation is necessary and unavoidable. Justice Black is on record as believing that the first amendment speaks in absolute terms,[95] but has not been able to convince his colleagues (nor anyone else, for that matter) that he is correct. Thus even where Justice Black sees absolutes, there are in fact none, and interpretation must be made, which means getting into the question of wisdom. The point, in short, is simply that evaluations of social wisdom ineluctably are a part of the constitutional adjudicative process, asseverations of Supreme Court Justices to the contrary notwithstanding. Judge Learned Hand put the matter in accurate perspective when he said: "Judges are seldom content merely to annul the particular solution before them; they do not, indeed they may not, say that taking all things into consideration, the legislators' solution is too strong for the judicial stomach. On the contrary they wrap up their veto in a protective veil of adjectives such as 'arbitrary,' 'artificial,' 'normal,' 'reasonable,' 'inherent,' 'fundamental,' or 'essential,' whose office usually, though quite innocently, is to disguise what they are doing and impute to it a derivation far more impressive than their personal preferences, which are all that in fact lie behind the decision. If we do need a third chamber it should appear for what it is, and not as the interpreter of inscrutable principles."[96] In other words, by composing an opinion in language with which lawyers are familiar and which makes them comfortable, the Justices both hide their creative role and seek to mask over the fact that they are ruling on what they think is wise social policy. Whether this is good or bad is not the purpose of this paper; it is merely to suggest that statements such as those quoted from Justices Taft, Frankfurter, and Douglas are statements mythical in nature and not in consonance with reality.

7. The Myth that the Court Is Encroaching on the Legislature

In part, this is the myth of "judicial legislation" mentioned above, which has as its basis that judges are supposed to "find" and do not "make" law. That judges can and do make law is, of course, as obvious a proposition as can be stated about the judiciary—whether it be in constitutional adjudications, in statutory interpretations, or in the development of the "common law." While it may be that lawmaking proclivities of judges are confined to interstitial matters, to "molecular" as compared to "molar" motion,[97] in any event, the judge does have a creative role in some degree, and in fact cannot escape having one. The myth to the contrary has not been followed by any thoughtful observer of the courts for decades. Federal Judge Charles E. Wyzanski, Jr., one of

---

95. *Ibid.*
96. HAND, THE BILL OF RIGHTS 70 (1958).
97. As Holmes, J., asserted in his dissent. Southern Pac. Co. v. Jensen, 244 U.S. 205, 221 (1917).

the better district court judges, put the matter in effective focus a few years ago: "Our law is no longer a judge-centered law. We find it hard to believe that, according to Maitland, a century and a half ago virtually all lawmaking that affected private persons was in the hands of fourteen judges of the High Court. Today even in England, and a fortiori in the United States, the judge has ceased to 'embody the law,' and is hardly its oracle."[98] Legislatures, in other words, and administrative agencies are latter-day developments. If any "encroachment" is taking place, it is by those two organs of government upon what, as Judge Wyzanski indicates, was the historical prerogative of courts.

Judge Wyzanski's observation about law creation in the Anglo-American legal system cannot be gainsaid, historically or contemporaneously. He spoke, however, in the main about the historical situation, of the times when the courts were central to the law-making process, before the rise of legislatures and the bureaucracy to their present prominence. Nevertheless, to the extent that courts make decisions today, in whatever category but surely in the area of constitutional interpretation, they cannot avoid having a creative function if they are to do their job at all. Cases, despite the oft-stated view to the contrary, are never on "all-fours" to previous cases. Factual situations can and do differ from case to case, so much so that the reasoning, as Dean Levi has said, is basically by analogy and the search is for the apposite analogy.[99] An analogous situation is never precisely the same situation, which is unfortunate for those who seek certainty in the law but fortunate for those who must work with and in the law. Furthermore, as Jerome Frank emphasized, in the later years of his career, one needs to be skeptical of the facts—to engage in fact-skepticism as well as rule-skepticism —if he is to attain any sort of an accurate picture of the judicial process.[100] Perhaps Bishop Hoadly, in his oft-quoted aphorism, summarized the situation as succinctly and as well as anyone when he stated in 1717: "Whoever hath an absolute authority to interpret any written or spoken laws, it is he who is truly the Lawgiver to all intents and purposes, and not the person who first wrote or spoke them."[101]

It is of more than incidental interest to wonder about the persistence of this myth. Why does it still influence the thinking of many commentators on the judiciary? Is there some deep-set psychological reason which makes many want to believe that judges can avoid law-making? Jerome Frank attempted an explanation in *Law and the Modern Mind*, a book which in all fairness must at this juncture be termed a brave, yet futile, effort to explain in Freudian terms some of the mysteries of the adjudicative process. Frank set forth what seemed to him to be the

98. Wyzanski, *History and Law*, 26 U. CHI. L. REV. 237, 240 (1959).
99. LEVI, *op. cit. supra* note 78; Levi, *The Nature of Judicial Reasoning*, 32 U. CHI. L. REV. 395 (1965).
100. FRANK, *op. cit. supra* note 78.
101. Quoted in GRAY, THE NATURE AND SOURCES OF THE LAW 102 (2d ed. 1931).

"basic myth": "The widespread notion that law either is or can be made approximately stationary and certain."[102] Frank called this an illusion, a myth.

A variation on the judicial legislation theme may be seen in those who admit the propriety of judicial review and even that judges can and do make law but who balk at certain decisions of the United States Supreme Court as unduly intruding upon the province of the legislature. In some respects, this variation is a restatement of Justice Frankfurter's and Justice Stone's notion that other branches of government must be considered to have the capacity to govern; such a notion was and is a resounding truism, even for Justice Stone and certainly for Justice Frankfurter. But the variation of the myth is somewhat more. Perhaps the most noteworthy recent instance came in *Wesberry v. Sanders*,[103] a 1964 decision which read article I of the Constitution as requiring districts of roughly equal population in the election of members of the House of Representatives. *Wesberry*, one of the progeny spawned by *Baker v. Carr*,[104] seems at first reading to be a rather clear judicial encroachment upon the clear legislative prerogative as spelled out in article I. But is it?

Whatever conclusion one reaches on *Wesberry*, there are of course numerous examples of the same thing, most of which, however, are of mere historical interest. Thus the 1930's saw the systematic invalidation of "New Deal" legislation, but the constitutional revolution of 1937 inaugurated a new set of doctrines. Possibly, it could be argued that Supreme Court interpretation of commerce clause matters in the absence of congressional legislation, as in state taxation or regulation of interstate commerce, is also an intrusion upon the legislative prerogative. If so, it has not convinced many, although Justice Black at times indicates that he believes the Court is not properly in the area.[105] And the late Edward S. Corwin argued that the decision in the *Steel Seizure Case* was as improper as the presidential seizure because if Justice Black, writing for the Court, was correct in his view, then only Congress could act in such industrial relations matters—and the Court's decision violated the command of the separation of powers.[106]

Such suggestions as these perhaps need not be taken very seriously, even though the judicial intrusion is as clear as, or clearer than in other cases. The cry of judicial legislation is at best a plaintive hankering for a bygone age—that never existed in the first place. It is the eternal cry for a "golden age"—one in which matters can be ordered, problems regulated, and the fuzziness in which most human questions are involved can be eliminated for cleancut solutions.[107] The next in our listing is of more substance, perhaps, but a myth nonetheless.

102. FRANK, LAW AND THE MODERN MIND (1930).
103. 376 U.S. 1 (1964).
104. 369 U.S. 186.
105. *E.g.*, McCarroll v. Dixie Greyhound Lines, 309 U.S. 176, 183 (1940).
106. CORWIN & KOENIG, THE PRESIDENCY TODAY 41 (1956).
107. *Cf.* FRANK, *op. cit. supra* note 102.

8. *The Myth that the Court Is Distorting the Federal System.*

Writing in 1962, the president of the American Bar Association, Mr. John C. Satterfield, asserted that "fundamental changes are being made in our form of government by judicial decisions."[108] His principal reference was to federalism and to the deterioration of the historical relationship between the states and the central government allegedly caused by judicial decisions. In this position Mr. Satterfield has some respectable company. Justice Harlan has been particularly vehement in this regard. For example, in *Reynolds v. Sims* he asserted that: "[N]o thinking person can fail to recognize that the aftermath of these [reapportionment] cases, however desirable it may be thought in itself, will have been achieved at the cost of a radical alteration in the relationship between the States and the Federal Government, more particularly the Federal Judiciary. Only one who has an overbearing impatience with the federal system and its political processes will believe that that cost was not too high or was inevitable."[109] Justice Harlan's position has been echoed by well-known professors of law; for example, Professor Philip Kurland of the University of Chicago, citing Mr. Justice Harlan's impassioned dissenting opinion in *Wesberry v. Sanders*,[110] maintains that "the Court has unreasonably infringed on the authority committed by the Constitution to other branches of government."[111]

There can be no question that major changes have taken place in the relative position of the state and federal governments since 1787.[112] It is becoming increasingly apparent that the states are not and cannot be viable political and economic units. The consequences are dual: On the one hand, there is a movement toward interstate cooperation by way of compact and other devices to enable local government to tackle social problems on a greater than state-wide basis;[113] but more importantly there is, on the other hand, the expanding power of the central government. That this latter trend has taken place is obvious, both from the lesson of history and from a survey of contemporary America. No one disputes this, however the trend may be deplored. What *is* disputed is the cause of the trend. Can it be traced to judicial decisions as the chief influencing factor? Not so: What the Court has done is to place a constitutional imprimatur upon changes that are wrought by

---

108. Satterfield, President's Page, 48 A.B.A.J. 595 (1962).

109. 377 U.S. 533, 624 (1964).

110. 376 U.S. at 48.

111. Kurland, *The Court of the Union or Julius Caesar Revised*, 39 Notre Dame Law. 636, 638 (1964). This article is cogently criticized in Hyman, *Concerning the Responsibility and Craftmanship of the Judge*, 14 Buffalo L. Rev. 347 (1965).

112. In 1958, thirty-six of the chief justices of the state supreme courts in conference assembled, "respectfully" urged the Supreme Court of the United States to exercise "one of the greatest of all judicial powers—the power of judicial self-restraint. . ." particularly with respect to the federal-state relationship. The report of the Conference of Chief Justices is reproduced in U.S. News & World Report, Oct. 3, 1958, p. 92. Effective refutation of the state chief justices may be found in Lockhart, *A Response to the Conference of State Chief Justices*, 107 U. Pa. L. Rev. 802 (1959); Rostow, *op. cit. supra* note 73.

113. See Dixon, *Constitutional Bases for Regionalism: Centralization; Interstate Compacts; Federal Regional Taxation*, 33 Geo. Wash. L. Rev. 47 (1964).

other, diverse influences, not the least of which is the growth of science and technology and the expansion of the corporate form of doing business.[114] Although it is doubtless accurate to note that the Supreme Court has been making decisions in matters long left to state control—notably in racial segregation and in voting matters—it is nonetheless true beyond peradventure that while doing so it has by and large merely promulgated a public policy that has the support, tacit or expressed, of the American people. Furthermore, the Court has at times tried to stem the tide toward greater centralized government, as in *Erie v. Tompkins*,[115] a decision that will eventually have to be overruled because it is not in consonance with the social realities of the nation.

If any one branch of the national government can be said to have an impact upon the federal system, it is Congress. The legislative policies established by the elected representatives of the people have had much more effect on the nature of federalism than have judicial decisions, particularly in the areas of economics and social legislation. These policies have been established, not because of some conspiracy of "creeping socialism," but because the "felt necessities of the times" produced pressures which made them unavoidable. A consistent failure on the part of state governments to accept the responsibilities of government in the twentieth century made it inevitable that the national government would be called upon to produce the programs demanded by the American people. Illustrations are many and need not be multiplied. One of the most noteworthy is the Civil Rights Act of 1964,[116] a statute that has enormous long-range implications for federalism. The interplay of congressional and judicial action may clearly be seen here. The statute, for example, provides in Title II for nondiscrimination in places of "public accommodation," reliance being placed upon the commerce clause for constitutional validity. When Title II was challenged the Supreme Court had no difficulty upholding it, even though the commercial organizations involved had only a remote connection to interstate commerce.[117] The point here is that it is the Congress, not the Court, which is effecting changes in federal structure. The Supreme Court *validates* the constitutional change, it is true, but that is a far cry from saying it is the cause. With respect to Negro relations within the country, the Civil Rights Act doubtless will have a more significant impact upon the pattern of racial discrimination in public schools than did *Brown v. Board of Education* and its progeny. Title VI of the statute, which provides for withholding federal aid from institutions that do not adhere to the congressionally-established norm of nondiscrimination on the basis of race, color, or creed, has in fact already had

114. See Miller, *Technology, Social Change, and the Constitution*, 33 Geo. Wash. L. Rev. 17 (1964).
115. 304 U.S. 64 (1938).
116. 78 Stat. 241 (1964).
117. Heart of Atlanta Motel, Inc. v. United States, 379 U.S. 241 (1964); Katzenbach v. McClung, 379 U.S. 294 (1964).

a greater effect.[118] Although it is probable that the Civil Rights Act could (or would) not have been passed had the Court not led the way with its racial decisions, what this means is that at times there is a reciprocating interaction between judicial and legislative (as well as executive) acts.

When the social bases of constitutional change are examined, as they must be if any accurate evaluation is to be made, then the mythical nature of the charge that the Supreme Court is distorting the federal system becomes clearly evident. What Justice Frankfurter once called "the unifying forces of modern technology"[119] have, with other forces such as war, had much more to do with the nature of the federal system than have judicial decisions. In addition, it should be recognized by anyone even casually conversant with the nature of law and government that public policies, however enunciated, are not likely to be effective unless the force of public opinion is behind them. Add to that the not-to-be-doubted factor of continuing and rapid change as a constant in the social order and the conclusion is unavoidable that the Supreme Court is not making fundamental changes in the American form of government. This is not to say that Court decisions are without effect, but merely to suggest that the context in which social and legal change takes place puts the lie to the charge by Mr. Satterfield and those who follow his line. The process is much more complicated than the simplistic model which he and Justice Harlan assert.

9. *The Myth that Court Decisions Have Contributed to the Growth of Crime.*

A spate of recent Supreme Court decisions, which, when taken together, apply segments of the Bill of Rights to the states and seek to improve the administration of the criminal law, has given rise to a tide of comment that the Court is "handcuffing the police" and is contributing to the increase in crime throughout the nation.[120] The indictment of the Court is that it severely and unnecessarily limits the power of the states to enforce their criminal laws.[121] As has been said by Mr. Keith Mossman, speaking as Executive Vice President of the National District Attorneys' Association:

> There has never in the history of this country been a greater need for effective law-enforcement. This country can no longer afford a "civil rights binge" that so restricts law enforcement agencies that they become ineffective and organized crime flourishes. Law enforcement agencies must not be handcuffed by the false and unrealistic application and expression of individual civil liberties to the point that law enforcement breaks down.[122]

---

118. Discussed in Miller, *supra* note 45.
119. Polish Nat'l Alliance v. NLRB, 322 U.S. 643, 650 (1944).
120. See, *e.g.*, Sondern, *Take the Handcuffs Off Our Police!*, Reader's Digest, Sept. 1964, p. 64.
121. See the collection of statements in Kamisar, *On the Tactics of Police-Prosecution Oriented Critics of the Courts*, 49 CORNELL L.Q. 436 (1964).
122. *Id.* at 447.

And a law professor:

> We are losing the war against crime despite unparalleled police forces and investigative agencies. . . .
>
> Why . . . ? Perhaps it is because criminal justice has become badly unbalanced. Too often it is justice for defendants without regard for the needs and problems of law enforcement and the public. . . . We too often forget that criminals are at war with society.[123]

And another law professor:

> I cannot answer the . . . point with any statistics of my own . . . but some simple logic is available to support the proposition that the *McNabb-Mallory* rule does, and is bound to have, a crippling effect upon law enforcement in any metropolitan jurisdiction saddled with the rule.
>
> . . . To prohibit police interrogation—which, in effect, is what the *McNabb-Mallory* rule does—means . . . that fewer crimes will be solved and successfully prosecuted. More criminals will remain at large, to commit other offenses. At the same time the deterrent effect of apprehension and conviction will be lost insofar as other potential offenders are concerned. The crime rate is bound to be greater under such circumstances, and I do not feel the need of statistics to support the conclusion.[124]

These state the proposition; it is a point of view echoed in many editorials throughout the nation and by police officials and others who have the responsibility of enforcement of the criminal law. How much substance is there to it? Do Court decisions handcuff the police, make it easy for criminals, and contribute to the rising incidence of crime? Is Professor Inbau correct when he says that "simple logic" will so indicate?

The short answer to such questions is that no data exist that will permit any accurate answers to be given. Professor Yale Kamisar has said: "Professor Inbau *may* be right—as far as he goes. Some would-be criminals *may* be emboldened by restrictive rules of evidence. Some *may* thereby be 'freed' to commit another crime another day. Some *may* even be attracted to a jurisdiction which has such rules."[125] (Emphasis added.) He then went on to say, in the course of an article disputing the contention that crime was increased because of judicial decisions, that so little is known about the cause of crime that "simple logic" is not very helpful. And so seems to be the case. The situation is similar to that which attributes the breakdown of historical federalism to judicial decisions. The conclusions are stated without buttressing evidence tending to show a causal relation. Until such evidence is produced, then, as with the previous myth, the notion that Court decisions are a substantial factor in the rise of antisocial behavior belongs at best in the realm of supposition and speculation. It is at most an hypothesis, not a fact; an

---

123. *Ibid.*
124. *Id.* at 455.
125. Kamisar, *supra* note 121, at 455.

opinion which *may* have some validity but which has not yet been authenticated.[126]

All of this, of course, is not wholly to condemn those who quickly assign blame to the Supreme Court. But the point is that what is needed is not only the control and effective handling of criminal activity, which no one disputes, but an understanding of its causes. Until that is forthcoming, it will not do to adhere to simplistic notions of cause-and-effect in social (or anti-social) activity. Blaming the Court for crime is analogous to the ancient Greeks blaming the gods for their troubles. The mythology concerning the Court assigns a malign influence to the Justices—a position not far from the Greeks attributing their misfortunes to Zeus. It is easier, although not very helpful, to assign blame to the Court. By doing so, one need not engage in what Learned Hand once called "the intolerable burden of thought," and one need not face up to the very real need for positive programs in criminal science.[127]

10. *The Myth that the Court Is All-Powerful.*

This discussion of myths eddying around the Supreme Court began with a myth which dealt with an alleged usurpation of power by the "Marshall Court" and its followers. We now turn to the other side of that question; namely, since the Court has assumed power to review acts of other government organs, what difference has it made? More particularly, what is the nature of that power and what are the effects of its exercise on the structure of government and the relationship of government to the individual? In many respects, questions such as these expand on matters discussed above, particularly in Numbers Eight and Nine. But the myth of the all-powerful nature of the Supreme Court goes beyond the question of federalism and the administration of the criminal law; it encompasses the entire spectrum of adjudication. A thorough analysis of the power of the Court would have to begin with the concept of power itself, and it surely is one of the most elusive and slippery terms in the lexicon of politics. Compare for example these definitions:

---

126. After the text was written, an announcement was made of a study to be conducted by the Department of Justice into the situation. In the newspaper account, the following statement appears:

Eight years after the Supreme Court's ruling in the Mallory case, lawyers in the Justice Department have come up with a disturbing discovery. They have learned that despite hundreds of court cases, volumes of congressional testimony and uncounted speeches, not much is known about the decision's effects on law enforcement. A maximum of emotionalism and a minimum of calm study have combined in the Department's view, to make the city's experience almost useless as a basis for advising Congress on legislating in this criminal area. Washington Post, Aug. 2, 1965, p. A-3.

127. The formation in July, 1965, of a national commission on crime, to be headed by the Attorney General, is an indication that at long last we may be getting some useful and usable data on crime. See N.Y. Times, July 26, 1965, p. 1. One should not be overly optimistic, however, if for no other reason than that the commission is heavily manned by lawyers. Lawyers have not displayed much insight into such social problems. See, for discussion, National Observer, August 1, 1965, p. 1.

> Power is participation in the making of decisions: G has power over H with respect to the values K if G participates in the making of decisions affecting the K-policies of H.[128]
> [Power is] the capacity of an individual, or group of individuals, to modify the conduct of other individuals or groups in the manner in which he desires.[129]

These are not satisfactory, but may suffice to indicate the nature of the concept. Power, in short, is the ability or capacity to make decisions affecting the values of others or to control their behavior.[130]

What can be said accurately about the power of the Supreme Court? We may begin with what seems to be the most justifiable conclusion, namely, that little is known to permit valid generalizations to be made about the power of the Court. Many commentators assert that the high bench does have much—sometimes pre-eminent—power. But most, if not all, of these statements are not based upon empirical data; rather, they are a priori pronouncements. We lack a sociology of judicial decision-making and do not know what in fact the impact of a Court decision is upon either the structure of government or upon the value patterns of the American citizenry. For this reason, if for no other, the notion that the Court is all-powerful may be said to be mythical; but that idea lacks any solid factual base. Alexander Hamilton knew this when he called the judiciary "the least dangerous branch."

Even with the scarcity of factual data which would prove a causal connection between judicial decision and social change, a second proposition may, however, be advanced: Some decisions receive widespread adherence but others are systematically disobeyed. It may be instructive to compare the reception given *Brown v. Board of Education* with that given *Baker v. Carr*, the reapportionment case. In the former, the pattern of refusal to adhere with what is sometimes called "the law of the land" has been notorious, both in the southeastern United States where no effort was made at all to live up to the *Brown* principle and in the remainder of the United States where "de facto" segregation is now rearing its ugly head.[131] *Baker*, however, got a much higher degree of approval, as the number of state legislatures which have been or soon will be reapportioned attests. Some of these came without further judicial decree, while others took additional court orders. What this would lead one to believe is that a Court decision receives approval—and thus the Court exercises "power" in the sense that it was defined above—when the public obeys. Further instructive examples of the impact of judicial decisions may be seen by comparing Supreme Court pronouncements in the church-state area—about the only situation in which impact analysis has been made of Court

---

128. Lasswell & Kaplan, Power and Society 75 (1950).
129. Tawney, Equality (1931).
130. See Dahl, *The Concept of Power*, 2 Behavioral Science 201 (1957).
131. For discussion, see Wright, *Public School Desegregation: Legal Remedies for De Facto Segregation* 40 N.Y.U.L. Rev. 285 (1965).

decisions—with Negro-voting decisions.[132] In both instances, the consequences seem to have been minimal insofar as alterations in institutional practices are concerned. In economic matters, such as anti-trust, little is known about how judicial decisions alter business practice. And so it goes with many other areas. The record, at best and so far as it is known, is spotty: Court decisions do trigger social change at times—but not always or even usually.

A third proposition regarding the power of the Court derives from the fact that the Court does not, in the usual sense of the term, have any enforcement power of its own. It must rely upon the good will and determination of the political branches of government to take action to see to it that judicial norms are applied; and it must rely upon the judges in lower federal courts and in state courts to put its decisions into effect.[133] The Supreme Court looses its bolts of lightning from Mount Olympus, and purportedly makes mere mortals quail; but the hard fact is that the Court must act through delegated commands (to lower court judges) or admonitions (to legislatures or administrators). When one adds to this the fact that the Court must await the bringing of a lawsuit by some proper plaintiff, it may readily be seen that its power is much less than it seems to be by reading the columns of, say, Mr. David Lawrence or Mr. Arthur Krock.

Over the nearly two centuries of American constitutional history one finds it difficult, even impossible, to locate any instance where the Supreme Court has been able to do more than postpone what a determined people or legislative majority wanted. Sometimes the avenue taken was constitutional amendment (as with the eleventh and sixteenth), but it more often was by way of the Court overruling or "distinguishing" prior decisions, (the "court-packing" hassle in the 1930's provides an apt illustration). In any event, neither the Constitution nor the Court has proved to be an insuperable barrier to what the American people wanted to do. This situation is intensified with the expansion of governmental powers, which means that judicial decisions in matters of statutory interpretation—particularly in the economic area—are always subject to congressional "review," even "overruling." Forty years ago John R. Commons could call the Supreme Court "the first authoritative faculty of political economy in the world's history,"[134] but today that is no longer valid. Ultimate power lies in the political branches of government when most important matters of political economy are concerned, and neither the Court nor the Constitution

---

132. On the church-state relationship, *compare* Beaney & Beiser, *Prayer and Politics: The Impact of Engel and Schempp on the Political Process*, 13 J. PUB. L. 475 (1964), with Patric, *The Impact of a Court Decision: Aftermath of the McCollum Case*, 6 J. PUB. L. 455 (1957) and Patric & Sorauf, *Zorach v. Clauson: The Impact of a Supreme Court Decision*, 53 AM. POL. SCI. REV. 777 (1959).

133. See Murphy, *Lower Court Checks on Supreme Court Power*, 53 AM. POL. SCI. REV. 1017 (1959).

134. COMMONS, LEGAL FOUNDATIONS OF CAPITALISM 7 (1924).

presents an obstacle to what Congress might want to do (short of some egregiously improper maneuver).

But saying all of this and dissenting from the view that the Court is all-powerful should not, it must be emphasized, lead one to the opposite error: that the Court has no power. The ignorance about the causal relation between decision and social change, plus the other matters discussed above, do, however, tend to bring the high bench into a better perspective. Moreover, when the Court is viewed as a component of the federal government and compared with Congress and particularly with the Executive, it is readily apparent that the Supreme Court has suffered a diminution of power relative to the other branches. The locus of governmental power, if it can be located at all, is now within the Executive Branch. "Government by judiciary," a term of opprobrium thirty years ago, now has become government by the Executive—the "administrative state."[135]

The upshot is that nothing definitive or concrete can be said that will precisely delineate judicial power. What is known would lead one to believe that it is not only the least dangerous branch; it is the least powerful as well. Lawyers, particularly law professors, and others who make a profession of following the Court may not know it, but they are really analyzing a nineteenth-century institution. The mythology to the contrary notwithstanding, the long-range tendency seems to be in the direction of even less power in the courts. The custody of the "rule of law" and even the making of constitutional decisions will ever increasingly become the province of the Executive and the Congress (with the primary emphasis on the former).

CONCLUSION

The mythology of the Supreme Court poses difficult, perhaps unanswerable, questions: Why are such beliefs current? Why, in the face of at least probable if not complete proof to the contrary, do substantial segments of the American people adhere to such notions? Merely asking such questions indicates, in the first place, that despite the millions of words that have been written about the Court very little is known with certitude concerning vital segments of its activity. What is seen by the public are nine middleaged or elderly men who periodically announce opinions, often in a delphic style, and who routinely listen to arguments of counsel. That is the public face, accompanied only by occasional speeches by individual Justices or by a rare acceptance of an extrajudicial assignment. The private face we are not privileged to witness, save in the biographies and collected papers of departed Justices. Of these doubtless the most revealing is Alpheus Thomas Mason's definitive study of Chief Justice Harlan Fiske Stone, who with Chief Justice Hughes presided over the constitutional revolution of the late 1930's

---

135. See, e.g., MORSTEIN MARX, THE ADMINISTRATIVE STATE (1957); WALDO, THE ADMINISTRATIVE STATE (1948).

and the early 1940's.[136] The result is that the Court as an instrument of governance and as an important decision-making body is wrapped in obscurity. Perhaps this is as it should be. But less defensible, in fact not defensible at all, is the failure of scholars (legal and otherwise) to study and develop viable insights about other aspects of the Court's activity—particularly the causal connection between judicial decisions and social change. This could be done, but it has not been done; and until it is accomplished an adequate picture of the Court will not be available.

Bronislaw Malinowski maintained that in primitive societies an intimate connection exists between the myth and everyday activity, including social organization.[137] Perhaps the same may be said about the United States, a highly industrialized urban nation which presumably is civilized.[138] Some observers believe the connection exists. Speaking of the United States Supreme Court, political scientist Alpheus Thomas Mason asserts that the Court has a "Janus-like" role which "maximizes rather than diminishes its effectiveness."[139] Myths, then, may serve a very useful purpose with respect to the Court, particularly the basic myth that judicial power, in the words of Chief Justice John Marshall, "is never exercised for the purpose of giving effect to the will of the judge; always for the purpose of giving effect to the will of the . . . law."[140] Myth thus becomes a recognized institution in the governing process. Alfred North Whitehead has stated: "The art of free society consists first in the maintenance of the symbolic code; and secondly in fearlessness of revision, to secure that the code serves those purposes which satisfy an enlightened reason. Those societies which cannot combine reverence to their symbols with freedom of revision must ultimately decay either from anarchy, or from the slow atrophy of a life stifled by useless shadows."[141]

The Supreme Court, it has been said, is both the most revered and the least understood of American governmental institutions.[142] "In our tripartite constitutional system, the Supreme Court is the Holy of Holies. In the public eye, Supreme Court Justices are 'brushed with divinity.' "[143] One may excuse the hyperbole in such statements, but nonetheless they are strongly felt, particularly by the priesthood. As Chief Justice Charles Evans Hughes once said, "I reckon him one of the worst enemies of the community who will talk lightly of the dignity of

136. MASON, HARLAN FISKE STONE: PILLAR OF THE LAW (1956).

137. MALINOWSKI, MAGIC, SCIENCE AND RELIGION 96 (1948) [pagination from 1954 paper edition].

138. However, I would not personally want to defend much of what goes on today in this country as being civilized. Compare, for example, BLAKE, GOD'S OWN JUNKYARD (1964) with DASMANN, THE DESTRUCTION OF CALIFORNIA (1965).

139. Mason, Myth and Reality in Supreme Court Decisions, 48 VA. L. REV. 1385, 1404 (1962).

140. Osborn v. Bank of the United States, 22 U.S. 738, 866 (1824).

141. WHITEHEAD, SYMBOLISM—ITS MEANING AND EFFECT 88 (1927).

142. Mason, supra note 139, at 1387.

143. Ibid.

the bench."[144] Cardozo thought the basic myth, as stated by Chief Justice Marshall in the previous paragraph, to be "inspired revelation."[145] One might be led to the conclusion that the judiciary, particularly the Supreme Court, is sacrosanct, beyond criticism. Is it? Should it be?

Whether the mystery about the internal workings of the Supreme Court is desirable or not raises difficult questions. The charismatic function and position of the Court has often been noted. Even such a hard-nosed legal realist as Thurman Arnold thinks that it is better not to point out that the Emperor is striding around in his birthday suit.[146] Perhaps the point of view was best stated, in another context, of course, by Charles de Gaulle: "There can be no prestige without mystery. In the designs, the demeanor, and the mental operations of a leader, there must always be a 'something' which others cannot altogether fathom, which puzzles them, stirs them, and rivets their attention."[147] That extra "something" about which de Gaulle spoke is the set of myths which envelop the Supreme Court in a foggy cocoon. Would it be improper to dispel it? *Could* it be dispelled? If indeed they are myths, then they are not really subject to rational discourse except by those who accept the idea that the Court is cloaked in myths. By their very nature, myths are rooted in the subconscious; they are irrational beliefs, but beliefs not likely to be eliminated by "rational argument." Further, not many people would be willing to engage in the intellectual efforts necessary. Accordingly, it may well be that the myths could not be eradicated, if indeed an attempt were to be made to do so.

Those who, like Thurman Arnold or Professor Martin Shapiro[148] or others, believe that the Supreme Court can be acceptable to the public at large only if its true nature is kept secret are engaging in "squid jurisprudence." For them, it seemingly is perfectly all right for sophisticates (eminent practicing attorneys, professors of law and political science, and the like) to know the truth about the Court, but that general knowledge of it would be harmful. Therefore, the facts about the Supreme Court should be kept from the public; they should be hidden behind a cloud of impenetrable ink. This assertedly will then permit the Court to retain its position in the value hierarchy of the American people, and to continue to make its portentous pronouncements on public policy. But as Morris R. Cohen said in an analogous situation, "to recognize the truth and to adjust oneself to it is in the end the easiest and most advisable course,"[149] elitist theory to the contrary

---

144. *Ibid.*
145. Cardozo, Law and Literature and other Essays and Addresses 11 (1931).
146. See Arnold, Fair Fights and Foul (1965).
147. Quoted by James Reston, N.Y. Times, Aug. 21, 1964, p. 28, col. 3.
148. Shapiro, *The Supreme Court and Constitutional Adjudication: of Political and Neutral Principles,* 31 Geo. Wash. L. Rev. 587, 600-01 (1963). *Cf.* Hyman & Newhouse, *Standards for Preferred Freedoms: Beyond the First,* 60 Nw. U.L. Rev. 1-5 (1965).
149. Cohen, Law and the Social Order 380-81 n.86 (1933). I am not, of course, suggesting that the "truth" is easily come by; quite the opposite is the fact. See Nagel, The

notwithstanding. "We live by symbols," as Justice Holmes said,[150] but that is no argument for deliberate obfuscation. Secrecy, as one Justice put it, may be "essential to the effective functioning of the Court,"[151] but that need only apply to the deliberations of the members of the Court—not to a description and analysis of its role and function in the American government. Planned obscurantism by an intellectual elite cannot be justified.[152]

STRUCTURE OF SCIENCE: PROBLEMS IN THE LOGIC OF SCIENTIFIC EXPLANATION (1961) (on the difficulty and complexity of "explaining" any happening or phenomenon).

150. HOLMES, COLLECTED LEGAL PAPERS 270 (1920).

151. Frankfurter, J., in AN AUTOBIOGRAPHY OF THE SUPREME COURT 244 (Westin ed. 1963).

152. Since the text was written, a radiant attempt to grapple with the complexities of obscurantism about the Supreme Court has been published. Mishkin, *The High Court, the Great Writ, and the Due Process of Time and Law,* 79 HARV. L. REV. 56, 62-70 (1965). Professor Mishkin, with apparent reluctance, joins those who would keep the Court obscured in mystery. But he does not do so happily—perhaps because he has thought more about the problem than have some of the other obscurantists.

3
THE MYTH OF NEUTRALITY IN CONSTITUTIONAL ADJUDICATION

(Coauthor: Ronald F. Howell)

That there is a pressing need for greater public information about how the Supreme Court operates cannot be doubted. Despite the plethora of books and articles about the Court, year after year, much remains to be learned, primarily because of two factors: the secrecy that surrounds the Court and its internal operations; and stubborn adherence to the pretense that judges are impartial arbiters of human disputes, far above the sweaty crowd.

No doubt some judges do try to be impartial but, however characterized, neutrality or objectivity in judges is an impossibility. The men called to the High Bench bring their personal philosophies with them, what Justice Oliver Wendell Holmes once called their "can't-helps"—as in the statement that one "can't help" believing a certain thing. Theodore Roosevelt and Richard Nixon, to name only two Presidents, knew that it was the personal philosophies of those nominated to the bench that were vastly more important than the law. As Roosevelt said, every time judges "interpret contract, property, vested rights, due process of law, liberty, they necessarily enact into law parts of a system of social philosophy." "The decisions of courts on economic and social questions," Roosevelt continued, "de-

"The Myth of Neutrality in Constitutional Adjudication" was originally published in 27 *University of Chicago Law Review* 661 (1960). Reprinted with permission.

pend upon their economic and social philosophy." As with Roosevelt, so with Nixon, who said his most important decision was that of naming Warren Burger Chief Justice. Nixon appointed four "strict constructionists" to the Court. That can only mean judges who would rule in accordance with Nixon's values.

The pretense is not only to the contrary; some thoughtful observers of the Court maintain that the primary task of the Justices is to enunciate "neutral" or "impersonal" principles of constitutional law. This essay analyzes one of the more noteworthy of those statements — Professor Herbert Wechsler's article in the Harvard Law Review—and suggests that Wechsler at best has merely restated the continuing problem of adjudication in the constitutional order. More explicitly, the important thing about a lawsuit is who wins and who loses—not, as Wechsler maintains, the reasons for the decisions. Professor Wechsler states an ideal that has never been reached in known human history. Given the state of the sociology of knowledge, his call for a search for neutral principles is, as Professor Leonard Levy once remarked, "comparable to a hunt for snarks and orcs." It is important, however, to know what he said, for he states what for many is still the conventional wisdom. That his position has adherents can only be attributable to the well-nigh infinite capacity of the human mind for self-delusion.

The teleological conception of his function must be ever in the judge's mind.—BENJAMIN NATHAN CARDOZO.

I. INTRODUCTION

IN TWO recent papers, responsible students of the United States Supreme Court have dealt extensively with so-called "neutral principles" of constitutional adjudication. The first was Professor Herbert Wechsler's Holmes Lecture delivered at the Harvard Law School in April 1959 and since published in the *Harvard Law Review*;[1] the other, labeled "A Reply to Professor Wechsler,"[2] is authored by Professor Louis H. Pollak of the Yale Law School. A third essay, by another highly regarded observer, Professor Henry M. Hart, Jr.,[3] is somewhat peripherally correlated with the other two. Both Wechsler and Pollak profess credence in the notion that neutral principles of adjudication can be agreed upon and should be followed by the nine men whose fate it is to sit on the highest bench. Hart holds a similar view, although he speaks of principles which are "impersonal and durable" rather than neutral. Because this position states at best a half-truth, this commentary has been written, not to engage in contentious debate but to point up another dimension to the concept of neutrality in constitutional decision-making. What follows suggests that neutrality, save on a superficial and elementary level, is a futile quest; that it should be recognized as such; and that it is more useful to search for the values that can be furthered by the judicial process than for allegedly neutral or impersonal principles which operate within that process.

Let us begin with a brief recapitulation of what each of the commentators has said. The position of each is easily stated. Wechsler adheres to these ideas: (a) the Supreme Court has a "duty to decide the litigated case . . . in accordance with the law . . . "; (b) the products of the fulfillment of this duty are to be

---

[1] Wechsler, *Toward Neutral Principles of Constitutional Law*, 73 HARV. L. REV. 1 (1959) (hereinafter cited as WECHSLER).

[2] Pollak, *Racial Discrimination and Judicial Integrity: A Reply to Professor Wechsler*, 108 U. PA. L. REV. 1 (1959) (hereinafter cited as POLLAK).

[3] Hart, *Foreword: The Time Chart of the Justices*, 73 HARV. L. REV. 84 (1959) (hereinafter cited as HART).

viewed, not as good or bad depending on the result, but in accordance with unstated other standards, these standards presumably to vary from factual situation to factual situation; (*c*) the Justices on the Court should employ a method which he describes as follows: "the maine constituent of the judicial process is precisely that it must be genuinely principled, resting with respect to every step that is involved in reaching judgment on analysis and reasons quite transcending the immediate result that is achieved . . ."; and further: it is "the special duty of the courts to judge by neutral principles addressed to all the issue[s]."[4] Finally, Wechsler tells us that the "virtue or demerit of a judgment turns, therefore, entirely on the reasons that support it and their adequacy to maintain any choice of values it decrees."[5]

Pollak's main effort is directed, not towards contradicting Wechsler in toto, but towards demonstrating that Wechsler is wrong in calling the recent Supreme Court decisions in racial matters violative of neutrality. He begins by accepting the concept of neutrality of constitutional litigation "on the assumption that what Professor Wechsler has in mind is exorcising, once and for all, 'the kadi . . . dispensing justice according to considerations of private expediency,'" although he does admit that Wechsler may really be "hunting larger game"[6]— without suggesting what that might be. Pollak reviews the *White Primary Cases*, the *Restrictive Covenant Cases*, and the *School Segregation Cases*, and is satisfied, contrary to Wechsler, that neutral principles determined the Court's decisions in those cases—even though these principles at times were hidden below the muddy water of clumsy judicial language.

Finally, Professor Hart, in building a case for the proposition that the present Court has taken on too much work and should lighten its load and thereby possibly produce opinions of higher quality, calls for what might be termed "due procedure" in the Supreme Court process. Saying that the Court is losing the "professional respect of first-rate lawyers,"[7] he ends hortatorily by sounding the tocsin: "But the time must come when it is understood again, inside the [legal] profession as well as outside, that reason is the life of the law and not just votes for your side. When that time comes, and the country gathers its resources for the realization of this life principle, the principle will be more completely realized than it now seems to be."[8]

---

[4] WECHSLER 6, 15, 16. At page 19, Wechsler summarizes his views as follows: "A principled decision, in the sense I have in mind, is one that rests on reasons with respect to all the issues in the case, reasons that in their generality and their neutrality transcend any immediate result that is involved. When no sufficient reasons of this kind can be assigned for overturning value choices of the other branches of the Government or of a state, those choices must, of course, survive. Otherwise, as Holmes said . . . 'a constitution, instead of embodying only relatively fundamental rules of right, as generally understood by all English-speaking communities, would become the partisan of a particular set of ethical or economical opinions. . . .'"

[5] WECHSLER 19–20. He goes on to say: "or, it is vital that we add, to maintain the rejection of a claim that any given choice should be decreed."

[6] POLLAK 5.   [7] HART 101.   [8] HART 125.

On one level these papers are exhortations to members of the Supreme Court to pull up their "judicial socks" and to act more as judges are alleged to act in an idealized view of the Anglo-American system of jurisprudence. This is the level of what can be called superficial or elementary neutrality. It seems to mean at least this: Decisions should be reached in constitutional cases, not in accordance with who the litigants were or with the nature or consequences of the results that flow from the decision, but by the application of known or ascertainable objective standards to the facts of the case. These standards are "neutral" because they have an existence independent of litigants; they are identifiable by Supreme Court Justices (and presumably by lawyers, although none of the three authors raises the specter of conflicting neutral principles); and they are usable in making decision and in writing opinions (though it should be said here that the three authors are never entirely clear whether it is the results or the opinions explaining those results that they are criticizing). In other words, the collective view of the three commentators is one of justice blindfolded, with even-handed application of known principle to known facts. So stated, the position is both an appealing and a familiar one. But it seems to ignore some basic elements of human activity and, accordingly, has at best only a very limited usefulness. Rather than providing any viable standards for gauging judicial decision-making, it merely restates the question.

Of the three, only Professor Pollak expresses any doubt about the principle of neutrality, and then only in passing. He took as his task the more limited purpose of evaluating Wechsler's allegation of judicial non-neutrality in the field of racial discrimination. He marks his adherence to the limited view of judicial neutrality, but notes in concluding his paper that Professor Wechsler's efforts "to capture and tame the concept are plainly unavailing,"[9] followed by a quotation from a recent address by Professor Myres S. McDougal:

The essence of a reasoned decision by the authority of the secular values of a public order of human dignity is a disciplined appraisal of alternative choices of immediate consequences in terms of preferred long-term effects, and not in either the timid foreswearing of concern for immediate consequences or in the quixotic search for criteria of decision that transcend the world of men and values in metaphysical fantasy. The reference of legal principles must be either to their internal—logical—arrangement or to the external consequences of their application. It remains mysterious what criteria for decision a "neutral" system could offer.[10]

It is on that note adumbrated but not developed by Professor Pollak that the following discussion is based.

At the outset it is desirable to define some terms. The word "neutral," according to the *Oxford Universal Dictionary*, when used as an adjective, has four meanings, two of which seem relevant for present purposes: "2. Taking neither

---

[9] POLLAK 34.

[10] McDougal, *Perspectives for an International Law of Human Dignity*, 1959 AM. SOC'Y INT'L L. PROCEEDINGS 107, 121 (1959).

side in a dispute; indifferent. . . . 3. Belonging to neither of two specified or implied categories; occupying a middle position between two extremes." Neutrality is defined as "a neutral attitude between contending parties or power" and "the condition of being inclined neither way; absence of decided views, feeling, or expression; indifference." And "objective" has *inter alia* this definition: "opposite to subjective in the modern sense: That is the object of perception or thought, as distinguished from the perceiving or thinking subject; hence, that is, or is regarded as, a 'thing' external to the mind."[11] (The terms, "neutrality" and "objectivity," are used synonymously in this paper, although philosophers would probably distinguish between them.)

The first point we want to make is this: Adherence to neutral principles, in the sense of principles which do not refer to value choices, is impossible in the constitutional adjudicative process. (We limit ourselves to constitutional adjudication at this time, although much of what is said here is applicable to litigation generally.)[12] Strive as he might, no participant in that process can be neutral. Even though this should be thought of as being self-evident, it is desirable to set it out in some detail. Before doing so, however, it should be noted that neutrality of *principle*, as distinguished from neutrality of attitude, is an obviously fallacious way of characterizing the situation. Principles, whatever they might be, are abstractions, and it is the worst sort of anthropomorphism to attribute human characteristics to them. Neutrality, if it means anything, can only refer to the thought processes of identifiable human beings. Principles cannot be neutral or biased or prejudiced or impersonal —obviously. The choices that are made by judges in constitutional cases always involve value consequences, thus making value choice unavoidable. The principles which judges employ in projecting their choices to the future, or in explaining them, must also refer to such value alternatives, if given empirical reference. A principle might, in Professor Hart's term, be "durable," but only because enough human beings want it to be so. Can there be neutrality of attitude in constitutional adjudication?

II. NEUTRALITY IN OTHER DISCIPLINES

The process of judicial decision-making is a species of human thought and human choice and should be viewed against the background of what is known about human knowledge and thought processes. The study of the United States Supreme Court is a significant facet of the study of man, both metaphysically and epistemologically. Although this is neither the time nor the place to review all of what is accepted in the sociology of knowledge, it is desirable and relevant

---

[11] OXFORD UNIVERSAL DICTIONARY 1323, 1350 (Onions ed. 1955).

[12] See the article by Julius Stone, *The Ratio of the Ratio Decidendi*, 22 MODERN L. REV. 597 (1959), for a discussion of the general idea. And see James, *Tort Law in Midstream: Its Challenge to the Judicial Process*, 8 BUFFALO L. REV. 315, 327 (1959): The distribution of responsibility in a tort is basically not a legal problem, but is "fundamentally a human, economic or social problem."

to indicate what some leading students of various other disciplines have concluded regarding neutrality or objectivity in thought and decision-making. In this section we shall set out, in very brief form, the opinions of a classical philosopher (Plato), a natural scientist (P. W. Bridgman), a physical chemist who is also a social philosopher (Michael Polanyi), a sociologist (Karl Mannheim), a social scientist (Gunnar Myrdal), a political philosopher (Leo Strauss), a historian (Isaiah Berlin), and a theologian (Reinhold Neibuhr). The consistent teaching of these respected observers is that neutrality or objectivity is not attainable, either in the social sciences or in the natural sciences. (Needless to say, it is rarely pretended to in the humanities.) Knowledge, therefore, is primarily *decisional* in nature. This means that the human agency cannot be eliminated from any subject to which man addresses his attention, that value preferences inescapably intrude to guide decisions made among competing alternatives. Professor Wechsler agrees that a judge must make a choice among conflicting values, but maintains that such a choice itself can be guided by adherence to neutral principles. This we deny, and we begin our discussion of the students of other relevant disciplines with a statement by sociologist Louis Wirth:

In studying what is, we cannot totally rule out what ought to be. In human life the motives and ends of action are part of the process by which action is achieved and are essential in seeing the relation of the parts to the whole. Without the end most acts would have no meaning and interest to us. But there is, nevertheless, a difference between taking account of ends and setting ends. Whatever may be the possibility of complete detachment in dealing with physical things, in social life we cannot afford to disregard the values and goals of acts without missing the significance of many of the facts involved. In our choice of areas for research, in our selection of data, in our method of investigation, in our organization of materials, not to speak of the formulation of our hypotheses and conclusions, there is always manifest some more or less clear, explicit or implicit assumption or scheme of evaluation.[13]

Plato stressed the distinction between rigorous apodictic knowledge and decisional knowledge, and believed the latter to be immensely more valuable than the former. In fact, Plato really doubted whether apodictic knowledge was possible other than within the pre-existing framework of decisional knowledge. By the former he meant that kind of definitional, axiomatic knowledge in which a valid syllogism culminates in a necessary conclusion and in which the mathematical equation $a = b$ permits predicate b to add nothing to subject a. Decisional knowledge, on the other hand, recognizes as unavoidable and indeed considers appropriate value-judgments grounded on value-preferences, choices, alternatives.[14] As theologian Robert Cushman recently commented:

Plato ... takes the position that there are various possible premises of thought because there are differing orders of reality with appropriately diverse avenues of

---

[13] Wirth, *Preface* to MANNHEIM, IDEOLOGY AND UTOPIA: AN INTRODUCTION TO THE SO-CIOLOGY OF KNOWLEDGE, at xx (Wirth & Shils transl. 1936).

[14] CUSHMAN, THERAPEIA: PLATO'S CONCEPTION OF PHILOSOPHY (1958).

apprehension. Therefore, what a man "knows," what he judges to be "real" is determined by which avenue he customarily employs and what data he usually accredits as actually "given" for reflection.[15]

Decisional knowledge is knowledge issuing from the dialectic.[16] And the dialectical process eventuates in a decision.[17] For, "if such knowledge were rigorous [apodictic], a decision . . . would have no legitimate part in judgments."[18] That "truth is no higher in honor than the value-judgment by which its discernment is implemented"[19] is an assertion we accept and from which we infer the necessity of a hierarchy of values.

So far as the physical sciences are concerned—those which in the popular mind are devoid of the "human element"—recent testimony by one of the more notable scientists, P. W. Bridgman, points to similar conclusions. Writing in 1959, Bridgman, Nobel Prize winner in physics and long highly regarded as a thoughtful analyst of human behavior, tells us that "even in pure physics . . . it is becoming evident that the problem of the 'observer' must eventually deal with the observer as thinking about what he observes."[20] Further, in a

---

[15] *Id.* at 261–69. At 261, 267 and 270, Cushman says: "The decisional character of working hypotheses means that, for Plato, the sum of available truth has a direct correlation with the totality of *bona fide* human preference. . . . But the truths which are derived by way of dialectic have, for Plato, a privileged position and significance as well as greater certainty. They possess greater certainty despite the fact that the truths of dialectic are decisional from first to last. . . . By "existential" it is here specifically meant only that the truths of dialectic are not available except through personal decision. . . . The way to truth is not one, but many. There are different avenues suitable to different spheres of reality. . . . Plato's analysis of the knowledge-process seems to suggest, then, that there is no achievement of knowledge which is not conditioned by a prior decision . . . about what is worth knowing. If this circumstance entails the consequence that there is an element of so-called "subjectivity" in knowledge, Plato accepts the inevitable with equanimity. . . . In Plato's view, the quest for certainty by way of *apodeixis* is both inadequate and futile."

[16] *Ibid.*

[17] Is it perhaps a valid hypothesis that the "dialectical process" in operation may inhere in a judicial conference of the Supreme Court, the outcome of which is a *decision?*

[18] CUSHMAN, *op. cit. supra* note 14, at 267.

[19] *Ibid.*

[20] BRIDGMAN, THE WAY THINGS ARE 2 (1959). See BRIDGMAN, THE LOGIC OF MODERN PHYSICS (rev. ed. 1957); JEANS, PHYSICS AND PHILOSOPHY (1942) (reprinted as an Ann Arbor Paperback, 1958).

"I will not attach as much importance as do apparently a good many professional lawyers to getting all law formulated into a verbally consistent edifice. No one who has been through the experience of modern physics . . . can believe that there can be such an edifice, but it seems to me that nevertheless I can sometimes detect an almost metaphysical belief in the minds of some people in the possibility of such an edifice. If one needs specific details to fortify his conviction that there is no such edifice, plenty can be found. . . . The situation . . . for the lawyer resembles somewhat the general situation for the scientist. We have seen that in the popular view the scientist assumes that nature operates according to certain broad sweeping generalities. This is paraphrased by saying that the scientist must have 'faith' that there are natural laws. We have not accepted this view. It seems to me that a better description of how the scientist operates is to say that he adopts the *program* of finding as much regularity as he

statement particularly relevant to the latter part of this paper, Bridgman states: "In my own case, pursuit of operational analysis has resulted in the conviction, a conviction which has increased with the practice, that it is better to analyze in terms of doings and happenings than in terms of objects or static abstractions."[21] If a physicist cannot divorce the personal element of preferences from his study, it would seem to be an *a fortiori* proposition that the social scientist (including the lawyer and judge) cannot.

Bridgman is weightily supported by Michael Polanyi, who, in two recent books,[22] argues that fact is inseparable from value and that the sciences cannot be severed from the humanities. How then does the personal factor manifest itself in the very structure of science? Polanyi discovers it wherever there is an act of appraisal, choice, or accreditation. Each science operates within a conceptual framework which it regards as the "most fruitful" for those facts which it "wishes" to study because they are "important," and it thereby chooses to ignore other facts which are "unimportant," "misleading," and "of no consequence."[23] Polanyi's position is aptly summed up in the following statement:

The ideal of a knowledge embodied in strictly impersonal statements now appears self-contradictory, meaningless, a fit subject for ridicule. We must learn to accept as our ideal a knowledge that is manifestly personal.[24]

Strong support for the views of Bridgman and Polanyi is found in actual laboratory "decision" in contemporary physics. In the theorem of uncertainty, Heisenberg's Principle of Indeterminacy, there is major substantiation for the hypothesis of dynamic "creativity" not merely in human interaction but also in the world of physical phenomena. Heisenberg's Principle is a "new law . . . regarding the behavior of those infinitesimal units of matter which are studied in micro-physics. Knowing the position and velocity of a body, we should be able to predict where it will be the next instant; but the particles in question

---

can in the operation of nature, without any prior commitment as to how much he will find. So too it seems to me that the lawyer should and can make no prior commitment about the pos- sibility of erecting a self-contained self-consistent verbal legal edifice, but all that he can strive for is as self-contained and logically consistent an edifice as he can erect." BRIDGMAN, THE WAY THINGS ARE 308–09 (1959).

[21] *Id.* at 3.

[22] POLANYI, PERSONAL KNOWLEDGE (1958); POLANYI, THE STUDY OF MAN (1958).

[23] See Earle, Book Review of Polanyi, *Personal Knowledge,* 129 SCIENCE 831 (1959).

[24] POLANYI, THE STUDY OF MAN 27 (1958). "Such a position is obviously difficult; for we seem to define here as knowledge something that we could determine at will, as we think fit. I have wrestled with this objection in a volume entitled *Personal Knowledge.* There I have argued that personal knowledge is fully determined, provided that it is pursued with unwavering uni- versal intent. I have expounded the belief that the capacity of our minds to make contact with reality and the intellectual passion which impels us towards this contact will always suffice so to guide our personal judgment that it will achieve the full measure of truth that lies within the scope of our particular calling." *Ibid.*

do not behave in this way, as sober bits of matter should. Statistical laws governing their behavior we can safely formulate but not the behavior of the single particle."[25] It does little good to retort that the failure is not that of the scientist but rather of his instruments, on the supposition that "some day" more reliable instruments will be invented to make exact predictability possible. Nor does it help to be told that completely reliable physical laws are lacking only because the observer adds something to the observed by the very act of observation. For, with Kant, that is precisely the point on which we would insist and will later apply to an analysis of the judicial process.[26]

What Bridgman and Polanyi (and Heisenberg) find valid in the physical sciences and are willing to carry over to the social sciences is buttressed by the conclusions of Karl Mannheim in his study of the sociology of knowledge. In *Ideology and Utopia* Mannheim confronts the problem of objectivity and decides that the contextual pattern "colored by values and collective-unconscious, volitional impulses"[27] is crucial, and then seeks a new type of objectivity in the social sciences not through the exclusion of evaluations but "through the critical awareness and control of them."[28] This assertion, which coincides in concept with the "operational" thesis of Bridgman noted above, seems to show the way to a more meaningful analysis of the judicial function in constitutional adjudication. (We shall return to it in Section IV, below.) Because constitutional law is for the most part political theory expressed in lawyers' language, the Justices of the Court in reaching their decisions manipulate juristic theories of politics. Mannheim's views of objectivity and neutrality in the area of politics thus are presently relevant:

When... we enter the realm of politics, in which everything is in process of becoming and where the collective element in us, as knowing subjects, helps to shape the process of becoming, where thought is not contemplation from the point of view of a spectator, but rather the active participation and reshaping of the process itself, a new type of knowledge seems to emerge, namely, that in which decision and standpoint are inseparably bound together. In these realms, there is no such thing as a purely theoretical outlook on the part of the observer. It is precisely the purposes that a man has that give him his vision, even though his interests throw only a partial and practical illumi-

---

[25] PATRICK, INTRODUCTION TO PHILOSOPHY 26 (1935). See NORTHROP, INTRODUCTION TO HEISENBERG, PHYSICS AND PHILOSOPHY: THE REVOLUTION IN MODERN SCIENCE 1, 25 (1958): "Unquestionably, one other thing is clear. An analysis of the specific experimentally verified theories of modern physics with respect to what they say about the object of human knowledge and its relation to the human knower exhibits a very rich and complex ontological and epistemological philosophy which is an essential part of the scientific theory and method itself. Hence, *physics is neither epistemologically nor ontologically neutral.*" (Emphasis added.) See also Bridgman, *The New Vision of Science*, Harper's Magazine, March 1929.

[26] KANT, *Preface to the Second Edition*, CRITIQUE OF PURE REASON (Everyman's ed. 1934).

[27] MANNHEIM, IDEOLOGY AND UTOPIA: AN INTRODUCTION TO THE SOCIOLOGY OF KNOWLEDGE 5 (Wirth & Shils transl. 1936) (Harvest Book).

[28] *Ibid.*

nation on that segment of the total reality in which he himself is enmeshed, and towards which he is oriented by virtue of his essential social purposes.[29]

Gunnar Myrdal, the Swedish political economist, places great importance on the idea that social scientists should work from explicit value premises; that is to say, a person should set out his personal preferences and predilections as clearly as possible when dealing with social data. By so doing, he will enable one who reads his exposition to evaluate what he says in the light of those preferences. It is only in this way, according to Myrdal, that any manageability and real intelligibility may be attained in handling social phenomena. The idea has been set out with some particularity in a collection of his essays entitled *Value in Social Theory*. Myrdal adheres to "the fundamental thesis that value premises are necessary in research and that no study and no book can be *wertfrei*, free from valuations."[30]

Quite apart from drawing any policy conclusions from social research or forming any ideas about what is desirable or undesirable, we employ and we need value premises in making scientific observations of facts and in analysing their causal interrelation. Chaos does not organize itself into cosmos. We need viewpoints and they presume valuations. A "disinterested social science" is, from this viewpoint, pure nonsense. It never existed, and it will never exist. We can strive to make our thinking rational in spite of this, but only by facing the valuations, not by evading them.[31]

"Analysis and prognosis," to Myrdal, "cannot be neutral, in the sense that they belong to a sphere of actual and possible causal relations which can be permanently separated from valuations and the programmes which they inspire."[32]

Myrdal's point has two facets: first, value preferences cannot be divorced from the study of social phenomena; and second, it is desirable for one who works in the field to set out the preferences he is seeking to further, for in this way a greater degree of objectivity is attained. "Specification of valuations aids in reaching objectivity since it makes explicit what otherwise would be only implicit. . . . Only when the premises are stated explicitly is it possible to determine how valid the conclusions are."[33]

---

[29] *Id.* at 170. At p. 119, Mannheim states: "The juristic administrative mentality constructs only closed static systems of thought, and is always faced with the paradoxical task of having to incorporate into its system new laws, which arise out of the unsystematic interaction of living forces as if they were only a further elaboration of the original system."

[30] MYRDAL, VALUE IN SOCIAL THEORY 261 (Streeten ed. 1958). See Streeten, *Introduction, id.* at ix, xxxiv–xxxvi, and particularly at xlv, where Streeten summarizes Myrdal's position in this way: "Analysis and prognosis cannot be neutral, in the sense that they belong to a sphere of actual and possible causal relations which can be permanently separated from valuations and the programmes which they inspire. . . . Analysis and prognosis presuppose programmes in the sense of interests which determine selection and appraisal of evidence. To ignore this side of the picture is analogous to adhering to naive empiricism in the theory of knowledge."

[31] MYRDAL, *op. cit. supra* note 30, at 54.

[32] Streeten, *op. cit. supra* note 30, at xlv.

[33] MYRDAL, *op. cit. supra* note 30, at 155.

Leo Strauss in *Natural Right and History*, along slightly different but contiguous lines, maintains that "historical objectivity" also is actually *abetted* by the retention of value-judgments:

The rejection of value judgments endangers historical objectivity. In the first place, it prevents one from calling a spade a spade. In the second place, it endangers that kind of objectivity which legitimately requires the forgoing [*sic*] of evaluations, namely, the objectivity of interpretation. The historian who takes it for granted that objective value judgments are impossible cannot take very seriously that thought of the past which was based on the assumption that objective value judgments are possible, *i.e.*, practically all thought of earlier generations. Knowing beforehand that all thought was based on a fundamental delusion, he lacks the necessary incentive for trying to understand the past as it understood itself.[34]

Moreover, in Strauss' assessment of the special positivism of Max Weber may be located the position of value judgments vis-à-vis the principle of neutrality.[35] "Reference to values is incompatible with neutrality; it can never be 'purely theoretical.' But non-neutrality does not necessarily mean approval; it may also mean rejection."[36]

An additional dimension to the limitations which must be faced in any analysis of human thought is set out by the historian, Isaiah Berlin, in this manner:

For it is plainly a good thing that we should be reminded by social scientists that the scope of human choice is a good deal more limited than we used to suppose; that the evidence at our disposal shows that many of the acts too often assumed to be within the individual's control are not so; that man is an object in nature to a larger degree than has at times been supposed, that human beings more often than not act as they do because of characteristics due to heredity or physical or social environment or education, or biological laws of physical characteristics or the interplay of these factors with each other, and with the obscurer factors loosely called psychical characteristics; and that the resultant habits of thought, feeling and expression are as capable of being classified and made subject to hypotheses and systematic prediction as the behavior of material objects. And this certainly alters our ideas about the limits of freedom and responsibility.[37]

Finally, Reinhold Neibuhr, without peer among native American theologians, has firmly denied that science is now able, or ever will be able, completely and perfectly, to analyze and predict the power and decisional factors in human relationships. His fundamental stricture against the "scientific approach" is that science cannot understand human motives, for "even the natural sciences are based on metaphysical suppositions." The *human* world, furthermore, is too dimensionally varied for any unilinear interpretation to have validity:

---

[34] STRAUSS, NATURAL RIGHT AND HISTORY 61–62 (1953).

[35] *Id.* ch. 2.

[36] *Id.* at 64.

[37] BERLIN, HISTORICAL INEVITABILITY 35–36 (1954). *Cf.* FRANK, FATE AND FREEDOM (1945).

The importance of hypotheses increases with the complexity and variability of the data into which they are projected. Every assumption is an hypothesis, and *human nature is so complex that it justifies almost every assumption and prejudice with which either a scientific investigation or an ordinary human contact is initiated.*[38]

What we have said thus far may appear to some to be an exercise in belaboring the obvious. Although the foregoing is but the briefest of summaries of what some of the seminal thinkers in their respective disciplines have said about neutrality and objectivity, the central inferences are clear: (a) choices among values are unavoidable in human knowledge and human activity; and (b) when those choices are made, they are motivated not by neutral principles or objective criteria but by the entire biography and heredity of the individual making them. The wholly disinterested person, be he judge or scholarly observer, does not exist; it can, nevertheless, be said that distinctions may be drawn between decisions in fact made by courts and those recommended by an outside observer who is not a participant in the process.

Professor Wechsler admits that value choices are inevitable, but diverges on the second point of *how* they are made.[39] What we suggest is that his quest for neutrality is fruitless. In the interest-balancing procedure of constitutional adjudication, neutrality has no place, objectivity is achievable only in part, and impartiality is more of an aspiration than a fact—although certainly possible in some degree. In making choices among competing values, the Justices of the Supreme Court are themselves guided by value preferences. Any reference to neutral or impersonal principles is, accordingly, little more than a call for a return to a mechanistic jurisprudence and for a jurisprudence of nondisclosure as well as an attempted denial of the teleological aspects of any decision, wherever made. The members of the high bench have never adhered to a theory of mechanism, whatever their apologists and commentators may have said, in the judicial decision-making process. Even in the often-quoted assertion by Mr. Justice Roberts about the duty of the Court to lay the statute against the Constitution to ascertain if the one squares with the other, one would indeed have to be naive to believe that this statement in fact described the process. Some reference to Supreme Court history will serve to substantiate the point.

III. Judicial Non-Neutrality

Throughout the history of American constitutional development may be found recurring evidence of the fact that Supreme Court Justices have been motivated by value preferences in reaching decisions. At no time have they resorted to neutrality or impersonality of principle in making choices between

---

[38] Niebuhr, Does Civilization Need Religion? 41 (1927) (Emphasis supplied.)

[39] *Cf.* Friedmann, Law in a Changing Society 47–48 (1959): "But if, as Professor Wechsler concedes, a value choice is inevitable and the Court should not be strictly bound by precedent, a 'principled' approach can mean little more than that the conflict of values should be frankly articulated and that the Court should not simply be guided by its preference in the case before it, but by consistency of reasoning."

competing alternatives. Although it is true that from time to time an individual justice has alleged aherence to such a posture—notably Mr. Justice Roberts in his statement in the *Butler* case[40]—the main thread clearly is contrary. The opinions of the members of the Court, particularly those often called the "strong" Justices, such as Chief Justice John Marshall, provide ample evidence of the purposive nature of constitutional adjudication since 1789. The history can be divided into three periods: (*a*) that to about the time of the Civil War, in which the thrust of Court decision was directed toward forging as strong a national union as law could produce; Chief Justice Marshall is of course the chief exponent of this period and this drive; (*b*) that from about 1870 to 1937, when the main focus of the Court's decisions was toward providing a favorable climate for business affairs, one free from adverse governmental control; Justice Field early set the tone for this period and the "conservatives" of the 1920's and 1930's embellished it; (*c*) the post-1937 period, beginning with the constitutional revolution of the 1930's and continuing with the intramural jousting between the Frankfurter and Black wings of the Court. In each of these, it is clear that something far different from neutrality motivated the Justices.

In making such statements, we do not wish it to be assumed that we are trying to rewrite history or to engage in seeking in the historical record only that evidence that will support the position set out in this paper. It is noteworthy in this connection that neither Wechsler nor Hart cites any valid examples of what they consider to be judicial reference to neutrality or impersonality of principle; while Pollak's effort to find neutrality in the recent race decisions simply does not wash. This failure may be traceable either to a fundamental oversight on the part of those commentators or to a complete lack of empirical data to buttress their positions. The latter seems the more likely.

A rundown of some of the better known constitutional decisions of the past will serve to underscore the proposition that non-neutrality has characterized the Court's decision-making. First, however, it is appropriate to point out that the rewriting of history is not merely the assumed prerogative of historians of the Soviet Union or of the fictional bureaucrats of George Orwell's *1984*. It has been the unconfessed though less flagrant practice of both historians since Thucydides and Justices of the Supreme Court. Historians must strive to be empirical while realizing they can never be "objective," Von Ranke not excluded.[41] Herbert Butterfield in his masterful *Whig Interpretation of History*[42] and Leo Strauss in his equally perceptive *Natural Right and History*[43] have ar-

---

[40] United States v. Butler, 297 U.S. 1 (1936).

[41] An interesting brief biography and criticism is Bourne, *Leopold Von Ranke*, 1 AM. HIST. ASSN. ANNUAL REP. (1896). See RANKE, WELTGESCNICHTE, 9 vols. (1883–1888). See also *Detachment and the Writing of History: Essays and Letters of Carl L. Becker* (Snyder ed. 1958).

[42] BUTTERFIELD, THE WHIG INTERPRETATION OF HISTORY (1950).

[43] *Op. cit. supra* note 34.

gued persuasively against the "historicist fallacy." That fallacy takes two forms. One is the pretense that history may be categorically outlined in accordance with discoverable "scientific" laws to permit its periodization and prognostication about its future. Proponents include Vico, Hegel, Marx, and Comte.[44] The other is to appraise a former historical era by the criteria of values that have become important since, or conversely, to assume that the standards of an earlier epoch were good for all time, and thus the present is condemned, since the world commenced its decline with the disintegration of the supposed medieval synthesis, or earlier.[45]

The United States Supreme Court cannot claim innocence where, for legal purposes, the rewriting of American history is concerned. Is any decision respecting the origins of the American Commonwealth more notoriously expedient and historically illogical than *Texas v. White?*[46] From the standpoint of every traditional definition of sovereignty, what *can* be "an indestructible union of indestructible states"? A more recent illustration of the judicial "rewriting of history," now valid for judicial purposes, is *United States v. Curtiss-Wright Export Corp.* (1936).[47] The decision spelled bad history but good law. Justice

---

[44] Giambattista Vico (1668–1747) structured world history into three stages: the Age of the Gods, the Age of Heroes, and the Human Age. While Vico insisted that we must attempt to understand an earlier period of history as the earlier period understood itself, by a sympathetic study of its language, law, myths, and poetry, he did commit the historicist fallacy in its first form—namely, by presupposing that history may be ordered in a discernible triad, and that the triad recurs. His doctrine of *ricorsi* (literally but not precisely "recurrence") stipulates that history progresses in spiral fashion, but that the triad is always repeated, actual historical units being grafted upon each stage. See VICO, LA SCIENZA NUOVA (1725).

G. W. F. Hegel (1770–1831) assumed that *Geist* (or "spirit" or God) imposes itself dialectically upon historical movement and that the tense head-on clash between the polarities of thesis and antithesis inevitably eventuates in a synthesis, which, at once, becomes the thesis attracting another antithesis. The final synthesis, somehow preordained, would, according to Hegel, be the "perfected" state (probably Germany), the ultimate realization of *Geist* on earth, "the march of God in the world." See HEGEL, THE PHILOSOPHY OF RIGHT (Knox ed. 1942); MORRIS, HEGEL'S PHILOSOPHY OF THE STATE AND OF HISTORY: AN EXPOSITION (1887).

Karl Marx (1818–1883) turned the Hegelian dialectic "upside-down." Dialectical idealism was transformed into dialectical materialism, but the dialectical process was retained: now, however, that which moved dialectically in history was not *Geist* but raw material (economic) forces. Marx maintained as inevitable that just as the bourgeois era had overcome and succeeded the feudal age, so would the communist world-state (the "final synthesis," the stateless, classless world) eventually replace the capitalist. This, to Marx, was the iron law of history. See MARX & ENGELS, THE COMMUNIST MANIFESTO (1848); MARX, DAS KAPITAL (1867). Also consult HOOK, TOWARDS THE UNDERSTANDING OF KARL MARX (1933).

Auguste Comte (1798–1857), the leading positivist of the nineteenth century, who developed his denial of metaphysics into a theology and was not averse to having a "church" built upon his principles, "scientifically" divided world history into three periods, the theological age, the metaphysical age, and the positive (scientific) age. See COMTE, POSITIVE PHILOSOPHY, 5 vols. (1830–1842); COMTE, POSITIVE POLICY, 4 vols. (1851–1854).

[45] See CARLYLE, A HISTORY OF MEDIEVAL POLITICAL THEORY IN THE WEST (1928) and TELLENBACH, CHURCH, STATE, AND CHRISTIAN SOCIETY (1940).

[46] 74 U.S. (7 Wall.) 700 (1869).

[47] 299 U.S. 304 (1936).

Sutherland, spokesman for the Court, proclaimed that at the time of the American Revolution sovereignty was transferred immediately from the British Crown to the United States in its collective capacity and competence. A direct transfer to the various states he would not contemplate. Yet the prevailing opinion of American historians, and the plain reading of historical events, show clearly that individual states considered themselves individually the recipients of sovereignty from the Crown *before* they delegated the authority they were willing for the government of the Union to exercise. In law, however, the value-opinion of Sutherland rather than any consensus of trained historians is controlling. And even in their reading of the historical record the Justices of the Court are not neutral.[48]

Judicial value-choice through personal-value-preference was most obvious, perhaps, in the period when a majority of the Court tried to stem the tide of the onrushing welfare state in the 1930's. Yet it was no less so in the pre-Civil War time and is certainly apparent in the flow of decisions since 1937. The rewriting of history by Mr. Justice Sutherland has been mentioned. Another opinion by the same judge indicates a clear case of non-neutral adherence to principles of economic theory. In *Adkins v. Children's Hospital*,[49] Sutherland, after maintaining that "the meaning of the Constitution does not change with the ebb and flow of economic events," went on to say that "to sustain the individual freedom of action contemplated by the Constitution is not to strike down the common good but to exalt it," for in no other way could the "good of society as a whole" be served. But there is no need to provide further documentation of the point that the "conservative" wing of the Court was non-neutral in the 1930's—that, in other words, they were "judicial activists."[50] The ideal is too well known and too widely accepted to require more than its statement. Suffice it only to say that the observation of Mr. Justice Holmes in *Lochner*,[51] that the majority was deciding that case on an economic theory not adhered to by most Americans, tersely and well illustrates the general point.

What we wish to emphasize here is that the embattled minority of Justices, who with the flip-flop of 1937 became the majority, were themselves actuated by belief systems no more neutral than their adversaries. One or two of the more

---

[48] It is, for example, rather doubtful that the historical record is so "inconclusive" as Chief Justice Warren asserted in Brown v. Board of Education, 347 U.S. 483 (1954), insofar as the framers of the fourteenth amendment had any intent regarding racially segregated schools. See Pollak, *The Supreme Court Under Fire*, 6 J. PUB. L. 428, 438–43 (1957).

[49] 261 U.S. 525 (1923). See MASON AND BEANEY, THE SUPREME COURT IN A FREE SOCIETY (1959).

[50] *Cf.* JACKSON, THE SUPREME COURT IN THE AMERICAN SYSTEM OF GOVERNMENT 57–58 (1955): "A cult of libertarian judicial activists now assails the Court almost as bitterly for renouncing power as the earlier 'liberals' once did for assuming too much power. . . . I may be biased against this attitude because it is so contrary to the doctrines of the critics of the Court, of whom I was one, at the time of the Roosevelt proposal to reorganize the judiciary."

[51] Lochner v. New York, 198 U.S. 45 (1905).

celebrated opinions by Mr. Justice Holmes will serve to indicate this. Thus, for example, in enunciating his famous "marketplace" theory of truth in the *Gitlow*[52] and *Abrams*[53] cases, Holmes followed what might be called a preference for the theories of the philosophers of the Englightenment. He stated the classical case for freedom of expression.[54] Thus if the development of substantive due process doctrine in the post-Civil War to Great Depression period of Court history reveals a judicial bias for the economic theories of Adam Smith and Ricardo, so too were the Holmes-Brandeis-Stone series of dissenting opinion illustrative of a set of preferences of those worthies.[55] The question is not whether the Justices during this time followed neutral principles, but rather what value preferences did they espouse.

If that be true in the two periods of time since the Civil War, then it was certainly also true in the pre-Civil War years, particularly those in which Chief Justice John Marshall exercised such a strong controlling hand on the course of Supreme Court decision. Beginning with *Marbury v. Madison*[56] and continuing for the next several decades, a series of landmark decisions issued from the Court. These had the consequence of forging strong legal chains of national unity, chains which became indissoluble with the civil strife of the 1860's. It is not only the "bad" (by hindsight, at least) decisions, such as those in the *Dred Scott*[57] case, that illustrated the point. A rundown of the leading constitutional decisions of the first part of the nineteenth century will show as much. Often Marshall seized upon a likely case to write an essay in political economy, sometimes with only incidental relevance to the precise legal issue before the Court. A ready examples is *McCulloch v. Maryland*.[58] And a comparison of the Marhsallian method in, say, the *Marbury* case with that in *McCulloch* or in *Gibbons v. Ogden*[59] will indicate that the Chief Justice chose his technique to suit the case at hand.[60] What Marshall started, Taney continued.

The process of non-neutrality continues today and will continue as long as the judiciary is a part of our governmental system. The alleged controversy

---

[52] Gitlow v. New York, 268 U.S. 652 (1925).

[53] Abrams v. United States, 250 U.S. 616 (1919).

[54] See Champney, *Liberty and Communication*, 13 ANTIOCH REVIEW 303 (1953).

[55] *Cf.* Howe, *Faith and Skepticism in American Constitutional Law*, PERSPECTIVES USA No. 9, p. 5 (1954). And for an illuminating comparison of the American and Australian practice, see Kadish, *Judicial Review in the United States Supreme Court and the High Court of Australia*, 37 TEXAS L. REV. 1, 133, 162–78 (1958).

[56] 5 U.S. (1 Cranch) 137 (1803).

[57] Dred Scott v. Sandford, 60 U.S. (19 How.) 393 (1857).

[58] 17 U.S. (4 Wheat.) 316 (1819).

[59] 22 U.S. (9 Wheat.) 1 (1824).

[60] For a discussion of Marshallian jurisprudence, see Frankfurter, *John Marshall and the Judicial Function*, in GOVERNMENT UNDER LAW 6 (Sutherland ed. 1956).

today over a "preferred freedoms" doctrine clearly demonstrates a conflict in values among members of the present Court, not one of whom can be said to be neutral in attitude. If the "activist" wing of the Court—Black, Douglas, Warren—is quick to speak up for individual liberties and personal freedoms, Frankfurter and the other espousers of judicial self-restraint are also furthering their own set of values. No real need for additional documentation of the point exists. It should, with a moment's reflection, be obvious.[61]

But in saying this—in stating that neutrality or objectivity is essentially impossible of attainment—it should not be inferred that we feel the judge is wholly free and that he does sit kadi-like under a tree dispensing "justice" by whim or caprice. It is one thing to attribute a degree of creativity to the judge and quite another to say that he is at liberty to roam at will. Most judges do not feel such a freedom, as Judge Cardozo said almost 40 years ago:

[L]ogic and history, and custom, and utility, and the accepted standards of right conduct, are the forces which singly or in combination shape the progress of the law. Which of these forces shall dominate in any case, must depend largely upon the comparative importance or value of the social interests that will thereby be promoted or impaired. One of the most fundamental social interests is that law shall be uniform and impartial. There must be nothing in its action that savors of prejudice or even arbitrary whim or fitfulness. Therefore, in the main there shall be adherence to precedent.[62]

There is enough evidence available to show, furthermore, the institutional influence that a judgeship has on the person who mounts to the bench. A man is transformed to some extent when he dons the black robe. And any analysis of the mountains of decisions which flow from our courts provides ample testimony to the high degree of adherence to precedent in the judicial process. This is true even of the United States Supreme Court, though members of that bench have often felt freer to disregard established doctrine than does a common law judge.[63] Another limiting factor on the activities of judges is the esteem in which they are held by members of the legal profession and by people generally. Judges, being human, want "to be liked."

Of this latter fact there seems to be rather strong inferential evidence in southern states, where lower federal court judges find themselves in the awkward position of wanting the respect and friendship of their neighbors off the bench at the same time that they are committed by their constitutional oath to render decisions often highly distasteful to those neighbors. The resolution of that dilemma, frequently casuistical and requiring considerable judicial legerdemain,

---

[61] It remains mysterious how there can be any serious talk about judicial neutrality in the face of the uncontroverted evidence, both historical and contemporaneous, that indicates precisely the contrary. The entire development of the common law, for that matter, reflects a conscious application of a process of normation by the English and American judges.

[62] CARDOZO, THE NATURE OF THE JUDICIAL PROCESS 112 (1921).

[63] For a recent analysis of overruling decisions, see Ulmer, *An Empirical Analysis of Selected Aspects of Lawmaking of the United States Supreme Court*, 8 J. PUB. L. 414 (1959).

has its amusing aspects. Major issues have been evaded or "distinguished."[64] Obvious judicial questions have been called "political" and therefore non-justiciable.[65] The desegregation decision has seldom been extended by these lower courts to other areas than education, even though the Supreme Court has applied the *Brown* ruling to public transportation, parks, golf courses, bath houses, and beaches. State efforts to avoid compliance have been upheld.[66] Per curiam opinions, often exhibiting judicial secrecy or judicial indecision, have been issued.[67] Professor Walter Murphy has characterized judicial behavior in terms usually employed to characterize government bureaucrats: "Officials down the line have interests, loyalties, and ambitions which go beyond and often clash with the allegiance accorded a given tenant in the White House." [8] Each judge obviously has his own ideas about correct public policy. Murphy continues: "The Supreme Court typically formulates general policy. Lower courts apply that policy, and working in its interstices, inferior judges may materially modify the High Court's determinations."[69] We feel that far too little research has been devoted to the policy-making role of these judges and to the personal *whys* of their decisions, and we favor converting such inferential evidence as there is into explicit, empirical findings.

We agree, moreover, that the bulk of American law is stable, quantitatively speaking. If Professor Wechsler is essaying to demonstrate that many cases can be relatively easily decided in accordance with principles derived from past experience, there can be little argument, as indeed there can be little purpose in underscoring the obvious. Numerous cases are considered with maximum dispatch through the issuance of per curiam opinions founded on fairly clear precedents—indicative, be it noted, of a preference for stability over change and also of an inescapable choice among the values involved in the controversy. So much of American law, which when first judicially tested seemed controversial and, to many, unconstitutional, has now been received into the corpus of law and is taken for granted. Yet in areas of law where definitive decisions have not been given, in areas criss-crossing so inextricably with policy formulation of one kind or another, "neutral" principles seem impossible because policy therein has not been finally formulated, because *decisions* have still to be made. It is with particular reference to those peripheral areas, occasioning so much publicity which suggests that American law is in constant flux, that we direct criticism

---

[64] *E.g.*, Bell v. Rippy, 146 F. Supp. 485 (N.D. Tex. 1956). A grimly amusing case, one displaying some degree of federal pusillanimity, is Williams v. Georgia, 210 Ga. 665, 82 S.E.2d 217 (1955), *rev'd. & rem.*, 349 U.S. 375 (1955), 211 Ga. 763, 88 S.E. 2d 376 (1956), *cert. denied*, 350 U.S. 950 (1956).

[65] See, *e.g.*, Dawley v. City of Norfolk, 159 F. Supp. 642 (E.D. Va. 1958).

[66] See, *e.g.*, Florida *ex rel.* Hawkins v. Board of Control, 162 F. Supp. 851 (N.D. Fla. 1958).

[67] This practice of the Supreme Court is criticized by Hart. See HART 100–01.

[68] Murphy, *Lower Court Checks on Supreme Court Power*, 53 AM. POL. SCI. REV. 1017 (1959).

[69] *Id.* at 1018. *Cf.* DE TOCQUEVILLE, DEMOCRACY IN AMERICA 271 (Bradley ed. 1945).

against any theory of allegedly neutral principles. It is precisely in these "new" areas (e.g., national security) that choice must be made among conflicting alternatives. We advocate merely that the value-preferences which determine the choice be stated explicitly. That done, the resulting judgment, were it not for the semantic problem, might even be termed "objective."[70]

In considerable measure Supreme Court Justices themselves are accountable for the recent public image of the judiciary as being everything but objective and neutral. Human nature being what it is, judges who confess that they are not neutral are more readily believed than judges who insist that they are. If the Supreme Court will not first defend its own honor, it is hardly to be expected that anyone outside the Court can do more than take the judges at their word. The issue of judicial neutrality versus judicial interventionism began to be embarrassing in American constitutional law in the 1930's, when the so-called conservatives accused the so-called liberals of judicial malpractice, and vice-versa. Actually the two groups were merely espousing almost opposite judicial values because they subscribed to almost opposite societal values. Far from arguing that judicial values should not reflect societal values, since we believe that they should, we contend only that the American people are entitled at the very least to have those values humbly confessed and assiduously articulated. This the Court did not do in the 1930's or the 1940's or the 1950's. The Suther-land-Stone feud concerning governmental regulation of business has been re-placed by the Black-Frankfurter feud concerning the breadth of fourteenth amendment due process. The substantive sphere of conflict has changed, but the procedural feud is still with us. And essentially it is reducible to the lack of consensus on the Court as to the appropriate role of the judiciary in an age in which no national consensus is apparent and no "public philosophy" has yet been enunciated.

The "liberals" of the 1930's and the 1940's could plead piously for the need of "judicial self-restraint" precisely because their battle had already been won, both in the legislatures and in the "public consensus."[71] It is easy, if somewhat sophistical, to insist that the function of the Court is to defer to the legislature in economic matters when the legislature is performing exactly as the Court majority would wish. Yet the liberals applied to their role no such self-restraint in the realm of civil liberties.[72] *That* battle had not been won. Here the Court's rationale was at least convincing, perhaps meritorious; its funda-mental premise as to the proper judicial *modus operandi* was clearly expressed:

---

[70] *Compare* STRAUSS, *op. cit. supra* note 34, *with* MYRDAL, *op. cit. supra* note 30, on this point; see also MANNHEIM, *op. cit. supra* note 27.

[71] We do not mean to imply that we believe that the Court should reflect what is often called "the will of the people," whatever that might mean. There can hardly be a system of "limited" government unless the will of the people, as reflected in legislative action, is subject to some restraint. *Cf.* Rostow, *The Supreme Court and the People's Will*, 33 NOTRE DAME LAW. 573 (1958).

[72] *Cf.* JACKSON, *op. cit. supra* note 45. See Rostow, *The Democratic Character of Judicial Review*, 66 HARV. L. REV. 193 (1952).

the business of the Supreme Court was primarily the business of civil liberties because the protection of such liberties was the prerequisite of insuring "justice under law" in a free society.[73] The protection of such liberties, moreover, ultimately raised philosophical problems with which nine Justices were admirably equipped to cope, even when, as a practical matter, the same nine men lacked the time, the knowledge, and perhaps even the constitutional authority to pronounce on a rate regulation of the Interstate Commerce Commission. The latter was the province of the Congress and of administrative experts skilled in the local and legal technicalities of the dispute.

A question that we would urge for consideration, however, is whether, in a supposedly free society, problems of a nation's economy present any fewer philosophical implications than problems of an individual's liberty. The obvious practical difficulties involved here we hastily acknowledge. Yet it is just as logical and as proper to call upon the Court to do its share in making corporatons and labor unions more responsible[74] and more responsive to the "public interest," as it is to limit its area of competence to elaborate dissertations on the "clear and present danger" test or on the meaning of "due process" and "equal protection of the laws" in particular situations. At any rate, such important considerations of the Court's function vis-à-vis the substance of law must await treatment until the Court, procedurally and methodologically, puts its own house in order. From the admission of the late 1930's that Justices were emphatically not neutral, we were confronted once more in the 1950's—and in many cases we were listening to the same men—with the adamant claim that Justices are or should be completely neutral beings.[75]

Assuredly we are not imputing to the Justices of the Supreme Court that kind of rational calculatedness that Hobbes and Bentham ascribed to the human animal. We recognize that judges, addicted like all men to Homer's nodding, cannot invariably act according to conscious rational design, enlightened or otherwise. In many domains of law judges are obviously, consciously or subconsciously, indifferent. The most desirable "progress" of the law has different significations for different judges, as it does for all men. And this suggests that certain provisions of the Constitution not only have varying meanings for individual Justices, but that they also have varying importance. During the past two decades, for instance, much commentary has been devoted to the problem of a possible "priority of liberties" in the Bill of Rights.[76] As Justice

---

[73] For a discussion, see McKay, *The Preference for Freedom*, 34 N.Y.U. L. REV. 1182 (1959).

[74] See Miller, *The Constitutional Law of the "Security State,"* 10 STAN. L. REV. 620 (1958); MILLER, PRIVATE GOVERNMENTS AND THE CONSTITUTION (1959).

[75] Note the curious evolution of thought by journalist David Lawrence, recounted in Bickel and Wellington, *Legislative Purpose and the Judicial Process: The Lincoln Mills Case*, 71 HARV. L. REV. 1 (1957).

[76] Justices Black and Douglas have "discovered" historical "proof" surrounding the formulation and ratification of the fourteenth amendment to justify and substantiate the inclusion of the total Bill of Rights within the protective confines of "liberty" guaranteed by the due process clause of that amendment. From an historical point of view, this discovery, to say the

Holmes earlier seemed most intense when deference to legislative action was posed for judicial advisement, so Justice Murphy later appeared most dedicated to his judicial duty when a civil liberties' dispute was being litigated. Other Justices have been most awake when commerce cases were being decided or when the right to privacy and other procedural guarantees were alleged to have been infringed. On the Court at the present time, Justices Black and Douglas are most alert when civil liberties seem endangered. Justices somewhat otherwise inclined look first to the protection of the "national interest" and thus have milder though not less decided views about legislation against subversion and disloyalty. A scholar-Justice like Frankfurter appears primarily committed to quite careful reflection upon any attempt to upset the federal balance. In each instance, a different political philosophy is furthered.

The personnel of the Supreme Court have historically differed from one another not only in value-preferences in given subject-matter areas, but also about the subject-matter areas they have deemed most significant. That they have done so, and will continue to do so, is inescapable and, though possibly to be lamented, probably not to be corrected. Here, at least, they operate "rationally" and "consciously" and may be expected to make their choices as explicit as a shrewd observer can extract from their implicit adumbrations. What is immeasurably more vexatious is to insist upon what may amount to the impossible: the demand that Justices articulate their value-preferences toward matters about which they are indifferent, uncertain, "subconscious," or irrational. To solve *that* problem would be the *summun bonum* not only in understanding the judicial process, but in understanding human nature itself. It is equally difficult to ascertain the judicial frame of mind during periods of Court retreat, as in an emergency. These constitute major lacunae in the thesis we here propound.

Finally, in the handling of the facts of a case, again there may be seen the influence of value preferences. That, contrary to popular opinion, facts do not speak for themselves should be axiomatic to any student of the judicial process.[77] The facts of a dispute, as brought forward by the briefs and record, as developed in oral argument, and as coming to the attention of the Court by way of judicial notice, are not themselves self-evident propositions requiring

---

least, is apocryphal. Failing victory in that attempt at historical rewriting, these Justices would "accept" a "priority of liberties," claiming that the substantive guarantees of the first amendment would, expediently, have to enjoy "priority" if the total Bill of Rights could not acquire for inclusion the approval of the Supreme Court majority. They fail either to realize or to be concerned about the fact that if the fourteenth amendment should embrace the procedural rights of the Bill of Rights, the criminal jurisdiction of the fifty states might be entirely disrupted. A proper "hierarchy of values" might appropriately include the Bill of Rights, but would not be restricted to the Bill of Rights. See Justice Murphy's dissenting opinion in Adamson v. California, 332 U.S. 46 (1947).

[77] *Cf.* Jerome Frank's "fact skepticism," for a discussion of which see Cahn, *Fact-Skepticism and Fundamental Law*, 33 N.Y.U. L. REV. 1 (1958). See FRANK, COURTS ON TRIAL ch. 3 (1949); PAUL, THE LEGAL REALISM OF JEROME N. FRANK (1959).

no interpretation. They exist only as contemplated by their recipient and are unavoidably colored by the reception given.[78] As (or more) important as the facts themselves in the judical process is the opinion based upon them—the reaction they evoke in human minds. "The assumption that events bespeak their character by merely happening has made for many strange reasonings in the history of jurisprudence. Events have meaning, it is true, but the meaning is always potential, or rather there are many meanings relative to many purposes. A situation is potentially meaningful in many directions, and which meaning is relevant is in part dependent upon a human judgment."[79] Advocacy thus consists as much—perhaps more—of persuading the judge to take a desired view of the facts as it is of the application of law to those facts. "To formulate the 'facts' in one way and not in the other is to get one kind of decision and not another."[80] The point, for present purposes, is that constitutional adjudication depends as much on "what are the facts?" as on "what is the law?" and far more than on "what are the neutral principles relevant to the decision?" Thus it can be said that judicial impartiality or neutrality, save again on the most elementary level, falls on two counts. Choices must be made between competing values; and choices must be made as to the interpretation to be placed on a set of "facts." Facts do not speak for themselves, and cannot be used by themselves for the establishment of value-judgments. As Reinhold Neibuhr puts it: "Every judgment of fact is a judgment of value."[81] And as Alfred North Whitehead has told us "Every proposition proposing a fact must, in its complete analysis, propose the general character of the universe required for that fact. There are no self-sustained facts, floating in non-entity."[82] Further: "The notion of mere fact is the triumph of the abstractive intellect. It has entered into the explict thought of no baby and of no animals. . . . A single fact in isolation is the primary myth required for finite thought . . . for thought unable to embrace totality. This mythological character arises because there is no such fact. Connectedness is of the essence of things of all types. Abstraction from connectedness involves the omission of an essential factor in the fact considered. No fact is merely itself."[83]

The point emphasized here is that there are no facts apart from a theory, and that, accordingly, a person's view of the facts is unavoidably colored by the

---

[78] See Krutch, *We Need More Than More Facts*, The New Leader, Sept. 27, 1954, p. 15; Krutch, *Value-Judgments Cannot Be Based on Facts Alone—And That's A Fact*, The New Leader, October 18, 1954, p. 15. Compare EASTON, THE POLITICAL SYSTEM 224 (1953): "[N]o factual proposition uttered by a human being can be devoid of all relevance to moral preconceptions."

[79] GARLAN, LEGAL REALISM AND JUSTICE 31 (1941). See Isaacs, *The Law and the Facts*, 22 COLUM. L. REV. 1 (1922).

[80] GARLAN, LEGAL REALISM AND JUSTICE 38 (1941).

[81] Niebuhr, *The Dilemma of Modern Man*, THE NATION, Feb. 22, 1947.

[82] WHITEHEAD, PROCESS AND REALITY 17 (1929).

[83] WHITEHEAD, MODES OF THOUGHT 12-13 (1938).

nature of that theory. Neutrality, thus, is unattainable in the constitutional adjudicative process, both on the level of (legal) principle and on the level of the facts of the dispute before the Court.

If that be true of the process of constitutional adjudication, then it is odd to find Professor Pollak maintaining that if the Court decisions in recent race cases "are not supportable on the basis of neutral constitutional principles, they deserve to be jettisoned."[84] Under the analysis suggested by the present writers, such a view would result in the rejection of all constitutional decisions. However, perhaps Pollak's concept of neutrality differs from that developed here and is more a statement of the ideal of the dispassionate rule of law in social affairs than a description of the judicial decision-making process. Thus he believes that Professor Wechsler is really calling for a "method of adjudication which is disinterested, reasoned, and comprehensive of the full range of like constitutional issues, coupled with a method of judicial exposition which plainly and fully articulates the real bases of decision."[85] Obviously this cannot state the actuality. As demonstrated above, ample evidence exists to indicate that the judicial method cannot be "disinterested." To call for it to be "reasoned" means little, for "reason" is a tool, not an end: the results of a process of "reasoning" depend entirely upon what premises (*i.e.*, values) are used in that process, just as the end product of Univac depends upon what is fed into it.[86] And it is highly unlikely that any method of judicial opinion-writing can plainly and fully enunciate "the *real* bases of decision." Surely enough psychological testimony is available to establish the fact that the "*real* bases of decision," in whatever context, are more unconscious than known to the decision-maker.[87] Surely it is manifestly impossible for a judge to tell us entirely what *really* motivated him.[88] Surely we have been able by now to pierce the facade of mechanical jurisprudence and to realize that the *real* bases of decision depend upon the total heredity and environment of the decision-maker.[89] Try as he might, the judge is not going to be able to do it, in any complete sense. What he can do, and what we suggest below that he consciously attempt to do, is to set out in explicit form his value preferences as he understands them.

---

[84] POLLAK 31.   [85] POLLAK 32.

[86] See, *e.g.*, Bridgman, *op. cit. supra* note 20; Polanyi, *op. cit. supra* note 22.

[87] For example, it has been said that important managerial decisions in business are made "subconsciously." McDonald, *How Businessmen Make Decisions*, Fortune, Aug. 1955, p. 132.

[88] Neither Cardozo nor Holmes nor Frankfurter, among the more literate of the judges, can describe in more than partially helpful generalities what the process is. See especially CARDOZO, THE NATURE OF THE JUDICIAL PROCESS 167–177 (1921) (on "subconscious forces").

[89] Compare the conclusion of some political scientists regarding foreign policy decisions: "In conclusion, we might summarize our comments on the nature of choice as follows: information is selectively perceived and evaluated in terms of the decision-maker's frame of reference. Choices are made on the basis of preferences which are in part situationally and in part biographically determined." SNYDER, BRUCK & SAPIN, DECISION-MAKING AS AN APPROACH TO THE STUDY OF INTERNATIONAL POLITICS 120 (1954).

It is with this background in mind that a recent statement by Mr. Justice Frankfurter of the constitutional adjudicative process is of interest:

We may not draw on our merely personal and private notions and disregard the limits that bind judges in their judicial function.... To practice the requisite detachment and to achieve sufficient objectivity no doubt demands of judges the habit of self-discipline and self-criticism, incertitude that one's own views are incontestable and alert tolerance toward views not shared.... These are precisely the presuppositions of our judicial process. They are precisely the qualities society has a right to expect from those entrusted with ultimate judicial power.[90]

What the Justice appears to be calling for here is not something called "neutrality" or even "objectivity," although he uses the latter word. Rather he seems to be saying that a judge should make conscious effort to evaluate all of the considerations present in a constitutional dispute, to comprehend "the full range of ... constitutional issues" in that dispute. If so, then there can be little quarrel with the proposition. With such a concept of neutrality no one can really disagree. But that involves what is at best a superficial or elementary sort of neutrality. Neither the Justice nor the professors have come to grips with the fundamentals of the constitutional adjudicative process.

IV. Towards a Purposive Jurisprudence

If, then, true neutrality in constitutional adjudication is a bootless quest, the important question which must be faced becomes: What *should* motivate judges faced with constitutional issues? A judge may try to be detached and objective, self-disciplined and humble, but he must ahdere to *some* standard. Certainly it is not something called "the intention of the framers," a filio-pietistic notion that can have little place in the adjudicative process of the latter half of the twentieth century—if, indeed, it ever did. A nation wholly different from that existing in 1787, facing problems obviously not within the contemplation of the Founding Fathers, can scarcely be governed—except in broadest generality—by the concepts and solutions of yesteryear. It is, of course, only those constitutional provisions of inherent ambiguity that pose problems of interpretation. Where the intention of the framers is clear—as, for example, on the number of Senators or in the establishment of two houses of Congress, or for the provision for a President and Vice-President—no interpretation is necessary.

---

[90] Rochin v. California, 342 U.S. 165, 170–172 (1952). In his essay on Marshall, *op. cit. supra* note 60, at 21, Frankfurter says: "It is important ... to appreciate the qualifications requisite for those who exercise this extraordinary authority, demanding as it does a breadth of outlook and an invincible disinterestedness rooted in temperament and confirmed by discipline. Of course, individual judgment and feeling cannot be wholly shut out of the judicial process. But if they dominate, the judicial process becomes a dangerous sham. The conception by a judge of the scope and limits of his function may exert an intellectual and moral force as much as responsiveness to a particular audience or congenial environment."

This is the sort of statement that *sounds* good on a first and rapid reading, but one which will not stand any sort of rigorous analysis. Mr. Justice Frankfurter's statement of the ideal, at the very least, fails to come to grips with the attainable. Compare a prior statement, possibly inconsistent, in Frankfurter, Law and Politics 13 (1939).

And it is not something called "reason," whatever that might mean to Professor Hart, through "the maturing of collective thought" which will develop "impersonal and durable principles of constitutional law."[91] No one, to be sure, can disagree with that sort of exhortation; it is to be equated with patriotism and motherhood and the "American way." But *what* principles? *Neutral* principles? There are no such things. *Impersonal* principles? Ditto. *Durable* principles? Some examples, please. Neither Hart, Wechsler nor Pollak has tackled the important (and difficult) problems of this era—those that can be summed up in these questions: What *is* the role of the United States Supreme Court in an era of positive government? What principles *should* guide the Justices in their difficult task of continuously updating the American Constitution? What the three commentators have done is, at best, to set out a partial restatement of the (unattainable) ideal of the Anglo-American system of jurisprudence, and, at worst, to ignore the questions relevant to the modern age.

The suggestion we make is for a *Teleological jurisprudence, one purposive in nature* rather than "impersonal" or "neutral." Only a brief statement of this proposal can be made here, since space limitations permit no more than the tracing of its main contours; a comprehensive development is planned by one of the present authors as a separate article.[92]

A basic difference between the society and government of today and those existing in the latter part of the 18th century is the entirely different posture that government takes with regard to social affairs. The United States is now well into the age of positive government, one in which it is widely agreed that government has affirmative jobs to perform. A consensus exists among the American people that social affairs are of a nature that, for many reasons, the intervention of the State is both necessary and desirable. Whether we call this a welfare State or a social service State, the central notion is clear: Only a dwindling minority of Americans espouse views of laissez-faire. At the same time, it has been proved necessary to reassign the respective roles of the governmental departments. Thus we find the growth in importance of the executive and the administrative branch of government, with a concomitant diminution of importance in both the legislature and the judiciary. These complementary developments present us with a point of departure for a discussion of the role of the Supreme Court in present day America.[93]

No further exposition is necessary of the obvious fact of the change in the nature of government to one positive in thrust (as opposed to the negative nature of laissez-faire government) and affirmative in responsibility. A few state-

---

[91] HART 99. Further elaboration of Professor Hart's views may be found in *Comment to Breitel, The Courts and Lawmaking*, in LEGAL INSTITUTIONS TODAY AND TOMORROW 40–48 (Paulsen ed. 1959), and in *Comment to Snee, Leviathan at the Bar of Justice*, in GOVERNMENT UNDER LAW 139–145 (Sutherland ed. 1956).

[92] Miller.

[93] For some elaboration of the statements made in this portion of the text, see Miller, *The Constitutional Law of the "Security State,"* 10 STAN. L. REV. 620 (1958).

ments may, however, be set out to indicate the functional realignment of the jobs of government. With the growth of administration to the point where it has with considerable validity been called a fourth branch of government, there has come a blurring of the sharp lines of demarcation of the traditional trichotomous division of government. The jobs done administratively now include all of those historically accomplished by the legislature, the judiciary, and the executive. The growth in scope and importance of administration is part of the overall aggrandizement in relative power of the executive branch of government. As Corwin has noted, the history of the presidency is one of steadily increasing power.[94] The analogue of this development is the downgrading in relative importance and power of both the legislature and the courts. The most that the legislature does today is to formulate broad policy guide lines for the conduct of our government. Its power of control over the details of government has been ceded to the administrators. Furthermore, it can be said that even in the formulation of policy, the Congress really is of lesser importance than the President and his advisers. It is, in fact, not too much to say that the Congress and the Chief Executive have swapped roles, so to speak: Now it is the President who proposes and Congress which vetoes, rather than the other way around.[95]

The executive in this scheme of affairs is of course the leader, not only of the legislative programs but also of the broad administration of policies formally announced by Congress. His own law-making power, often exercised without specific grants of power from Congress, enables him further to take over the ostensible role of Congress. For the most part, it is the executive branch, including the administrative agencies, which, in the resolution of the myriad of claims by individuals on the government and the requirements that government imposes upon individuals, effects the nexus between the broad policy guide lines set out by Congress and the complex facts of everyday life in an industrialized and urbanized society. As we are being told with increasing frequency by qualified observers, more and more the administrator is replacing the judge in this fundamental task.[96] Historically, the judge did this job, and in fact legislated as he did so. The development of the common law was the result. Today, the courts have lost power in the same way as has the Congress. While still of great importance, relative to administration they simply are not so influential as once they were.[97] The job of judges has become one of deciding

---

[94] CORWIN, THE PRESIDENT: OFFICE AND POWERS ch. 1 (4th ed. 1957).

[95] The point was made by a perceptive journalist, DOUGLASS CATER, THE FOURTH BRANCH OF GOVERNMENT (1959). See Senator Clifford P. Case of New Jersey's *Comment to Newman, A Legal Look at Congress and the State Legislatures*, in LEGAL INSTITUTIONS TODAY AND TOMORROW 92–99 (Paulsen ed. 1959).

[96] See, *e.g.*, the remarks of Justice William O. Douglas, *Legal Institutions in America, Id.* at 274–299: "Today the administrative agency is supreme in state and federal governments." *Id.* at 274.

[97] See the interesting essay by one of the better known federal judges, Wyzanski, *History and Law*, 26 U. CHI. L. REV. 237 (1959), particularly at 240–42.

the pathological case—the case that has not been satisfactorily resolved by one of the other branches of government, Congress, the executive, or the administrative. With regard to constitutional issues, without making reference to many questions of statutory interpretation which obviously also result in important examples of policy-making by the courts, the federal judiciary speaks in instances where there is a clash of values that cannot be resolved politically. These values usually revolve around a failure on the part of government to satisfy an individual that a governmental demand is a reasonable one. The Court's role in this type of situation, which is its most important function, is that of articulating a broad norm, one which fits the facts of the case before it and also transcends that particular dispute.[98] In this process, it is acting as a national conscience for the American people, more than as an arbitrator of the insignificant disputes of insignificant people.[99] Through the medium of the law case, a process of normation[100] by adjudication takes place. A standard is erected toward which men and governments can aspire.

Professor Lon Fuller has demarcated two basic forms of social ordering; in the absence of one or the other of these, nothing resembling a society is possible: *"organization by common aims* and *organization by reciprocity."*[101] The adjudicative process has traditionally seemed to work most efficiently in cases involving reciprocity. In a contractual relationship, for instance, a thing of value, material or otherwise, is granted by one party to another in return for some thing of presumptively equal value. We say "presumptively" because in an earlier era of negative government, buttressed in economic theory by the tenets of doctrinaire economic liberalism, legally equal values were in fact not always economically equal values. Reference is made to the Court's sustained use of the fiction of "liberty of contract" to thwart state or federal attempts to establish minimum wages, maximum hours, and acceptable working conditions in the reciprocal business relations of management and labor.

The demise of the "liberty of contract" doctrine, and therewith the transition to the positive, service, welfare State, left the way clearly open for the adjudica-

---

[98] One of the bases for considerable current criticism of the Supreme Court, both on and off that bench, is that it undertakes to decide too many cases, many of which are thought by the critics to be unimportant. The academic critics are epitomized by Professor Hart, who espouses the views of his former colleague, Mr. Justice Frankfurter. A biting critique of the Hart-Frankfurter position is set out in Arnold, *Professor Hart's Theology,* 73 HARV. L. REV. 1298 (1960).

[99] See, *e.g.,* Ribble, *Policy Making Powers of the United States Supreme Court and the Position of the Individual,* 14 WASH. & LEE L. REV. 167, 184–5 (1957). See the statement by Mr. Justice Harlan that it is the policy of the Court to choose its cases "in the interest of the law, its appropriate exposition and enforcement, not in the mere interest of the litigants." Harlan, *Manning the Dikes,* 13 RECORD 541 (1958).

[100] The term is that of Karl Llewellyn. See Llewellyn, *The Normative, The Legal, and the Law Jobs: The Problem of Juristic Method,* 49 YALE L. J. 1355 (1940).

[101] Fuller, *The Forms and Limits of Adjudication,* Remarks before the Jurisprudence Round Table at the Annual Meeting of the Association of American Law Schools, December 29, 1958. This paper, in revised form, will be incorporated in a book to be entitled *The Principles of Social Order,* which will be published by Professor Fuller in the near future.

tive process to be employed to abet that other form of other ordering: organization by common aims. As yet, adjudication has adjusted itself less efficiently to this new form. One reason is that "organization by common aims" implies a national consensus, which on most controversial issues is not yet determined by the American people and is also undetermined by one spokesman of that consensus, the Supreme Court. Another and probably more significant reason is that "organization by common aims" involves "polycentric" questions, *i.e.*, questions not easily settled by the adjudicative process because of their unavoidable intersection with problems not primarily "legal" and "constitutional."[102] On the other hand, "organization by common aims" as a motive for social ordering, for social cooperation, has seemed in this century and in this country to be the only viable means of effectuating doctrines of social justice, a feature of the "national consensus" to which the American people now appear committed. Yet "common aims," suggesting common agreement, touch precisely those "polycentric" questions with which heretofore the Supreme Court has been deemed ill-equipped to deal.

The position taken by Hart and Wechsler is based on a view of life and the social process in which litigants (and others) are in agreement on the basic essentials—the goal values—and all that remains is the settlement of preferred ways to reach those ends. Put another way, their position is bottomed on a theory of a fundamental harmony of interests of all members of the American community. But that is precisely what may *not* be present in most important constitutional litigation, such as racial relations, where disagreement is over ends or goals and not the means or tactics to attain them; the administration of the criminal law, where an anti-social being is jousting with something called society; and in many of the civil liberty cases, where again the disagreement is over fundamentals. To posit a society with a harmony of interests is to rearticulate a fundamental tenet of the American democracy; to speak otherwise is to question, at least in part, one of the underpinnings of the constitutional order. Nevertheless that, in essence, is what is present here, and serves to explain, at least partially, the counting of votes—as Hart says—of "one up (or down) for civil rights" and so on. To put it in other terms, it is the difference between a Hobbesian view of the social process and that of, say, Burke, Locke or Rousseau.

The essential thing to recognize about the social process is that it is not governed by something called "reason," as Hart intimates, but is a set of interlocking and interacting power relationships; it is not ruled in accordance with "neutral principles" or as a result of common adherence to what is desirable.[103] "While philosophic saints in their ivory towers construct ideal societies,

---

[102] Fuller borrows the term "polycentric" from POLANYI, THE LOGIC OF LIBERTY (1951).

[103] The social process of course includes the judicial process, particularly as it relates to the resolution of constitutional questions. Constitutional law, accordingly, is much more than "lawyers' law," and can even be considered of such importance that it should not be left to the lawyers—at least not wholly so.

'burly sinners rule the world.' "[104] To some extent, thus, civil rights determination in the judicial process is a resultant of an evaluation of power relationships in the social process; and civil liberties receive protection when it is convenient for society to protect them or when the issue with which the liberty is concerned is one in which the major social groups are in basic agreement. Compare, in this regard, the position of Mr. Justice Douglas, who looks upon the first amendment as the enunciation of absolute principle, with the interest-balancing position of, say, Mr. Justice Frankfurter, who concedes the necessity of value-choice in adjudication. Who, then, is the "activist"; who the exponent of self-restraint? The answer, of course, is that both—plus their colleagues—are activists in the sense that conscious use of decisional power makes it inevitable. Both Douglas and Frankfurter see the Court as a power organ in a social power process, the former desiring to use it affirmatively, the latter more willing to rely on the end-products as they come tumbling out of the social decision-making spigot, so long as those results do not unduly upset him.[105] Thus Douglas can, at least in part, be said to hold to a Hobbesian view of the judicial process, with Frankfurter being more a follower in the Burkean or Lockean tradition.[106] The comparison is not exact, but does serve to describe two diverging views of the role of the Court.

In many aspects of the American social scene the commitment of the people is less to the democratic ideal than it is to the furtherance of their own parochial interests. While it can be said that a spirit of cooperation, not competition, prevails in most of the nation,[107] in some respects something less than even "antagonistic cooperation" is the rule. It is in these sharp cleavages that the Court reflects, in its cliques and its decisions, the warring factions of the American people. Negro-white relations and the criminal law have been cited; they are joined in large extent by labor-management relations and other im-

---

[104] PATTERSON, JURISPRUDENCE 558 (1953).

[105] Compare Mr. Justice Frankfurter's opinion in Rochin v. California, 342 U.S. 165 (1952) (forcible use of stomach pump by police officers is conduct "that shocks the conscience . . . [and is] too close to the rack and screw . . .") and in Louisiana v. Resweber, 329 U.S. 459 (1947) (execution of felon by electrocution after first attempt failed because of power trouble does not offend "a principle of justice 'rooted in the traditions and conscience of our people' ") How these opinions by Mr. Justice Frankfurter can be reconciled, in so far as judicial neutrality is concerned, is a mystery. Even more mysterious is Frankfurter's assertion in the *Resweber* case that he saw his duty as that of enforcing "that consensus of society's opinion which, for purposes of due process, is the standard enjoined by the Constitution." Such a view of the constitutional adjudicative process is not substantiated by history or practice. See, for an instructive analysis of due process, Kadish, *Methodology and Criteria in Due Process Adjudication —A Survey and Criticism*, 66 YALE L. J. 319 (1957).

[106] Consult STANLIS, EDMUND BURKE AND THE NATURAL LAW (1958); CONE, BURKE AND THE NATURE OF POLITICS: THE AGE OF THE AMERICAN REVOLUTION (1957); CANAVAN, THE POLITICAL REASON OF EDMUND BURKE (1960). See PATTERSON, JURISPRUDENCE § 4.16 (1953), for a comparison with John Locke.

[107] See, *e.g.*, MONTAGU, THE NEXT DEVELOPMENT IN MAN (1952). *Cf.* SIMON, PHILOSOPHY OF DEMOCRATIC GOVERNMENT 123 (1951): "[In a democratic state] deliberation is about means and presupposes that the problem of ends has been settled."

portant social disputes. In some of the fundamental issues growing out of these relationships can be found differences, not in details or in tactics, but in end-values or purposes. And while it can be said that a political counterpart of Adam Smith's invisible hand *may* operate, so as eventually to get the "common good" furthered (a doubtful proposition, in any event), still what might be called "the individual good" often must suffer in the process. When those "individuals" so suffering are sufficiently numerous and can exercise a considerable power leverage, then their *political* battles, in the American system, often tend, as we have been told by Tocqueville and Dicey, to become *judicial* in nature. The *judicial* area is, thus, a *political* battleground—either because, as in the case of the Negro, the legislature is foreclosed to him, or because, as in labor relations, the legislature delegates its responsibility—and there should be little wonder that the results are hailed as victories for one side or another, both by laymen and lawyers. Reason, Hart to the contrary, in these instances, if not in others, is emphatically not "the life of the law"; rather, it is the language of political battle. And the Court *is* a power organ, which aids in the shaping of community values, whether avowedly so as in the hands of a Douglas or whether abashedly so when Frankfurter seeks to convince us that he is an apostle of "self-restraint."[108] Whatever its decision—even a denial of certiorari or taking refuge within the doughy contours of "political questions"—the Court is institutionally a part of a government with affirmative orientation: In a welfare state, it is also concerned with "welfare." The only question is not whether it should be so but whether it should be *outwardly* so, and whether it should try to be so systematically, rather than in a helter-skelter manner.

The role, then, of the Supreme Court in an age of positive government must be that of an active participant in government, assisting in furthering the democratic ideal. Acting at least in part as a "national conscience," the Court should help articulate in broad principle the goals of American society.[109] The process is not a novel one; it has characterized the activities of the Supreme Court in the past, and the suggestion here is that it become outwardly so. Historically, the Court has espoused such goals as the free market, political democracy, and fairness in governmental activities affecting individuals. Today there is an equal need for more conscious normation on the part of the members of the Court.

---

[108] Something that neither Frankfurter nor his followers have answered is what happened to his vaunted sense of self-restraint in the recent race cases, involving certainly the most poly-centric of social questions. Why didn't the Justice dissent or at least utter one of his well-known concurring opinions?

[109] The Court as a "national conscience" is discussed by Bryce, by Curtis, and by Ribble: BRYCE, THE AMERICAN COMMONWEALTH 273 (1913), and the recent analysis by Howell, *James Bryce's "The American Commonwealth,"* 9 J. PUB. L. 191 (1960); CURTIS, LIONS UNDER THE THRONE (1947) and his essay in SUPREME COURT AND SUPREME LAW 170–198 (Cahn ed. 1953); and for Ribble see his article cited in note 99, *supra.* See also Rostow, *The Supreme Court and the People's Will,* 33 NOTRE DAME LAW, 573 (1958).

In this process it is the *effects* of a given decision that become important. But is it here that the judges of today, as well as those of yesterday, operate in areas of personal ignorance. We lack a sociology of judicial decision-making, and do not really know, save in an impressionistic, helter-skelter manner, just what the impact on the value position of Americans is of a decision of the United States Supreme Court.[110] The need is thus apparent for a greater use of the data of the social sciences by the judiciary in reaching their decisions. The judge as policy-maker and norm-articulator must manipulate more than the legal doctrine.

It is in this connection that P. W. Bridgman's concept of operational analysis becomes of importance: *thought in terms of consequences.* As Bridgman put its:

In general, an operational analysis appears as a particular case of an analysis in terms of activities—doings or happenings. In my own case, pursuit of operational analysis has resulted in the conviction, a conviction which has increased with the practice, that it is better to analyze in terms of doings or happenings than in terms of objects or static abstractions. Many professional philosophers will doubtless object that this begs the whole question, for it assumes that an analysis in terms of doings or happenings is possible. Whether this objection is valid in any ultimate sense we leave unexplored, at least for the present, but I believe it possible to analyze at a level where the immediate emphasis is on doings or happenings. . . .

Analyzing the world in terms of doings or happenings, as contrasted with analyzing in terms of things or static elements, amounts to doing something new and unusual.[111]

It may be doubted that this latter sentence is true so far as what judges have actually done is concerned. In the annals of American constitutional adjudication, those men we call the great judges have habitually analyzed and thought in terms of consequences. Although their decisions are often couched in terms of adherence to "the law," nevertheless to some degree they have been engaging in operational thinking. In the main, we are suggesting in this paper that operational thinking become the outward rule, rather than the hidden actuality.

Hence we suggest that judicial decisions should be gauged by their results

---

[110] The point is well made in FRANKFURTER, SOME OBSERVATIONS ON SUPREME COURT LITIGATION AND LEGAL EDUCATION 17 (1954): "Take a problem that has been confronting the Supreme Court, Sherman Law regulation of the movie industry. A number of decisions have been rendered finding violations under the Sherman Law. Does anybody know, when we have a case, as we had one the other day, where we can go to find light on what the practical consequences of these decisions have been? . . . I do not know to what extent these things can be ascertained. I do know that, to the extent that they may be relevant in deciding cases, they ought not to be left to the blind guessing of myself and others only a little less uninformed than I am."

Compare CARDOZO, THE GROWTH OF THE LAW 116–17 (1924): "Some of the errors of courts have their origin in imperfect knowledge of the economic and social consequences of a decision, or of the economic and social needs to which a decision will respond. In the complexities of modern life there is a constantly increasing need for resort by the judges to some fact-finding agency which will substitute exact knowledge of factual conditions for conjecture and impression."

[111] BRIDGMAN, *op. cit. supra* note 20, at 3.

and not by either their coincidence with a set of allegedly consistent doctrinal principles or by an impossible reference to neutrality of principle. The effects, that is to say, of a decision should be weighed and the consequences assessed in terms of their social adequacy. Alternatives of choice are to be considered, not so much in terms of who the litigants are or what the issue is, but rather in terms of the realization or non-realization of stated societal values. What those values might be, we do not now set forth. Rather we contend that judges have always done this, in greater or lesser degree, overtly or covertly, consciously or unconsciously; and that now it should become a matter of conscious choice. The reports are replete with statements indicating that judges think in terms of effects, as well as of such other matters as precedent. The proposal here is that this should become recognized, on and off the bench, as the hallmark of the constitutional adjudicative process. Disputes are and should avowedly be settled in terms of the external consequences of their application—with those consequences spelled out in some degree of particularity. In making this suggestion, we call for a return to a Marshallian view of the Court.

At least two attempts—completely dissimilar in approach—have seriously been made to postulate a set of teleological criteria for the judiciary. These propose the affirmative utilization of the judicial process for definite, designated ends. The two proposals are those broached by M. S. McDougal, who often in collaboration with Harold D. Lasswell has published a series of essays calling for a "policy-oriented" law, the latest of which was directed toward the need for such an international law; and by Alexander M. Pekelis, whose article calling for a "jurisprudence of welfare" has lain neglected for over fifteen years.

McDougal's position is summed up in the concept of what he calls "human dignity":

By an international law of human dignity I mean the processes of authoritative decision of a world public order in which values are shaped and shared more by persuasion than coercion, and which seeks to promote the greatest production and widest possible sharing, without discriminations irrelevant to merit, of all values among all human beings.[112]

While McDougal has at no time published a detailed exposition of his ideas, still it is apparent that he considers the judicial process to be one of "authoritative decision" which should be concerned with furthering the law of human dignity. For "outcomes" and "effects" are important aspects of the power process, and a "law of human dignity will insist upon the most flexible interpretation of . . . inherited doctrines for promoting the application of authority to particular events in ways that enhance the overriding values of a world public order of freedom, security, and abundance, as such values are at stake in differing types of particular events and contexts."[113] The point emphasized

---

[112] McDougal, *supra* note 10, at 107.

[113] *Id.* at 130.

here is not an evaluation of the merits of the McDougal "law of human dignity," but that it is a serious attempt to project a set of criteria by which an affirmatively-minded judiciary may think in terms of consequences and evaluate their decisions teleologically.

As with McDougal, so with Pekelis. In a single terse essay[114] he picks up the thread of judicial freedom and judicial creativeness—which had been brandished by so many legal realists, who, perhaps overwhelmed by their audacity, failed to follow the implications of their finding—and asks "judicial freedom for what?" The problem is no longer that of description but instead it is that of "the shaping of legal reality" following a "quest for extra-legal guidance." Such guidance has been found in economics (as in *Wickard v. Filburn*)[115] and in political science (as in *Schneiderman v. United States*).[116] Even in the private law categories, Pekelis tells us, it is clear that "the crucial issues . . . cannot be solved by legal syllogisms only, or without making a more or less conscious choice between alternative social policies." He then makes his plea for a *jurisprudence of welfare*, based on "that minimum knowledge of social science which would enable [judges] to exercise a common-sense control. . . ." For "unless we are resigned to a government by technicians, and ready to submit to a totemistic symbolism evolved by the social sciences, we must be ready to learn their language. . . ." Judges (and lawyers) must be able to use social-science material in making their decisions. Although welfare is "an ambiguous concept," "it assumes as its end the ethical and political ideals professed by our society and attempts to find in the arsenals of judicial doctrine and social science the means for their realization." Welfare jurisprudence is the rejection of "an issueless life and an issueless jurisprudence," and is more of a mode of inquiry than an answer to the problems of our time. It is "a call for the growth of systematic participation of the judiciary—burdened with responsibility and stripped of its pontifical robes—in the travail of society."[117]

Both of these formulations are attempts to build on the shambles of classical jurisprudence left after the attack of the legal realists had crumbled the edifice of the "phonograph" theory of justice. The authors of them call not for neutrality but for the open taking of sides by the judiciary so as to further the ideals of American democracy. Forward looking, they reject, expressly or implicitly, the notion that neutrality can be of any real help in the judicial, and social, process. The call for "systematic participation . . . in the travail of society" is fundamentally at odds with the published views of the three commentators whose papers are under discussion. McDougal and Pekelis seek to replace the haphazard system now in operation with one dominated by conscious design.

A judicial process in terms of consequences is both unavoidable in the

---

[114] PEKELIS, LAW AND SOCIAL ACTION 1–41 (1950).

[115] 317 U.S. 111 (1942).   [116] 320 U.S. 118 (1943).

[117] PEKELIS, *op. cit. supra* note 114, at 5, 6, 9, 14, 31, 39, 40.

American legal system and to be desired. Thus the job of the American lawyer is to help build such an affirmative jurisprudence. This does not mean that the judge should sit like a kadi under a tree, dispensing justice by whim or caprice. Rather it means that the judge is to be engaged in "operational analysis"—in purposive directional thought—which is both a recognition of the creative nature of his job and a consideration of the forces that limit that creativity.

A teleologically-oriented jurisprudence is not, it should be stressed, a device to provide the answers to a given set of circumstances. Rather, it is a method—a mode of inquiry, a way to approach constitutional questions. It is opposed to a mechanistic view of the social and the judicial processes. It seeks to provide purposive direction to the flow of social events. By asking the welfare or the human dignity question, the judge must think in terms of consequences and will help in providing some guiding lights for the attainment of the democratic ideal.

In such a purposive posture, the data heretofore considered useful in judicial decision-making will perforce have to be supplemented with relevant facts and principles from the social sciences. To the legal doctrine must be added what is known in the pertinent social science disciplines. If, for example, a judge is to make a decision on the economic question of the nature of the American market economy, as is necessary in antitrust cases, he will probably have either to emulate Judge Wyzanski in the *Shoe Machinery* case[118] and appoint an economist as one of his "law" clerks or find some other means of determining what is useful and necessary to know about that case.

Finally, judicial decision-making in terms of consequences emphatically does not mean that the judiciary is a "tool of the State." If a judge acts in conscious affirmation of a set of values, it is just as likely that he will oppose the position of the State as to uphold it. Saying that in an age of positive government, all organs of government must be avowedly purposive in their actions, is not to postulate a subservient judiciary.[119] Just as in the days of the "nightwatchman State," the judiciary can be independent, even while admitting its deep and continuing involvement in societal affairs.

V. Conclusion

All nations face the same basic problems: external security and internal order. Both of these are interdependent. But all governments do not resolve these problems in the same way. In the American constitutional order, the values of personal freedom and individual liberty are given as much importance as anywhere else in the world and more importance than in most of the world. In the attainment of these goals, the judiciary has as important a role to play as any other organ of government. Perhaps it is even more important than the

---

[118] Discussed in Freund, *The Supreme Court and American Economic Policy*, THE JURIDICAL REVIEW 142, 159–162 (1959). The case is United States v. United Shoe Machinery Corp., 110 F. Supp. 295 (D. Mass. 1953), *aff'd per curiam*, 347 U.S. 521 (1954). See KAYSEN, UNITED STATES v. UNITED SHOE MACHINERY CORPORATION: AN ECONOMIC ANALYSIS OF AN ANTITRUST CASE (1956).

[119] See FRIEDMANN, LAW IN A CHANGING SOCIETY 59–62 (1959).

legislature or the executive. For while it is true of course, as we are often told by Mr. Justice Frankfurter, that the other branches of government also have the capacity to govern, it is the courts that can best protect the rights of minorities which tend to become submerged in the political processes of government. The other branches of government, precisely because they are more political and thus more susceptible to the prevailing winds, may and do find it difficult at times to withstand the pressure of majority opinion. A majority, as De Tocqueville and John Stuart Mill have indicated, can be despotic. It is, accordingly, the quintessence of democracy for an appointive judiciary to further the ends of the integrity of the individual.

One final word: "Reason," Professor Hart to the contrary notwithstanding, is not "the life of the law." A part of the law, to be sure. But the life? No. As used by Hart, "reason" is an ambiguous term. If he is referring to logical derivations from abstract general principles, then he is not describing the judicial process. If, however, he is referring to a process of disciplined observation, coupled with a recognition that choices must be made among alternatives and a cognizance of the consequences of the decision, then Reason is certainly of great importance. It is certainly not a "life principle," whatever that might mean. But Professor Hart, and Professors Wechsler and Pollak, do state an ideal, one which Chief Justice John Marshall once stated as follows:

Courts are mere instruments of the law, and can will nothing. When they are said to exercise a discretion, it is a mere legal discretion, a discretion to be exercised in discerning the course prescribed by law; and when that is discerned, it is the duty of the court to follow it. Judicial power is never exercised for the purpose of giving effect to the will of the judge; always for the purpose of giving effect to the will of the legislature; or, in other words, to the will of the law.[120]

In the course of a slashing critique of what he calls Professor Hart's "theology," Thurman Arnold, a central figure in the legal realist movement of the 1930's, says that the ideal is of "tremendous importance."[121] For without a continuing pursuit "of the shining but never completely attainable ideal of the rule of law above men, evolved solely from Reason," says Arnold, "we would not have a civilized government. If that ideal be an illusion, to dispel it would cause men to lose themselves in an even greater illusion, the illusion that personal power can be benevolently exercised. Unattainable ideals have far more influence in molding human institutions toward what we want them to be than any practical plan for the distribution of goods and services by executive fiat."[122]

---

[120] Osborn v. Bank of the United States, 22 U.S. (9 Wheat.) 738, 866 (1824). For Cardozo's comment on this statement, see CARDOZO, THE NATURE OF THE JUDICIAL PROCESS 169–170 (1921) See also BLACK, THE PEOPLE AND THE COURT (1960).

[121] Arnold, *supra* note 98.

[122] *Id.* at 1311. For a discussion of "reason" and its role in human thought, see Alexander, THE WESTERN MIND IN TRANSITION (1960): "Like Kierkegaard, Nietzsche was motivated by the conviction that abstract reason cannot solve the basic problems of human existence. 'Reason,' Nietzsche wrote in his *Thoughts Out of Season*, 'is only an instrument and Descartes, who

What this seems to mean is that sophisticated people[123] should recognize the personal power of federal judges but that the creative role of the judge should not be divulged, else the nation will suddenly succumb to totalitarianism. As such, it has a familiar ring: it is the same argument used against the legal realists of two or three decades ago.[124] It has no more validity today than it had then. Morris Cohen put the matter succinctly many years ago:

When I first published the foregoing views [on judicial legislation] in 1914, the deans of some of our law schools wrote me that while the contention that judges do have a share in making the law is unanswerable, it is still advisable to keep the fiction of the phonograph theory to prevent the law from becoming more fluid than it already is. But I have an abiding conviction that to recognize the truth and adjust oneself to it is in the end the easiest and most advisable course. The phonograph theory has bred the mistaken view that the law is a closed, independent system having nothing to do with economic, political, social, or philosophical science. If, however, we recognize that courts are constantly remaking the law, then it becomes of the utmost social importance that the law should be made in accordance with the best available information, which it is the object of science to supply.[125]

Legal fictions permeate law and the legal process. They are useful to the extent that they serve desirable ends. The "shining . . . ideal of the rule of law above men, evolved solely from Reason" is partially fictional in nature. It is a useful fiction. But the alternative is not despotism: the range of social choice is far greater than Thurman Arnold's over simplified "either-or" dichotomy. A recognition of what Holmes called "the secret root from which the law draws all the juices of life," by which he meant "considerations of what is expedient for the community concerned,"[126] provides a more viable point of departure for a jurisprudence of the age of the positive State.[127]

---

recognized only reason as the supreme authority, was superficial.' He succinctly said that the true statement should read *vivo, ergo cogito* and not the Cartesian *cogito, ergo sum*. Reason is in the service of life, of the will to live. . . . The common element in these two so opposite philosophies is their denial that scientific abstractions can solve the actual concrete problems of human existence. Both represent a reaction against the belief of three centuries that the eventual salvation of mankind lies in science." *Id.* at 196.

[123] It is not explained why no danger exists if only Arnold and other sophisticates see the illusory nature of the ideal, but that it is dangerous for people generally to become aware of it. Isn't there an equally "shining" ideal that members of a democratic society have the capacity to make up their own minds and to guard against self-deception? Arnold is engaging in the even greater illusion that deception of the "masses" is proper in a democracy. *Quaere* also just what relevance Arnold's remarks about "executive fiat" have in the cirsumstances? His juxtaposition of the two pole positions involves the use of a resounding *non sequitur.*

[124] See, *e.g.,* Wade, *The Concept of Legal Certainty,* 4 MODERN L. REV. 183 (1941).

[125] COHEN, LAW AND THE SOCIAL ORDER 380–81 (1933) (a collection of previously published essays).

[126] HOLMES, THE COMMON LAW 35 (1881).

[127] Can it not be said that the Supreme Court may legitimately serve as part of an "aristocracy of talent," in Carlyle's phrase, in helping build that jurisprudence during the ensuing decades? (The term comes from CARLYLE, PAST AND PRESENT 29 (Everyman's ed. 1941).)

4
A NOTE ON THE CRITICISM OF SUPREME COURT DECISIONS

The essay reprinted here supplements Chapter 3. Much of the commentary upon the Supreme Court and the decisions the Justices render reflect a tendency to judge the results reached by the niceties of internal consistency with an edifice of legal doctrine. Law, however, should be evaluated by the results it achieves, as Dean Roscoe Pound said in 1908. The basic problem is that many commentators still seek to achieve an internal, logical consistency, rather than weighing considerations of social advantage. A decision can be logically arbitrary but sociologically nonarbitrary.

Generally, scholarship about the Supreme Court tends to reflect what the philosopher Morris Raphael Cohen once termed "absolutistic legalism." Legalism is indeed the prevailing ideology of the American legal profession. The tendency is to think of law, including constitutional law, as a separate and discrete entity, apart from the pull and tug of politics and economics and other matters. In jurisprudential terms, this means that analytical positivism is the basic belief. The same holds true for Great Brit-

"A Note on the Criticism of Supreme Court Decisions" was originally published in 10 *Journal of Public Law* 139 (1961). Reprinted by permission of the *Emory Law Journal* (formerly *Journal of Public Law*) of the Emory University School of Law.

ain, from which American law derived. According to Professor J.A.G. Griffith of the London School of Economics:

> A man who has had legal training is never quite the same again . . . is never able to look at institutions or administrative practices or even social or political policies, free from his legal habits or beliefs. It is not easy for a lawyer to become a political scientist. It is very difficult for him to become a sociologist or a historian. . . . He is interested in relationships, in rights in something and against somebody, in relation to others. . . . This is what is meant by the legalistic approach. . . . [A lawyer] will fight to the death to defend legal rights against persuasive arguments based on expediency or the public interest or the social good.

As in Great Britain, so in the United States. Legal commentary, including criticism of Supreme Court decisions, is not immune from that attitude. This essay points out in brief form what is wrong with such a posture.

The doctrines which best repay critical examination are those which for the longest period have remained unquestioned.[1]

—A. N. WHITEHEAD

I. INTRODUCTION

LAWYERS, as we all know, have both the right and the duty to criticize governmental officials, not excluding those who work on courts. In recent years, the spate of critical comment on the performance of the United States Supreme Court has reached a flood. It emanates both from within‘ and without the legal profession and at times is both informed and responsible. The lay critics, at least as numerous and often more vociferous than the lawyers, outwardly reflect the operation of the old saw that "it all depends upon whose ox is being gored" by a particular decision. Lawyers, circumspect by nature and apt to try to find other motivations for their sometimes anguished and sometimes approving reactions, do not seem to be immune from that principle. But more likely than not it is the client, whose fees are the main source of a given lawyer's income, whose ideas the lawyer tends to reflect. That is no crude example of economic determinism, but merely an obvious conclusion from an evaluation of the published statements of members of the bar, be they "liberal" or "conservative." It is the academic lawyers—those few whose good fortune it is to profess the law in the nation's several score law schools—who are supposedly free from client-induced bias and who should thus be able to render the type of disinterested criticism of judicial decisions so sorely needed.

Commentary about court decisions is in fact one of the main activities of some law professors. Carrying on from their student law review days, in which intensive and extensive training was received in doctrinal exegesis, the law teacher fills the pages of the law journals with heavily footnoted, oft-times readable accounts of what judges have done with particular disputes. (In this focus of attention, the academic lawyer stands imprisoned by the common-law heritage, which glorified the law-making proclivities of judges but which denigrated those by legislators and administrators, and tends to shy away from other equally [or more] important segments of the law-making process.) Often the comment takes the form of determining whether or not a given judge erred in his decision, in evaluating the result in terms of accepted doctrine (the "conventional wisdom," in Galbraith's mordant term), and in setting out what must have been the "real" reasons for the decision as distinguished from those stated in the opinion. The value of such exercises is obvious; it is helpful to others in the teaching profession for their classroom and research activities, to students who might stray from the casebook to the library and even get beyond the hornbook shelf, and sometimes to practitioners and to judges who must deal with the disputes in which people become involved—and which they cannot settle without resort to the ritual of official action. But it is a value and an aid only to the extent that legal periodicals are read—by no means a self-evident proposition, except by the writers of the papers and the editors who print them.

Nevertheless, at times law journal articles *do* get read. Witness, for example, the gaggle of papers, essaying opinions on Supreme Court adjudication and the replies thereto which have been published in recent months. One of these is the mellifluously written but puzzling comment by Dean Erwin N. Griswold appearing in the November 1960 issue of the *Harvard Law Review*.[2] In that paper, Dean Griswold defended his colleague, Professor Henry M. Hart, Jr., against the biting thrusts of sometime legal realist, quondam law professor, and former judge, Thurman Arnold.[3] Several other articles of the genre have appeared; they are listed in the footnote.[4] One may be permitted the hope that the various authors, having shot their opening volleys, will now move on to other weapons in their arsenals and come up with a different level of criticism. In the present brief note, I should like to make comment on three points: (a) time and official decision-makers, (b) the pathological decision, and (c) criteria for Supreme Court criticism. In so doing, an attempt has been made not to duplicate what others have said, and what I have myself

---

[2] Griswold, *Of Time and Attitudes: Professor Hart and Judge Arnold*, 74 HARV. L. REV. 81 (1960).

[3] Arnold, *Professor Hart's Theology*, 73 HARV. L. REV. 1298 (1960).

[4] Including the following: Wechsler, *Toward Neutral Principles of Constitutional Law*, 73 HARV. L. REV. 1 (1959); Pollak, *Racial Discrimination and Judicial Integrity: A Reply to Professor Wechsler*, 108 U. PA. L. REV. 1 (1959); Mueller & Schwartz, *The Principle of Neutral Principles*, 7 U.C.L.A. L. REV. 571 (1960); Miller & Howell, *The Myth of Neutrality in Constitutional Adjudication*, 27 U. CHI. L. REV. 661 (1960); Black, *The Lawfulness of the Segregation Decisions*, 69 YALE L.J. 421 (1960); Bickel & Wellington, *Legislative Purpose and the Judicial Process: The Lincoln Mills Case*, 71 HARV. L. REV. 1 (1957); Brown, *Process of Law*, 72 HARV. L. REV. 77 (1958). No effort has been made to list all of the articles published in legal and other periodicals, of which there are a large and growing number.

said in another place,[5] but to add a little to the on-going debate about the Supreme Court and its role in the American democracy.

II. On the Idea that Judges Work too Hard

Professor Hart believes that Supreme Court justices have too many decisions to make in the time at their disposal, and compiles statistics to buttress his conclusion. He also thinks that better opinions and decisions would emanate from the Court if the justices had more time to ponder their problems—thus permitting the "maturing of collective thought"—but fails to document that belief empirically. Judge Arnold disagrees with both beliefs and tells us that Hart, having never been a judge (but only a clerk to a judge), misconceives the judicial decision-making process. Dean Griswold, who has neither been a judge nor a law clerk, sides with Hart.

This sort of dispute has a historical counterpart—and not so long ago. In 1937 President Roosevelt, more than mildly unhappy with some Court decisions, said that the justices were too old and didn't have the energy or stamina to keep up with their docket. He proposed to add some younger men to the high bench to help the "nine old men." In the *brouhaha* that resulted, Chief Justice Hughes and his colleagues said that they were not too old to do their job, and proved it to the satisfaction of Congress. But the last laugh, of course, went to the President, whose policies soon received judicial approbation (entirely coincidentally, to be sure, and supposedly without any causal connection to the "Court-packing" plan) and who soon had the opportunity to replace old men with younger. A scant quarter-century later, we are again faced with the proposition that the justices do not do their jobs properly because they do not have enough time (age is not mentioned). But since the Court has long ago abdicated any sustained scrutiny of executive and legislative decisions, it is now the bar, academic and practicing, that decries the performance of the nine men. Also in that category are the majority of the chief justices of the various state supreme courts.

The state judges have opined that the Supreme Court has gone too far, particularly with respect to some of its recent decisions on federalism, in its law-creating as distinguished from its law-finding actions.[6] In circumspect language and backed up by memoranda from five University of Chicago law professors, these critics have attempted to stem a flow of decisions they do not like.[7] (It is somewhat amusing to note the acceptance that judges do "make law," but with the immediate rejoinder that

---

[5] Miller & Howell, *supra* note 4.
[6] The views of the state chief justices may be found in 8 U. Chi. L. S. Rec. (Supp. 1958).
[7] *Ibid.*

they shouldn't make too much.[8] But how much is too much?) Professor
Hart tells us that the Court is losing "the professional respect of first-rate
lawyers"—but does not identify any in that category. Professor Herbert
Wechsler wants adherence to "neutral principles" of constitutional law—
but fails to tell us when the Court ever did so. Professors Bickel and Wellington bemoan opinions having all the vacuity of "desperately negotiated
documents"—but do not reveal preferred examples of judicial opinion-
writing. And Dean Griswold warns that the case-load of the Court must
be reduced or superficial opinions will continue to emanate from the
Court. (At just what period in its history, one is forced to ask, did the
Supreme Court justices write "good" opinions?)

Now it may be true that judges do work too hard. But is it really relevant? Who doesn't work hard? The President? Congressmen? Heads of
the agencies? Top policy-makers? Practicing lawyers? The point is that
hard work is the lot of the highest governmental decision-makers generally, none of whom have the time to permit that maturing of thought so
extolled by Hart and Griswold. And lawyers, as a whole, have too much
to do—the better ones, at any rate. Even some law professors work too
hard. There is a need for "reflective deliberation" by all members of the
legal profession—and by all high-level policy-makers. Why single out the
justices and bewail only their fate? Do their decisions have greater impact? Are they of more significance? Important judicial decisions certainly
are, but hardly more so than those made by men in the high echelons of
the public administration.

Is a decision easier for a conscientious congressman to make than for
an equally conscientious judge? Is it less difficult to decide about nuclear
disarmament than it is to determine whether public schools should be
racially separated? Should there be any less mature collective thought
given to measures to protect the dollar in international exchange than
to the severance of DuPont ownership of General Motors stock? Is it
harder to be a justice on the Court than a Secretary of State or of Defense?
I suggest not. More, complex as the problems are that confront the judiciary, those officials do have one great advantage over other public
officers—their decisions are retrievable. A rehearing can be granted;
former holdings can be overruled; the impact is much slower. But the
President would have found it difficult to recall troops sent into action in
Korea in 1950; and a decision not to produce a given weapon can have
enormous, irretrievable consequences. *His* guesses must be right. This is
not to denigrate the judiciary, but merely to say that one grows a trifle
weary of the solicitude for judges and the absence of same for other offi-

---

8 See Kadish, *A Note on Judicial Activism,* 6 UTAH L. REV. 467 (1959). *Cf.* Lockhart,
Response to the Conference of State Chief Justices, 107 U. PA. L. REV. 802 (1959); Black,
supra note 4.

cials. And one wonders how long lawyers will continue to look upon judicial decisions as being so important as to merit the great preponderance of scholarly commentary, to the systematic slighting of the decisions of administrators.

Should the number of court-made decisions be reduced? The short answer to that is that it cannot be. The question is: *Who* should make them? If not the Supreme Court, then who? For made they will be. That is unavoidable. Should the final say rest with state judges? Lower federal judges? Administrators? In what instances? By what criteria? Such questions as these receive little attention. The critics cry: Don't work so hard; cut out the nonessential; reflect and ponder and produce judicial gems of enduring quality. But while some suggestions have been made to reduce the workload, no comprehensive examination of the problem has been made. Diversity of citizenship cases, habeas corpus, FELA—these and a few others have been relegated to the unimportant by some observers, suitable to be left to decision by those whose time is less precious. But even so, how much time *is* necessary for judicial decision-making? And would the excision of the listed categories of disputes make any real difference in the final results of the cases that are decided? Did judges make better decisions when dockets were less crowded? How busy were the justices who rendered *Dred Scott v. Sandford? United States v. Butler?* the *Japanese-Exclusion Cases? Danbury Hatters?*

In final analysis, the criticisms of the Court cited above seem to be based on the view that there is something lacking from the opinions that judges write as distinguished from the decisions themselves. But is the *quality of opinions* the truly important matter here? Isn't it, rather, the *quality of decision-making?* Can it be that the critics are hiding their dislike of the results reached through an attack on the opinions written to explain and/or justify those results? After all, the end we want from the judiciary is wise decisions, not well-parsed window dressing. If not, why is there no constitutional or statutory requirement for explanatory opinions? We should not mistake the judicial custom of explanation for the judicial *raison d'être*. In other words, it may be less the rationale than the decision that distresses the academic critics, who may be more favorable to a "result-oriented jurisprudence" than they care to admit.

But *what* decisions are wise? How can they be determined? By what standards? Dean Griswold asserts that the result "must seem to be sound" "in terms of the law as it has been received and understood...." He thereby echoes Wechsler who maintains that the "virtue or demerit of a judgment turns . . . entirely on the reasons that support it and their adequacy to maintain any choice of values it decrees," and Hart who avers that "reason is the life of the law and not just votes for your side." But nowhere do these commentators postulate criteria other than those generalized views: they say to the judge: "decide in accordance with the law"—as if the law was certain and all that was needed was the selection of relevant doctrine.

Let us pause to analyze that a bit. It was precisely because the justices in the 1930's were deciding cases "in terms of the law as it has been received and understood" that President Roosevelt and others so severely castigated the Supreme Court. The Griswold-Wechsler-Hart position can only be based on the assumption that a sort of Platonic heaven of legal concepts exists from which a judge may select the one principle appropriate for the case before him. But it is because judges do have a choice between inconsistent propositions that the judicial process is invoked in the first instance. A principle of doctrinal polarity is present in all constitutional litigation; at least two equally appropriate rules are always available from which judges may make their choices.[9] After all, if a Platonic heaven of concepts were "true," then it must be said that lawyers, before they become judges, can also locate it and identify the "neutral principles" or "the law as it has been received and understood," and advise their clients accordingly. Since they do not and since they advise continuation of litigation, the only conclusion is that half of America's lawyers appearing before the Supreme Court take their cases there for pettifogging reasons.

But surely those lawyers who lose Supreme Court cases are not shysters nor have they made an error in choice of neutral principle or the law. For of course there is more uncertainty in the process than that. What the academic critics are espousing is the construction of a verbally consistent doctrinal edifice, a system logically consistent within itself but one with a disregard of the consequences (other than doctrinal fidelity) of those decisions. A mechanistic view of human affairs dies hard, even after it has been partially repudiated in the natural sciences—and never validly transferred from the physical to the social sciences.

The problem, in sum, is one of the wisdom of decisions, not their rationale. And the time that judges need—and all officials should have—is that required to make a judgment that is wise in the circumstances. But will more time give more wisdom to the Court's product? Who can say? What can be said is that there is no escape from the view that it is the decisions themselves—the results, the "votes"—and their effects on the value-position of Americans that are important. "Reason" as logic, as Holmes long ago stated, is not the chief end to be held in mind; reason must refer "to a process of disciplined observation, coupled with a recognition that

---

9 As Cardozo noted long ago; see *e.g.*, his PARADOXES OF LEGAL SCIENCE (1927). In constitutional law, Professor T. R. Powell's thinking "was infused . . . by the principle of polarity. . . ." Freund, *Thomas Reed Powell*, 69 HARV. L. REV. 800, 802 (1956).

choices must be made among alternatives and a cognizance of the consequences of the decision."[10] And the result "must seem to be sound," that is, be "wise," not so much in terms of "the law" but in terms of the realization or furtherance of societal, including individual, values—only one of which is that adherence to regularity of official social control that we call law.

III. ON THE CONCEPT OF THE PATHOLOGICAL DISPUTE

Any society uses a large number of techniques for the resolution of the myriad of differences and disputes that arise among its members. By far the greatest number of these are informal, *i.e.,* unofficial, in nature. The range of social controls is broad, and they are variously imposed. If social control is defined as the process by which individuals are persuaded or compelled to conform to standards or values imposed by others, it takes place "when a person is induced or forced to act according to the wishes of others, whether or not in accordance with his own individual interests."[11] Of these means of molding human behavior, law is but one of many: As Huntington Cairns has put it, "in the world of order, law appears as one of the instruments which stabilize and modify modes of activity. It is one of the means of social control. . . . In its widest and most useful sense . . . [social control] includes every way through which human society exercises a modifying influence upon itself or any part of itself."[12] The point sought to be made here is elementary, but often lost sight of: whereas law may be considered to be one of the main social controls, the law suit is relatively rare in occurrence. Despite the seemingly immense amount of litigation, resort to the official dispute-settling organ (the judiciary) usually takes place only after all of the other social controls have been tried and found wanting. The norm is the unofficial settlement of human differences of all types; the exception is judicialization. Not only do people bypass the official dispute-settlers through the use of private judiciaries (*e.g.,* arbitration), but far more often the differences are resolved by face-to-face dealing—by negotiation, by compromise, by other techniques of a similar nature. Law enters this picture of normality only indirectly and informally.

As far as the Supreme Court is concerned, the implication is that the law suit, and particularly the litigation of a constitutional nature that gets Court attention to the extent of a ruling on the merits, may be taken to represent the exceptional—the "pathological"—situation in social affairs. The term *pathological* is used not in its medical sense as a morbid physical condition, but in the sense that social conditions have broken down to the

---

10 Miller & Howell, *supra* note 4, at 694.
11 SOCIAL CONTROL 3 (Roucek ed. 1957).
12 CAIRNS, THE THEORY OF LEGAL SCIENCE 22 (1941).

point that someone other than the immediate parties must settle a dispute or controversy. It also refers to the situation in public law when a given controversy cannot be settled by the avowedly political branches of government, whether those disputes are between segments of government (in which event they are usually called "political questions" and evaded by the Supreme Court) or between an individual and government. In the terminology of Professor Lon L. Fuller, a constitutional case that gets the scrutiny of the highest bench is always "polycentric" in nature[13]—in that it concerns a question that is only ostensibly legal. A polycentric question is one in which more is involved than consequences for the value position of two private individuals. It permeates into and is derived from the very interstices of society. A clear illustration of present-day interest is the series of cases in which the Court has been engaged in redefining the status of the Negro in American society.

The meaning for the Griswold *et al* position is significant: in his essay the Dean concedes that "there must be occasions when judgment is so nicely balanced that it is finally resolved by a sense of ultimate values," making reference to the Holmesian "can't helps" in so doing. But in the constitutional case, it is always a "can't help" that is involved; there is always a conflict in ultimate values present, making inevitable a judicial choice between competing goals. That this choice cannot be by reference to neutral or impersonal principles, as Wechsler and Hart enjoin us to believe, or through a "disinterested exposition and development of the law of the land," as Griswold maintains, must be the point of departure for any serious critical examination of Supreme Court decisions. The ideal of the "Rule of Law," as usually understood, simply does not suffice.[14] For *so far as the particular dispute and the litigants then before the Court are concerned,* there is no law governing the case until the justices have spoken. It is relevant, thus, to ask: Can there be a "rule of law" in a substantive sense? If that concept is limited, as it usually is, to aspects of procedural "regularity," then to the extent that a principle of doctrinal polarity exists, the task of constitutional decision-making is inescapably a creative one. In that litigation, if not in other types, relevant applicable doctrine tends always to run in inconsistent multiples, in pairs of opposites. There, accordingly, can be no pre-existing law "as it has been received and understood" by which a given case then before the Court may be determined. Even though one may easily agree with Dean Griswold

---

[13] Fuller, The Forms and Limits of Adjudication (mimeographed 1959) (to be published in revised form in a book to be entitled THE PRINCIPLES OF SOCIAL ORDER). See Fuller, *Adjudication and the Rule of Law,* in PROCEEDINGS OF AMERICAN SOCIETY OF INTERNATIONAL LAW 1 (1960); and see Llewellyn, *The Normative, the Legal, and the Law Jobs: The Problem of Juristic Method,* 49 YALE L.J. 1355, 1375-76 (1940) (on the "trouble case").

[14] That the rule of law is not a static concept is revealed in INTERNATIONAL COMMISSION OF JURISTS, THE RULE OF LAW IN A FREE SOCIETY (Marsh ed. 1960). See also FRIEDMANN, LAW IN A CHANGING SOCIETY ch. 16 (1959).

in his assertion of the need for "intellectual detachment and disinterested-ness, rare qualities approached only through constant awareness of their elusiveness and constant striving to attain them," it should not and cannot be forgotten that, as Michael Polanyi put it, "the ideal of a knowledge em-bodied in strictly impersonal statements now appears self-contradictory, meaningless, a fit subject for ridicule. We must learn to accept as our ideal a knowledge that is manifestly personal." [15] All constitutional questions be-ing polycentric, they can be approached only by facing the unavoidable requirement of valuations and value-judgments, and never by an impossible effort to evade them. There is no middle ground between teleology and attempted mechanism in the judicial process—and mechanism is neither appropriate nor possible. The ideal espoused by the academic critics is one of those doctrines which, as Whitehead has reminded us, "best repay criti-cal examination" precisely because it has remained unquestioned for a long period of time.

Judges are, in sum, those officials who operate in officially-established organizations which are maintained to help decide the socially-exceptional case. In this job, judging, as with politics, is the "art of the possible" rather than the attempted realization of the impossible. The question is not: Should the judge be disinterested? For that he cannot be. Rather, the question is: What are the interests (the values, goals, aims, ends, prefer-ences, what have you) that can be furthered by the judicial process? What can a judge hope to attain by way of the attitude he brings to his impor-tant task? We have elsewhere answered this latter question in the follow-ing manner:

> In the interest-balancing procedure of constitutional adjudica-cation, neutrality has no place, objectivity is achievable only in part, and impartiality is more of an aspiration than a fact—although certainly possible in some degree. In making choices among competing values, the Justices of the Supreme Court are themselves guided by value preferences. Any reference to neutral or impersonal principles is, accordingly, little more than a call for a return to a mechanistic jurisprudence and for jurispru-dence of nondisclosure as well as an attempted denial of the teleological aspects of any decision, wherever made. The mem-bers of the high bench have never adhered to a theory of mech-anism, whatever their apologists and commentators may have said, in the judicial decision-making process.[16]

The other question—what interests can be furthered by the judicial process —involves the larger question of the criteria for rational Supreme Court criticism.

---

15 POLANYI, THE STUDY OF MAN 27 (1958).
16 Miller & Howell, *supra* note 4, at 671.

IV. On the Needs of Judicial Criticism

The upshot is that it is high time for general acceptance of the fact that the Emperor has no clothes. We should no longer beguile ourselves with the attractive but unattainable quest for realization of the rule of law above men and above society. All of us now know that the Emperor is striding around in his birthday suit, and while it may be possible, it serves no useful or desirable purpose to act as if he were fully clothed. More than verbal acceptance must be given to that view of the judicial process; one cannot be both a legal realist and a mechanist. A "result-oriented jurisprudence" is both unavoidable and to be desired; *it is the only tenable conception of the judicial process.* It is unavoidable because "intellectual disinterestedness in a judge" is more than "a pearl of very great price, achieved only by continual care and striving"; it is unattainable. Not only do "the greatest sometimes succumb," they *always* succumb to some degree. The amount of failure to reach the ideal doubtless varies from judge to judge, but the failure is always there, being inherent in the process of human thought and human choice. (In like manner, criticism of judicial decisions, whether lay or professional, must always itself be based on some set of value preferences of the critic. Those valuations may be conscious or they may be unconscious, but present they are, ineradicably.) And a result-oriented jurisprudence is desirable, for the judiciary is itself a part of a government of affirmative orientation; in the age of the welfare state, it too is concerned with welfare.

The needs of rational criticism of the constitutional adjudicative process may be outlined as follows:

1. A result-oriented jurisprudence cannot be avoided, whether by the judicial decision-maker or the critic. The fundamental requirement thus is: What are the values that can be furthered by the judicial process? That central question can be broken down into separate segments, including:

(a) The flow of information to the bench: How it gets there; who is responsible for producing it; and most important, what is relevant among all the data available?

(b) The criteria for judgment of a given dispute: By what standards should the dispute be determined?

In these two questions, constitutional scholarship has thus far done little to produce the quantity or quality of studies needed to clarify and illuminate them. The justices themselves have also been of little help; from Marshall to Warren, the essays in political theory that the justices write have not been noteworthy for their communicative qualities.

(c) The effects of past decisions: What changes have Court decisions made in the behavior patterns of the American citizenry? Have changes in attitude been instigated? To what extent does a given decision tend to realize the values (the ends) that can be furthered by the judicial process?

Here, again, very little of a significant nature has been produced by way of scholarship. We lack a sociology of judicial decision-making, save in scattered instances.

(d) The basic role of the Court in the age of the Positive State: Too little attention has been paid to the fact that the society that is the United States today differs in type as well as degree from that in existence in 1787 —and even in the first decades of the nineteenth century, when the original role of the Supreme Court was being fought out. The too easy assumption apparently is that the Court's job does not change, even though social affairs have been completely transformed and other branches of government markedly altered.

2. Since the Court is a social institution, it is necessary to know the basic goals of the American people—the "national purpose," as it has recently been put.[17] A result-oriented jurisprudence must take this into consideration. Conversely, the Court can aid in the continuing process of refining and updating those basic goals. In its decisions, as we have had recent clear illustration,[18] the Court can act as a "national conscience" —in conscious normation. The activity is reciprocal: the Court must know the national aspirations, and it helps to set them. The enduring values of a democratic polity are both relevant to judicial decision-making and partially established by that process.

The clarification of these matters can best be accomplished with a systematic approach to the problem, not a piecemeal stab here and there at isolated cases and doctrinal categories. For it is only when the over-all contextual problem is solved that the details take on meaning and can themselves be analyzed and explicated in a rational way. The Supreme Court has to be viewed as a social institution endowed with important social responsibilities and as a unit of government which cooperates as much as or more than it conflicts with other branches of government. Study of the Supreme Court forces lawyers, as Professor Paul Freund has

---

[17] The appointment of a presidential commission in 1960 to articulate the goals of Americans is a high-level recognition of the great need for that sort of clarification. See REPORT OF THE PRESIDENT'S COMMISSION ON NATIONAL GOALS, GOALS FOR AMERICANS (1960). The published product of that group is at best disappointing, if not somewhat pathetic, and indicates that the hard thinking in this regard is yet to be done. Of course, the goals of national life are not something to be constructed in a committee. The point in the text is that goal values of Americans must be known if rational decision-making is to take place anywhere in government, including the Supreme Court. Cf. Kristol, *Keeping up with Ourselves*, 49 YALE REV. 509 (1960); Miller, *The Public Interest Undefined* (to be published in the Fall 1961 Issue of the *Journal of Public Law*).

[18] The group of cases dealing with the race question. Cf. GREENBERG, RACE RELATIONS AND AMERICAN LAW (1959).

said,[19] to become philosophers. It also forces them to become sociologists and political economists, psychologists and political theorists.

V. Conclusion

To summarize what has been said, legal thought can either be in terms of its internal consistency with a set of principles or in terms of the external consequences of decisions. There is no halfway-house. In other words, legal thought is either mechanistic or it is teleological. If the former is desired, then it must be wholly abstract, and it can provide no basis for growth. But law, like society, changes and grows; it is a process, not a static system. There can be no escape from teleology in the constitutional adjudicative process. The true and only valid question, thus, is: What ends (purposes, goals, values) can and should be furthered by adjudication? Is doctrinal purity the main one? Or is it human welfare and human freedom? The suggestion here is that our hard-working judges, in their decisions in socially pathological disputes, should purposively strive for the affirmative goal of maximum human welfare.[20]

A final note: The argument is often made that the Supreme Court and the Constitution serve a symbolic function and that harm would result from general dissemination of the idea that the Court is a "political" as well as "legal" institution. It is better, so this theory goes, to hide the creative nature of judgment and to employ a fiction of legal certainty. To dispel the ideal of the rule of law above men and above society would, it is felt, cause severe harm to democratic institutions. One might label this a jurisprudence of nondisclosure, one which operates with a "squid function"—that of discharging an impenetrable cloud of ink to hide the facts about the judiciary. While recognizing the sincerity of those who espouse it, nevertheless there are a number of persuasive arguments against its employment. How, for example, it can be reconciled with a theory of democracy is difficult to perceive. For it is a fundamental tenet of a democratic society that power should be responsibly exercised—that it should be accountable—and it scarcely can be if the facts of power-exercise are concealed. Furthermore, in all probability concealment is not really possible, for the truth will surely out—eventually if not at once— and at the cost of even greater disillusionment. And for those whose right and duty it is to seek and state the truth as they see it—the scholars of the nation—that cause is hardly served by a policy of ignoring or hiding

---

[19] Freund, On Understanding the Supreme Court (1949).

[20] This term is deliberately left undefined. An attempt will be made to put some content into it, and such other roughly synonymous terms as "human dignity," in a future article. That paper will be a sequel to Miller & Howell, *The Myth of Neutrality in Constitutional Adjudication*, 27 U. Chi. L. Rev. 661 (1960).

the facts, however unpalatable they might be or however destructive of the conventional wisdom.[21]

---

[21] For a recent statement of squid-jurisprudence, see HAYEK, THE CONSTITUTION OF LIBERTY 206 (1960): "If the ideal of the rule of law is a firm element of public opinion, legislation and jurisdiction will tend to approach it more and more closely. But if it is represented as an impracticable and even undesirable ideal *and people cease to strive for its realization,* it will rapidly disappear." (Emphasis added.) But of course it is a complete non sequitur to maintain that the result of a healthy skepticism about the possibility of attaining the rule of law will be its disappearance. Hayek assumes his answer in his statement of the problem. See also Cooperrider, *The Rule of Law and the Judicial Process,* 59 Mich. L. Rev. 501 (1961), in which it is recognized that the judicial process is filled with uncertainty but in which, again, Professor Cooperrider asserts that too much skepticism would destroy adherence to the rule of law. This, again, is not satisfactory, for several reasons: (a) one has to be very clear about the meaning on the concept in order to say that, and there simply isn't that much agreement on it; (b) while it is of course true that justice must not only be done, it must appear to be done, the greatest peril to the rule of law is not so much a cleansing skepticism as it is a series of "unwise" decisions; (c) it is obvious that people generally do not include judicial opinions in their normal reading matter; hence it is unlikely that there will be widespread dissemination of the mysteries of the judicial process; (d) an unsupportable and unchallenged dogma—such as Cooperrider and Hayek advocate—can scarcely help liberate the human mind to face the burgeoning problems of the future.

5
ON THE CHOICE OF MAJOR PREMISES IN SUPREME COURT OPINIONS

One of the unexplored areas of criticism of Supreme Court opinions is the way the Justices accept certain major premises. Perhaps it is not explorable, for much of what we know about the Court is what the Justices choose to tell us. But that is not nearly enough to give a full understanding. A constitutional decision, as Justice Oliver Wendell Holmes said in 1905, depends "on a judgment or intuition more subtle than any articulate major premise." Judges—all lawyers—pursue both an inspirational or intuitive and a logical method. They choose their premises on faith or assume them subconsciously, and then use a form of syllogistic reasoning to reach a result.

Of fundamental importance, then, in achieving understanding of the Supreme Court is the Justices' choice of major premises. This essay suggests that that choice is the most important consideration. If it is in fact unknowable, then the obvious conclusion is that there is a large area of ignorance about the Justices and the Supreme Court. In 1962, Dean Eugene V. Rostow

"On the Choice of Major Premises in Supreme Court Opinions" was originally published in 14 *Journal of Public Law* 251 (1965). Reprinted by permission of the *Emory Law Journal* (formerly *Journal of Public Law*) of the Emory University School of Law.

of the Yale Law School said that "there is an inescapable Bergsonian element of intuition in the judges' work — in their ordering of 'facts,' in their
choice of premises, in their formulation of the postulates we call 'rules' or
'principles,' in their sense of the policy or policies which animate the trend,
or change it." So there is. The result is that in many key cases of constitutional law, it is difficult, if not impossible, to predict with certainty what
the result will be. It is easy enough to forecast some of the Justices — they
who are judicial ideologues — but often there is a middle group of the nine
men who simply are unpredictable. In large part, this is because we cannot
tell in advance the premise an individual Justice will assume when making
his decision.

The very considerations which judges most rarely mention, and always with an apology, are the secret root from which the law draws all the juices of life. I mean, of course, consideration of what is expedient in the community concerned. Every important principle which is developed by litigation is in fact and at bottom the result of more or less definitely understood views of public policy; most generally to be sure, under our practices and traditions, the unconscious result of instinctive preferences and inarticulate convictions, but nonetheless traceable to views of public policy in the last analysis.

—Holmes, The Common Law
35-6 (1881).

Introduction

OF CONTINUING FASCINATION TO LAWYERS, particularly those who make up the academic branch of the profession, is the manner in which courts operate, or, as Judge Benjamin Nathan Cardozo put it, "the nature of the judicial process." True for all courts, it is particularly so for the United States Supreme Court—a governmental organ the activities of which have occupied and continue to occupy the time and energies of some of the most brilliant legal minds this country has produced. The nine middle-aged or elderly men who constitute that Court at any particular point in time are the object of additional intense scrutiny by other governmental officials, by members of the press, and by political scientists and some economists and sociologists. Doubtless this is because those people recognize what lawyers at times have to be reminded of: that the Supreme Court in its constitutional decisions (and often in matters of statutory interpretation) has a creative, not mechanical, task. Its decisions, furthermore, have large consequences for the manner in which values are shaped and shared within the nation. In this respect, the Court cannot escape being "political"—not, be it said, in the invidious sense of that term, but because the nine Justices unavoidably are participants in the political arena.[1]

Recognition that the task of constitutional adjudication is often, perhaps always, creative, is merely the beginning and not the end of analysis. A few

---

[1] For recent discussion, see SHAPIRO, LAW AND POLITICS IN THE SUPREME COURT (1964).

decades ago, when the movement in American jurisprudential thought labelled "legal realism" was at its apex, probably it was enough to maintain and demonstrate that judicial decisions were not brought by legal storks, but were the product of the mental processes of very human men. The legal realists were a cold douche to the orthodox notion of the adjudicative system. *Law and the Modern Mind* epitomized the attack upon the pretense that law judicially enunciated was the product of the application of the one relevant known rule to the facts of a given social dispute that ended up in court.[2]

But if judges can and must make law if they are to do their job—and no thoughtful observer of the day denies it—left unanswered are the difficult questions: How much? when? what law? The legal realists cut through the intellectual miasma of mechanical jurisprudence but failed to come to grips with these other equally—or more—important questions. Holmes, in an oft-quoted statement which was truistic when made, once said that of course judges legislate, but that they were confined from "molar to molecular" motion; they could, in his view, fill in the interstices of already established policy (by legislature or by Constitution) but were not permitted to legislate "wholesale." This was not because of anything written in statute or constitution, but apparently because of inherent limitations in adjudication, which is essentially an *ad hoc,* piecemeal approach to social problems, of emanations from the doctrine of separation of powers, and of an intuitive feeling that by attempting too much the courts could be greatly damaged. Holmes answered the question of "how much?" by saying "a little bit"; the "when" he left unanswered; "what law" he left for individual decisions (and basically for the legislature). So, too, with Frankfurter who, while faithfully echoing his master's position failed to grasp the simple fact that Holmes spoke for different times and different problems, published numerous statements (some very passionate indeed) calling for "judicial self-restraint" (but who in fact was neither consistent nor clear in what he meant by that posture).[3] Not so, however, for other members of the Court (and other judges), the majority of whom are today actively, even avowedly, participating in a process of progressive updating of the Constitution (and thereby making law), much to the consternation of some commentators.[4]

The question of how much, when and what creativity should occur in constitutional adjudication cannot be answered categorically. Many commentators, however, do essay partial opinions on the matter. Today these tend to fall into two camps, neither of which may be said to have a pipeline

---

[2] FRANK, LAW AND THE MODERN MIND (1930), discussed in LEVI, AN INTRODUCTION TO LEGAL REASONING (1949).

[3] *Cf.* Grant, *Felix Frankfurter: A Dissenting Opinion,* 12 U.C.L.A.L. REV. 1013 (1965).

[4] See, for discussion, Miller, *Notes on the Concept of the "Living" Constitution,* 31 GEO. WASH. L. REV. 881 (1963).

to revealed truth—those who with Justices Frankfurter and Harlan espouse the view of limited judicial action by calling for "judicial self-restraint" and those who follow the "activist" lead of Chief Justice Warren, Mr. Justice Douglas, and (sometimes, although not outwardly) Mr. Justice Black. It would be idle to count noses on this division of critical opinion, if indeed such were possible, although it seems fair to say that both sides have a considerable number, many of whom have not been loath to make their views known, and also that no one has as yet produced a thorough-going, systematic explication of the role of the Supreme Court in the modern era. Ascertaining who is in either camp, for that matter, is far less important than asking the question of why a judge (or a commentator) takes a particular position on a specific issue. How, that is to say, does a judge choose his point of departure in writing his opinion? We are seldom enlightened on that score, either on the general question of activism/self-restraint or upon the particular issues of specific cases. In this brief paper, I should like to examine the problem thus posed by using a few selected Supreme Court opinions as the raw material. What follows, accordingly, is a discussion of the question of how choices of major premises are made by judges in particular cases. The life of the law is not logic, as Holmes long ago noted, but he was neither so assertive nor so clear as to why and how major premises were chosen. Speaking in 1899, however, he said in a passage which may cast some light on the question: "I sometimes tell students that the law schools pursue an inspirational combined with a logical method, that is, the postulates are taken for granted upon authority without inquiry into their worth, and then logic is used as the only tool to develop the results."[5] If for "law schools" we read "courts," then the question under scrutiny herein is the manner in which judges adopt postulates in their opinions.

At the outset, three matters are emphasized. First, a focus upon the judicial opinion only gives a distorted picture of the process; there is more to adjudication than what judges choose to tell us, although it is also true that our knowledge about the process is still in a relatively primitive stage.[6] Most of the discussion of constitutional adjudication, however, has been concerned with parsing the opinions of the Justices. At least two further dimensions must be developed in any meaningful explication of the process: (a) an evaluation of the societal impact of decisions; this involves inquiry into the consequences of alternatives of adjudication,[7] and (b) an appraisal of the extent to which the Justices have flexibility in choosing among alternatives of decisions; this involves, among other matters, what

---

[5] HOLMES, COLLECTED LEGAL PAPERS 238, (1920).

[6] Compare the statement of Chief Justice Roger Traynor: "How many lawyers have any real awareness of how courts arrive at a decision?" The answer he seemed to give was that not enough lawyers had such an awareness. See Traynor, *Badlands in an Appellate Judge's Realm of Reason*, 7 UTAH L. REV. 157, 158-9 (1960).

[7] See Miller, *On the Need for "Impact Analysis" of Supreme Court Decisions*, 53 GEORGETOWN L.J. 365 (1965).

Professor Walter Murphy has called "judicial bargaining."[8] In short, by looking only to the opinions the Justices write, commentators upon the Supreme Court have slighted other, probably equally important, aspects and thus have as yet failed to produce meaningful rules *about* constitutional law (as compared to rules *of* constitutional law). Second, although Professor Ernest J. Brown recently maintained that we "cannot explore the minds of Justices, and what they do not put on paper we do not know,"[9] nevertheless it may be possible to construct some working hypotheses about judicial behavior. For Justices who have left the bench and whose collected papers are available for scholarly analysis, such hypotheses may be more valid than for others who have not been so frank or for members of the present Supreme Court. In other words, what the Justices put on paper includes writings other than the judicial opinions; these other papers may include internal memoranda to other members of the Court, letters to friends, diary entries, and the like.[10] In addition, behavioral scientists may be able to lend insight into the complex workings of the Supreme Court.[11] Third, our attention herein is not upon all of the methods apparently or ostensibly employed by Supreme Court Justices in deciding and explaining cases. Judicial methodology in constitutional cases includes, but is not limited to, at least two principal approaches: (a) The "interest-balancing" technique which may be seen in such diverse matters as state power to tax or regulate interstate commerce, legislation contested as violative of due process, and First Amendment freedoms.[12] It may be noted in passing that Mr. Justice Black of the present Court has castigated this approach, particularly with respect to First Amendment cases.[13] Be that as it may, it is apparently often employed by the Justices. Our interest here is not upon that method, save peripherally as a question may be presented as to why a Justice chooses one method over another. (b) Application of more-or-less rigid rules or standards to factual situations. It is this method which is under scrutiny here. In its most extreme form it may be said to fall into the category of what Roscoe Pound once denounced as mechanical jurisprudence"[14] and what Jerome Frank once said consisted of the following formula: $R(ule) \times F(acts) = D(ecision)$.[15] Judge Frank then went on to demonstrate the inadequacy of such a stark formulation. In this he was correct, in my judgment, but nonetheless to some extent constitutional adjudication

---

[8] MURPHY, ELEMENTS OF JUDICIAL STRATEGY (1964).

[9] Brown, *Quis Custodiet Ipsos Custodes?—The School-Prayer Cases*, SUP. CT. REV. 1, 32 (1963).

[10] One of the most revealing accounts of what some Justices choose to tell us may be found in MASON, HARLAN FISKE STONE: PILLAR OF THE LAW (1956), a book which some reviewers thought told too much about the mysteries of the Court.

[11] See JUDICIAL BEHAVIOR (Schubert ed. 1965).

[12] See, *e.g.*, Frantz, *The First Amendment in the Balance*, 71 YALE L.J. 1424 (1962).

[13] See, *e.g.*, Black, *The Bill of Rights*, 35 N.Y.U.L. REV. 865 (1960).

[14] Pound, *Mechanical Jurisprudence*, 8 COLUM. L. REV. 605 (1908).

[15] See FRANK, COURTS ON TRIAL (1949).

does evidence, in the opinions of some of the Justices, an $R\times F=D$ approach, not, to be sure, in its simplistic form but, rather, in the purported application of known rules to cases brought before the Court. The choice among these "rules" is the crux of the problem—and the object of scrutiny here.

I do not mean to suggest that these two methods exhaust the techniques of adjudication. As Cardozo put it with respect to the task as he saw it as Chief Judge of New York's Court of Appeals, "there are more methods to be applied than one," a recognition which "in itself is a forward step and a long one upon the highway to salvation."[16] Furthermore, the choice of methods is the judge's; and judgments may be shaped in accordance with the method chosen. Methods, accordingly, are means to an end, not ends in themselves. There is no magic in interest-balancing in and of itself; it is a way of describing what a judge believes went on in his mind when the decision was crystalized. But the choice that is made as to method may well determine the end that is reached. Supreme Court Justices seldom, if ever, enlighten us as to why a particular method is chosen, but surely that question is as important to an understanding of the decision (and opinion) as is the explication of the method in the opinion itself. In any event, the limited inquiry to which this paper is addressed is those cases in which the Supreme Court purportedly applies known rules or principles in the resolution of disputes. What will be said below may also have some relevance to the analogous question of choice of methods.

THE OFFICE OF THE OPINION

Oddly enough, given the plethora of discussions as well as millions of opinions of judges, an initial question must concern the proper office of the judicial opinion: What should it contain and how should it be written? Most Supreme Court decisions, of course, are issued without opinion; these consist of the bulk of denials of certiorari and even of the appeals which are dismissed "for want of a substantial federal question."[17] Furthermore, a number of decisions on the merits are issued *per curiam*, that is, without formal opinion and usually without an indication of the vote. Of the relative handful of cases annually which do get consideration of oral argument and opinion writing, only a few have important constitutional implications. The question, accordingly, comes down to this: what is the proper office of the judicial opinion in those few constitutional cases which get decision on the merits?

---

16 CARDOZO, THE GROWTH OF THE LAW 64 (1924).

17 Does a dismissal for want of a substantial federal question constitute a ruling on the merits of the case? It has been so asserted. See WRIGHT, FEDERAL COURTS 431 (1964), citing STERN & GRESSMAN, SUPREME COURT PRACTICE 164 (3d ed. 1962). The latter authors cite Barton v. Sentner, 353 U.S. 963 (1957), a per curiam affirmance of a district court judgment. The case hardly stands for the broad proposition stated by the foregoing authors.

The essence of the law is thought to be "reason," law being as Aristotle said, "reason unaffected by desire." But this both fails to answer the question in that it does not tell us what "reason" might be and assumes too much about human behavior in that "desire" is eliminated. The concept of reason has not been fully explored by legal scholars, although it is often used as though it had some sort of definitive meaning. Lord Coke, in his famous controversy with King James, asserted that only lawyers could understand the "artificial reason" of the law; hence, even the King had to give way to the interpretation of judges. If the law, in the context of judicial opinions, is the exemplification of a reasoned process of decision—a rational decision making process—then the opinions written by judges should at least set forth how that process operated in particular cases. Do they?[18]

The short answer to that question is no. Ideally, the judicial opinion could and should provide a basis for understanding why and how the decision was reached; at the same time, it should be a means of forecasting what might happen in the future in similar situations. But that is the ideal; the reality falls far short of attainment of even those minimal goals. An additional function of the opinion is to provide a basis for independent evaluation by scholars and others interested in the subject matter. This it does do, whether the scholarly commentator concludes that the Justices have not done their job properly or whether the commentator approves what is said. Thus some critics of recent examples of the Supreme Court's jurisprudence have been at least caustic in their evaluations of opinions; perhaps the climax of this came in Professor Philip B. Kurland's savage attack upon the Court in a recent issue of the *Harvard Law Review*,[19] characterized by Anthony Lewis of the *New York Times* as "one of the most sarcastic, all-inclusive attacks directed at the Supreme Court in recent years."[20] Others have defended the Supreme Court, but in more restrained language. My point here is that both those who disapprove and those who approve of Court opinions tend, by and large, to look only to those opinions as the sole source of research and reach their conclusions about the opinions and decisions on the basis of their consonance (or lack of consonance) with some ideal—an often unarticulated ideal, one might add.

A considerable literature has accumulated in recent years concerning this type of scholarly activity. The seminal paper is probably Professor Herbert Wechsler's *Toward Neutral Principles of Constitutional Law*. Wechsler's

---

[18] On the general question, see The American Society for Political and Legal Philosophy, Freund, *Rationality in Judicial Decisions*, NOMOS VII 109 (1964); DIESING, REASON IN SOCIETY (1962); Mayo & Jones, *Legal-Policy Decision Process: Alternative Thinking and the Predictive Function*, 33 GEO. WASH. L. REV. 318 (1964).

[19] Kurland, *Foreword: "Equal in Origin and Equal in Title to the Legislative and Executive Branches of the Government,"* 78 HARV. L. REV. 143 (1964). Professor Kurland's frontal assault upon the "activist" philosophy of the Supreme Court in recent years culminates, but doubtless does not end, a number of academic criticisms of the Court made for the most part by professors who have had some exposure to the late Justice Felix Frankfurter.

[20] N.Y. Times, Nov. 15, 1964, p. E-5.

main point was that "the main constituent of the judicial process is precisely that it must be genuinely principled, resting with respect to every step that is involved in reaching judgment on analysis and reason quite transcending the immediate result that is achieved."[21] That point of view has been variously disputed by others, among them the present writer,[22] the main thrust of whose effort may be summed up in the statement that they see the constitutional adjudicative process as far more complex than apparently Professor Wechsler believes it to be. He has stated an ideal (unattainable, in my judgment) that the judicial opinion be the published apotheosis of articulated reason.

That judicial opinions, in any field of law but particularly in those large questions of public policy we call constitutional law, do not attain that ideal is obvious from reading in any standard law school casebook. What, then, may reasonably be expected from judges? If law is the embodiment of reason, then we might expect a coherent statement of the reasons why a given decision was reached. But even here we apparently cannot succeed. The most we get from a judge is a delineation of what factors he considered important (or desirable to divulge) in coming to a decision, written in language with which lawyers are familiar. We often do not even get that. Opinions are often what Professors Bickel and Wellington a few years ago castigated (wrongly) as "desperately negotiated documents."[23] Often they are the process of "negotiation" or of "bargaining," as has been demonstrated,[24] but this is merely to label the process, not to condemn it. Inasmuch as most opinions have to be hammered out on the anvil of compromise, the net result is a document which is satisfactory to more than one (up to nine) but which, as a consequence of getting such agreement, displays either the ambiguities of language settled on by compromise or a watered-down substitute for a strong statement of principle.[25] It is not likely that the Supreme Court has ever operated in any substantially different manner; nor will it change its methods in the foreseeable future. Those who call for "principled decision-making" are foredoomed to frustration. Like it or not, the Supreme Court is not and cannot be so circumscribed, unless it is to forego entirely its historical role in constitutional adjudicating. Within the area of its competence (self-ordained, to a considerable extent) it is as close to a set of Platonic guardians as may be seen anywhere. Learned Hand,[26] among others, didn't like this—but true it is nonetheless.

As Morris R. Cohen said three decades ago, "we cannot pretend that

---

[21] 73 HARV. L. REV. 1, 15 (1959).

[22] Discussed in Shapiro, *The Supreme Court and Constitutional Adjudication: Of Politics and Neutral Principles*, 31 GEO. WASH. L. REV. 587 (1963).

[23] Bickel & Wellington, *Legislative Purpose and the Judicial Process: The Lincoln Mills Case*, 71 HARV. L. REV. 1, 3 (1957).

[24] Murphy, *supra* note 7; Mason, *supra* note 9.

[25] *Ibid.*

[26] HAND, THE BILL OF RIGHTS 70 (1958): "For myself it would be most irksome to be ruled by a bevy of Platonic Guardians, even if I knew how to choose them, which I assuredly do not."

the United States Supreme Court is simply a court of law. Actually, the issues before it generally depend on the determination of all sorts of facts, their consequences, and the values we attach to these consequences. These are questions of economics, politics and social policy which legal training cannot solve unless law includes all social knowledge."[27] From this it follows that the Supreme Court opinion cannot be an exercise in simple explanation of a result, if indeed such were possible, as Ernest Nagel has demonstrated.[28] Many in fact are "state papers" of considerable magnitude and importance. Furthermore, as opinions (even decisions) apparently are often the resultant of a process of negotiating and bargaining, as well as an evaluation of the consequences of the decision, the opinions, accordingly, must reflect the cautious ambiguities or high-level abstractions in which many major statements of public policy are couched. As a pronouncement of public policy, the opinions (and decisions) of course transcend the individual litigants—whose function it was to provide the vehicles by which such statements can be made—and thus they must be phrased with a degree of generality which would permit their application in other instances. They are examples of statecraft, not of routine private problem-solving.

In that limited sense, the Supreme Court opinion in constitutional cases does provide a basis for understanding how the result was really reached and a means for prediction of future decisions. As such, the opinion helps to make the decision palatable or tolerable to the legal profession and others who are interested in the outcome. Failures to attain the unrealizable ideal of fully "rational" judicial opinions has provided a basis for attack by critics of the Court in recent years. But these critics never indicate just when the Court ever wrote "better," i.e., more rational, opinions, and lay themselves open to the possible charge that it is the result they disapprove rather than the means of reaching it. The critics thus may well be among those Dean Griswold labelled as "result-oriented."[29]

In any event, as Professor Brown has indicated, the opinion is about all we presently have of substance to employ in dealing with the Court. The remainder of this paper is confined to an appraisal of a few Supreme Court constitutional opinions in an effort to develop the inquiry concerning choice of major premises by judges. But, as noted above, the opinion as a "state paper" is more than an exercise in simple explanation of a result; accordingly, it would be necessary to go outside the opinion and utilize the as yet dubious findings of behavioral science to construct viable hypotheses which would fully explain a Supreme Court decision. We begin with a proposition which should be obvious, but which merits restatement: the

---

[27] COHEN, REASON AND LAW 83-4 (1950) (pagination from paperbound edition 1961).

[28] NAGEL, THE STRUCTURE OF SCIENCE (1961).

[29] Griswold, *Of Time and Attitudes: Professor Hart and Judge Arnold,* 74 HARV. L. REV. 81 (1960).

fact that major premises (constitutional premises) tend to travel in pairs of opposites.

PAIRED OPPOSITES

If, as Cardozo said, "the thing that counts chiefly is the nature of the premises,"[30] the important matter to perceive is that relevant or apposite premises in constitutional cases tend to be multiple rather than single. Oliphant and Hewitt maintained almost 40 years ago that in litigation "two conflicting major premises can always be formulated, one embodying one set of interests, the other embodying the other."[31] They spoke mainly of private law cases, but their insight may be applied to public law, including constitutional law, as well; in fact, the observation may be even more evident in constitutional than in other types of cases. A convenient label for this characteristic is the Principle of Doctrinal Polarity.[32] So labelled, it of course is familiar learning, but one which needs restating. Furthermore, it is one of the basic assumptions upon which the adversary system is built. In other words, a high degree of uncertainty exists in the adjudicative process insofar as application of "the law" is concerned, higher even than that which Judge Cardozo was willing to grant when he asserted that nine-tenths of the cases that came before the Court of Appeals were "predetermined in the sense that they (were) predestined—their fate pre-established by inevitable laws that follow them from birth to death."[33] To him, the judge had a relatively small area of "free activity." That may have been accurate when Cardozo wrote those views—although I am inclined to think he exaggerated the situation—but if so, it is not valid today. If Cardozo (and others) are correct, then how does one explain the *quantity* of appeals in American courts? Cardozo did not essay an explanation; and I am not aware of anyone who has. Is there one? What are the alternatives? Four seem possible: appeals are taken because (a) judges know more law than lawyers; or (b) lawyers are misleading their clients; or (c) neither judges nor lawyers are sure of the law, which must be created anew in each decision; or (d) clients demand appeals for frivolous or other reasons, even in the face of known or probable eventual defeat. Of those alternatives, two may be dismissed summarily: judges, speaking generally, do not know more law than lawyers; and lawyers, again speaking generally, are not misleading their clients about the state of the law. At times, particularly when large sums of money may have to change hands, no doubt a client will demand an appeal from an adverse judgment in the trial court, in which event it will be taken even in the

---

[30] CARDOZO, THE GROWTH OF THE LAW 62 (1924). *Cf.* O'Meara, *Natural Law and Everyday Law*, 5 Natural L.F. 83 (1960).

[31] Oliphant & Hewitt, *Foreword* to RUEFF, FROM THE PHYSICAL TO THE SOCIAL SCIENCES at xv (1929).

[32] See McDOUGAL, *The Ethics of Applying Systems of Authority: The Balanced Opposites of a Legal System,* in THE ETHICS OF POWER: THE INTERPLAY OF RELIGION, PHILOSOPHY, AND POLITICS 221 (Lasswell & Cleveland eds. 1962).

[33] CARDOZO, *supra* note 30, at 60.

face of probable defeat simply because retention of the money for the period of the appeal is financially advantageous. But these instances must be of a relatively small number. So perhaps Cardozo was not correct, in which event there is a much higher degree of uncertainty than he was willing to admit. This seems to be a valid generalization, even though there doubtless are many exceptions.[34] For, as Professor Grant Gilmore has noted, the proliferation of decisions has resulted in a breakdown of traditional ideas of precedent and *stare decisis*.[35] True enough for private law categories, it is also valid for public law. For example, as Kenneth Culp Davis has demonstrated, in the field of administrative law the Supreme Court's handling of "standing" and other problem areas has resulted in a multiplicity of doctrines.[36] It is a poor lawyer indeed who cannot, as a consequence, find "authority"—that is, precedent—for the result his client desires once a human dispute has gone beyond the stage of settlement informally and has been submitted to the official organ for dispute settling, a court.

Put another way, the cases which come to courts tend often, if not always, to be the "trouble" or "hospital" cases, to use Llewellyn's labels.[37] They represent the pathological in society. They are not typical.[38] Lawyers (and legal educators), by concentrating on courts and on the pathological in society, have ignored the indubitably vast role of law in the routine ordering of human affairs. We lack a sociology of law in any real sense, and by concentrating on the abnormal have obscured normality. Perhaps a good deal of the ill repute of law and lawyers may be traced to this over-concentration. All but a minute portion of human disputes are settled extra-judicially—by negotiation, by some sort of give-and-take, by one party giving in to the other, by the range of techniques through which social control is imposed. Those which cannot be so settled must be referred to the courts, which are the organs of government established for

---

[34] See, however, Mayo & Jones, *supra* note 18, at 379: "Some decisions purportedly offering a deliberate choice may, for all practical purposes, be essentially 'determined'," citing Cardozo; Clark & Trubek, *The Creative Role of the Judge: Restraint and Freedom in the Common Law Tradition*, 71 YALE L.J. 255, 256 n.7 (1961); and Dahl, *Decision-Making in a Democracy: The Supreme Court as National Policy-Maker*, 6 J. PUB. L. 279, 293 (1957).

[35] Gilmore, *Legal Realism: Its Cause and Cure*, 70 YALE L.J. 1037 (1961).

[36] DAVIS, ADMINISTRATIVE LAW TREATISE (1958).

[37] Llewellyn, *The Normative, the Legal, and the Law Jobs: The Problem of Juristic Method*, 49 YALE L.J. 1355, 1375-76 (1940). See Miller, *A Note on the Criticism of Supreme Court Decisions*, 10 J. PUB. L. 139 (1961).

[38] As Professors Mishkin and Morris put it: "A lawsuit is an extraordinary event. The vast bulk of transactions between private individuals and between citizens and the government move smoothly through intended steps to ultimate conclusions acceptable to all sides. When disagreement does arise—whether on the merits of a claim or out of failure to pay it—it is usually resolved without resort to the institutional deciders known as courts. . . . Even if a lawsuit is commenced, efforts at negotiation usually continue and suits are frequently settled. Litigation to a conclusion is the exception." MISHKIN & MORRIS, ON LAW IN COURTS 1 (1965).

that purpose. The pathological dispute, accordingly, represents a situation where the parties are at loggerheads, each advancing a certain value or set of values inconsistent or in conflict with the other's. This may be seen with particular clarity in constitutional adjudication. Examples are easily found. The Negro desires better treatment from government, only to run into another value system (that of the whites); urban voters want better representation and come into conflict with rurally dominated legislatures; states wish revenue in order to maintain the diversity to be furthered by federalism, and come up against the commerce clause and the commitment to uniformity; those caught in the toils of the criminal process want a literal and complete interpretation of the Bill of Rights, while the policeman (and the "nice" people) prefer to deal with crime expeditiously even at the risk of unfairness to a few; the alleged criminal wants a fair trial, but the newsman wants to print anything he wishes; and so it goes in an unending stream of value conflicts over basic principles that exist in the constitutional litigation that gets to the Supreme Court.

What is here called the pathological dispute, which is characterized by a concomitant inability of the parties to compromise and settle extra-judicially, may be added to the proliferation of decisions to provide ample evidence to substantiate the validity of the Principle of Doctrinal Polarity. What this means is that a Supreme Court Justice in every case which is presented to him for decision on the merits, whether review is denied or not, represents a situation of multiplicity of premises from which one may be chosen as the point of departure for writing the opinion. The task of the Justice, it thus is obvious, is not to search in Jhering's "heaven of legal concepts" for the one principle or rule which precisely fits the case at hand. He must face up to the burden of choice among conflicting premises, choices which, when made, have the characteristic of creating new principle (or premises).[39] Every decision thus is law creating as well as law applying. Each constitutional decision on the merits has at least a partial element of "new-ness," of creativity. As Dewey put it, "Whenever there is genuine deliberation, there are alternatives at almost every step of the way."[40] Reference to some Supreme Court opinions will illustrate the point.

ILLUSTRATIVE DECISIONS

In a recent essay Dean E. V. Rostow maintained that "there is an inescapable Bergsonian element of intuition in the judges' work—in their ordering of "facts," in their choice of premises, in their reformulation of the postulates we call "rules" or "principles," in their sense of the policy or policies which animate the trend, or change it."[41] While Dean Rostow

---

[39] Cf. Levi, *The Nature of Judicial Reasoning*, 32 U. CHI. L. REV. 395 (1965); Freund, *supra* note 18.

[40] DEWEY, LOGIC: THE THEORY OF INQUIRY 163 (1938).

[41] Rostow, *American Legal Realism and the Sense of the Profession*, 34 ROCKY MT. L. REV. 123, 144 (1962).

is not very clear as to what he meant by "intuition," at the very least his statement may be taken to mean that he agrees that the task of the judge is to choose from among premises. That choice may well determine the outcome of the case—insofar as the opinion reveals the judge's mental processes. Consider, in this connection, the following statement by Mr. Justice Potter Stewart dissenting in the 1962 decision, *Kennedy v. Mendoza-Martinez*:[42]

> The Court's opinion is lengthy, but its thesis is simple: (1) The withdrawal of citizenship which these statutes provide is "punishment." (2) Punishment cannot constitutionally be imposed except after a criminal trial and conviction. (3) The statutes are therefore unconstitutional. As with all syllogisms, the conclusion is inescapable if the premises are correct. But I cannot agree with the Court's major premise—that the divestiture of citizenship is punishment in the constitutional sense of that term.

Here, then, is a classically clear instance of the point being discussed: how two major premises, mutually inconsistent, are available to Supreme Court Justices. The critical question which is posed by Mr. Justice Stewart's statement goes, as he says, not to the result reached or to the logic (reasoning) from premise to conclusion. Rather, the question is: which premise, to use his term, is "correct"? How does an observer, be he lawyer or scholarly commentator or layman, determine whether Mr. Justice Stewart or Mr. Justice Goldberg (who wrote the opinion of the majority) is the proper one to be chosen? What were the criteria of choice? As to the latter question, neither wrote about why the premise he chose was superior to the alternative. On this, we are left without guidance or insight.

In his dissenting opinion, Mr. Justice Stewart thus made explicit what is implicit in other cases. Examples, while available in plethoric quantity, need not be multiplied; a trio will suffice: *Mapp v. Ohio, Sinclair Refining Co. v. Atkinson,* and *Marbury v. Madison*.[43] Collectively they demonstrate what Holmes noted long ago: "General propositions do not decide concrete cases. The decision will depend on a judgment or intuition more subtle than any articulate major premise."[44] In *Mapp*, Mr. Justice Harlan pointed out in dissent that the Court had two legal questions (premises) to choose from in order to dispose of the controversy. Said he: "In overruling *Wolf* the Court . . . has simply chosen between two Constitutional questions. Moreover, I submit that it has chosen the more difficult and less appropriate of the two questions."

The *Sinclair Refining* case did not deal with constitutional interpretation; rather, it involved the meaning to be given to several labor statutes in the

---

[42] 372 U.S. 144 (1963).

[43] Mapp v. Ohio, 367 U.S. 643 (1961); Sinclair Refining Co. v. Atkinson, 370 U.S. 195 (1962); Marbury v. Madison, 1 Cranch (5 U.S.) 137 (1803).

[44] Lochner v. New York, 198 U.S. 45, 76 (1905).

context of a dispute between a company and a union. As such, one might believe that the "rule" or "premise" to be applied would be relatively clear, certainly more so than if the problem was to extract a rule from past decisions (as in common law cases) or from such vague constitutional pronouncements as "due process of law" or "no establishment of religion." But the contrary was evident in the judicial disposition of the case, as Professor Paul Freund has shown in an instructive essay on rationality in judicial decisions.[45] Writing for the majority, "Justice Black took the Norris-La Guardia Act as the primary datum; held the railway cases inapposite; and stressed what would be the legislative character of a repeal of Section 7 [of the Norris-La Guardia Act], which Congress had declined to do."[46] In dissent, Mr. Justice Brennan took as his point of departure "a pattern of legislation and asked not whether the earlier provision had been repealed but whether it could be 'accommodated' with the later legislation."[47]

Marbury needs no present restatement. Suffice it merely to note that Chief Justice Marshall's confident assertion that it is "emphatically" the province of the judiciary to say what the law is can be matched with a contrary proposition, equally valid under the Constitution and certainly valid in the context of the facts of the *Marbury* case, that it is the province of Congress to say what the law is and that it is only in cases in which there are clear and unmistakable conflicts with the fundamental law can a statute be invalidated. Some eminently respectable modern authority has enunciated such a view: For example, in *The Bill of Rights*,[48] the late Judge Learned Hand questioned the basis of *Marbury* as well as a number of latter-day decisions.

From such cases as these, as well as many—perhaps most—others that the Supreme Court decides, the conclusions are obvious (and far from novel). They include:

1. Each constitutional case decided by the Supreme Court has an element of creativity in it. The same may be said for other cases as well, those which shape common law doctrine, those in which statutes are central, those in which the relationship to the public administration is at issue. Learned Hand, in a review of Cardozo's *The Nature of the Judicial Process*, said as much in 1922: "The pretension of. . . . [an English-speaking judge] is, or at least it has been, that he declares pre-existing law, of which he

---

[45] Freund, *supra* note 18.

[46] *Id.* at 124.

[47] *Id.* at 125. All of which serves to indicate that the judicial task in statutory matters is no less complex and little or no less creative than in common law or constitutional cases. *Cf.* Frankfurter, *Some Reflections on the Reading of Statutes*, 47 COLUM. L. REV. 527 (1947).

[48] HAND, THE BILL OF RIGHTS (1958). The introduction to the paperbound edition by Judge Charles E. Wyzanski, Jr., seems to answer most of Judge Hand's criticisms. See Wyzanski. *Introduction* to HAND. THE BILL OF RIGHTS v-xiv (Atheneum paperbound edition 196?).

is only the mouthpiece; his judgment is the conclusion of a syllogism in which the major premise is to be found among fixed and ascertainable rules . . . . Yet the whole structure of the common law is an obvious denial of this theory. . . ."[49] Judges may and must thus exercise the "sovereign prerogative of choice" from among conflicting premises. But old ideas die hard, and it seems likely that the "pretension" of which Hand spoke still states the conventional wisdom. Certainly it does for those who engage in such "intellectual" tasks as writing hornbooks and compiling "restatements" of law.

2. From this it follows that in constitutional adjudication on the merits the law can never be certain in any significant sense. Nevertheless, predictability is present in the sense that close observers of the flow of Court decisions can usually develop an intuitive "feel" for what is likely to happen.[50]

3. The opinions the Supreme Court Justices write usually do not reveal the reasons why a certain premise is chosen.

4. From this it follows that we will not get "reasoned" opinions from Supreme Court Justices unless and until they see fit to delineate the reasons why a choice of premises is made. (This assumes a judge can make such a statement, in itself a dubious proposition. Whether any humans, including judges, can validly state their motivations and what influences their decisions is doubtful.)

5. In like manner, the choice a given Justice makes as to the method to be employed—interest-balancing, etc.—is not explained in the opinions of Justices. And this is true even though the method that is chosen may well have a major influence in shaping the result. One example will illustrate the point: Mr. Justice Black's continuing battle against interest-balancing and against finding rights beyond those set forth in the Constitution, exemplified most recently in *Griswold v. Connecticut*, the decision which invalidated an anti-contraceptive statute.[51]

6. The resulting intellectual problem is to construct valid hypotheses which, when tested empirically, will serve to explain choices of both method and premise. This task is one which lawyers must confront and resolve in some manner which will permit predictions of the Supreme Court's future decisions. At present this is done by long-continued study of Court opinions plus an intuitive feeling of the direction the Court is moving. Are

---

[49] 35 HARV. L. REV. 479 (1922).

[50] For that matter, predictability is not necessarily an absolute value. Some of the recent criticisms of the Court may be read as complaining that some decisions have become too predictable! In this connection, compare Wechsler, *supra* note 21, with Kurland, *supra* note 19.

[51] 85 Sup. Ct. 1678 (1965).

data available which will allow the construction of tenable hypotheses? Some political scientists have so asserted.[52]

THE PROBLEM RESTATED

We have seen enough to say that judges have freedom of choice among conflicting premises to apply in individual cases. So, too, with commentators: the premises from which they begin their discussions of judicial opinions are, in Holmes's words, "taken for granted upon authority without inquiry into their worth, and then logic is used as the only tool to develop the results." Professor Geoffrey Hazard recently made the point in this manner:[53]

> Legal realism has demolished the edifice of Victorian legal certainty. . . . None may mourn this development and none should suppose that the demolition job is completed. But having eschewed formulae and set out in quest of the "facts," legal scholarship, it seems to me, has come up with a blank page on which the judges and scholars write what they please. Decision turns on a "balancing" of the "relevant considerations," without much indication of why the considerations are relevant, what weights are to be given them, or where the fulcrum is. In this state of affairs, mid-Twentieth Century adjudication, although intoned in modern and even scientific language, seems hardly different from the Moslem curb-stone disposition. And seeking to obey the law has become in many fields a process of divination.

The point is well taken, although perhaps a bit overdrawn. The problem is clear: to find some middle-ground between the polar positions of (a) "Victorian legal certainty," which is untenable, and (b) what Mr. Justice Frankfurter called "kadi justice," decisions made on the whim of a given decision-maker, which negates the idea of the rule of law. Is there a way out of the dilemma?

Two, possibly three, alternatives may be suggested, only one of which reveals any feasibility: (a) hiding the nature of judicial creativity behind a facade of ostensible non-discretion so that the American people will continue to accept the Court as an authoritative decision-maker, the idea being that if it becomes generally known that the Justices do not act only in response to rigid, authoritative guides the people will lose faith and confidence in the Court; (b) insisting that the Justices develop "neutral" or "impersonal" principles of law in their decision making; and (c) avowedly facing up to the problem of judicial value judgments and asking that the Justices state the values they are seeking to further in their decisions. Since governments, including courts, are not in the habit of ordering their affairs so as to fit neatly into any particular political theory but tend to make incremental adjustments in institutions and policies as needs arise, no one of these choices (assuming all are tenable) is likely to be followed. Further-

---

[52] See JUDICIAL BEHAVIOR (Schubert ed. 1965).
[53] HAZARD, RESEARCH IN CIVIL PROCEDURE 8-9 (1963).

more, a *tour d'horizon* of constitutional adjudication, historically and contemporaneously, leads to the conclusion that all three alternatives are in
part followed (and have been followed) by the Supreme Court; in other
words, insofar as the written opinions reveal the process, constitutional
decision making is a melange made up of the application or development
of principle, an intuitive assessment of the impact of the decision, plus
a simultaneous cloaking of the result so that it seems to be the working
of inexorable antecedent commands and logic even though, because little
or no attention is paid to the reasons for choice among premises, the logic
is questionable.

The point is beautifully illustrated in the Connecticut birth control case
decided in June 1965, *Griswold v. Connecticut*. The facts are simple. At
issue was the validity of a statute which made it a crime to use "any drug,
medicinal article or instrument for the purpose of preventing conception";
defendants, officers of the Planned Parenthood League, were convicted
under the Connecticut accessory statute after they gave information, in-
struction, and medical advice to married persons as to the means of preventing conception. Found guilty as accessories, and fined $100 each, defen-
dants appealed on the grounds that the accessory statute as applied violated
the Fourteenth Amendment. With Justices Black and Stewart dissenting,
the Supreme Court reversed the Connecticut Court of Errors and declared
the birth control statute invalid. Six opinions were rendered, two by the
dissenters. The main thrust of Mr. Justice Douglas, who wrote for the
Court, and of concurring Mr. Justice Goldberg, who was joined by Chief
Justice Warren and Mr. Justice Brennan, was the assertion of a constitutional right of privacy of married persons "older than the Bill of Rights—
older than our political parties, older than our school system,"[54] "a personal right 'retained by the people' within the meaning of the Ninth Amendment."[55] Mr. Justice Harlan also concurred but would have struck down
the statute on due process grounds as violative of a basic value "implicit
in the concept of ordered liberty," a somewhat odd position for a judge
who a year previously had accused his colleagues of using the Constitution
as a "panacea for every blot upon the public welfare" and making the
Court "a general haven for reform movements."[56] Similarly, Mr. Justice
White could find no rational basis for the statute and maintained that it
deprived persons affected of liberty without due process of law. Apparently
—although this is unclear—Justices Douglas and Goldberg would apply
the "penumbral" right of privacy, formed by an "emanation" from the
specific guarantees of the Bill of Rights and imbedded in the Ninth Amendment, to the states through "absorption" or "incorporation" into the due
process clause of the Fourteenth Amendment.

All of this was anathema to Justices Black and Stewart. Mr. Justice

---

[54] Griswold v. Connecticut, *supra* note 51, at 1682.
[55] *Id.* at 1690.
[56] Reynolds v. Sims, 377 U.S. 533 (1964).

Black accused the majority of resorting to the discredited *Lochner-Coppage* line of substantive due process decisions[57] and thereby substituting their ideas of the wisdom of public policy for that of the state legislature. Not being able to find a specific right of privacy in the Constitution, he concluded: "this Court does have power, which it should exercise, to hold laws unconstitutional where they are forbidden by the Federal Constitution. My point is that there is no provision of the Constitution which either expressly or impliedly vests power in this Court to sit as a supervisory agency over acts of duly constituted legislative bodies and set side their laws because of the Court's belief that the legislative policies are unreasonable, arbitrary, capricious or irrational."[58] So, too, with Mr. Justice Stewart, who called the statute an "uncommonly silly law" but who thought it would be judicial legislation to strike it down.[59]

Here, then, is the development of principle, certainly as "neutral" and "impersonal" as one may wish, even though it is couched in language of such high-level abstraction that its application in other cases is difficult to predict.[60] But that does not make it much different from, say, "due process of law" or "equal protection of the laws" or "no establishment of religion," constitutional terms which have never been thought to be useless because of inherent vagueness. A constitutional right of privacy, "penumbral" rather than implied, furthermore does not differ essentially from a constitutional right of association or a constitutional right to travel, both of which have been found in the Bill of Rights.[61] So, principle there is, as neutral as there has ever been.

Furthermore, we find the Justices stoutly denying that they are sitting in judgment on the wisdom of the birth control statute. "We do not," said Justice Douglas, "sit as a super-legislature to determine the wisdom, need, and propriety of laws that touch economic problems, business affairs, or social conditions."[62] But since the law directly concerned "an intimate

---

[57] This is the line of cases repudiated by the Court in the late 1930s and early 1940s. For discussion, see McCloskey, *Economic Due Process and the Supreme Court: An Exhumation and Reburial*, SUP. CT. REV. 34 (1962).

[58] Griswold v. Connecticut, *supra* note 51, at 1701.

[59] Which only goes to prove, if proof were necessary (which it isn't), that the Justices can themselves contribute to the folklore surrounding the Court and Constitution. On this, ARNOLD, THE FOLKLORE OF CAPITALISM (1937) and THE SYMBOLS OF GOVERNMENT (1935) are classics. I have attempted to show some of the mythology surrounding the Court in Miller, *Some Pervasive Myths About the United States Supreme Court*,—ST. LOUIS U.L.J.—(1965).

[60] The call for "neutral principles," discussed in Shapiro, *supra* note 22, can never result in the development of principles which do not call for judicial creativity in their application, simply because any such principle must be framed in abstract language. For that matter, neutrality is itself a bootless quest, as I have said in a previous paper, Miller & Howell, *The Myth of Neutrality in Constitutional Adjudication*, 27 U. CHI. L. REV. 661 (1960).

[61] See NAACP v. Alabama, 357 U.S. 449 (1958); Kent v. Dulles, 357 U.S. 116 (1958).

[62] Griswold v. Connecticut, *supra* note 51, at 1680.

relation of husband and wife and their physician's role in one aspect of that relation," he found no difficulty in sitting as a censor of the "wisdom, need, and propriety" of the anti-contraceptive statute. Mr. Justice Douglas thereby was able at one swoop to hide the fact of judicial law-making behind a smokescreen of covering verbiage and to face up to the problem of stating the values his decision furthered, namely, that the "intimacies" of the marital relation were beyond state control. (That this proposition is itself ambiguous is, of course, obvious, as will be noted below.) Mr. Justice Black boggled at this, asserting that general application of the Douglas method would "amount to a great unconstitutional shift of power to the courts"[63]—in other words, he accused his colleague of "judicial legislation" which tended to break down the doctrine of separation of powers and of federalism. In so doing, he maintained that amendment was the only proper manner to effect constitutional change, thereby eliminating at one stroke most of American constitutional history.[64] Without going into the fascinating question of the role of the Court in updating the Constitution, it may be said that a Justice who can read history to say that the Fourteenth Amendment incorporated all the Bill of Rights is not in a very good position to chide his brethren for putting new content into the Constitution.[65] Mr. Justice Black also takes an absolutistic position on First Amendment freedoms, believing them to be beyond governmental interference, but refuses to read the First Amendment literally in its entirety; after all, that amendment does say "*Congress* shall make no law . . . ," yet the learned Justice has no trouble reading "Congress" to mean "the states."[66]

All of this is at least faintly amusing. We take the Supreme Court, its members, and its decisions much too seriously. Lawyers and laymen alike have built up an aura of awe and mystery around the Court and look upon it with a reverence which, to a cool-minded person, is more than a little astonishing. No doubt there are many reasons for this, reasons which could only be discovered by probing into the psyche, individual and collective, of the American people. However, it is easy enough to poke fun at

---

[63] *Id.* at 1702.

[64] Black's opinion is illustrative of some of the mysteries of the Court and of some of the obvious inconsistencies of the Justices. For him to deny the validity of the concept of the "living" Constitution is most astonishing, to say the least.

[65] *Cf.* Powell, *The Logic and Rhetoric of Constitutional Law,* in ESSAYS IN CONSTITUTIONAL LAW 85 (McCloskey ed. 1957). See the opinion by Black, J., in Adamson v. California, 332 U.S. 46 (1947) in which he asserted that the Fourteenth Amendment incorporated all of the Bill of Rights.

[66] Nor do his brethren, for that matter, who have since Gitlow v. New York, 268 U.S. 652 (1925) progressively "absorbed" or "incorporated" most of the important parts of the first eight amendments into the due process clause of the Fourteenth Amendment. Just how "due process" has anything to do with such matters as an establishment of religion has never been explained. *Cf.* Frankfurter, *Memorandum on "Incorporation" of the Bill of Rights into the Due Process clause of the Fourteenth Amendment,* 78 HARV. L. REV. 746 (1965).

the Justices and to demonstrate their inconsistencies. A number of commentators have done so. But our inquiry herein is not that; rather, it is: how did the Justices attain or explain the premises from which they started in constructing their opinions. On this, none of the six who wrote opinions are helpful; their words do not illumine the intellectual process. Their opinions, in this respect, consist of little more than the statement of conclusions embellished with citations and paragraphs which fill up space but which do not explain. "Reason," it may be said, is absent, if by reason is meant a meaningful delineation of the factors which led any of the several justices to their conclusions.

In this, the Justices in *Griswold* did not operate in a substantially different fashion from the time honored manner in which judges have always acted in the Anglo-American legal system and particularly in the field of constitutional adjudication. The premises were taken, as Holmes said, "without inquiry as to their worth." In this, it may be noted, judges appear to act much as natural scientists are said to operate. As Professor Henry Margenau recently put it, "Deductive science (in contra-distinction to descriptive sciences like geography or botany) begins with fundamental, *unproved* propositions which are verified only in their several consequences. The scientist does not seek to prove these axioms; rather, he accepts provisionally, judiciously but without proof, hoping that their *consequences* agree with the facts. Nor is his attitude toward them one of avoidance or tolerance. He cannot get going without them . . . ."[67] If that be so, and I am willing to accept the statement, it may be useful to compare the scientist with the judge as to method. The similarities are obvious: both begin with fundamental, unproved propositions—for the scientist these may be called axioms, for the judge the term may be a premise or "the law" (to take the classical view) or a principle or standard; for both, they cannot "get going without them," which for the judge means that while "general propositions do not decide concrete cases," neither can they be decided without them.[68] But the obvious similarities may well end there, for two reasons: (a) the precision in which scientific axioms or laws are stated as compared with the vagueness or ambiguity of most legal premises; and (b) the extent to which the propositions are tested by their consequences is not so clear in adjudication. Both of these reasons bear at least peripherally upon our inquiry herein.

First, the precision with which the proposition is stated differs for a basic reason. Legal premises (propositions, etc.) are and must be couched in language of high-level abstraction because they must be sufficiently

---

[67] MARGENAU, ETHICS AND SCIENCE 7-8 (1964).

[68] See M. R. COHEN, *supra* note 27, at 63: "Without the use of concepts and general principles we can have no science, or intelligible systematic account, of the law or any other field. And the demand for system in the law is urgent not only on theoretical but also on practical grounds. Without general ideas, human experience is dumb as well as blind."

flexible to permit their application in differing factual situations and because by being ambiguous they allow for growth to take place.[69] Legal propositions thus differ from scientific axioms in that the former are always in a state of "becoming," while the latter are settled within the frame of reference in which the scientist operates. The point is illustrated by comparing the constitutional right of marital privacy enunciated by Mr. Justice Douglas in *Griswold* with, say, Newton's laws of motion. Morris R. Cohen put it this way: "law is essentially concerned with norms that regulate, rather than uniformities that describe, human conduct. The laws that natural science seeks to discover . . . are uniformities which if valid at all cannot be violated. . . . But it is of the very essence of legal rules that they are violable and that penalties or sanctions are provided for their various violations. They do not state what always is, but attempt to decide what ought to be."[70] The "ought" element in law is that which, when meshed with the "is," brings about creativity in judicial decision making; in constitutional law the degree of creativity seems to be very high indeed.

When we look to the second possible difference between scientist and judge, it is clear, as Margenau notes, that the scientist tests by consequences. Do judges also? On this point, it seems to be fairly certain that they do, although often they hide this behind covering verbiage in the opinion. As hypothesized in a previous paper:[71] "Choices are made by Justices from among conflicting principles (or inconsistent interests) not because of compelling law, but because of an evaluation of what the impact of given decisions is thought to be."[72] If this hypothesis is valid, then judges as well as scientists test their propositions by their consequences. The difference is that the scientist can rigidly control the environment in which his test is made, while the judge usually must proceed by way of intuitive guesses of what the consequences will be.[73] But it does seem clear, as a general proposition, that not only in constitutional adjudication, but in all types of judicial decision making, the judge looks forward to an

---

[69] See Kayton, *Can Jurimetrics be of Value to Jurisprudence?*, 33 GEO. WASH. L. REV. 287, 302 (1964).

[70] COHEN, LAW AND THE SOCIAL ORDER 205 (1933).

[71] Miller, *supra* note 7.

[72] Obviously, the "impact" must and does take into consideration the imperatives of the legal system.

[73] Mr. Justice Frankfurter put the matter cogently in an off-bench statement on anti-trust adjudication, a statement which can be expanded to cover other areas of judicial cognizance: "Take a problem that has been confronting the Supreme Court, Sherman Law regulation of the movie industry. A number of decisions have been rendered finding violations under the Sherman Law. Does anybody know, when we have a case, as we had one the other day, where we can go to find light on what the practical consequences of these decisions have been? . . . I don't know to what extent these things can be ascertained. I do know that, to the extent that they may be relevant in deciding cases, they ought not to be left to the blind guessing of myself and others only a little less uninformed than I am." FRANKFURTER, SOME OBSERVATIONS ON SUPREME COURT LITIGATION AND LEGAL EDUCATION 17 (1954).

evaluation of the impact of the decision upon certain value patterns. As two astute legal scholars have recently said, "American jurisprudential thought, certainly since the famous lectures of Holmes on the Common Law, has reflected an ever-increasing tendency to look forward to the consequences of decision rather than backward to first principles."[74]

If judges, then, are at least partially "result-oriented" in their decision making—a proposition which I believe cannot be gainsaid—it is readily apparent that certain consequences and conclusions follow. These may be stated in brief form:

1. The judiciary has no method by which consequences may be ascertained in any systematic way.[75]

2. Judges accordingly need some institutional means to test the effects of alternative decisions and to be able to evaluate *prior to decision* what those effects will be. Unless some such prognosis can be made about the possible effects of alternative decisions, an individual litigant may well be harmed. Some Justices—for example, Louis D. Brandeis—were willing to risk such harm and even let individuals suffer in the greater interest of certainty in the law. Said Mr. Justice Brandeis, dissenting in *Burnet v. Coronado Oil & Gas Co.*: In constitutional matters "the Court bows to the lessons of experience and the force of better reasoning, recognizing that the process of trial and error, so fruitful in the physical sciences, is appropriate also in the judicial function." Also: "It is more important that the applicable rule of law be settled than that it be settled right."[76] The difficulty here is that the learned Justice's attempt to transfer a methodology from the physical sciences to adjudication simply will not wash: law deals with human beings and it seems to be asking too much—as Mr. Justice Brandeis does—for the individual to sacrifice his interests for what is considered to be a greater good (legal certainty). There is no way to retrieve a decision with harmful consequences. It is, in short, important that the applicable rule of law be settled *and* be settled right. To do so will require some sort of institutionalized prescience to enable judges to foresee the consequences of alternative decisions.

3. If judges are to be given such assistance and if ever an adequate description and explication of the adjudicatory process is to be made, attention must be paid to the insights and teachings of other disciplines,

---

[74] Mayo & Jones, *supra* note 18.

[75] See FRANKFURTER, *supra* note 73; Mayo & Jones, *supra* note 18, at 436-54; Miller, *supra* note 7; BREDEMEIER, LAW AS AN INTEGRATIVE MECHANISM, IN LAW AND SOCIOLOGY 73 (Evan ed. 1962):

the court needs an analysis of cause-and-effect relationships. It needs a way of ascertaining both the *past* relationship between the alleged act of the defendant and the alleged injury of the plaintiff, and the probable future relationship between the decision and the activities of defendant and plaintiff and all persons similarly situated.

[76] 285 U.S. 393, 406-08 (1932).

particularly the behavioral sciences.[77] To do this, it will be necessary to construct rules *about* law and the legal process as distinguished from rules *of* law. Traditional legal lore and learning offers no promise of being able to do this task; but the behavioral sciences, once they have transcended their present primitive stage of development, are another matter. Unless, as Holmes said, the study of law is to incorporate all knowledge,[78] which perhaps it should, the need is evident for a synthesis which will enlarge understanding of the Supreme Court and its role in the American polity, a synthesis which will gather together and blend the disparate strands of learning from law and from economics, politics, sociology, and psychology. I am not suggesting that such a blend must be produced in order to enable lawyers to continue to operate as advocates and counsellors, although it seems evident that even here it would be helpful, but do advance the proposition that an adequate understanding of adjudication (and of law) must encompass these added dimensions.

4. The choices judges make from among the premises available to them in any particular case are to be explained only when scrutiny is made, not only of the judicial opinion itself, but the entire context (all of the "inputs") in which the decision is made—if, indeed, any real explanation is ever to be forthcoming. We should not be sanguine that it will be, for we may have to live with a situation which will not and cannot permit a full description and explication of adjudication.

5. There are, in this connection, those who are quick to assert that a complete exposition of the creative nature of the adjudicatory process would not be desirable. Thus Professor Archibald Cox, writing in 1947, maintained that "Society will not long tolerate the wisest judge who, knowing no master, decides cases only according to his individual sense of justice."[79] And Professor Martin Shapiro, while noting the discretion of judges and their value-laden decisions, asserts that effort should be expended in giving the courts the appearance of value-free decision making in order to enhance the acceptability of their work.[80] Others have made similar statements. This point of view, which I have elsewhere labelled "squid jurisprudence," that is, hiding the facts of judicial creativity behind a cloud of impenetrable ink, got its effective answer years ago by Morris Raphael Cohen; said he:[81]

---

[77] *Cf.* Miller, *On the Interdependence of Law and the Behavioral Sciences*, 43 TEXAS L. REV. 1094 (1965).

[78] HOLMES, *The Profession of the Law* (1886), in SPEECHES 22 (1913):
If your subject is law, the roads are plain to anthropology, the science of man, to political economy, the theory of legislation, ethics, and thus by several paths to your final view of life . . . To be master of any branch of knowledge, you must master those which lie next to it; and thus to know anything you must know all.

[79] Cox, *Judge Learned Hand and the Interpretation of Statutes*, 60 HARV. L. REV. 370, 373 (1947).

[80] Shapiro, *supra* note 22.

[81] COHEN, LAW AND THE SOCIAL ORDER 380-81 (1933) (collection of previously published essays).

When I first published the foregoing views [on judicial legisla-
tion] in 1914, the deans of some of our law schools wrote me
that while the contention that judges do have a share in making
the law is unanswerable, it is still advisable to keep the fiction of
the phonograph theory to prevent the law from becoming more
fluid than it already is. But I have an abiding conviction that to
recognize the truth and adjust oneself to it is in the end the
easiest and most advisable course. The phonograph theory has
bred the mistaken view that the law is a closed, independent system having nothing to do with economic, political, social, or
philosophical science. If, however, we recognize that courts are
constantly remaking the law, then it becomes of utmost social
importance that the law should be made in accordance with
the best available information, which it is object of science to
supply.

6. If, as Cohen says, "the law should be made in accordance with the
best available information" (and this would include the question of choice
of premises), then two further conclusions seem apposite: (a) the present
system of information flow to the courts, including the Supreme Court,
does not adequately insure that "the best available information" does get
to the courts and is employed, should it get there, by judges. This seems
to be particularly true when courts make decisions in economic areas.[82]
A corollary of this conclusion is that there is no evidence which would
lead one to believe that judges have the competence to make pronouncements in areas of, say, economic importance. The fact is that the situation
may be quite the contrary.[83] (b) Legal education, even as now constituted
with the many changes which have come about in the past thirty years,
is not up to the task of producing lawyers who are knowledgable not only
in the technical doctrine of the law but who have some expertise in closely
relevant allied matters as political economy.[84]

CONCLUSION

A high degree of discretion is accorded to judges in the American legal
system, much higher than the myth would have it. The Justices of the
United States Supreme Court are particularly noteworthy in this respect.
But this is hidden—or, at least, has been hidden—behind a facade of non-
discretion and of the inexorable demands of antecedent law. The mythical
nature of that viewpoint has long been known, although the conventional
legal wisdom either still restates it or has not yet produced a viable substitute. When the question is posed as to the reasons why justices adhere
to certain premises in particular cases it readily becomes evident that there

---

[82] See Massel, *Economic Analysis of Judicial Antitrust Decisions*, 20 A.B.A.
ANTITRUST SECTION 46 (1962); MASSEL, COMPETITION AND MONOPOLY (1962).

[83] As Mr. Justice Frankfurter said in a candid, off-bench statement, *supra*
note 73.

[84] *Cf.* Miller, *The Impact of Public Law on Legal Education*, 12 J. LEGAL ED.
483 (1960).

is a paucity of meaningful knowledge which would enable one adequately to answer the question. In this essay, it has been suggested that premises are chosen because of an intuitive unscientific evaluation of the effects or consequences of alternative decisions. This was proffered as an hypothesis, rather than as a definitive answer. Evidence to substantiate that hypothesis may never be forthcoming, but an examination of merely the opinions that Supreme Court justices write leads one to the conclusion that such "forward looking" is present in the adjudicative process. However, we may possibly be faced with the proposition that, as Thomas Reed Powell argued,[85] judicial "reason" in constitutional law cases is not markedly different from the "reasoning" all people employ. If that be so, and if the "artificial reason" of the law Lord Coke extolled is in fact a myth, considerable alteration will have to be made in the usual picture of the Supreme Court.

One further question remains: If Supreme Court justices do enjoy that much discretion and if they in fact do attempt to evaluate the social impact of alternative decisions, what theory should guide or canalize that discretion? The question becomes acute, for with an opportunity to choose (and assuming that choices are not predetermined by environmental or hereditary factors) a justice must select both the facts he considers most important, in itself not a mechanical task, and the goals or purposes he will seek to further. The work of Chief Justice Taft on the Supreme Court exemplifies the problem: here was a judge who, according to present-day historians, avowedly pursued the protection of the "property interests" of the country and who also fought retirement in order to help stave off "the Bolsheviki" from taking over the nation.[86] Not that these sentiments were openly stated in his opinions; they were not—but they were revealed in private correspondence since made available. And it is precisely this which would seem to be behind the statement by President Theodore Roosevelt in 1908: "The decisions of our courts on economic and social questions depend upon their social and economic philosophy."[87] If it is assumed that Supreme Court decisions do have some lasting importance on the manner in which American values are shaped and shared—and this is not such a self-evident proposition as some may believe—the thing to know about judges is their philosophy.

The question of the theory which should guide or canalize the discretion of Supreme Court Justices in their choice of premises cannot be answered (at this time, at least) save in high-level abstractions. Two legal theorists who agree on the need have not been able to set forth more than the broadest of generalities: Felix Cohen, writing in the early 1930s, asserted

---

[85] See Powell, *The Logic and Rhetoric of Constitutional Law*, in ESSAYS ON CONSTITUTIONAL LAW (McCloskey ed. 1957).

[86] See MASON, THE SUPREME COURT FROM TAFT TO WARREN (1958); MURPHY, WIRETAPPING ON TRIAL (1965).

[87] Quoted in COHEN, AMERICAN THOUGHT: A CRITICAL SKETCH 163 (1954).

that the purpose of the law (and of adjudication) was to achieve "the Good," but he did not give specificity to that nebulous concept;[88] and Myres McDougal has more recently called for a "law of human dignity" without stating the particularized content of the formulation.[89] This is not to disparage their efforts, but merely to point up the difficulties. (They at least tried; others are content to retire into a verbal fog of "interest balancing" and deference to the political branches of government.) A trip down the ladder of abstraction to more particularity in goals to be pursued by the judiciary has not yet been made. It will not be made unless (and until) the American people demand a clear articulation of the ideology of the nation.[90] For a nation of avowed pragmatists, that will not soon be forthcoming. Perhaps it never will be done, in which event students of the United States Supreme Court will have to continue to put up with the dubious insights derived from study of their greatest source of date—the judicial opinion. That the opinion is a poor vehicle for understanding the Court cannot be gainsaid. Perhaps it is better to proceed this way—to leave the Court as a riddle wrapped in an enigma inside of a mystery—but I doubt it. In any event, a constitutional decision seems to "depend on a judgment or intuition more subtle than any articulate major premise."[91]

---

[88] COHEN, ETHICAL SYSTEMS AND LEGAL IDEALS (1933).

[89] *E.g.*, McDOUGAL AND ASSOCIATES, STUDIES IN WORLD PUBLIC ORDER (1960).

[90] "Ideology" as defined in SHKLAR, LEGALISM (1964) at pp. 1-28. *Cf.* F. S. COHEN, THE LEGAL CONSCIENCE 145-46 (Kramer ed. 1960):

There is a special reason why most judges will not willingly uncover, even in the privacy of judicial chambers, their basic valuations. For the custom of the realm and the defense of the status quo require that judges should appear to be unsusceptible to the wayward gusts of human emotion. The law is supposed to be objective, impersonal, and firmly grounded in the indubitable. On the other hand, everybody knows—especially judges and lawyers and law professors—that men's views of what is good and bad vary atrociously from place to place and from year to year.

[91] Holmes, J., in Lochner v. New York, 198 U.S. 45, 76 (1905).

6
THE POWER OF THE SUPREME COURT IN THE AGE OF THE POSITIVE STATE

(Coauthor: Alan W. Scheflin)

Part of the conventional wisdom maintains that the Supreme Court has great power. Some have called it the highest legislative chamber in the nation. Although there is no question that the Court can and does make law, and does so routinely, its ability to make its decisions alter the behavior patterns of the citizenry is by no means as obvious as some unthinking persons believe. Quite the contrary: the Justices have power (in the long run if not in the short run) only to the extent that their decisions are accepted by other governmental officials and by the people generally.

In this essay, originally published in two parts, the principal inquiry is into the basis for whatever power the Supreme Court does have. (Chapter 7 is devoted to an analysis of the actual power of the Court.) Does the symbolic role of the Court as an impartial tribunal far above the sweaty mob, not prey to the drives and emotions of ordinary mortals, have anything to do with the Court's position as a power-wielder in the governmental structure? The answer suggested here is that it does not; the people are interested in the results—in who wins or loses—and not in how those results were reached. As a part of the essay, the answers to a questionnaire sent to a number of leading scholars are presented.

Those who believe there is great significance to the symbolic position of the Justices impartially dispensing justice by and large do not believe that the ordinary person has the moral stamina to withstand the knowledge that judges are human. These commentators would knowingly hide the operations of the Court in a fog of mythology rather than permit its operations to be exposed for all to see. That, in short, is an elitist position that fits uneasily at best in a polity that both calls itself a democracy and seeks to achieve that ideal.

PART ONE

The time is past in the history of the world when any living man or body of men can be set on a pedestal and decorated with a halo.

. . . .

It is not good, either for the country or the [Supreme] Court, that the part played by the Court in the life of the country should be shrouded in mystery.‡

INTRODUCTION

THIS ARTICLE is in two parts. In main thrust, it is concerned with the power (in a political sense) of the United States Supreme Court in the modern era. Part One, published here, is a discussion of the symbolic role of the Court and the alleged need that it outwardly adhere to the Blackstonian declaratory theory of law. In this preliminary foray into a complicated subject matter, we intend no more than to suggest a few hypotheses which may, when subjected to empirical test, result in a greater understanding of the High Bench. Part Two, which will appear in a subsequent issue, considers the necessity for the Court to adapt itself to changing reality if it is to retain whatever power it may presently have. Running through both essays is the theme that much more factual data is required before an adequate understanding of the Court can be attained. Both parts of this article attempt to identify some of

‡Frankfurter, *The Supreme Court and Public,* 83 FORUM 329-30 (1930).

the many factors affecting the prestige and power of the nine men who sit in the Marble Palace; hence, the subtitle, "a preliminary excursus."

The essential question is one of political power, by which is meant the ability or capacity to make decisions affecting the values of Americans.[1] The prestige of the Court, the esteem in which it is held, can be of importance only insofar as it is capable of translation into power in a political sense. That the Court exercises such power is assumed without argument, and there remains only the question as to how much and on what occasions.

We do not intend to "talk lightly of the dignity" of the Supreme Court[2] but merely to try to ascertain some truths about it. No suggestion is made that the truth is easily come by. Far from it. Difficulties are initially presented by rigid internal secrecy which, Justice Frankfurter maintained, is "essential to the effective functioning of the Court."[3] Furthermore, as Ernest Nagel has observed, there is no such thing as a simple and, at the same time, adequate explanation of any phenomenon or institution.[4] To know government, including the Supreme Court, one must know history and economics, sociology and political science, law and psychology, and divers other matters. Nonetheless, it is possible to broach a greater understanding of the Court and at least pose some of the questions upon which correct and vitally important answers are dependent.[5]

---

[1] See LASSWELL & KAPLAN, POWER AND SOCIETY 75 (1950); ROSINSKI, POWER AND HUMAN DESTINY (1965); RUSSELL, POWER (1938); Fuller, *Irrigation and Tyranny,* 17 STAN. L. REV. 1021 (1965).

[2] The phaseology is taken from a statement by Charles Evans Hughes, who said: "I reckon him one of the worst enemies of the community who will talk lightly of the dignity of the bench." Quoted in Mason, *Myth and Reality in Supreme Court Decisions,* 48 VA. L. REV. 1385, 1387 (1962).

At the outset, it is desirable to postulate a basic value position: that it is the duty of legal scholars to pursue the "truth" even though truth may well be "subversive of the established order." Aiken, *A Virtue in Question,* New York Review of Books, June 9, 1966, p. 10, 11. See Szent-Györgyi, *Science, Biology and Human Relations,* The Minority of One, May 1966, p. 10, 11.

[3] Frankfurter, *Justice Roberts and the "Switch in Time,"* in AN AUTOBIOGRAPHY OF THE SUPREME COURT 244 (Westin ed. 1963).

[4] See NAGEL, THE STRUCTURE OF SCIENCE: PROBLEMS IN THE LOGIC OF SCIENTIFIC EXPLANATION 26 (1961).

[5] As Mr. Justice Frankfurter opined, "in law also the right answer usually depends on putting the right question." Estate of Rogers v. Commissioner, 320 U.S. 410, 413 (1943). "[A]nswers are not obtained by putting the wrong question and thereby begging the real one." Priebe & Sons v. United States, 332 U.S. 407, 420 (1947).

This may be done even though relevant factual data is simply not available to enable one to "prove" his conclusion definitively.

One of the hallmarks of the mid-twentieth century is an apparent need to re-define terms and re-evaluate the operating principles of the disciplines which play a basic role in structuring our lives.[6] Change is in the air, a constant of the social and intellectual order. Accordingly, re-examination of the legal system, haphazard and incomplete though it may be, has roots running at least as far back as the legal realist movement of the 1920s and '30s; it is a part of the "revolt against formalism" noted by Morton White.[7] The realists, by destroying nineteenth century conceptualism, left the legal system in general and the judicial process in particular, in a state of intellectual disarray. They were not system builders; they were iconoclasts who ripped the facade off classical jurisprudence but who did nothing to replace it with a more acceptable (that is, intellectually satisfying) conception of the nature of the judicial process. As Professor Wilfred Rumble has said, "their dissatisfaction with the traditional standard of judicial behavior was never translated into an explicit and sustained examination of the norms which ought to replace *stare decisis* as the regulator of judicial decisions."[8] We do not undertake such an examination here; what follows has a far lesser goal—a suggestion of the unfulfilled need for empirical data about the Supreme Court accompanied by a further suggestion that the Court has lost, and will continue to lose, power vis-à-vis the other organs

---

[6] Several examples come to mind: in literature, the rise of the existentialist novel picturing the despair and anguish of individual existence and the impotence of a "community ethic" to solve the responsibility for one's own essence; in the dramatic arts, the theatre of the absurd bringing to the stage essentially the same point the existentialist writers have dwelt upon; in philosophy, the abdication of the role of system-builder and explainer of the function of man, with a resultant rise of linguistic analysis and ordinary language philosophy in an attempt to ascertain the nature of a philosophical question; in religion, the God-is-dead movement challenging the efficacy of traditional religion in a secular age to perform its role as moral conscience for man and his spiritual mentor; in science, new breakthroughs to new levels of understanding especially in the areas of internal medicine and space technology; and in society, the frequent riots on college campuses, the civil rights movement, and the turn toward the new hallucinogenic drugs and the insights they purportedly give.

[7] WHITE, SOCIAL THOUGHT IN AMERICA 11 (1949). See COMMAGER, THE AMERICAN MIND 359-90 (1950).

[8] Rumble, *The Paradox of American Legal Realism*, 75 ETHICS 166 (1965). (Emphasis in original.) See also Rumble, *Legal Realism, Sociological Jurisprudence and Mr. Justice Holmes*, 26 J. HIST. IDEAS 547 (1965).

of government (particularly the Executive) in this era of the Positive State.[9]

NATURE OF THE INQUIRY: A MATTER OF JURISPRUDENCE

"[T]he question of jurisprudence," it has recently been asserted, is "what, in general, is a good reason for decision by a court of law."[10] At best, this is a dubious proposition. Aside from the difficulty that concealed within its simplistic veneer lurk several very different and very troublesome inquiries,[11] there remains the fact that it can only be based upon the unwarranted assumption that the judiciary is still the center of the legal universe, something which has not been true in Anglo-American law for decades. Perhaps at one time analysis of adjudication could validly be termed *the* problem for jurisprudents, but the governmental emphasis now has shifted in official decision-making to legislatures and, of even more importance, to the Executive Branch. Accordingly, even though, as Dean Levi recently noted, legal education (and thus, the law reviews and scholarly discourse) is still "court oriented,"[12] that orientation is excessive and increasingly non-reflective of legal reality. Hence, although this paper further adds to the already too large literature on the Supreme Court, in main thrust it suggests that further single-minded casuistry about the Court is on the whole unrewarding in attaining a greater understanding about the judiciary and that the need, accordingly, exists for empirical data and hypotheses which will add more meaningful dimensions to the sparse existing learning. We should take as our goal the increase in *understanding* of the Supreme Court, rather than the more limited task of being able better to *predict* the course of judicial decision, although no doubt greater understanding will

---

[9] The concept of the Positive State is outlined in Miller, *Constitutional Revolution Consolidated: The Rise of the Positive State*, 35 GEO. WASH. L. REV. 172 (1966).

[10] Dworkin, *Does Law Have a Function? A Comment on the Two-Level Theory of Decision*, 74 YALE L.J. 640 (1965). (Emphasis in original.)

[11] Professor Dworkin continues by noting that the question of what is a good reason for a decision by a court is one way of asking "what is law?" *Ibid.* But that seems too simple a formulation. The question, "What is law?", is itself reducible to at least the following questions: (1) What is a legal system? (2) What is a valid law? (3) What is the essence, or nature of law? (4) What is a good reason for a judicial decision? (5) What are the pre-conditions for the maintenance of a legal order? See Sartorius, *The Concept of Law*, LII/Z ARCHIVES FOR PHILOSOPHY OF LAW AND SOCIAL PHILOSOPHY 161, 162 (1966).

[12] Levi, *Law Schools and the Universities*, 17 J. LEGAL ED. 243, 248 (1965).

lead to more accurate predictions.   As Professor Lon L. Fuller recently said:

> There may be said to exist two philosophies of science.   The one sees the aim of science as *understanding*; the other as *prediction*. The first regards prediction as a by-product of understanding; we acquire the ability to predict events as our minds penetrate into the causes that underlie the happenings of nature.   The adherents of the opposed theory see "understanding" as an illusory, metaphysical trapping superfluously tacked on the essential goal of acquiring predictive knowledge.[13]

Fuller opts for understanding.   The point here is simply that there is a pressing need for a true conception of the nature of the Court as a politico-legal institution in a broader societal matrix before we can predict what that institution will do.   The need therefore is for data *about* the Court and its effect on the populus.   There is abundant criticism of the Court today purely on the grounds that it has abandoned its (assertedly) proper institutional role and has encroached upon the private domains of the other organs of government.   Such criticism, we suggest, is meaningless without a settled notion of what the proper role of the Court is vis-à-vis the other organs of government.   It is to further that initial inquiry that we call for data about the Court in its institutional setting so that a greater understanding of what the Court is *supposed to do* may be obtained.

To accomplish that greater understanding will require drawing upon insights and learning from allied disciplines, particularly the behavioral and social sciences.   But here, as in the better known casuistical exercises about the Supreme Court, the necessary insights are scanty at best and non-existent at worst.   Available are some tentative explorations into the *terra incognita* of judicial behavior but nothing of a comprehensive and systematic nature.[14]   Neither the lawyers (and political scientists) who confine their study of the high tribunal to the published opinions of the Justices nor their colleagues in the behavioral sciences have yet produced the answers.[15]   Students of the Court are just now beginning to ask some

---

[13] Fuller, *An Afterword: Science and the Judicial Process*, 79 HARV. L. REV. 1604, 1623-24 (1966).   (Emphasis in original.)

[14] See, *e.g.*, SCHUBERT, JUDICIAL BEHAVIOR: A READER IN THEORY AND RESEARCH (1964).

[15] How many lawyers, questioned Chief Justice Roger J. Traynor, have any "real

of the correct questions.[15a] By and large these questions are non-casuistical and non-doctrinal; they provide a means of breaking out of the narrow navel-gazing that has so preoccupied legal studies in the past (and even the present) and enable one to perceive the Court as a unit of government and a societal institution. First of all, some attention must be paid to the question: *What is a question* (or problem)? The task of identifying the correct questions itself is not an easy exercise, as Felix Cohen demonstrated in 1929 and as Mayo and Jones have recently developed.[16]

THREE TENTATIVE HYPOTHESES

To provide a point of departure for what follows, a recent paper of Professor Paul Mishkin on the *Linkletter* case[17] has been selected as a statement of the point of view substantially at variance with what is suggested below.[18] In his article Professor Mishkin, in the context of a recent criminal law decision, thoughtfully analyzes the problems inherent in prospective overruling of constitutional doctrine by the Supreme Court. During his exposition he asserts that there is symbolic value in the Blackstone "declaratory" theory of law, which he believes may be "in part myth [but] . . . which can be sacrificed only at substantial cost."[19] Apparently the cost he has in mind is public disrespect for, and lack of confidence in, the Supreme Court. In other words, we understand him to say that if it became generally known that the Justices were something less than the coldly rationalistic, automatonistic judges extolled by Blackstone, the prestige (and thus the power) of the Court would plummet. The image, in short, is deemed an important element of the power of the Court. His assertions are made without reference to empirical data, and therefore his conclusions, it seems, are derived intuitively rather than "scientifically." With all deference, intuiting conclusions about the prestige and resultant power of the Supreme

---

awareness of how courts arrive at a decision?" Traynor, *Badlands in an Appellate Judge's Realm of Reason,* 7 UTAH L. REV. 157, 158 (1960).

[15a] See text accompanying note 96 *infra.*

[16] COHEN, *What is a Question?,* in THE LEGAL CONSCIENCE: SELECTED PAPERS OF FELIX S. COHEN 3 (L. Cohen ed. 1960); Mayo & Jones, *Legal-Policy Decision Process: Alternative Thinking and the Predictive Function,* 33 GEO. WASH. L. REV. 318 (1964).

[17] Linkletter v. Walker, 381 U.S. 618 (1965).

[18] Mishkin, *Foreword: The High Court, the Great Writ, and the Due Process of Time and Law,* 79 HARV. L. REV. 56, 62-70 (1965).

[19] *Id.* at 63.

Court does not meet the requirement of reliable information upon which judgments may be made and a greater understanding reached. The same thing may be said about the need for hard factual data in evaluating the Court, as has been said by the Court itself in rendering opinions. For example, the reluctance to issue true advisory opinions is based, according to Professor (later Justice) Felix Frankfurter, precisely upon the lack of a factual context in which the legal concepts may be seen.[20] This does not mean, of course, that the Court does not issue advisory opinions; it does on occasion but does not call them that.[21] However, the opinion is at least partially couched in a factual setting. The point here is that Professor Mishkin's conclusions are not convincingly supportable except upon an empirical foundation. Professor Mishkin is not directing himself toward a closely reasoned conceptual theory about the basis of a constitutional (or other) doctrine where the process of argumentation is of prime importance. Nor is he attempting to give an historical explanation of a phenomenon of the Court where citation to leading authorities is decisive. Rather, he is attempting to explain a public reaction to the existence and activity of an august governmental body and is drawing conclusions from an intuitive idea of how people regard the Court. In short, Professor Mishkin is asking the kinds of questions that he, by himself, cannot answer since he is directing his inquiry beyond reason and beyond history to contemporary fact. And without those facts there is little support for his opinion.[22]

We certainly do not mean to suggest that Professor Mishkin's analysis is not a useful discussion containing valuable insights. However, given the dearth of empirical inquiry, the difficulty is

---

[20] See Frankfurter, *A Note on Advisory Opinions*, 37 HARV. L. REV. 1002 (1924).

[21] See, *e.g.*, Johnson v. New Jersey, 384 U.S. 719 (1966); Miranda v. Arizona, 384 U.S. 436 (1966). Insofar as Linkletter v. Walker, 381 U.S. 618 (1965), and Tehan v. United States, 382 U.S. 406 (1966), purport to settle a *general*, as distinguished from a *particular*, rule, they too may be considered as a form of advisory opinion. In other words, they determined the fate of all those caught by the prospective overruling determination without the benefit of a specific ruling on the merits of each individual case.

[22] The fallacy involved has been referred to as the "intuitionist fallacy." Professor Mishkin is asking us to accept his position without offering empirical data to back up his conclusions. If we suppose that someone else comes along and asks us to believe the contrary, also without data, we may believe either one since there is no criteria for proper choice. This puts one in the same situation as the fabled donkey who, in trying to choose which of two piles of hay to eat where both piles were the same distance away, died on the spot before he could make up his mind which one to choose.

an inability to speak with any authority about matters resting solely upon facts that are not presently in evidence. This is only a small part of the larger problem of ascertaining the role of the Supreme Court in the American polity.

In an attempt to discover what some students of the Court *believe* about the symbolic value of the declaratory theory of law, a questionnaire was sent to a selected group of people, including lawyers, political scientists, and a newspaperman. The questionnaire, which is reproduced in the appendix,[23] was drafted in somewhat imprecise terms, so as to cover greater ground without imposing upon the recipients' time. Approximately 150 letters were sent and replies were received from about one-third, some very brief (just a few words) and some quite long and extensive.[24] While no effort was made to question lay members of the public, there was an attempt to reach both the "activists" and the advocates of "self-restraint." Of some interest, perhaps, in this search for critical fact is that there were no replies from the most vociferous modern critics of the Court.

We are well aware of a great many difficulties in our survey. Perhaps the major defect is that it does not poll the layman but rather attempts to ascertain what members of the profession, and especially students of the Court, are thinking about the problems discussed by Professor Mishkin. There is a pressing need for empirical data reflecting the lay opinion on these matters[25] since the "hearsay" we have gleaned is far from sufficient to settle the matters in issue. The other major defect, if it can be called a defect, is the vague and ambiguous nature of the questions. Thus, the first question, which calls for an opinion as to *why* the judiciary is held in high esteem, assumes that the Court *is* widely respected and does not differentiate whether such regard is for the activities of the Court or for its general institutional setting. The second and third questions, which request opinions about the necessity or desirability of public ignorance of "legal realism," assume that a unified set of beliefs constitute

---

[23] See page 301 *infra.*

[24] A few of the more thoughtful and provocative of the replies are reproduced beginning at page 302 *infra.*

[25] Since the main text was written, we have become aware of some as yet unpublished studies which do attempt to assay lay opinion about the Supreme Court and its decision-making. Dolbeare, *The Public Views the Supreme Court,* in LAW AND POLITICS IN THE SUPREME COURT (Jacob ed. 1967); Dolbeare & Hammond, The Political Party Basis of Attitudes Toward the U.S. Supreme Court, 1966 (unpublished manuscript, The University of Wisconsin).

that philosophy; such a set of beliefs of course does not exist. But this ambiguity was intentional and has had the advantage of allowing more freedom in answering. The questions, sent to students of the Court, were not intended to "count noses" scientifically on basic propositions but rather to serve as a vehicle for the expression of thoughts on the topics mentioned in the questions.

The results of the survey, admittedly sparse and by no means unanimous,[26] seem to indicate that experts hold the following *beliefs* about the Supreme Court and the symbolic value of the declaratory theory: (1) the American people generally have little or no knowledge about how the Court operates; (2) they probably do not care and would not take the trouble to find out; and (3) they are probably more interested in *what* the Court has done in a substantive sense, rather than how it accomplishes the result. No one, it is important to note, knew of any studies which had developed empirical evidence on these matters.

A First Hypothesis

From the survey, the following tentative hypothesis has been formulated: *The prestige of the Supreme Court has little or nothing to do with its symbolic role as such—court qua court, nine wise men, cult of the robe, et cetera—but rather with what it does.* Stated another way, it is hypothesized that the American people accord a high respect to the Supreme Court when there is basic agreement with the results the Court reaches in its decisions. From this hypothesis it follows that since prestige is important only insofar as it contributes to its power, the Supreme Court's power depends upon *what* it does and not *how* its decisions are made.

Even among those who make a practice of studying and following the course of Court decisions, in other words, there seems to be considerable agreement that what in recent years has been termed "principled decision-making"[27] is of importance only to the cognoscenti—and, of them, only to a relatively small percentage. The

---

[26] No attempt has been made to collate the results of the survey in neat tables. What is suggested in this paper gives the tenor of the bulk of the answers. Some dissents were received. See Appendix, page 302 *infra*.

[27] By and large this group is made up of votaries in the cult of Justice Frankfurter. What they have failed to see will be developed more fully in Part Two, namely, that the Supreme Court as they envisage it never existed and also that they are calling for a return to mechanical jurisprudence, however sophisticated its current version may be.

handful who seek an *elegantia juris*—those who demand the aesthetic satisfaction of closely reasoned, appropriately documented opinions written in immortal prose and ideal fashion—do not seem to represent anyone other than themselves. They do not speak for those lawyers and persons who must predict what the Court will do and rely on what it has done, because predictability is a function of change and of understanding and not aesthetic symmetry. Predictability does not depend upon the perfectly symmetrical legal system which progresses by deduction but rather upon the ability to read correctly the temper of the age and to calculate the logarithm between legal doctrine and social change. In final analysis, those who seek symmetry alone are asking for the impossible. They mistake the nature of adjudication, historical and contemporaneous, and fail to accord necessary emphasis to the fact that the Court in its constitutional adjudications is as much—or more—a political organ than a legal body. In short, there is a consistent failure to note that judicial decisions in constitutional cases *should* be evaluated more by whether they meet standards of sociological arbitrariness than by their logical consistency.[28] This is not to say, of course, that one should applaud sloppily written opinions but merely to point out that, as the Court itself said in connection with public utility rate-making, "it is the result reached not the method employed which is controlling . . . ."[29] Furthermore, throughout American history the Justices themselves apparently have been more interested in results than in methodology. One need only compare the reasoning used by Chief Justice Marshall in different opinions to find evidence for that proposition; brief reference to *Marbury's Case*[30] and *McCulloch's Case*[31] will quickly reveal how he changed his method to suit the problem. At no time in American constitutional history can it be said that the demand for "principled decision-making" has been fulfilled. This should not be taken to mean that such an ideal should not be striven for, but simply that here, as otherwise, a man's reach inevitably exceeds his grasp. Perhaps it would be better to take as the ideal something within the capacities of the human mind and something which is more in

---

[28] See Miller, *Mulkey v. Reitman: A Brave But Futile Gesture?*, 14 U.C.L.A.L. Rev. 51 (1966).

[29] Federal Power Comm'n v. Hope Natural Gas Co., 320 U.S. 591, 602 (1944) (opinion of the Court by Douglas, J.).

[30] Marbury v. Madison, 5 U.S. (1 Cranch) 137 (1803).

[31] McCulloch v. Maryland, 17 U.S. (4 Wheat.) 316 (1819).

accord with what people apparently want from courts. Furthermore, this does not mean that judges are free to rule according to their personal whims; they are bound by the institutional setting of the Court, part of which is adherence to the received norms from the past. However, those pre-existing norms cannot be said to be *specifically* controlling, for constitutional rules and principles run in pairs of opposites. A ruling on the merits may be said to synthesize *creatively* the choice made from those opposites.

A Second Hypothesis

If one assumes the validity of the first tentative hypothesis, then a second may be suggested: *The Supreme Court has power to the extent that it articulates deep-set valeus (preferences) of the American people.* Obviously, this is closely allied to the first, for if the prestige (or power) of the Court is more dependent upon what is decided than how the Justices reason, then it ineluctably follows that power varies with the result reached. In other words, decisions on different issues have a differing impact upon the manner in which people order their affairs. It is one thing to say that the Court has an impact upon the litigants before it; usually (although not necessarily always)[32] it doubtless does have. The Danny Escobedos, Dollree Mapps, Clarence Gideons, and many other individuals, are eloquent testimony to that. But it is quite another thing to say, as is sometimes done, that "the law of the land" thus enunciated is followed generally. The decision of the Court, in *most* cases, can affect only the parties before it. Whether others read and heed it is another matter.

At the outset, it may be said with confidence that very little is in fact known about the actual societal impact of judicial decisions, or, put another way, about the causal connection between social change and judicial action.[33] There has been much loose talk about such a connection, but the studies are well-nigh non-existent, save for the church-state relationship problem where some political scientists have made studies.[34] Much has been made about the allegedly

---

[32] See Note, 67 HARV. L. REV. 1251 (1954); Note, 56 YALE L.J. 574 (1947).

[33] See Miller, *On the Need for "Impact Analysis" of Supreme Court Decisions,* 53 GEO. L.J. 365 (1965).

[34] *E.g.,* Beaney & Beiser, *Prayer and Politics: The Impact of Engel and Schempp on the Political Process,* 13 J. Pub. L. 475 (1964).

key role the Supreme Court has played in American history; and as recently as the 1930s "government by judiciary" could seriously be suggested.[35]   Would the nation be different today had *Marbury*[36] and *McCulloch*,[37] *Gibbons*[38] and *Cooley*,[39] *Missouri v. Holland*[40] and *Nebbia v. New York*,[41] *Jones & Laughlin*[42] and *Steward Machine*,[43] *Darby*[44] and *Wickard*,[45] *Shelley*[46] and *Brown*,[47] *Baker*[48] and *Reynolds*,[49] been decided differently—or had not been decided by the Supreme Court at all?   Suppose the social problems inherent in those judicial decisions had been decided politically, as they would have in other democratic nations, would the net result be fundamentally different?

In many respects the question is idle and impossible to answer. The Court did exist and did make decisions; the nation has changed from situation *A* in 1787 to situation *B* in 1967.   However, it seems clear that historians simply cannot supply an answer to such a question.   In another sense, it of course is commonly assumed that the fact of the Court's acting as ultimate constitutional interpreter *has* made a difference.   John R. Commons could call it "the first authoritative faculty of political economy in the world's history."[50] Boudin and others maintained that this made ours a "government by judiciary"; a president of the American Bar Association asserted as recently as 1962 that fundamental changes are being wrought in the fabric of government by the Court,[51] a view echoed by Justice John M. Harlan.[52]   Many others, in and out of the law, have made similar pronouncements.   Even the cool-minded Holmes, who saw

---

[35] BOUDIN, GOVERNMENT BY JUDICIARY (1932).
[36] Marbury v. Madison, 5 U.S. (1 Cranch) 137 (1803).
[37] McCulloch v. Maryland, 17 U.S. (4 Wheat.) 316 (1819).
[38] Gibbons v. Ogden, 22 U.S. (9 Wheat.) 1 (1824).
[39] Cooley v. Board of Wardens of Philadelphia, 53 U.S. (12 How.) 299 (1851).
[40] 252 U.S. 416 (1920).
[41] 291 U.S. 502 (1934).
[42] NLRB v. Jones & Laughlin Steel Corp., 301 U.S. 1 (1937).
[43] Steward Mach. Co. v. Davis, 301 U.S. 548 (1937).
[44] United States v. Darby, 312 U.S. 100 (1941).
[45] Wickard v. Filburn, 317 U.S. 111 (1942).
[46] Shelley v. Kraemer, 334 U.S. 1 (1948).
[47] Brown v. Board of Educ., 349 U.S. 294 (1955).
[48] Baker v. Carr, 369 U.S. 186 (1962).
[49] Reynolds v. Sims, 377 U.S. 533 (1964).
[50] COMMONS, LEGAL FOUNDATIONS OF CAPITALISM 7 (1924).
[51] See Satterfield, *President's Page*, 48 A.B.A.J. 595 (1962).
[52] See Reynolds v. Sims, 377 U.S. 533, 624 (1964) (Harlan, J., dissenting). See also Norman v. Baltimore & O.R.R., 294 U.S. 240, 381 (1934) (McReynolds, J., dissenting).

things whole and who was not likely to be deluded by images of judicial grandeur, could say that the Court has made a great difference in the nature of federalism—even though he asserted that little difference would result if the Court lost its power to declare acts of Congress and the Executive unconstitutional.

Against that array of talent, one would be temerarious indeed to suggest a contrary view. The essential question involves the relationship between legal and social change; here the most that can be said is that we simply do not know the impact the Supreme Court has had on the structure and nature of American society. No empirical data exists to show a causal connection. What is available are the ipse dixits of a number of observers. The Court, accordingly, *may* have made a difference, but no one can tell precisely what that difference is. It will not do, in other words, to make grand pronouncements like Professor Felix Frankfurter, who said in 1938:

> We speak of the Court as though it were an abstraction. To be sure the Court is an institution, but individuals, with all their diversities of endowment, experience, and outlook, determine its actions. The history of the Supreme Court is not the history of an abstraction, but the analysis of individuals acting as a Court who make decisions and lay down doctrines, and of other individuals, their successors, who refine, modify, and sometimes even overrule the decisions of their predecessors, reinterpreting and transmuting their doctrines. In law also men make a difference. It would deny all meaning to history to believe that the course of events would have been the same if Thomas Jefferson had had the naming of Spencer Roane to the place to which John Adams called John Marshall, or if Roscoe Conkling rather than Morrison R. Waite had headed the Court before which came the Granger legislation. The evolution of finance capital in the United States, and therefore of American history after the Reconstruction period, would hardly have been the same if the views of men like Mr. Justice Miller and Mr. Justice Harlan had dominated the decisions of the Court from the Civil War to Theodore Roosevelt's administration. There is no inevitability in history except as men make it.[53]

The difficulty with this statement is at least two-fold: first, it reveals a philosophy of history which itself is in dispute.[54] Men make a

---

[53] FRANKFURTER, LAW AND POLITICS 62 (1939).
[54] See FRANK, FATE AND FREEDOM (1945).

difference, says Professor Frankfurter, but how does he know?[55] Here, again, is another example of the intuitionist fallacy: Why, one is forced to ask, is there any solid basis for believing that "men make a difference?"

Whatever conclusion one draws on the "inevitability in history . . . as men make it," historical interpretation, it seems clear, is bound up with value judgments: "the search for causalities in history is impossible without reference to values [for] . . . behind the search for causalities there always lies, directly or indirectly, the search for values."[56]   Furthermore, when we view the past and attempt to achieve an understanding of it, it can only be through the eyes of the present.   The historian is unavoidably a product of the age in which he lives and is bound to it by the conditions of human existence. Even the words he uses—words like democracy or capitalism or property—have present-day connotations from which he cannot divorce them.   Finally, causation itself as a legal concept is complex and difficult.   Whether it is in the context of the present inquiry of the relationship between judicial decision and social change or in such matters as establishing tort liability, legal causation is far different from causation in the laboratory, where within rigidly limited circumstances a natural scientist can "cause" certain results through the operation of known, invariable "natural" laws.

However, adapting the scientific method to the problem of causality in human affairs in order to support assertions is a most difficult task, perhaps ultimately impossible.   "The craving for an interpretation of history is so deep-rooted that, unless we have a constructive outlook over the past, we are drawn either to mysticism or to cynicism."[57]   In present context, the Frankfurter position tends toward mysticism; to be able to avoid cynicism, it seems to be necessary to have available, at the very least, deep and continuing studies into the manner in which the American people "obey" Supreme Court edicts.   Without such studies, one can give meaning to history if he so chooses, but what he is stating will tend to be merely a re-

---

[55] "How can one discover in history a coherent sequence of cause and effect, how can we find any meaning in history, when our sequence is liable to be broken or deflected at any moment by some other, and from our point of view irrelevant, sequence?" CARR, WHAT IS HISTORY? 130 (1962).

[56] Quoted in *id.* at 141. See Miller & Howell, *The Myth of Neutrality in Constitutional Adjudication,* 27 U. CHI. L. REV. 661 (1960).

[57] Quoted in CARR, *op. cit. supra* note 55, at 144.

flection of his personal valuations.   One sees meaning—or historical causation—where one wants to see it.

But we should not be optimistic that such studies will be made. Legal scholars, whether lawyers or political scientists or others who have singled out the Supreme Court for scrutiny, have been anything but quick to produce the necessary data.   One searches the literature in vain for anything more than sporadic forays into the uncharted sea of "impact analysis."[58]   In the main, such studies have been in the area of the influence Court decisions have had on the church-state relationship.   Although these, too, are far from definitive, one may conclude from them that the Court's pronouncements have had at best a highly discontinuous impact; in some areas, they have been obeyed, in others, ignored.   When one adds to this the concomitant fact that, at the very time that the Supreme Court was uttering the decisions about walls high and impregnable between church and state, the federal government was entering into systematic subsidization of church-related (as well as other) schools, one wonders just what the Supreme Court's power is.[59]   It seems small indeed.

On the other hand, how does one explain the well-nigh unanimous acceptance of *Baker v. Carr*[60] and its progeny?   There can be no question here that the Court has wrought significant changes in the composition of state legislatures and the House of Representatives.   However, when one compares the public reaction to that series of cases with that which followed *Brown v. Board of Education*,[61]

---

[58] See Miller, *On the Need for "Impact Analysis" of Supreme Court Decisions,* 53 GEO. L.J. 365 (1965).   Professor Walter Murphy has stated flatly: "No serious student of public law has ever doubted the immense power of the Justices . . . ."   Murphy, *Deeds Under a Doctrine: Civil Liberties in the 1963 Term,* 59 AM. POL. SCI. REV. 64, 75 (1965).   We doubt the validity of Murphy's statement insofar as the power of the Court is concerned; at best, we simply *do not know* just what the power of the Justices is, has been, or will be.   Perhaps, as Whitehead once said, "the doctrines which best repay critical examination are those which for the longest period have remained unquestioned."   WHITEHEAD, ADVENTURES OF IDEAS 228 (1933).   Judicial power is one of those doctrines.   For further discussion, *compare* Dahl, *Decision-Making in a Democracy: The Supreme Court as National Policy-Maker,* 6 J. PUB. L. 279 (1957), *with* Levy, *Judicial Review, History and Democracy: An Introduction,* in JUDICIAL REVIEW AND THE SUPREME COURT 1 (Levy ed. 1967).   See also COMMAGER, MAJORITY RULE AND MINORITY RIGHTS (1943).

[59] See S. 2097, 89th Cong., 2d Sess. (1966), introduced by Senator Sam Ervin of North Carolina, which would seek to require the Supreme Court to decide the validity of disbursements to church-related schools.   See *Hearings Before the Subcommittee on Constitutional Rights of the Senate Judiciary Committee,* 89th Cong., 2d Sess., pts. 1-2 (1966).

[60] 369 U.S. 186 (1962).

[61] 349 U.S. 294 (1954).

he is forced to the conclusion that the pattern of adherence to judicial prescription is uneven. Even on reapportionment, moreover, we do not know with any certainty just what the *ultimate* impact will be, for there have been few if any studies made to determine whether different legislative decisions will result after reapportionment, as compared with the different identity of the legislators.[62]

Whether one can explain the discontinuous reception given Supreme Court decisions is the question. Can it be on any other basis than that decisions are "obeyed" when they are in consonance with the deep-felt preferences of the people? No other equally tenable suggestion seems available. Historically speaking, furthermore, it is difficult, perhaps impossible, over the nearly two centuries of Supreme Court history to find *one* instance where the Court has been able to do more than postpone what a determined people or legislative majorities wanted. It may well be that at times the Court helped the people to know what they wanted—by articulating the "national conscience"[63]—and thus had influence.[64] But this is a far cry from saying that it *caused* constitutional or social change. The second tentative hypothesis, accordingly, appears to have validity.

A Third Hypothesis

Our third hypothesis complements the first two: *The Supreme Court has power to the extent to which the avowedly political branches of government—Congress, the President, the state governments—affirmatively respond to the norm announced by the Court.*

[62] One might hypothesize that legislative decisions, whether on the state or national level, are the resultant of a parallelogram of conflicting *group* forces and that, accordingly, a rural-urban dichotomy would be far too simplistic if it were taken to mean that because legislatures are now made up of more representatives from urban areas the ultimate decisions will be different than they would have been if rural America had retained control. See McCONNELL, PRIVATE POWER AND AMERICAN DEMOCRACY 91-118 (1966); TRUMAN, THE GOVERNMENTAL PROCESS 213-391 (1951); ZIEGLER, INTEREST GROUPS IN AMERICAN SOCIETY (1964).

[63] We make no statements regarding the manner in which the Justices do or should ascertain the "national conscience."

[64] Speaking very broadly, one may discern three functions of the Supreme Court: (1) validating constitutional change and thereby updating the Constitution, see Miller, *Notes on the Concept of the "Living" Constitution*, 31 GEO. WASH. L. REV. 881 (1963); (2) interpreting statutes, particularly in socio-economic areas, see Miller, *Constitutional Revolution Consolidated: The Rise of the Positive State*, 35 GEO. WASH. L. REV. 172 (1966); (3) norm-setting or acting as the national conscience, see Cox, *Foreword, Constitutional Adjudication and the Promotion of Human Rights*, 80 HARV. L. REV. 91 (1966); Miller, *An Affirmative Thrust to Due Process of Law?*, 30 GEO. WASH. L. REV. 399 (1962).

Defiance of a judicial edict is far from unknown; but even more familiar is indifference to what a court has said. The judicial command runs to the parties only and binds only them; anyone not before the bar of the court can with impunity ignore the decision and await the application of the principle or rule there enunciated to him in a proper case. This is the nub of the problem: a Supreme Court decision in a constitutional matter states the *law of the case* and not the law of the land, as is often asserted. Judges are inherently limited by their inability to articulate *general* norms. Their creativity is not only confined "from molar to molecular motion"; in final analysis it can affect only the particular interests of the litigants then before it—unless and until others, without direct command and without possibility of sanction, are willing to abide by it. And this observation is valid even though it may be clearly predictable that the Court and lower courts will decide the same way in a similar future case. Legislative commands, on the other hand, are *general*; they affect all in similar circumstances.

The difference, while technical, is important: one does not violate the rule in, say *Brown v. Board of Education,* unless and until someone within the jurisdiction in question brings an action with similar facts; but one does violate Title VI, say, of the Civil Rights Act of 1964 by not adhering to the legislative and administrative commands. The law enunciated by the Supreme Court in *Brown,* was the "law of the land" only because one could, by following the prediction theory of law, forecast the same result should other cases be brought. Not so, however, with the general congressional norms, even though subsequent determinations have to be made that violations *in fact* occurred. There has been much loose talk in recent years about a Court decision stating the "law of the land," but the talk is just 'that —loose. No matter how much one approves certain results, the commands of the judiciary are aimed only at those before the court except, of course, in the case of a class action (or in the Supreme Court's supervisory power over lower federal courts).[65] This is un-

---

[65] On class actions, see Note, 71 HARV. L. REV. 874, 928-43 (1958). See newly amended FED. R. CIV. P. 23 and Notes of the Advisory Committee thereon. As will be developed in Part Two, the function of the litigant in constitutional litigation is solely that of getting the case to the Court. Once that is performed, he largely becomes irrelevant, even though the decision will affect him directly. The pronouncement of the Court, furthermore, is limited to the litigants; and that is true even though the Court, as Mr. Justice Harlan has said, chooses its cases "in the interests of the law,

fortunate for those who applaud the recent activism of the Supreme Court, but true it is, nonetheless. On the other hand, it is in accord with the wishes of those who advocate a quietistic role for the Court.[66]

A Supreme Court pronouncement in a constitutional case in effect delegates authority to others—legislatures, executives, administrators, and judges in lower courts (federal and state)—to carry out the terms of the edict in other situations. Other than judges in lower federal courts, whether they do so is required neither by the Constitution nor the Court decision; nor is it a requirement of statutes, discretion in the delegate being the rule.[67] It depends, ultimately, upon the willingness of those who occupy positions in the political branches of government to recognize the Court decision and to follow it up with official action.[68] Whether they do so seems to be a resultant of

---

its appropriate exposition and enforcement, not in the mere interest of the litigants." Harlan, *Manning the Dikes*, 13 RECORD OF N.Y.C.B.A. 541, 551 (1958).

On the supervisory power over the federal courts, *compare* Cheff v. Schnackenberg, 384 U.S. 373 (1966), *with* Green v. United States, 356 U.S. 165 (1958). In this area, the Court's "legislative power" is at its peak.

[66] Compare BICKEL, THE LEAST DANGEROUS BRANCH; THE SUPREME COURT AT THE BAR OF POLITICS (1962).

Of course, a decision can have an immediate wide influence, as witness the aftermath of *Baker v. Carr*. And a cumulative effect may be seen in a series of decisions, as in racial segregation, which in total impact tends toward a general norm. Furthermore, the Court in such cases as Miranda v. Arizona, 384 U.S. 436 (1966), has announced detailed guidelines in certain aspects of criminal law administration, a decision which is at once a form of "advisory opinion" and an apparent attempt to legislate "a detailed set of operational procedures." See Schwartz, *Retroactivity, Reliability, and Due Process: A Reply to Professor Mishkin*, 33 U. CHI. L. REV. 719, 758 (1966). The ultimate impact of *Miranda* and its companion, Johnson v. New Jersey, 384 U.S. 719 (1966), is yet to be determined.

[67] For an assertion that ours is emphatically "a government of men, not of laws," see HORSKY, THE WASHINGTON LAWYER 68 (1952). In other words, there is a large element of discretion within the public administration. See 1 DAVIS, ADMINISTRATIVE LAW TREATISE § 4.16 (1958, Supp. 1965). And what is true of the public administration is a fortiori valid for the legislatures.

An instructive insight into the power of the Court, particularly as it relates to the public administration and to lower federal courts, may be found in a case decided after the text was written, Cascade Natural Gas Corp. v. El Paso Natural Gas Co., 87 Sup. Ct. 932 (1967). In that decision, the Court, after finding that the Antitrust Division of the Department of Justice had "knuckled under" to one of the litigants, went to the extraordinary length of ordering the removal of the federal district judge from further participation in the case.

[68] Whether official action is forthcoming would seem in turn to depend, at least in part, upon the extent to which interest groups within American society can bring influence to bear upon the political processes. See authorities cited in note 61 *supra*. Other factors may, of course, bear upon what is done politically following a Supreme Court decision; we make no attempt to indicate here what they may be, but merely

political factors, rather than legal commands: the difference between President Jackson's (perhaps apocryphal) sneer at Chief Justice Marshall's decision and President Eisenhower's use of armed forces in Little Rock in 1957 reveals the uncertainties of the process. Here, as elsewhere, Bishop Hoadly's dictum is apposite: he who has the power to interpret the law is more truly the lawmaker than he who originally states the norm.

The racial segregation situation again provides illustration. Despite such decisions as *Cooper v. Aaron*[69] and *Bailey v. Patterson*,[70] cases in which the Court tried to establish a general norm, segregation, *de facto* or *de jure*, is still a "litigable issue." The tribulations experienced in the administration of Title VI of the Civil Rights Act of 1964 are ample evidence of that. In the field of administrative law, other evidence exists. For example, several years after the *Phillips* decision of the Court in 1954, the Federal Power Commission had still not adhered to it.[71] For that matter, it is by no means clear that the President, as a constitutional matter, must follow congressional commands, as the history of presidential impounding of appropriated funds indicates.[72] Furthermore, the commands issued by the Court are not necessarily "followed" by lower courts, as Professor Walter F. Murphy has shown,[73] and as the following episode evidences:

Walton Hamilton tells the story of the effectiveness of Tumey v. Ohio, 273 U.S. 510 . . . . When he was caught in some "speed trap" in Pennsylvania and taken before a justice of the peace, he asked the J.P. how much of the fine the J.P. got. When the reply "five dollars" was forthcoming, Mr. Hamilton mentioned that this was

point out that political recognition of judicial decisions is not automatic, an obvious fact of which little is known.

[69] 358 U.S. 1 (1958).

[70] 369 U.S. 31 (1962). In the *Bailey* case, the Court expressly stated: "We have settled beyond question that no state may require racial segregation of interstate or intrastate transportation facilities.. . . . The question is no longer open; it is foreclosed as a litigable issue." *Id.* at 33.

[71] Phillips Petroleum Co. v. Wisconsin, 347 U.S. 672 (1954), referred to by James M. Landis in *Hearings of the Subcommittee on Administrative Practice and Procedure of the Senate Committee on the Judiciary*, 86th Cong., 2d Sess. 316 (1960).

[72] See Miller, *Presidential Power to Impound Appropriated Funds: An Exercise in Constitutional Decision-Making*, 43 N.C.L. REV. 502 (1965). The congressional remedy in such instances seems solely that of impeachment. See also Berger, *Executive Privilege v. Congressional Inquiry*, 12 U.C.L.A.L. REV. 1043, 1111-17 (1965).

[73] Murphy, *Lower Court Checks on Supreme Court Power*, 53 AM. POL. SCI. REV. 1017 (1959).

unconstitutional. "Who said that?" he was asked. Upon learning that it was the United States Supreme Court, the J.P. shrugged and said, "Oh well, I didn't think it was any Pennsylvania court."[74]

Anyone who has been caught in a speed trap in Georgia in recent years knows that this is not an isolated incident. As Professor George Braden phrased the matter, "We do not know how effective a Supreme Court decision is, or in what manner its effect is transmitted."[75] Those who, in the American framework of government, must or should listen to the commands of the Court, may choose to follow them or not depending upon whether it is politically or philosophically palatable to do so. Certainly little or nothing is known about the manner in which *official* behavior follows judicial edict[76]—and official behavior is what is important, for it is still by and large true that the Constitution runs against governments only. The behavioral patterns of persons, both natural and artificial, are little concerned with judicial norms—excluding, of course, the litigant (s) before the Court in a specific case.[77]

The requirement for an affirmative response to a Supreme Court decision prompts the further question: To what extent, if at all, is there is a constitutional *duty* on the part of government (or its officials) to take action? Some recent decisions of the United States Supreme Court and of the California Supreme Court suggest that a concept of constitutional duty may be in process of "becoming." Even though the notion is as yet inchoate, it is nevertheless possible to read such decisions as *Burton v. Wilmington Parking Authority*,[78] *United States v. Guest*,[79] *Katzenbach v. Morgan*,[80] *Evans v. Newton*,[81] *Griffin v. School Board*,[82] and *Mulkey v. Reitman*[83] as at least imply-

---

[74] Braden, *Legal Research: A Variation on an Old Lament*, 5 J. LEGAL ED. 39, 41 n.1 (1952).

[75] *Ibid.*

[76] Such ignorance prevails even in the area of administrative law. See Miller, Book Review (of JAFFE, JUDICIAL CONTROL OF ADMINISTRATIVE ACTION), 34 GEO. WASH. L. REV. 970 (1966).

[77] For example, a survey in 1964 found that most school districts in Kentucky had not adhered to the Court's prayer decisions. See N.Y. Times, Aug. 30, 1964, § 1, p. 70, col. 5.

[78] 365 U.S. 715 (1961).

[79] 383 U.S. 745 (1966).

[80] 384 U.S. 641 (1966).

[81] 382 U.S. 296 (1966).

[82] 377 U.S. 218 (1964).

[83] 50 Cal. 2d 881, 413 P.2d 825 (1966). See Cox, *supra* note 64; Miller, *An Affirmative Thrust to Due Process of Law?*, 30 GEO. WASH. L. REV. 399 (1962).

ing that, if at any time a state could prevent racial discrimination, its failure to do so is state action. That proposition, stated in more positive terms, means that the fourteenth amendment imposes a duty upon states to take action to prevent racial discrimination. Under the principle of *Bolling v. Sharpe*,[84] a like duty would then be imposed in areas of racial discrimination upon the federal government. In other words, the Constitution not only carries negative prohibitions; freedom is as much positive as negative.[85]

In recent decades it has become clear beyond peradventure that a massive realignment of function has been taking place within each of the three branches of government set up by the Constitution. The most basic alteration, perhaps, is the rise of the "administrative state"—the Positive State—headed by a presidency ever growing in power. Accomplished through the medium of delegations from Congress, the public administration now does and increasingly will represent the real power center of government. A consequence has been a diminution in relative power of Congress[86] and also a lessening in the power of the United States Supreme Court, particularly over economic policy questions. The principal implications of the new alignment of function and power will be more fully discussed in Part Two; suffice it now to say that it has become apparent in the new adjustment of roles that the three branches must of necessity cooperate more than compete: "Government in the Positive State means that the separation of powers, which historically has helped to protect liberty through the inevitable frictions brought about by the 'checks and balances,' cannot be permitted to stymie the reasonable realization of the aims of the people of that State."[87] The suggestion here is that a concept of constitutional duty on the part of government, and thus of governmental officials, is now being created as a serendipitous by-product of some of the recent decisions of the

---

[84] 347 U.S. 497 (1954).

[85] "For an individual to have freedom *to* participate and to attain the goals imbedded in the concept of human dignity, it is necessary that he have freedom *from* both the arbitrary exercise of power and the inadequate social conditions which make it improbable that he can achieve that plane. The social basis of liberty, in the sense that affirmative duties are imposed on the State, has thus far received relatively little attention from constitutional scholars . . . ." Miller, *An Affirmative Thrust to Due Process of Law?*, 30 GEO. WASH. L. REV. 399, 425 (1962). (Emphasis in original.)

[86] See the several essays collected in THE CONGRESS AND AMERICA'S FUTURE (Truman ed. 1965).

[87] Miller, *An Affirmative Thrust to Due Process of Law?*, 30 GEO. WASH. L. REV. 399, 427 (1962).

United States Supreme Court and other courts. In the language of the Declaration of Delhi, made in 1959 by the International Congress of Jurists:

> The International Congress of Jurists . . .
>
> . . . .
>
> Recognizes that the Rule of Law is a dynamic concept for the expansion and fulfillment of which jurists are primarily responsible and which should be employed not only to safeguard and advance the civil and political rights of the individual in a free society, but also to establish social, economic, educational and cultural conditions under which his legitimate aspirations and dignity may be realized. . . .[88]

However, it is one thing to say that an abstract official duty to take action may exist, but quite another to determine who may be able to enforce it. In some few cases a proper plaintiff has been located and permitted to bring—and to win—actions designed to enforce such a duty. The prime example, perhaps, is the *Prince Edward County* case,[89] although surely *Baker v. Carr*[90] and its progeny would also indicate that the problem is not an insuperable one (assuming, of course, that one agrees that *Baker* is *in its effects* the enunciation of a duty to reapportion). However the inchoate notion of constitutional duty is resolved, the inability of the Supreme Court to do much more than issue grand pronouncements and then hope for acquiescence places a great responsibility upon the officials of the avowedly political organs of government, both federal and state. The Court articulates the ideals of the American democracy, but those ideals can become hollow if not followed by affirmative response by the other governmental officials. Whether they are does not depend upon judicial adherence to the declaratory theory, or even in making reasoned, principled decisions.[91] It would seem, thus, that the third tentative hypothesis advanced has considerable validity.

---

[88] INTERNATIONAL CONGRESS OF JURISTS, THE RULE OF LAW IN A FREE SOCIETY 3 (1960). See Thorson, *A New Concept of the Rule of Law*, 38 CAN. B. REV. 239 (1960). For a discussion of the affirmative obligations of government, see Ackley, *Foreword: The Employment Act After Twenty Years: The Legal Basis for Managing the Economy*, 35 GEO. WASH. L. REV. 170 (1966).

[89] 377 U.S. 218 (1964). See United States v. Jefferson County Bd. of Educ., Civil No. 23345, 5th Cir., Mar. 29, 1967 (affirmative duty of states to effect school integration).

[90] 369 U.S 186 (1962).

[91] *But see* EDELMAN, THE SYMBOLIC USES OF POLITICS 32, 108 (1964).

In Summation

We have suggested three hypotheses concerning the power of the United States Supreme Court. Each would require much study and empirical data to be validated. Even so, each seems to be tenable as a working hypothesis. And each offers a way of more significant thinking about the Court than the intuitive propositions usually advanced, propositions which are largely based upon nothing more than reading of Supreme Court opinions. What conclusions, if any, may be drawn from such an analysis?

That question will be developed in Part Two. At present, we summarize some of the implications of the foregoing investigation. The first is to suggest one painfully obvious inference: Using the texts of judicial opinions as the sole source of data concerning the Court, its operation, and its power, simply will not suffice to provide the minimal informational needs upon which to base conclusions. Although, as Professor Ernest J. Brown said in the course of discussing a Supreme Court opinion, we "cannot explore the minds of Justices, and what they do not put on paper we do not know,"[92] what they do put on paper in their published opinions is not enough to answer the critical questions. All that such verbiage does is to permit the scholarly disputation with which we are all familiar but which does not lend true understanding or clarity to the judicial process. "The fact is," in the words of Felix Frankfurter, "that pitifully little of significance has been contributed by judges regarding the nature of their endeavor . . . ."[93]

It follows that legal training alone is of little help, for most of it is still concerned with analysis of appellate court opinions; as for constitutional law, analysis of Supreme Court opinions is almost the entire scrutiny. Those opinions being at best poor vehicles, data must perforce be produced from outside of the traditional confines of the legal profession. One should not be sanguine on that score, for little of significance has thus far been produced.[94] Some intel-

---

[92] Brown, *Quis Custodiet Ipsos Custodes?—The School-Prayer Cases*, 1963 SUP. CT. REV. 1, 32.

[93] FRANKFURTER, OF LAW AND MEN 32 (1956). He went on to say: " and, I might add, that which is written by those who are not judges is too often a confident caricature rather than a seer's version of the judicial process of the Supreme Court." *Ibid.*

[94] Little has been added to our knowledge of the nature of the judicial process since Holmes published THE COMMON LAW in 1881 or Cardozo his THE NATURE OF THE JUDICIAL PROCESS in 1921.

lectual stirrings, however, are visible and should eventually add to
our knowledge about the high tribunal.[95]   Questions such as the
following must be asked and answered:

> Much of the commentary about the Supreme Court . . . does not
> pose the proper questions. Few, perhaps none, of those who par-
> ticipate in today's debate about the Court reach the tough prob-
> lems. . . . The time has come [to make] . . . concerted effort to
> analyze the Court as dispassionately as possible. Such questions
> as the following [are] . . . in need of development: (1) the data
> relevant to the decisional process; (2) impact analysis of Court
> decisions; what difference does a decision make in the practices of
> the American people? (3) what are the factors which have in-
> fluenced the Court? (4) what are the preferred means of getting
> information to the Court? (5) are there aids that could be estab-
> lished through which the Court could receive assistance in making
> decisions? (6) what are the "social realities" which the Court
> should consider? (7) what are the goals which the Court does, and
> should, seek? (8) what is the relationship—and what should it be—
> of the Court to other units of government? (9) what insights can
> students of the sociology of knowledge and of human cognition
> bring to an understanding of the thought processes of the Justices?
> and (10) what are the criteria (principles) which should operate
> as standards of judgment by the Justices (and of evaluation of
> the Court's work by commentators)?[96]

Of course, some of the commentary about the Court has dealt at least
in part with certain of these questions. For the most part, however,
they remain unanswered. As a result, our knowledge about law and
legal institutions, including the Supreme Court, is roughly comparable to that in the natural sciences of 100 to 150 years ago, before
scientific knowledge was revolutionized by Darwin and Mendel, by
Planck and Einstein, and the others who precipitated the scientific
revolution. Law and lawyers are in a pre-Darwinian stage, perhaps
even in a pre-Newtonian and pre-Copernican stage.[97]   As yet, there
is not even an accepted taxonomy. While doctrinal analysis is

---

[95] Most of these studies tend to be by political scientists, rather than lawyers (practicing or academic). A study of the reasons for the paucity of instructive and illuminating studies of the judicial process, particularly by the legal profession, would
itself make a valuable contribution.

[96] Miller, Book Review (of BICKEL, THE LEAST DANGEROUS BRANCH), 9 HOWARD L.J.
188, 190 (1963).

[97] See Miller, *Public Law and the Obsolescence of the Lawyer*, — U. FLA. L. REV. —
(1967).

necessary and should be continued, it alone cannot give us an adequate understanding of the Court.[98]

A third point underscores what has been said previously: there is a need for hard factual data about the attitudes and preferences of the American people toward the Supreme Court. It will not do to make a priori pronouncements about the symbolic role of the High Bench unless and until we actually know that the American people give any thought to (1) the Court itself or (2) its methodology. On this, our knowledge is almost completely lacking.[99]

Implicit in the three hypotheses set forth above is the idea that the Court must innovate, that is, that it must routinely face the rigors of the "sovereign prerogative of choice" in making decisions. This, as Arnold Toynbee has recently stated, is the principal way in which human affairs, including law (although he did not mention law), are to be distinguished from scientific pursuits: "What element is it in human affairs that makes impossible . . . the exact mathematical prediction that is so brilliantly successful in our calculations about non-human nature? Evidently our unknown quality in the realm of human affairs is a human being's apparent power of making

---

[98] Perhaps some of the gaps in our knowledge *about* the law and the legal process, as compared with knowledge *of* rules and doctrines, may be traced to the failure of undergraduate colleges to include the requisite courses in their curricula. Jurisprudence in the sense of knowledge about how law operates in the social system should be part of the prescribed education of all undergraduates; no one can be said to have a liberal education without it. Compare Barkman, *Law-in-the-Liberal Arts: An Appraisal and A Proposal for Experimentation*, 19 J. LEGAL ED. 1 (1966).

[99] One study of courts in Wisconsin which is of relevance here concludes: "Public acquiescence to judicial actions in the realm of policy-making hardly seems to be a function of the 'priestly' image promulgated by Lerner and Frank; neither is it a function of the "Blackstonian" image proclaimed by Mishkin and Arnold. In the face of widespread disagreement with the substance of judicial innovations in public policy areas, public support seems a matter more of acquiescence or ignorance rather than positive endorsement, and of respect for the judiciary as one kind of government official rather than as a distinctive office embodying unique functions and status. Indeed, in our interviews judges were typically respected as dignified representatives of the people and the state, as men of distinguished achievement, rarely as aloof guardians of immutable, constitutional principles." Ladinsky & Silver, *Popular Democracy and Judicial Independence: Electorate and Elite Reactions to Two Wisconsin Supreme Court Elections*, 1967 WIS. L. REV. —.

This study, buttressed by a few others, of course actually "proves" little or nothing about the United States Supreme Court. What it does indicate, at least in part, is that untested assumptions and pronouncements about the Court will not suffice, insofar as they relate to the attitudes and preferences of the American people. Empirical information must first be obtained. This does not mean that the Court need change its methodology, but merely that commentary upon the Court should transcend the doctrinal exegeses now so prevalent. See Miller, *On the Need for "Impact Analysis" of Supreme Court Decisions*, 53 GEO. L.J. 365 (1965).

choices."[100]   And choices inevitably involve, insofar as law is concerned, something quite different from the declaratory theory of law. That theory is based upon the proposition that there is but one "true" principle or rule to be applied in a given factual situation. The entire history of the adversary system is impressive testimony to the contrary, at least with respect to appellate litigation (which, of course, is the great bulk of the Supreme Court's work). Put another way, the adversary system in appellate courts requires choices by judges, choices which inevitably mean that innovation must take place.[101]

Fifth, it is of vital importance in any analysis of the Supreme Court today that it be seen as a part of government quite different from that contemplated in 1787, a government which exists in a society wholly different from that of the late 18th century. The declaratory theory of law is a product of a pre-industrial age, of an agricultural, even feudal, society. The United States today, pre-eminent in wealth and power, straddles the continent and knows no earthly frontiers so far as public policy is concerned. This, then, means the proliferation and dominance of *public* law, rather than the private law of pre-Civil War times. In legal systems which are private-law oriented and which exist in an essentially static society, one can think of law in terms of a closed system of concepts. Not so, however, with a public-law dominated system, existing in an age of constant and even cataclysmic change: the requirement is to look upon law as "process"—for the ends to be achieved, for the goals to be sought. The industrial revolution, Herbert Rosinski has said, has transformed man's way of life "from an 'existence' into an unending 'process.' "[102] Public law is an unending process, an endless succession of partial solutions to public policy questions. The legal profession has not yet come to terms with the growth and domination of public law, but this must be done if ever an adequate theoretical formulation of law in the modern era is to be produced.[103]

Constitutional law, in the sixth place, is a flow of decisions—judicial, legislative, and executive—and also of certain habits and

---

[100] TOYNBEE, CHANGE AND HABIT 5 (1966).

[101] See Miller, On the Choice of Major Premises in Supreme Court Opinions, 14 J. PUB. L. 251 (1965).

[102] ROSINSKI, POWER AND HUMAN DESTINY 93 (1965).

[103] See generally Miller, Public Law and the Obsolescence of the Lawyer, — U. FLA. L. REV. — (1967).

patterns of behavior which can be given the label of custom. Open ended, it is always in a state of "becoming." The fiction of the declaratory theory clouds truth and does not enable the Court to receive the assistance that it needs if it is to continue to perform its high functions. Thurman Arnold to the contrary notwithstanding,[104] briefs cannot be written before the Court on any other theory than that the Justices have choices to make between competing rules or principles of equal persuasiveness (provided, of course, that the case is not a frivolous one). But whether the members of the Court will want to be open in decribing their decision-making is quite another matter; quite possibly, they will not privately face up to the discretion they have.[105] Some judges may wish to proceed "by denying change"[106]—the time-honored way of common-law judges. As Holmes said in 1897,

> I think that the judges themselves have failed adequately to recognize their duty of weighing considerations of social advantage. The duty is inevitable, and the result of the often proclaimed judicial aversion to deal with such considerations is simply to leave the very ground and foundation of judgments inarticulate, and often unconscious . . . .[107]

But weighing considerations of social advantage is what legislators are supposed to do.[108]

---

[104] See note 113 *infra* and accompanying text.

[105] See FRANK, LAW AND THE MODERN MIND 32-41 (1930); SHKLAR, LEGALISM 101 (1964).

[106] See DIESING, REASON IN SOCIETY 154 (1962).

[107] Holmes, *The Path of the Law*, 10 HARV. L. REV. 457, 467 (1897). He went on to say: "I cannot but believe that if the training of lawyers led them habitually to consider more definitely and explicitly the social advantage on which the rule they lay down must be justified, they sometimes would hesitate where now they are confident, and see that really they were taking sides upon debatable and often burning questions." *Id.* at 468.

[108] Dr. Judith Shklar put the matter in effective focus in her recent book: "All judges must sooner or later legislate—create rules either unconsciously or openly. The codes of several European countries directly provide for this possibility, and in the United States it is an accepted aspect of every stage of judicial activity. From Austin to Gray, moreover, writers on jurisprudence have urged judges to face the facts of life candidly, to accept the responsibilities the community has placed upon their shoulders, and to make rules that seem to them useful and intelligent. To the judge, however, these are frightful occasions. By training and professional ideology he is tied to a vision of his function that excludes self-assertion and places a premium on following existing rules impartially. His natural impulse is to find a rule at any cost, or at least to assimilate his decision to a rule as closely as possible. He may even openly evade responsibility . . . . [I]t is obviously of great importance to him that the rules he relies on be based on universal agreement among either the experts, the wise, or the

Finally, truth is to be valued for itself alone, even though it may "lie at the bottom of a well." However subversive of the established order it may be, truth is an ultimate value. As a nation, we are deeply committed to it; thoughtful citizens become disturbed when, for example, the credibility of government is challenged. If truth, in final analysis, is subjective, then that fact should be faced and dealt with. The truth about the Supreme Court of the United States is difficult to ascertain. Enveloped in secrecy in its deliberations, issuing few public pronouncements other than written opinions which are often "desperately negotiated documents" or the products of a process of bargaining, the Supreme Court is further submerged in a fog of myth and ritual. It has not received sustained attention from scholars who will study it as an institution and as an instrument of government with "a legitimate political function to perform."[109] As with the avowedly political organs of government, its power rests ultimately upon whether the decisions it makes, as Frankfurter wrote, "rest on fundamental presuppositions rooted in history to which widespread acceptance may fairly be attributed."[110] Or as Professor Alexander Bickel has said, "The Court should declare as law only such principles as will—in time, but in a rather foreseeable future—gain general assent."[111] If one replaces the "should" of that statement with a "can," then it would seem that Professor Bickel would tend to agree with the tenor of this paper. In any event, candor about government is desirable: why should a few intellectually sophisticated scholars bamboozle the people back home? That is "squid" jurisprudence—hiding the truth about the Court behind a

---

whole people. Otherwise the rule becomes a mere opinion—a thought he does not wish to entertain. . . . In the United States the extent of judicial lawmaking is both greater and more frankly recognized than anywhere else. Nevertheless, this does not mean that our judges like the system. It is well known that Judge Learned Hand and Justice Frankfurter have expressed a deep aversion to the notion that even in constitutional questions the courts take any legislative initiative. Preferably they should rely on the legislature to have the last say whenever possible, and when that has failed they should place their trust in community sentiment." SHKLAR, LEGALISM 101-02 (1964). See STONE, SOCIAL DIMENSIONS OF LAW AND JUSTICE 678 (1966): "Citizens left to believe that burdens flowing from a judgment inevitably flowed from pre-existing law, when in fact decision on the law might have been the other way, are in a sense being deceived. The right to know the architect of our obligations may be as much a part of liberty, as the right to know our accuser and our judge."

[109] Alfange, *The Relevance of Legislative Facts in Constitutional Law,* 114 U. PA. L. REV. 637, 639 (1966).

[110] Quoted in BICKEL, *op. cit. supra* note 66, at 238-39.

[111] *Ibid.*

cloud of inpenetrable ink.[112]   While doubtless it is desirable to maintain secrecy about the internal deliberations of the Court, we too have an abiding conviction that truth is better than fiction.   We feel, further, and will attempt to demonstrate in Part Two, that unless the Supreme Court adjusts itself to changing reality, it will plummet in power.

Appendix

The following is a questionnaire which was sent to selected students of the Supreme Court in an effort to elicit opinions about the role of the Court.

1. In your judgment, what is the basis for the high esteem in which the Supreme Court is held by the American people generally?   Is there a difference with other courts—*e.g.*, state courts or trial courts?

2. Would it harm the Court as an institution if people generally adhered to the beliefs of the "legal realists?"   Why?

    a. In this connection, do you know of any studies which have been made to develop empirical evidence on the question?

3. If the "legal realist" view of the judicial process is reasonably valid, *should* it be kept from the public even though known to the intellectually sophisticated?   Why?

    a. In this connection, is there a utilitarian function to the ideal of a "government of laws and not of men?"   Thurman Arnold says that "briefs could not be written before a court on any other premise.   This very simple ideal is essential to the public acceptance of our judicial system and to all steps in the judicial process."[113]   What do you think?

---

[112] The late Morris Raphael Cohen gave effective refutation to the squid jurisprudents when he stated: "When I first published the foregoing views [on judicial legislation] in 1914, the deans of some of our law schools wrote me that while the contention that judges do have a share in making the law is unanswerable, it it still advisable to keep the fiction of the phonograph theory to prevent the law from becoming more fluid than it already is. But I have an abiding conviction that to recognize the truth and adjust oneself to it is in the end the easiest and most advisable course. The phonograph theory has bred the mistaken view that the law is a closed, independent system having nothing to do with economic, political, social, or philosophical science. If, however, we recognize that courts are constantly remaking the law, then it becomes of the utmost social importance that the law should be made in accordance with the best available information, which it is the object of science to supply." Cohen, Law and the Social Order 380-81 n.86 (1933).

[113] The quotation from Thurman Arnold is taken from a letter of March 23, 1966, from him to the senior author of this article and is used with permission. Similar views may be found in Arnold, Fair Fights and Foul (1965). See Miller, Book Review, 15 Am. U.L. Rev. 160 (1966).

The following are eight of the replies received from recipients of the questionnaire. They are reprinted as received. It must be emphasized that while permission to print these replies has been granted by each of the writers, none of them has read the text of this article; in no way should they be considered as approving (or disapproving, for that matter) anything contained therein.

I

Question 1

Respecting "the basis for the high esteem in which the Supreme Court is held . . . ," I am going to read "basis" as "factors accounting for," and I am going to assume that your reference to "American people, *generally*" means that you realize that the Court is not held in "high esteem" by some groups, *e.g.*, strong supporters of segregation, but that you do not want me to address that aspect of your question. I will not therefore directly touch that question. But, I think what I have to say will necessarily have implications for *who* holds *how much esteem* for the *Supreme Court* (or some person or persons within it) through *selected periods* of *time*.

Turning, then, to the "factors accounting for" the Court's high esteem, I must generalize without systematic empirical foundations, thus to some extent merely speculate about the causative agents. Some people may hold the Court in high esteem because they study its work very carefully with great understanding and perceptivity, are thus well aware of the difficulties it faces when problems of choice are presented to it, and appreciate, indeed may admire, the attempts of the Court (and individual justices) to be as frank and candid about the premises of its decisions as it can. For example, this group might hold high esteem for the Court because of the frankness with which the policy components of the choice which the Court faced in *Barr v. Matteo* [360 U.S. 564 (1959)] were stated in the several opinions. Esteem and respect could derive here from understanding and appreciating the difficulty which the Court faced in resolving a problem for which there is no pat answer, and from the conviction that the Court was honestly, conscientiously, in the finest judicial tradition searching for the solution which was most in accord with the values of the national community. (My guess is that this group is not large in number, being composed principally of professionals and academics. The vast majority of the American people probably do not study the Court closely enough to react to the kind of variables that influence close students of the Court.) Some people may hold the Court in high esteem merely because it is identified as part of the United States Government. Some may hold it in high esteem simply because they defer to and esteem established authority. (The reverse may also be true of some people, *i.e.*, anti-authoritarians holding authorities in low esteem.) Some people may hold the Court in high esteem because they believe (basically because it is reputed to be so) the Court has an expertise and wisdom deserving of such esteem. Finally, some people may hold the Court in high esteem because they believe it has some means, of which few men are gifted, of "finding" the law. The most general hypothesis I would advance, however, is that the esteem of the Court (the degree to which the population holds supportive attitudes toward it) is a function of the extent to which the population regards the outcomes of the Court's decision-making as indulging or depriving their own values, both their purely personal values and their ideological values. This hypothesis may be in need of further refinement. Conceivably supportive attitudes are a function of the congruence between the Court's conceptions of problems, values at stake, models of cause and effect or probability relations, alternatives, and predictions, and the population's conceptions of these components of a policy choice. It is also quite likely that over time the court builds up or tears down a "bank" of supportive attitudes upon which it may draw in times of stress. Consult David Easton's discussion of the relation between system outcomes and supportive inputs to governmental systems in EASTON, A SYSTEM ANALYSIS OF POLITICAL LIFE (1965).

I have no doubt, I might add, that new insights would be realized from a sustained, careful effort to put the question, "what is the basis for the high esteem . . ." into a form that is operational for the purpose of an empirical research study of American attitudes toward the Court. I think such a study would conclude that most of the talk about esteem of the Court is exceedingly loose.

Respecting attitudes toward trial courts and state courts, my hypothesis is that they do not enjoy as much esteem as does the United States Supreme Court, even from the population in their own jurisdictions.

Question 2

As to the second question, I assume that what is meant by "harm" is decreased esteem for the Court. But I do not know what to assume is meant by "beliefs of legal realists." If this expression means that judges use their purely private and personal value system as criteria for deciding cases to the exclusion of community values (statutes, rules, etc. included), I think this belief by people generally would lead to a decrease in esteem for the Court. If "beliefs of legal realists" means that the legal realists hold that legal propositions do not decide concrete cases, but that judges make a policy analysis or react in an idiosyncratic way, my answer differs. I do not believe that the Court's esteem would suffer because people believed the Court made a policy analysis, at least among the people who do not believe that the "law" is to be "found." The Court's esteem would suffer, I believe, if people believed that the Court's decisions were *merely* the resultant of idiosyncratic reactions of individual justices. I would also hope that the Court's esteem would not suffer merely because in a given case its decision appears to be an example of a relatively mechanical application of pre-existing rules to facts. In some instances highly programmed (minimum discretion) decisional systems may work better than less highly programmed ones. Of course the reverse may be true. But to say which approach is better we must appraise the operation of both types of decisional systems in terms of criteria of "working well." It is of course a most difficult question whether to decide a particular case relatively mechanically, or, perhaps at the price of overruling past cases, to decide it after a full-fledged policy analysis. But, to sum up, with these qualifications I do not believe esteem for the Court would suffer if people generally adhered to the beliefs of the "legal realists." Indeed, more realism among the population might lead to increased esteem for the Court.

I will go one step further: justifying decisions by question-begging use of legal citations, or legal mumbo-jumbo, or vague appeals to metaphysical concepts may lead to loss of esteem for the Court. I believe that the population steadily is becoming more intelligent and rationalistic and is increasingly demanding rational decisions from legal process. Perhaps it is mostly my personal value system that is speaking, but I also believe that people in general share my belief in the principle of accountability respecting public officials. This principle calls for visible decisions—visible in the sense of who made them, when, and for what reasons. To fail to give the felt reasons, or to obscure them, offends the accountability principle. Moreover, hidden decisions are very often a reflection of an arrogant attitude toward people generally. It is, I hope, apparent why I believe that a realistic view of legal process should not be kept from the public. In fact I think it is decidedly healthy to tell the people the truth, and I think the Court is the best agency to do the telling. Possibly, the bar and legal educators are remiss in failing to launch a general educational program designed to acquaint the population at large with the difficulties of choice that the Court faces, and to develop an appreciation for its role. Such a program might do wonders for improved esteem.

Question 3

As to the government of laws and not of men idea, and whether it serves a utilitarian function, the first proposition is too loosely stated. It invites one to formulate a dichotomy—no discretion in the Court at one extreme, and unlimited discretion in the Court as the other. The truth lies somewhere in between, but not always at the same place in between. We are dealing with a continuum, not with a simple dichotomy. Now I think there is often utility to a decisional system so highly programmed that discretion in individual applications is held to a minimum (discretion in such a system is largely that of the designer of the system) because it may produce quicker, less expensive decisions. Moreover, it may appear very impartial. But such a system may in fact be dysfunctional in some instances. The quick inexpensive decision may prove to be neither quick nor inexpensive if it is so poor that its effects breed the necessity of many other decisions. Moreover, detachment and impersonality can lead to dehumanization. Of course, similar pro and con comments can be made of the use of highly discretionary decisional systems in some contexts. So I answer the first question in *3a* as yes and no, it depends.

I think Thurman Arnold clearly overstates his point. Certainly when one drafts a brief one acts on expectations that certain legal propositions will be invoked by the Court. (Lawyers are not always successful, however, in predicting the doctrinal propositions which a court may feel are relevant; see Mermin's recent study of a very important Wisconsin case [MERMIN, JURISPRUDENCE AND STATECRAFT (1963)].) But surely Arnold does not act on the expectation that the only acceptable decision "under the law" which the Court may render is the one Arnold urges. Surely he doesn't assume that the opposing attorney is stupid, or uninformed, or mistaken, or asking the Court to act illegally. I don't think Arnold is saying any of these things, although his choice of words might permit such inferences. Rather, I think he means, or should mean, that without well-founded expectations that certain value standards are accepted by the Court as limits on their discretion, argument would be meaningless. I agree. But I would add that meaningful arguments might still be made although the Court felt that it faced a brand new issue, and that all legal analogies were of no help. To argue in terms of what public policy should be is not to abandon the idea of a government of law. To the contrary, the practice of advancing arguments respecting what policy should be defers to the idea of a government of law. Any such argument asks a properly constituted institution of legal process to prescribe a legal proposition to govern a case for which no rule particularly tailored to the case exists. This situation is perhaps most apparent, and perhaps the most extensive in scope, example of creative law-making. But law-making also takes place in deference to legal principles. Legislatures must legislate in accordance with constitutional principles. If the case of the Court construing constitutional provisions against completely new fact situations is cited, I concede that no legal proposition may be influential on the merits (although of course many legal propositions will have been influential in developing the record and defining the issue). Even when this is true, and the Court feels that it is making new law without the aid of legal propositions, it does not have to retreat to an idiosyncratic approach. We expect our law makers (judges included) to make law, but to make law that they conscientiously believe is good for the community. We expect them, then, to make a complete policy analysis. In making that analysis there are some general principles which may serve as guides to decision, although they do not dictate decision. One such principle is to carefully formulate the problem for decision (get the facts, its dimensions, etc.—this means formulate not merely the legal problem but also its societal counterpart). Another principle says identify the social values at stake. Another says formulate realistic alternatives. Another says estimate the efficiency of these alternatives. And a final one says choose the alternative which maximizes the public interest. I don't mean to minimize the difficulties that may attend such an open-ended approach. But I do mean to assert that in our tradition this approach is not lawless, nor without constraints upon personal idiosyncracy, but upon the contrary honors the ideal of the Rule (not rules) of Law.

Thurman Arnold, I'm afraid, has seriously over-simplified the problem.

Ernest M. Jones
Professor of Law
University of Florida

II

Question 1

Those who hold the Supreme Court of the United States in uniquely high esteem, distinguishing it in this respect from the state courts and the inferior federal courts, do so because the Supreme Court of the United States exercises the power of judicial review over decisions of state courts and enactments of federal and state legislatures. Public hostility to the Court stems primarily from the same source. As the Court exercises the power more militantly, more and more of those in the middle of the road will tend to join this group of adverse critics of the Court. To the extent that the Court hesitates to exercise its power, it avoids this danger, but disappoints the expectations of its strongest supporters. From the point of view of its own prestige, as well as the point of view of its proper function, the most important thing that the Court does is to exercise its unique power responsibly. (I give a nod of respect but disagreement to the view that the most important thing the Court does is "not doing.")

Question 2

Responsible exercise of the power of judicial review must be responsive to the needs of the society in which we live if the Court is to maintain its prestige. Public allergy to the law itself as an institution stems primarily from its engagement with considerations that appear to be irrelevant to these needs. The same may be said of the Supreme Court. The irrelevant considerations which can damage the Court's prestige are, of course, quite varied. In earlier decades, the Court was probably judged more by the results reached in a particular case than by the public rationalization in the Court's opinions, but advances in public education and in communications have altered this balance and are continuing to alter it. No amount of public loyalty would permit the fabled emperor's lack of clothing to go unnoticed if a television camera were trained on him. For the same reasons, unsatisfactory rationalization of its results becomes increasingly damaging to the Supreme Court of the United States as an institution. Thus, an opinion that seeks support in non-existent legislative intent, whether of the framers of the Constitution or one of its amendments, or of the Congress that enacted the Wagner Act or the Taft-Hartley Act, not only is unlikely to produce a sound decision; even if it does, it carries potentiality of damaging the Court's good repute.

Upon rereading question 2, I realize that my answer does not meet it directly. What I am saying is that more and more people are coming to adhere to the beliefs of the "legal realists." In answer to question 2a, I do not know of any empirical study on this subject. In further answer to the basic question, I feel sure that the present Court would fare better among "legal realist" critics than among critics clinging to disproved abstract conceptions of the role of legal institutions. But if the public is only partly transformed, neither is the Court's adherence to "legal realism" perfect nor complete. This entire answer, of course, makes certain implicit assumptions about what "legal realism" is.

Question 3

I do not believe that what courts actually do can long be kept from the public. And to the extent that the "legal realist" view of the judicial process is valid, I do not believe that it can permanently be kept from the public, when known to the intellectually sophisticated. Assuming that the truth could be confined to the latter group, I do not believe that it should. Thus, for two reasons, I answer question *3* in the nega-tive. Since the true nature of the judicial process cannot be kept from the Court's "intellectually sophisticated" adverse critics, any attempt by the Court itself or by its supporters to conceal the truth will naturally be characterized as intellectual dishonesty and deceitfulness by those hostile to the Court. Whether or not the general public can be made to understand the complexities of the judicial process as it exists in fact, the public can certainly understand accusations of this kind. Thus, in the long run, I believe that honesty is the best policy for the judiciary. Even assuming that the Court *could* conceal the true nature of its functions, I believe that it would be un-fortunate for the Court to do so. The Court is, after all, responsible to the public if only indirectly, through the limited powers that the executive and legislative exercise over the judicial branch. While a dictatorship by the judiciary is a most unlikely event, elimination of the pressures of public criticism by shrouding the work of the Court is undesirable for other reasons. First, it would certainly facilitate judicial sur-render to improper assertions of power by the executive or the legislative branch. Second, it would impair social interests in certainty and predictability of the law made by Supreme Court decisions. If the published opinions of the Court are to be regarded only as buffers against the onslaught of public opinion, then the well-advised client should disregard those opinions. And the line that divides the "intellectually sophisti-cated" from everyone else can never be really a line anyway. We certainly cannot assume that all members of the Bar will fall on the proper side of it, and we can expect a similar division in the ranks of politicians, civil servants, and the public itself. The prospect of a not-so-intellectual practicing attorney attempting to advise a similarly unblessed governmental official on the basis of Supreme Court opinions that were written to conceal rather than reveal the springs of judicial action poses an obvious threat of total chaos.

Thurman Arnold is at least half right. I would say rather that briefs can be and are written on the premise that ours is a government of laws as well as men. The Constitution, legislation and judicial precedent all play important roles, but we would be foolish to believe that electronic data retrieval can ever replace the creative role of adjudication. This is obviously even more true of the Supreme Court of the United States, because of its powers of judicial review, than it is of any other court. Realism does not require rejection of the role played by laws; it requires, rather, recognition that laws without the intervention of courts are only part of the story. Any lawyer who wrote a brief before the Supreme Court of the United States exclusively on the basis of cold precedent, without regard for the creative function of the Court, would in most cases have left the job only partly done.

Thomas S. Currier
Professor of Law
University of Virginia

III

Question 1

I suspect that the basis for high popular esteem of the United States Supreme Court is in large measure popular acceptance of (a) the declaratory theory of law, removing from popular imagination any discomforting doubts which would naturally attend an explicitly recognized value-making and means-to-ends-choice-making role, plus (b) the popular image of the blind goddess with the scales, or the stalwart male figure with the sword, signifying—to the man in the street, at least—the idea of impartial adjudica-tion, demanding simply fair application of already known, existing doctrine. I have no Gallup poll to back me up, and don't know whether any of the pollsters' past questions supply empirical data or not. I would cite the general fact—I think it to be a fact—that most of the really hot public controversies about the judicial role have arisen not out of disputes over the correctness of integrity of the adjudicative role (notable exceptions, of course: *e.g.*, Sacco and Vanzetti), but over the lawmaking role when that has come sharply to public attention (child-labor decisions, Dred Scott, invalidation of New Deal Legislation).

Question 2

I think you must ask, which legal realists? It would harm the Court and the country if popular opinion adopted the sophomoric cynicism or inside-dopester weaknesses of some fringe realists (*e.g.*, Pearson and Allen). Healthy government with some substantial popular base should be advanced and not harmed by a maturely realistic appreciation of how institutions should operate in order to fulfill the abiding values of the society; in such a context, if realism hurt the Court, it would be only because the Court was not behaving well. Of course, healthy, popular-based government requires unifying symbols, and symbols add an emotional dimension to views of institutions: that is largely their function. But society has to run with a good deal of emotion as well as reason; the question must be, whether it is emotion responsibly disciplined by reason. I am sorry that I don't know of empirical studies to back me up. There are some disquieting empirical studies on the other side of the coin: of the dubious attachments of common opinion (notably of young people's opinion) to values like Bill-of-Rights values, which need sound emotional underpinnings for survival.

Question 3

Again, your question can't be answered without very careful definition of just who are the realists whose sophistication is in issue. And, again, a healthy legal order which seeks a substantial popular base, can't run simply on empty symbols or unreal concepts; though it will probably always be a race with catastrophe, I see no other workable tack to take except the Jeffersonian one of educating at least a broad spectrum of the people to the extent that they know something of how to define where their real interests lie and how to look after them. I think the Court would be stronger for there being a broadly pervasive, responsibility realistic understanding of (a) the considerable measure of policy-making discretion which has always resided in it and must continue to reside in it, coupled with (b) the consequent need for defining standards (*e.g.*, a meaningful presumption of constitutionality) to which to hold the Court in exercising its discretion and in not improperly trenching upon the legislative and executive branches.

(a) There is utilitarian function to the idea of a "government of laws and not of men," if the phrase is taught as spelling the demand upon public officers to exercise judgment by criteria derived from broad community ideals, tested by application of reason to facts and to acute definition of involved interests and values, and not derived from the peculiar or parochial experience or prejudice of the particular officials. If the phrase is taken to mean an appeal to the "brooding omnipresence," then dependence on it seems to me sophomoric, if only because in the long run it won't work.

Willard Hurst
Professor of Law
University of Wisconsin

IV

Introduction

I am delighted to hear that you plan to have a go at Mishkin, with whom I also disagree (at least in part). I first came into the prospective overruling angle when I was at the University of Virginia Law School in the fall semester '64, and had a chance to exchange ideas with Tom Currier of the Law School on some jurisprudential aspects of his pre-*Linkletter* article [*Time and Change in Judge-Made Law: Prospective Overruling*, 51 VA. L. REV. 201 (1965)]. I think Tom and I are agreed that in the choice between certainty/consistency/predictability/stability and flexibility/creativity/social-adaptation/justice, there are certain basic values or interests inherent in our whole case law system, which *normally* operate to support the former set of demands (though Tom's list of these values at 235-37 is not quite the same as mine). The prospective overruling problem arises because in some situations some of these values may turn out to work *against* their normal implication of adherence to precedent. When this happens, these errant values must still be weighed against the others by an *ad hoc* consideration of the instant case. Consequently there is practically nothing that can be said at the general level as to how the weighing of values should turn out. But perhaps it *can* be said that if the instant problem itself has any special features which have the effect of "loading" one of the values being weighed (as in my view the *Linkletter* situation ought to "load" the value of equality), then that should be enough to tip the balance.

The *Linkletter* opinion is itself so close to this approach that all that I can really say by way of criticism is that when it came to the ultimate *ad hoc* weighing of values which such an approach demands, the Court's weighing of the values involved came out differently from mine. But there is one thing which perhaps affected the result. The above analysis would imply that prospective overruling is always a sometime thing, with retroactivity continuing to be the norm: and this corresponds with what I understand to have been the use of the device up to now. In the *Linkletter* litigation this position seems to have been somehow switched around, so that there was (as it were) a presumption that *Mapp v. Ohio* [367 U.S. 643 (1961)] would operate only prospectively, and the appellant was put in the position of having to show reasons why this presumption should not apply.

I am, of course, at a disadvantage in discussing prospective overruling. In Australia we have no such animal. My own experience is limited to my brief flirtation with the Currier article, and some equally brief preliminary work with my own teacher, Julius Stone, on the prospective overruling section of his SOCIAL DIMENSIONS OF LAW AND JUSTICE 658-67 (1966). Similarly, with regard to your questionnaire, I am inclined to think that anything I can say will have little value, because of my limited and largely impressionistic awareness of relevant American conditions. Such insight as I may be able to bring to the problem would stem, I think, from two sources. One is my own crude but continuing attempt to articulate the contrasts between Australian and American judicial systems, both as to technique and social impact. The other is my own long perplexity over your questions 2 and 3, not so much as raised by legal realism itself, but rather as raised by my own involvement with Stone's position now most fully set out in Chapters 6-8 (especially Chapter 7) of his LEGAL SYSTEM AND LAWYERS' REASONING (1964).

For me, those chapters raise two fundamental but still unsolved questions. *First*, Stone's position (which I entirely accept) does not require us (as "realism" did) to reject the orthodox concentration on rules and precedents altogether: it requires us to see that certainty/consistency etc., and flexibility/creativity etc., are both important aspirations of the legal system, and that *by working with the orthodox precedent apparatus*, judges do in fact manage to achieve realization of both of them. But exactly how is the balance to be struck in *stating* this position? In particular, how is the certainty/consistency set of demands (to which I would add rationality and "soundness" of argument) to be stated without plunging us back into the overemphasised orthodoxy that the "realists" pried us free from? (Obviously the importance of Wechsler's "neutral principles" [WECHSLER, *Toward Neutral Principles of Constitutional Law*, in PRINCIPLES, POLITICS AND FUNDAMENTAL LAW 3 (1961)] is that they represent an attempt, though a verbally muddled one, to solve precisely this problem.) *Second*, if "realism" (or Stone's extension and modification of it) is right, should we say so? This last is, of course, exactly your question *3*; and as far as I can see we still haven't managed to produce any better discussion of it than the crude Demogue-and-Wurtzel chapters in FRANK, LAW AND THE MODERN MIND (1930). Stone, I think, would regard the whole of pages 652-96 of his 1966 book referred to above (and especially perhaps pages 677-78) as an attempt to help us with these very questions; but for my part I am still just as perplexed as ever. At any rate for what they are worth, *my* answers would be as follows.

Question 1

In Australia, law and government tend generally to be seen as rather remote from relevance to ordinary daily life. Legal and governmental functions are seen as important, but they tend to be left to their specialist functionaries: "ordinary" men are concerned with ordinary things. This means, of course, that along with apathetic unconcern for the doings of lawyers and politicians there goes a good deal of respect, of the kind accorded to any specialist in an esoteric but important field. Yet for both lawyers and politicians, this respect is coupled with a certain degree of scepticism and even contempt, such men being seen as "manipulators."

There are, however, projected onto this mixture of favourable and unfavourable popular attitudes, certain hierarchical value-ascriptions originating within legal circles themselves. Judges tend traditionally to be seen as more dignified, wiser and more just, possessed of higher intellect and higher integrity, than ordinary lawyers; and ability and dignity are also assumed to increase in an ascending scale as we move progressively from magistrates' courts to the highest judicial tribunal. Consequently as to most judges, and a fortiori as we near the top of the judicial hierarchy, judges tend to be freed from the "manipulative" stigma which attaches to lawyers generally, and popular respect for them is correspondingly more unreserved. Finally, the respected status which judges thus occupy allows them to speak out extrajudicially from time to time, as spokesmen of "official" public opinion on controversial issues; and these extrajudicial pronouncements further enhance their public image as "ideology makers." This last function, in Australia at least, tends not to be exercised by judges of the (federal) High Court, but by a few particular judges of the State Supreme Courts; but perhaps the enhancement of the public image of the judicial office extends to all holders of that office.

All this, I should guess, is more or less true for all common law countries; and represents a kind of minimum model for the answer to your question. For the United States, however, this model needs to be supplemented (and in part modified) by reference to further important factors.

A first factor, particularly striking for an outsider, is the high degree of "law awareness" in the American community. Not just legal philosophers, but people generally, regard the idea of law as fundamental to American society; and this must appreciably enhance the popular respect for lawyers which is present even in my "minimum" model. *Second,* this "law awareness" is particularly striking in relation to the Constitution. In Australia the constitution is no more revered (and hardly any better known) than if it were an ordinary Act of Parliament (as in fact it is); in the United States it is popularly reverenced to a degree that amazes the outsider. As a foreign jurisprude, I like to believe that U.S. law-awareness in general, and Constitution-awareness in particular, have a deep historical linkage with the origins of the whole polity in a people's rebellious choice of its own destiny, based on a natural law ideology—which, of course, I disapprove of as a positivist almost as much as I do as a Britisher! Whatever the explanation, the popular reverence for the Constitution is real, and must rub off on the institution whose work is primarily associated with the Constitution. The President's symbolic identification with the "idea" of the Constitution is a major source of *his* high esteem; the Supreme Court has its own kind of identification with the same symbolic "idea," and it reaps the same rewards in public assumptions. *Third,* this factor acquires special importance from the fact that the workload of the Court is in fact almost wholly confined to its constitutional functions: where, as in Australia, the "Constitutional" court is also the highest national court of appeal in "ordinary" litigation, it tends (even in its constitutional work) not only to function in fact much more like an "ordinary" court, but to be regarded as such. *Fourth,* within the framework of its "constitutional" functions, the Supreme Court does in fact have occasion to pass judgment on almost every aspect of American litigation, consequently touching almost every aspect of American social life. Supreme Court Justices then tend to be projected as ultimate arbiters of every aspect of "the American way of life." What makes this fourth point not inconsistent with my third is that, *fifth*, almost all the Supreme Court's work is widely and intelligently reported in the press. If fully reported the diversity of *our* High Court's "ordinary" appellate work might give it, too, the image of an ultimate arbiter of life in general. In fact, however, press coverage is given only to those of its judgments which are thought to touch on either "vested" or general popular interest, mainly in the constitutional and criminal law fields; and even then the reportage is usually garbled to the point of unintelligibility. By contrast the United States Supreme Court owes much to its press coverage. *Sixth*, in Australia almost all law graduates go into "ordinary" professional practice. Consequently all our judges, including High Court judges, are still drawn from the ranks of men who have successfully practised at the bar. (On three or four occasions, as with the present Chief Justice, a man has been appointed straight from the political office of Commonwealth Attorney-General, but even this is always at least plausibly referable to the appointee's former outstanding career as a practising lawyer.) This means that we can still maintain, with a substantial degree of truth, the myth that judges (and particularly High Court judges) represent the best and most talented of our legal profession. In the U.S., the distribution of good law graduates through a wide range of governmental, academic and other occupations in addition to "ordinary" law has founded a similarly wide range of sources from which judicial appointees are drawn; and occasionally, of course, the selection reaches outside the range of law graduates altogether. The myth equating judges with "the best lawyers" then becomes less maintainable; and Supreme Court Justices may to that extent get less respect than their Australian brethren. But this, I think, is offset by the fact that the American practice also means that it is almost a matter of course for appointees to be men already marked out as outstanding personalities in the public eye.

I gather from my discussions with Stone that he would want to elaborate very considerably on the fourth factor I mentioned above. I would not exactly disagree with his elaboration, but I would tend to regard it as of inspirational rather than reportive value. Roughly, the elaboration would run like this. Mishkin's approach to the Court's symbolic function harks back finally to the old maxim that it is more important that a matter be settled than that it be settled right. But what we should rather say is that it is more important that a matter should be settled *as right as possible for the time being* than that it be not settled at all. At page 795 of SOCIAL DIMENSIONS OF LAW AND JUSTICE, Stone comes close to this view in discussing the "demand of justice" that the legal system should provide institutionalized outlets for the unavoidable tensions of a pluralistic society: "The Supreme Court of the United States, in those very aspects at which British lawyers sometimes look askance, offers a supreme example of this provision. The very varied outlooks and talents and capacities of its members often spell discord. Yet its very discord may symbolize the will of so richly complex a people to live under broadly agreed principles, and also to sublimate the bitter disagreements which broad principles so often yield in application." In now wanting to expand this suggestion, I gather he would say that most members of the American community now realize that the fundamental policy issues that the Supreme Court has to deal with are not capable of legalistic answers, nor of any absolutely right answers capable of lasting for all time. In face of these problems, he would say, the Supreme Court represents an expedient which appellate courts in other countries may yet have to follow: a resort in effect to the "wise men" syndrome in the hope that the settled policies for the time being, while necessarily imperfect, will be the best available.

Question 2

In answering your second question, I shall take "legal realism" to refer to all the views—from "extreme" realism to (at least) its more moderate latter-day versions—which in fact recognize a substantial measure of judicial creativity, and a substantial degree of illusoriness in the legalist's rule-and-precedent structure. I simply do not believe that *popular* acceptance of any of the views thus included would do any sub-stantial harm to the efficiency or prestige of the Court as an institution. In the "minimum model" which I constructed from Australian conditions, such a view if popularly held would no doubt increase the weight of the "manipulative" slur as an ingredient in popular attitudes; but I believe the overall balance of factors in this minimum model would still be in favour of respect. Of the specific American factors which I added to this minimum model, the first and second do not (in my natural-law-tending explanation of them) entail a belief in "law" or "Constitution" as a specific set of black-letter rules; the focus of respect is rather on the "idea" or "spirit" of law as a means of rational guidance of a country's destiny, and a substantial measure of judicial creativity is perfectly consistent with this. My third and fourth factors, insofar as they focus on the functions that the highest tribunal is believed to perform, are I think in no way affected by any beliefs about the techniques employed in performing those functions. (As to the "ultimate arbiters" angle of my fourth point, see below.) My fifth point, as to press coverage, perhaps suggests a basic flaw in your whole second question, or at any rate a reason for difficulty in trying to answer it: namely that the full press coverage of the United States Supreme Court does already, I think, import a good deal of "realism," with no notable ill effects.

My sixth point perhaps suggests different answers for Australia and the U.S. What it does is crudely to contrast two alternative bases of respect for high appellate judges: the Australian "best lawyers" basis, and the American "outstanding personalities" one. These nationally-oriented equations are of course extremely rough, and each alternative factor is confined to a minor subsidiary role in popular attitudes. But for what it is worth, I suppose that "realism" popularly imbibed would somewhat detract from the "best lawyers" basis for respect (insofar as it might make legal qualifications less important to good adjudication), and would correspondingly enhance the importance of the "outstanding personalities" basis. To this extent "realism" might actually strengthen popular respect for the U.S. Court.

This leads me to consider Stone's "wise men" version of my "ultimate arbiters" point. The *belief* that he would seem to ascribe to most American citizens is: Ultimate policy problems are not finally or permanently soluble; all we can do is to work out guidelines for them from time to time; in the U.S. we do this by leaving the job to a bench of nine wise men representative of different ideologies. And, he seems to say, most Americans would add to this belief the evaluation: This is the best solution any nation could devise.

Now, I suppose I must agree that *many* American citizens would hold the above *belief*; but I think the above *evaluation* would be added only by those who think that by and large the Court's results are *right*. Many other Americans would also hold the above *belief*, but would add the different evaluation: Surely there must be something better we could do. I also think that, in addition to these two classes of citizen-approving believers in the "wise men" syndrome and disapproving believers, there would be many other citizens who would not share the above *belief*. But these, too, would be divided into approvers and non-approvers of what the Court does.

No doubt popularization of "realism" would tend to shift the balance between believers and non-believers in the above *belief*; there would clearly be more "be-lievers." But within the changed belief framework, it seems to me that the balance between approvers and non-approvers would not be substantially altered. Possibly Stone would even say that more of popular "realism" would spread both belief and favourable evaluation; if so, I would disagree. But while I do not think more "real-ism" would diminish popular criticism of the Court, I don't think it would increase it either. In other words, whether or not judges are or should be "result-oriented," I think that popular evaluations of judges clearly are so oriented.

So much for the effects of widespread "realism" on *popular attitudes*. Thus far, in effect, I see no real problem. But if we interpret the words "people generally," as used in your question, to include the Supreme Court Justices themselves, I become very much more worried. In relation to *our* High Court, my estimate is that most of our judges do in fact exercise a substantial degree of creativeness, but that they do not in fact (with one probable exception on the present bench) "generally adhere to the beliefs of the 'legal realists' "—nor to any view placing substantial stress on judicial creativity. If this were to change, I do not believe that there would be any striking change in the patterns of judicial behaviour of our present generation of judges; but I honestly do fear that the next generation might be the worse for it. I do not know. But my fears are prompted by the very things that trouble me, and also many other observers, with regard to your Supreme Court, where I think it is fair to say that there is a fairly widespread judicial belief in something like "realism."

My worries are twofold, and the first of them relates precisely to the effect on "the Court as an institution." It is, I think, the same kind of worry as Bodenheimer expresses at the tail end of *his* piece [*Birth Control Legislation and the United States Supreme Court*, 14 KAN. L. REV. 453 (1966)] on *Griswold v. Connecticut* [381 U.S. 479 (1965)], where *he talks* about "the spectacle of nine philosopher Kings at war with each other," and pleads for "a strengthening of the *institutional* approach by the Court, as distinguished from an exclusively individualistic attitude toward . . . constitutional interpretation." It seems to me that this excess of personal sound and fury is the main complaint to be made about the Supreme Court in recent years. In part, I suppose, the same comprehensive press coverage as I was praising earlier is responsible for throwing individual Justices under a personal limelight to which they feel that they must play up; and perhaps all we academics in our Law Review commentaries also encourage this. But I think also that judicial imbibing of "realism" must share a part of the blame for the tendency to write as nine individuals rather than as an institution. The present pattern translates the "star" system from the movies to the Court. It may be, as I suggested earlier, that this does no harm to the prestige of the institution, and may even enhance it; but I think it does no harm to the prestige of the institution itself.

My second worry is epitomised in my anxieties [*Constitutionalism and Comstockery*, 14 KAN. L. REV. 403 (1966)] over the Douglas opinion in *Griswold v. Connecticut*. Whether or not I am right in thinking that Stone wants to modify "realism" by finding *some* place, in his account of the judicial process, for certainty/consistency etc., *I* certainly want to do this. Lawyer-like patterns of argumentation, careful rational work within a framework built up by precedent—in short, all that Mishkin wants to preserve in *appearance* for symbolic reasons, I want to preserve as *reality* for substantial evaluative reasons. I don't want to say that judges should be creative but should seem orthodoxly judicial; I want to say that they should be creative but should also *be* orthodoxly judicial. Our High Court, under the last Chief Justice, Sir Owen Dixon, went through a period when by and large it managed not only to *be* creative while stressing an appearance of legalistic values, but actually to get its creativeness out of its legalism. I still can't quite say how this conjuring trick is done, but whatever the secret, that is what I want all judges to do. Harlan, I think, is capable of it; but generally the present Supreme Court seems so concerned with "what it is doing in fact" that it ceases to be sufficiently concerned with the craftsmanship of opinion-writing. Perhaps for the immediacy of the moment "result-orientation" *is* enough; but for long-run contributions to a legal tradition, it just won't do.

Question 3

Again, I see no adequate reason why "realism," or whatever modification of it is reasonably valid, should be kept from the public; I really don't believe it will make much difference one way or the other. Most of this is covered in my answer to question 2. But again, if "the public" be taken to include the Justices themselves, I have serious doubts, and just don't know the answer.

I suppose the main arguments *for* full disclosure are (a) truth is truth and must always be told, and (b) Pound's old axiom that "Much will be gained when courts have perceived what it is that they are doing, and are thus enabled to address themselves consciously to doing it the best that they may." Three or four years ago I would have taken these two arguments as conclusive. The main arguments that I now see pressing against these are (c) power corrupts (a judge who *knows* he is being creative may become *sweepingly* creative; a judge creating unconsciously within the leeways of an "authority" system will be confined from molar to molecular motion, etc.); and (d) on the "realist" view the whole burden of choice of decisions—with full awareness that these are to constitute the only justice available, both for the individual litigants and for whole masses of the community—bears down personally on the individual judge. The Blackstonian myth, which cushions and seems to ease the pressure of this responsibility, may be the only thing that makes it bearable. My anxiety here is for what Stone calls (SOCIAL DIMENSIONS OF LAW AND JUSTICE 683) "the overall psychic economy of the man who is a judge, who has to perform not merely in this case today, but in an endless series of cases, day after day, and year after year." Perhaps both (c) and (d) are rather fanciful, and it may be that I would finish up still following (a) and (b). But the points I raised in the final paragraphs of my answer to question 2 are also relevant here, and not at all fanciful. I really think that if "public" includes "judges," your question *3* is an agonising problem.

In spite of what I have said so far, I do not entirely reject Mishkin's plea for the "symbolic" value of the Blackstonian declaratory theory. But, as already hinted, my real reason for wanting judges to preserve adherence to precedents and sound patterns of argument from them is that I think these things are important in their own right. And here I find that I must after all drag in my own version of the Currier list of "values" affecting prospective overruling.

In my version, I would want to say that the judicial process (indeed "law" in general) is not merely a device for producing the most just and expedient solutions to social problems, but a *rational* device for doing this: "law" does import a commitment to rationality in problem-solutions. "Rationality" here has Max Weber's double sense of referring (a) to the basing of decisions on consistent, well-grounded, and "principled" intellectual operations, and (b) to the organization of legal institutions and their facilities and personnel so as to achieve a maximum of coordination and efficiency and a minimum of friction and expense (in the sense in which economists speak of the "rationality" of an industry). Now, (a) imports values of *consistency* in statement from one case to another; of *equality* of treatment from one suitor to another; and of what the current crop of ethical philosophers call *"universalizability"* in the value-judgments that we take as a basis for decisions; and (b) imports values of *stability* in social arrangements, *certainty* in judicial pronouncements, and *efficiency* in the handling of the Court's workload. All six values do demand that right results be reached not just anyhow, but by reasoned elaboration of precedent.

Now if I can take the symbolic value of the phrase "a government of laws and not of men" as a shorthand reference to all these things that I see involved in the idea of "law" as a rational endeavour—or even simply as referring to the need for "reasoned elaboration" of precedent as a *means* to judicial creativeness—then I would agree that the "government of laws" ideal does have a utilitarian function, as helping to ensure the implementation of my six "rational" values. Similarly if the "premise" that Arnold has in mind is to be taken in this broad sense, I would agree with him. If, as Arnold's presence in your question leads me to suspect, the reference is merely to Mishkin's notion that we should preserve an *appearance* of "government of laws" by going through the motions of "reasoned elaboration" etc., for symbolic reasons for re-affirming our ritual commitments to the "rational" law way of doing things, then I would also agree that this might have a utilitarian function. Somewhere within my overall view of the reasons for our need of "reasoned elaboration," there would be a place for this symbolic ritual reason; but it would be a very subsidiary reason, and one that I would prefer not to mention at all. For I think that *this* reason does get us back to "Demogue's belief in the importance of deluding the public," and what *I* want to find is a way of saying that the good judge is both a precedent man *and* a creative one, *without* being thereby committed to saying that he is "deluding the public."

Anthony R. Blackshield
Lecturer in Jurisprudence
Faculty of Law
The University of Sydney

V

Question 1

The American people have appeared always to maintain a remarkable respect for law. Perhaps part of the reason for this is, as Tocqueville suggests, that in a democratic society law is looked upon as the creation of the people, and, therefore, those who claim to share in the process of self-government are inclined to approve of law that they have putatively helped to make. Perhaps it is also that the general level of affluence that has been characteristic of American society has established a respect for the *status quo,* and law inevitably stands for the preservation of the *status quo.* In any event, the Supreme Court, as the authoritative interpreter of federal law—which, in the popular conception, may often be equated with American law—serves as a convenient focal point for this public esteem and reaps the benefit of it. Moreover, and probably more important, the Supreme Court, as the branch of the national government most clearly responsible for the support and defense of the Constitution, shares in the amazing reverence that the American people have always had toward that document.

There is an aura of infallibility attached to final judgments, and simply because the Supreme Court is final, as Justice Jackson noted, it is considered authoritative. Thus, it appears to be held in higher esteem than any other court in the nation. Similarly, state appellate courts, capable of reversing trial court judgments and more isolated in their activities, are more respected than lower state courts. I think it is true that federal courts, in general, are more highly thought of than state courts, and I believe that the greater respect is due to the fact that they represent the whole nation rather than merely a part. I doubt that this would hold true, however, in any of the states of the South.

Question 2

The views of the legal realists, as even Professor Mishkin's article makes clear, have undoubtedly won general acceptance in law schools and among lawyers. The qualifications and reservations that are frequently expressed in the law reviews are not in any real sense a rejection of realism, but merely a shift in emphasis to place stress on the existence of certainty and stability, factors which most realists did not deny, but which, in contrast to the Blackstonian theory, they refused to consider as necessarily controlling. While this acceptance of legal realism has caused members of the bar to look upon the actions of courts in a different light, it has not appeared to cause a significant lessening of respect for the judicial process. Holmes, by all odds the most influential of the realists, could hardly be said to have held law or the courts in disrespect—he simply insisted that judges not be allowed to use legal certainty as an excuse for blocking the attainment of social goals generally thought to be essential.

The point is that if the triumph of legal realism has not denigrated the Supreme Court as an institution in the eyes of its most attentive and critical constituency, why should it be expected to have this effect in the eyes of the general public? The "declaratory theory" of the judicial process is a functional myth to the extent that is generally believed that the only alternative to a legal system in which judges merely find law is a system of judicial arbitrariness and irresponsibility. But I am far from certain that the general public views either the legal system or the work of the Court in terms of these simplistic alternatives. I would surmise, instead, that there is a vague but substantial awareness that the Supreme Court does not merely inexorably apply existing law regardless of the social consequences, but that it acts, and must act, with considerations of the public good firmly in mind—that is, that it acts, and must act, politically. In this regard, the most potentially dangerous myth is the one you describe in your article [Miller, *Some Pervasive Myths About the United States Supreme Court*, 10 St. Louis U.L.J. 153, 162 (1965)] as "the myth that the Supreme Court is to be equated with a court of law." Citizens desire litigation to be decided, for the most part, according to settled and accepted rules, and do not want courts to depart from these rules for insufficient reasons—that is, for reasons unconnected with the general public good. While it is, of course, true that cases even in such mundane areas as contract and tort can involve vital questions of public policy, the cases of this type that occupy most of the time of the "courts of law" are usually of far less general significance, and may be disposed of in accordance wtih Brandeis' observation that, in most areas, "it is more important that the law be settled than that it be settled right." The Supreme Court, on the other hand, has the authority, which it is expected to exercise, to limit its jurisdiction to cases other than the ordinary. By definition, therefore the cases that come to it for decision, especially cases of constitutional law, do not have importance solely for the parties, but, as in reapportionment or civil rights, may have ramifications that are crucial to the entire nation. Thus, while "courts of law" should not be expected to decide a high percentage of cases involving Negro and white litigants in favor of the Negro, the Supreme Court, hearing, with few exceptions, only those Negro-white cases involving crucial constitutional questions of justice and deprivation of civil rights, may justifiably be expected to decide much more frequently in favor of the Negro, so long as settled rules operate to perpetuate a system of racial injustice.

I know of no studies that provide any direct empirical evidence on this question. Without exception, every statement that I make here is based on nothing more substantial than intuition.

Question 3

Whether legal realists should keep the truth to themselves or should allow it to reach the public depends on the extent to which the public is disabused of the notion that it is unwarranted for the Supreme Court to decide cases even partially on the basis of extralegal considerations. There need be, therefore, no conscious suppression of the views associated with "legal realism," provided only that care be taken that revelations of the political aspects of the work of courts, and particularly the Supreme Court, be accompanied with at least implicit assurances that the law-making function of the judges is entirely proper and, in fact, utterly indispensable, that considerations in constitutional cases are different from those in ordinary litigation, demanding a correspondingly different judicial response, and that nothing in this judicial activity necessarily detracts from the dignity of the law. In this light, there is perhaps more danger to be apprehended from the stubborn denial that courts perform a political function than from the chance that the word will get out to the uninitiated. As Martin Shapiro put it in a brief but cogent argument against the preservation of the "declaratory theory" [*Stability and Change in Judicial Decision-Making: Incrementalism or Stare Decisis?*, 2 Law in Transition Q. 134-136 (1965)]: "[I]f scholars continue to state that courts are not political, the consequences are going to be worse for the courts than from freely admitting that they are . . . . The present situation is one in which the public knows the courts are political, but thinks that they should not be, need not be, and are currently in a state of aberration from their normal condition of apoliticism." One of the weaknesses in Mishkin's argument, which was much more exaggerated in the preceding Foreword to Harvard's annual survey by Philip Kurland, was its expressed resentment over the claim of political scientists that constitutional law is within the scope of their discipline. My answer to Kurland's contemptuous remark that he is not yet ready to turn constitutional law over to the political scientists is simply that, as a political scientist, I am not yet ready to turn the field over to lawyers, certainly not to lawyers who would deny the Supreme Court any legitimate political role. The Supreme Court is a branch of the national government, and, as such, it shares part of the responsibility for governing. It is entitled to be judged by the people on the basis of how well it fulfills that responsibility, not on the basis of how little it makes law.

The ideal expressed in the phrase, "government of laws, and not of men," is a meaningful and useful standard for judging the legal order. It loses its meaning, however, if it is read literally. Laws exist, at best, in the form of words, and words cannot govern. Only men, interpreting the words, can perform that function. What the ideal instead repudiates is arbitrariness—the kind of arbitrariness that Frankfurter spoke of when he declared in his *Terminiello* [*v. Chicago*, 337 U.S. 1, 11 (1949)] dissent: "We do not sit like a kadi under a tree dispensing justice according to considerations of individual expediency." To state that law is political is not to assert that it may be based on whim or caprice, or judicial will, or individual expediency. The public may properly demand that law be based on reason, but reason is not limited to the application of precedent. It was neither arbitrariness nor lack of reason that led the Court to discard *Plessy v. Ferguson* [163 U.S. 537 (1896)] or *Colegrove v. Green* [329 U.S. 549 (1946)], for example, and it is neither arbitrariness nor lack of reason that causes the Court to be influenced by questions of public policy. Of course, briefs could not be written on the premise that judicial decisions will be arbitrary, but there is a great amount of room between the Blackstonian theory and simple arbitrariness, and it is far from impossible that "a government of laws" can be well served by a politically sensitive judiciary.

Professor Dean Alfange, Jr.
Department of Government and Law
Lafayette College

VI

Question 1

Since the Supreme Court deals in such significant measure with the ordinary political conversation of the people, it is small wonder that in the press and in the popular imagination it has a firmer place than that of "private law" courts. But I think that the high esteem the Court enjoys is a precarious status. Should it step on too popular a toe, the esteem will be soon dissipated. Nevertheless, and this is what makes the Court remarkable, even those who may be opposed to its results will sometimes come to its aid because they are awed by its vestigial function as the only Olympus in American life; *e.g.*, defense of the Court by Walter Craig of the American Bar Association during the Goldwater campaign, the defense by some New Dealish groups of the Court in the court-packing battle.

Question 2

I don't think it would hurt the Court in the slightest if people generally adhered to the beliefs of the "legal realists" because the legal realists didn't believe anything except that judges didn't believe what they said. I think alienation and non-commitment are such majoritarian attitudes in our national life that emphasis on the fact that judges are motivated by extra-legal factors would, in the final analysis, not really startle anybody. The layman doesn't care what courts do but only what they decide. That what they decide is not inevitably compelled is not widely known but I think it should be.

As in so many areas, that which everybody knows has not yet been reduced to empirical monotony. I daresay it soon will be. I for one am hardly inclined to await passionately the day when social scientists publish answers, the nature of which has usually been suggested by the questions. The real need for empirical research is not to find out flabbly facts as to what people think about the Court, contingent as that must necessarily be, but to do some serious thinking on how we can give the rich yield of social science data we now possess to the Supreme Court and its bar so that it will be usable and meaningful.

Question 3

This question is impossible to answer since there is no such thing as a "public." There are various elites with their various concerns and to the extent that they are affected by the Court they are well aware of its workings.

Thurman Arnold is quite right. The trouble with extra-legal materials as an essential confessed element in Supreme Court adjudication is that they simply do not cohere within the existing structure of the Court. See the discussion about the use of social science materials in the *School Segregation Cases*. If the frankest possible aware of the character of the Court as a political institution is sought, then the frankest re-thinking of the inutility of the adversary process must be engaged in. If politics, economics, psychology and other arts are the real living juices of the Court's work then perhaps non-lawyers should argue the cases before the court. Indeed, perhaps the adversary process should be abandoned. If one is not ready to abandon it, as I am not, then I think one should not expect lawyers to jump too far out of their legal skins. At least if one expects it, one is bound to be disappointed.

Jerome A. Barron
Associate Professor of Law
George Washington University Law School

VII

Question 1

I would say that the basis of the high esteem in which the Supreme Court is held by the general American public is compounded of several factors: (a) the public need for a firm, central "father-image," which in our form of government is divided between the President, the Court and certain Senators; (b) the mystery surrounding the Court— mystery in the sense that the general public cannot and will not understand its opinions and functions; (c) the constant repetition in text books and newspapers of the glamour of the Court—the pictures of the nine robed Justices, the publicity attending certain Justices from time to time, the reiterations of the fact that they are at the apex of our judicial system, etc., etc. All of these factors combine to make the Court an integral part of our folklore of secular infallibility that is seemingly essential to a stable form of government. State courts and trial courts are too localized, too fragmented, and too close to the people to share in this public esteem.

Question 2

I don't think the Court as an institution is either aided or harmed by the public's "adherence" to any particular legal beliefs, realist or otherwise. It is a mirage to say that the general public has any discernible comprehension of the beliefs of the legal realists or of the judicial restraint school. The public thinks of and reacts to the Court in gross political terms, usually of awe or of derision. To the extent that it is possible to guess, I would imagine those terms are more of a "realist" nature but I can't escape feeling that the beliefs of the legal realists are beyond the pale of public comprehension. I know of no empirical studies of this nature, however.

Question 3

I firmly believe there is no valid basis for keeping from the public any view of the judicial process, including the legal realistic view. Every view is entitled to public airing; and the more that is written about the ways of Supreme Court adjudication the better. But the nature of this subject is such that only a tiny fraction of the public, in addition to the intellectually sophisticated, will ever read or be influenced by such revelations. To get to the public, such revelations must appear in newspapers or popular periodicals like Reader's Digest or Life. But the numbers of people who actually read and absorb material in such popular form are infinitesimally small. They are so few, in fact, that I can see no real purpose served in discussing whether the public should be made aware of the legal realist view. That view is so sophisticated that it will continue to be confined for the most part to intellectual or legal circles, with occasional but not too significant public airings.

In conclusion I would say that, to the extent there is meaningful public revelation of the legal realist viewpoint, the Court will not suffer in public esteem. The legal realist concept is much nearer than any other to the actual operation of the Court and indeed is more consistent with a public understanding of the Court's functions. The public myth of the Court as an Olympian tribunal may remain, but the myth is made more meaningful once it is understood that the Court actually moves in political and practical paths.

Eugene Gressman
Attorney-at-Law

VIII

Question 1

The Supreme Court is venerated because it is the apex, the pinnacle.

It is elementary psychology, it seems to me, that Americans always admire and praise anything that is the best of its kind, or the topmost of its kind, even if it isn't very good. Thus H. L. Mencken tells us (with his remarkable insight and inimitable style),

> Here, as always, the worshipper is the father of the gods, and no less when they are evil than when they are benign. The inferior man must find himself superiors, that he may marvel at his political equality with them, and in the absence of recognizable superiors *de facto* he creates them *de jure*.

And so the godship of the Court is fathered by the public that they may marvel— no less if the Court is evil than if it is benign.

Clearly the same kind of psychology obtains with other public officials of all sorts and levels. Public opinion polls are often published in which people are asked what occupation they regard as most prestigious; the answer is always "Justice of the Supreme Court"—not of some lower court. But the element of "I know the great man and I'm just as good as he is" extends to all levels of officialdom. Today I was at lunch with a retired Judge of the Superior Court. All of the waiters wanted to reach across the counter and shake hands with him, and say "Hello, *Your Honor*," and got great and genuine pleasure from doing so. Seated next to us was the manager of the main office of a large bank. The waiters all addressed him by name, but paid no further attention to him. He probably makes four times as much money as the judge ever got as judge, and wields forty times as much power as the judge ever had.

Question 2

As usual, I go back to Holmes.

The question is, do judges really have power to legislate only interstitially—are they confined from molar to molecular motion?

I submit not; at least that they have not so confined themselves in recent years.

The turning-point came, I think, when the court, walking on eggs in the School Segregation Cases, found that its public image was such that it *could* get away with revolutionary changes in the doctrines. The success that it had in that field must have encouraged it mightily to take the other revolutionary changes in the areas of criminal-law enforcement and reapportionment. Obviously they have been successful in those areas too in obtaining public acceptance and legislative-judicial enforcement of doctrines that are law only because nine men, or a majority of them, think they are right. I think Douglas in his WE, THE JUDGES [(1956)] quoted somebody as saying, "Power is a heady thing, my boy." And so it is.

Obviously, then, if the general public—and especially minor public functionaries (I am thinking particularly of state legislators)—felt that they could get across to the general public the ideas of the legal realists (that the Emperor has not got any clothes on) then the Court as an institution would be immeasurably harmed in the sense that its power would be much curtailed. If the fiat of the Court were to be critically examined for its public acceptability, then the Court would not be nearly so powerful as it is.

Moreover, the Court's public image is sustained and fostered each time it has one of the successes such as it had in the areas of school segregation, criminal-law enforcement, and reapportionment. Success begets success; more power begets more power.

This makes the Court much more able *and much more willing* to legislate in other areas that are not so "important" legally—because they do not involve constitutional questions—but may be much more important practically and economically. I speak of the rewriting of statutes, especially regulatory and economic statutes. Theoretically, "If Congress does not like our legislation, it can repeal it—as it has done a number of times in the past." (Jackson, J., concurring in *United States v. PUC*, 345 U.S. 295, 320-21 (1953)). But does this not become immeasurably more difficult for Congress to do when the public image of the Court is such that a Congressman who votes to overrule the Court—even when the Court has trodden on an area which constitutionally belongs to Congress—will inevitably be charged with sacrilege? (Compare Senator Dirksen on school prayer.)

Question 3

It seems to me that the "legal realist" view of the judicial process is unquestionably valid, but there is no way ever to make it known to the public, even if you wanted to. It is not a question of revealing to the public something which is known to an intellectual elite. It is a question of ever getting the public to see the obvious. Mencken concludes the article quoted above by saying,

> The one permanent emotion of the inferior man, as of all the simpler mammals, is fear—fear of the unknown, the complex, the inexplicable. What he wants beyond everything else is security. His instincts incline him toward a society so organized that it will protect him at all hazards, and not only against perils to his hide but also against assaults upon his mind—against the need to grapple with unaccustomed problems, to weigh ideas, to think things out for himself, to scrutinize the platitudes upon which his everyday thinking is based.

People will applaud Willie Mays every time he hits another home run, and they will continue to venerate the Supreme Court, regardless of what you try to teach them. Both are part of the national mystique. The Supreme Court, Jackie Kennedy, movie stars, and champion athletes, will be in the same position in the minds of the public until you and I are dust, and longer. I should add astronauts.

Arnold is of course quite mistaken, and there are plenty of legal realists around who write briefs on quite a different basis. A lot of them are in the Solicitor General's office and they write briefs every day on the premise that this is a government of men and not of laws. They sometimes invite the Court to make new law on the basis of a newspaper article. (I can give an example or two if desired.)

I haven't any idea what a survey of Solicitor General's briefs would show; but I suspect that the quickest way to debunk Arnold's statement would be to review all of the briefs filed in one term by the Solicitor's office, or even review all of the briefs filed in two or three terms by Arnold's firm. An even quicker, although perhaps not so convincing, way would be simply to go to Stern & Gressman (both of whom are ex-functionaries of the Solicitor General's office) and read in there [STERN & GRESSMAN, SUPREME COURT PRACTICE (1950)] that argument in the Supreme Court is different from argument elsewhere.

Illustrations of the truth of—and the lack of complete insight in—the quotation in Mishkin's footnote 25 [Mishkin, *The Supreme Court, 1964 Term,* 79 HARV. L. REV. 56, 62 n.25 (1965)] . . . are within everybody's experience. Many a disappointed litigant has accused the *particular judge* of venality or dishonesty or stupidity, and many a one has announced, "I'll take the case to the Supreme Court of the United States." None has ever announced—except Senator Dirksen—that he would take the case from the Supreme Court to the people.

And so it is quite true to say that "to the 'ipse dixit' of a court, however just or impartial, men are not so constituted as to afford the same ready obedience and respect," but the problem is that every man is ready to believe that he has been subjected to the ipse dixit of a trial court, but they always think that the Supreme Court is infallible because it is final, and therefore "willingly acquiesce." (Not so, of course, some of the sophisticated "instituitonal litigants" referred to by Mishkin; but to them, Congress is available, as in the bank merger act.

Anonymous
Attorney-at-Law

PART TWO

> Government is not a machine, but a living thing. It falls, not un-
> der the theory of the universe, but under the theory of organic
> life. It is accountable to Darwin, not to Newton. It is modified
> by its environment, necessitated by its tasks, shaped to its functions
> by the sheer pressure of life. . . . Living political constitutions
> must be Darwinian in structure and practice.
>
> —Woodrow Wilson‡

INTRODUCTION

IN Part One of this article,[1] three hypotheses which, of necessity,
were unsupported by empirical foundation,[2] were tentatively advanced in an attempt to suggest some ways of thinking about the
institutional position of the United States Supreme Court.[3] It was
noted that *a priori* assertions about the Court and its power are
wholly inadequate and that scholarship must go beyond the confines
of judicial opinions if a full understanding of America's peculiar

---

‡ WILSON, CONSTITUTIONAL GOVERNMENT IN THE UNITED STATES 56-57 (1908).

[1] Miller & Scheflin, *The Power of the Supreme Court in the Age of the Positive
State: A Preliminary Excursus* (pt. 1), 1967 DUKE L.J. 273.

[2] A modest survey of students of the Supreme Court revealed that no studies developing the necessary empirical data were known to exist. See *id.* at 301-20 (Appendix).

[3] The hypotheses are as follows: (1) The prestige of the Supreme Court has little
or nothing to do with its symbolic role, but rather with what it does (*id.* at 281-83);
(2) The Supreme Court has power to the extent that it articulates deep-set values
(preferences) of the American people (*id.* at 283-88); and (3) The Supreme Court has
power to the extent to which the avowedly political branches of government affirmatively respond to the norm announced by the Court (*id.* at 288-94).

contribution to the science of government is to be developed. In short, a sociology of constitutional adjudication is needed.

In this part of the article, attention is directed to three propositions concerning the need for the Supreme Court to adapt itself to the exigencies of changing reality if it is to retain (or regain) whatever power it has (or may have had). While these propositions are not intended to follow from the prior hypotheses as a matter of inexorable logic, they are related to and are not inconsistent with what has been said before. Taken together, with the reminder that much more factual data is required, they indicate the need for adaptation to the demands brought on by a rapidly changing society.[4] The propositions hereinafter discussed include the following: (1) Outward or ostensible adherence to the declaratory theory of law is not necessary for the integrity and continuing viability of the constitutional adjudicatory process; (2) The adversary system is not adequate to the needs of the Court; and (3) The Court in the years ahead must direct itself to the problems of a changing social milieu.

A First Proposition

The first proposition may be stated as follows: *Adherence to the declaratory theory of law is probably not necessary for the integrity and viability of the constitutional adjudicatory process.* We say "probably" because we know of no hard "evidence" to validate or invalidate the statement. However, the assertion seems to be a fair conclusion deducible from the flow of Supreme Court decisions in recent decades and bolstered by the observation that at those times when the Court has ostensibly adhered to the declaratory theory (for example, during the early years of the New Deal) its position has been threatened.[5] Moreover, if as Professors Mishkin and Morris maintain in *On Law in Courts,*[6] the declaratory theory is dead, some

---

[4] Change is built into the American social structure. *Compare* LAPP, THE NEW PRIESTHOOD: THE SCIENTIFIC ELITE AND THE USE OF POWER (1965), *with* PRICE, THE SCIENTIFIC ESTATE (1965), 1966 DUKE L.J. 622. See Miller, *Notes on the Concept of the "Living" Constitution,* 31 GEO. WASH. L. REV. 881 (1963), and Miller, *Technology, Social Change, and the Constitution,* 33 GEO. WASH. L. REV. 17 (1964), for discussions of the factor of change as it relates to the Constitution.

[5] See, *e.g.,* United States v. Butler, 297 U.S. 1 (1936). *Butler* and similar cases invalidating New Deal legislation led to the Court packing plan of 1937.

[6] MISHKIN & MORRIS, ON LAW IN COURTS 57 (1965). The roots of the declaratory theory can be traced back to Flaundres and Wife v. Rycheman, Y. B. Hill. 18 & 19 Edw. 3, pl. 3 (1344-45), in PIKE, YEAR BOOKS OF THE REIGN OF KING EDWARD III, YEARS 18 AND 19, at 374, 378 (1905), in which a lawyer argued "I think you will do as others

additional support for the above proposition is available. As Professor Wolfgang Friedmann has asserted, "The Blackstonian doctrine of the 'declaratory' function of the courts, holding that the duty of the court is not to 'pronounce a new law but to maintain and expound the old one,' has long been little more than a ghost."[7] The decline of the declaratory theory permits attention to be diverted "from the stale controversy over whether judges make law to the much more complex and controversial question of the limits of judicial lawmaking."[8]

Nevertheless, it is evident that the declaratory theory continues to obscure legal scholarship by providing the standard by which judicial decisions are often evaluated. The reasoning of judges, which has long fascinated lawyers and students of the judiciary, has been the subject of numberless written comments. Most of what is printed in legal periodicals today, for example, may be said to consist of efforts to analyze the manner in which judges reach decisions. Very often, the net conclusion of such writings is that the judge reached the correct result but for the wrong reasons.[9] The author then proceeds to set forth what seem to him to be better reasons. This is exegesis upon judicial texts, casuistry about what judges say are their reasons for decisions. Lawyers, particularly law professors who follow the Supreme Court, seize upon the newly issued opinions of that tribunal and then, in heavily footnoted scholarly disputations, gnaw over what the Justices say. The commentators are apparently more interested in the *method* than the *result*. Not so the layman, who either for reasons of indifference or because of innate canniness apparently ignores the opinions and looks to the results.

Similarly, the usual law school casebook or textbook makes little or no reference to the "policy" aspects of legal decisions or the lawmaking proclivities of judges. Witness also the activities of the American Law Institute which purports to "restate" legal doctrine in a series of black-letter propositions, presumably to aid judges in

---

have done in the same case, or else we do not know what the law is." Judge Hillary answered, "It is the will of the Justice" but Chief Justice Stonore broke in and said, "No; law is that which is right." See also Linkletter v. Walker, 381 U.S. 618, 623 n.7 (1965).

[7] Friedmann, *Limits of Judicial Lawmaking and Prospective Overruling*, 29 MODERN L. REV. 593 (1966).

[8] *Id.* at 595.

[9] Illustrations are legion. For a recent example, see Horowitz & Karst, *The Proposition Fourteen Cases: Justice in Search of a Justification*, 14 U.C.L.A.L. REV. 37 (1966).

finding and declaring the law à la Blackstone. While it is, as Professor Friedmann asserts,[10] an exercise in sterility to debate the question of judicial creativity, an explanation of the operation and basis of the declaratory theory is necessary to round out the development of this article.

According to Blackstone, the judge is "sworn to determine, not according to his own private judgment, but according to the known laws and customs of the land; not delegated to pronounce a new law, but to maintain and expound the old one."[11] Only in this way, according to the theory, can the litigants, and society at large, be assured that the same acts will be treated the same way and that, in essence, reliance may be placed on law.[12] If law is to be a guiding principle in society and the matrix within which the affairs of men may be legitimately conducted, it must be obeyed, and "to be obeyed or followed, must be known; to be known it must be fixed; to be fixed, what is decided today must be followed tomorrow."[13] The declaratory theory posits the principle of *stare decisis* as the only effective means for maintaining stability in the legal system, protecting reliance, and checking judicial caprice by restricting the limits within which the judge may operate.

The declaratory theory also is said to serve another useful function. Professor Mishkin has stated that, as a symbolic expression of the judicial process, it accounts in large measure for the prestige of the courts. There is, he asserts, a "strongly held and deeply felt belief that judges are bound by a body of fixed, overriding law, that they apply that law impersonally as well as impartially, that they exercise no individual choice and have no program of their own to advance."[14] However, whatever role the symbolic conception plays

---

[10] Friedmann, *supra* note 7, at 595.

[11] 1 BLACKSTONE, COMMENTARIES *69. Compare BACON, OF JUDICATURE: "Judges ought to remember, that their office is *jus dicere*, and not *jus dare*; to interpret law, and not to make law, or give law. Else will it be like the authority, claimed by the Church of Rome, which under pretext of exposition of Scripture, doth not stick to add or alter; and to pronounce that which they do not find; and by show of antiquity, to introduce novelty."

[12] This position appears to be the main thrust of Professor Lon Fullers' eight principles of legality. See FULLER, THE MORALITY OF LAW 33-39 (1964).

[13] Kaufman, *A Defense of Stare Decisis*, 10 HASTINGS L.J. 283, 284 (1959).

[14] Mishkin, *The High Court, The Great Writ, and the Due Process of Time and Law*, 79 HARV. L. REV. 56, 62 (1965). For another criticism of Professor Mishkin's article, see Schwartz, *Retroactivity, Reliability, and Due Process: A Reply to Professor Mishkin*, 33 U. CHI. L. REV. 719 (1966).

Thurman Arnold maintains that "the ideal of a government of laws rather than

in the relationship between the public and the law as announced in courts, surely there is a negative side to it. Even if it could be demonstrated that the symbol is valuable, it obviously conceals truth. Merely by being a symbol, it necessarily obscures the real foundation of what is symbolized. Nevertheless, Professor Mishkin maintains that if the declaratory theory "be in part myth, it is a myth by which we live and which can be sacrificed only at substantial cost."[15] While acknowledging that the truth behind the symbol ought not be obscured to anyone wishing to learn and taking the trouble to understand, he goes on to say:

> At the same time, I see no affirmative virtue in the destruction of essentially sound and valuable symbols in order to promulgate a part of a more sophisticated—and indeed over-all more accurate—general view. Such partial truths do not necessarily represent a gain in wisdom over the more elementary general view, and the destruction of the symbol does involve real loss. Though I know that judges are human and quite distinct individuals, I am not in favor of their doffing their robes, for I think there is value in stressing, for themselves and for others, the quite real striving for an impartiality I know can never be fully achieved.[16]

The trouble with this position is multiple. First, it assumes that truth about the judiciary (whatever it may be) can be kept from the people at large. As education spreads and as the mass media reach into every home, that assumption is dubious at best. Second, where does an elite, however defined, acquire its warrant or license to keep the truth from others?[17] Third, it is difficult to grasp what "real

---

men is a necessary one. Briefs could not be written before a court on any other premise. This very simple ideal is essential to the public acceptance of our judicial system and to all steps in the judicial process." Letter from Thurman Arnold to Arthur S. Miller, March 23, 1966 (quoted with permission). However, briefs could not be written before an appellate court on any other premise than that the law is sufficiently uncertain to permit opposing arguments. See Miller, *On the Choice of Major Premises in Supreme Court Opinions*, 14 J. PUB. L. 251 (1965).

[15] Mishkin, *supra* note 14.

[16] *Id.* at 63 n.29.

[17] For, "in the long run . . . any government institution must rest upon a full understanding of its function and operations by the public; . . . concealment, deception or ignorance weakens and eventually will destroy an institution." Letter From Professor Thomas Emerson of the Yale Law School to Arthur S. Miller, May 12, 1966 (used by permission).

An unexplored area of constitutional concern is the meaning for the first amendment's freedoms of expression, as well as the meaning for democratic government generally, of a government which "manages" news, pursues secrecy policies, at times is not candid, and otherwise pollutes the stream of information to the people. The

loss" would occur if the truth were known about the judicial process. To call it a loss is to fall into the Holmesian fallacy of looking at the law solely through the eyes of the "bad man."[18] Law, if it means anything, must mean more than the workings of the judicial process.[19] One must visualize the social role of law in the myriad of day-to-day transactions of people, rather than in those disputes which are sent to lawyers or which end in judicial decision.[20] Fourth, to our knowledge no one has suggested that judges doff their robes. Candor does not require that pomp and ceremony be eliminated or that the awesome dignity of the Court be discarded. We cheerfully concede that there is some value in the outward trappings of courts.[21] Fifth, again we know of no one who has ever suggested or implied that judges should not strive for "impartiality." But is that effort to achieve what Frankfurter called "an invincible disinterestedness"[22] to be attained by adherence to the declaratory theory? We think not. Moreover, the connection which impartiality has with the alleged need for adhering to the declaratory theory is not self-evident.[23] Sixth, the perpetuation of error at the expense of truth is dangerous because the error may be forgotten as error and believed

---

"market place" theory of truth becomes at least shaky, if not repudiated. See, *e.g.*, Dennis v. United States, 341 U.S. 494, 503-05 (1952); Abrams v. United States, 250 U.S. 616, 630-31 (1919) (Holmes, J., dissenting).

[18] Holmes, *The Path of the Law*, 10 HARV. L. REV. 457, 459 (1897).

[19] See HART, THE CONCEPT OF LAW *passim* (1961), for an exposition of the "good man" theory.

[20] See Miller, *A Note on the Criticism of Supreme Court Opinions*, 10 J. PUB. L. 139 (1961).

[21] It is not at all clear why the Supreme Court enjoys prestige as a result of the rituals or myths which surround it. The prestige may derive from the mystery of the Tribunal. *Cf.* Reston, *The Mysterious Ways of Lyndon Johnson*, N.Y. Times, Aug. 21, 1964, p. 28, col. 3 (quoting President Charles de Gaulle): "There can be no prestige without mystery. . . . In the designs, the demeanor, and the mental operations of a leader, there must always be a 'something' which others cannot altogether fathom, which puzzles them, stirs them, and rivets their attention."

The Court may also satisfy the psychological needs of persons. See FRANK, LAW AND THE MODERN MIND 243-52 (1931).

[22] Frankfurter, *John Marshall and the Judicial Function*, in GOVERNMENT UNDER LAW 6, 21 (Sutherland ed. 1956).

[23] Frankfurter seemed to say as much in his well-known majority opinion in Rochin v. California, 342 U.S. 165 (1952): "We may not draw on our merely personal and private notions and disregard the limits that bind judges in their judicial function." *Id.* at 170. "To practice the requisite detachment and to achieve sufficient objectivity no doubt demands of judges the habit of self-discipline and self-criticism, incertitude that one's own views are incontestable and alert tolerance toward views not shared." *Id.* at 171. "[T]hese are precisely the presuppositions of our judicial process. They are precisely the qualities society has a right to expect from those entrusted with ultimate judicial power." *Id.* at 172.

as truth; fictions have a way of becoming pernicious. Deliberate obfuscation will ultimately destroy; planned obscurantism by an intellectual elite cannot be justified. Finally, it may well be that the truth, however much it is hidden, will out, sooner or later; and it is better for the revelation to occur sooner so that conscious efforts to deal with it may be undertaken.

The declaratory theory rests upon at least two erroneous premises. The first and most obvious fallacy is the assumption that the law is not a creation of men but rather exists as some form of Platonic Idea.[24] The second, and perhaps more crucial, error upon which the theory is based is the assumption that the judicial process operates at an ideal level. This premise, however, is simply not true.[25]

In addition to resting upon two erroneous premises, the declaratory theory is also subject to attack upon another ground. There exists today the very real and very perplexing problem of the proliferation of precedents.[26] The geometric progression of reported cases, estimated at over 100,000 pages of reported judgments or 70 million words per year issuing from state courts of last resort and federal courts,[27] has the effect of making it possible to find case support for almost any theory or argument. *Stare decisis* loses meaning when alternate lines of authority exist in opposition to each other; the force of a guiding criterion is no longer available.[28] It is only when one line of authority exists, which is seldom in fact true, that *stare decisis* is operative because only then does it provide a criterion for decision.[29] What is really at stake is the nature of the adversary system itself. But in a more limited fashion, the prolifera-

---

[24] See Cooperrider, *The Rule of Law and the Judicial Process*, 59 MICH. L. REV. 501, 507 (1961).

[25] See Breitel, *Ethical Problems in the Performance of the Judicial Function*, in CONFERENCE ON JUDICIAL ETHICS 64, 67-68 (University of Chicago Conference Series No. 19, 1965): "[The adversary system] . . . with the altogether proper commitment of the lawyer to his client and his client's cause, all but absolute, is not exactly akin to the asceptic techniques of the laboratory . . . . The popular notion that judges are mere declarers of what is in the books, all laid down clearly and simply, is not confined to the laity. It obtains too with large segments of the bar. And judges still believe it."

[26] See Gilmore, *Legal Realism: Its Cause and Cure*, 70 YALE L.J. 1037, 1041 (1961).

[27] STONE, LEGAL SYSTEM AND LAWYERS' REASONINGS 13 (1964).

[28] This phenomenon has been called the "principle of doctrinal polarity." Miller, *A Note on the Criticism of Supreme Court Opinions*, 10 J. PUB. L. 139, 144 (1961). With several lines of authority the doctrine becomes multipolar.

[29] It is the choice between *conflicting* doctrinal principles that makes any decision creative. See Schaefer, *Precedent and Policy*, 34 U. CHI. L. REV. 3, 4 (1966).

tion of precedents weakens the declaratory theory by making the doctrine of *stare decisis,* which is its backbone, impracticable.

With such serious defects, it might be wondered how the declaratory theory has attained acceptance, both within the profession and with certain segments of the laity. Part of the reason is that it neatly fits into the mainstream of western thought epitomized in Newtonian mechanics and Cartesian philosophy. The declaratory theory has an illusion of certainty, a mechanical appeal that is almost mathematical. The classic treatment of legal reasoning bears out this thesis. It is commonly believed that legal thinking is a deductive-analogistic process in which prior cases are related by analogy to the case at hand and conclusions deduced therefrom.[30] But if this is true, what does the lawyer argue when the precedents are clearly against him? How does he argue policy? How does he present statistics to the court? Indeed, it is at this point that one may rightfully ask: "How can courts, supposedly by logical deduction from non-contemporaneous legal propositions, and without entering upon social and ethical inquiries, reach conclusions so well adapted (on the whole) to contemporary problems?"[31] Julius Stone finds the answer by a thorough examination of what he calls "the categories of illusory reference" which, in the process of legal reasoning, "serve as devices permitting a secret and even unconscious exercise by courts of what in the ultimate analysis is a creative choice."[32] By thus attacking the logical form of the traditional doctrine of legal reasoning, Stone manages to show that there cannot be, in effect, strict deductive reasoning in law. This circumstance forces the judge to base his decision on other considerations, such as public policy and statistical facts, though he may not want to do this.[33] It is this inherent problem in the judicial process that may in large

---

[30] Dean Levi categorizes legal reasoning as a three-step process "described by the doctrine of precedent in which a proposition descriptive of the first case is made into a rule of law and then applied to a next similar situation. The steps are these: similarity is seen between cases; next the rule of law inherent in the first case is announced; then the rule of law is made applicable to the second case." LEVI, AN INTRODUCTION TO LEGAL REASONING 2 (1949). Reasoning, thus, is by example or analogy. See generally Schaefer, *supra* note 29.

[31] STONE, *op. cit. supra* note 27, at 240.

[32] *Id.* at 241.

[33] As Holmes pointed out, "perhaps one of the reasons why judges do not like to discuss questions of policy, or to put a decision in terms upon their views as lawmakers, is that the moment you leave the path of merely logical deduction you lose the illusion of certainty which makes legal reasoning seem like mathematics." Holmes, *Privilege, Malice, and Intent,* 8 HARV. L. REV. 1, 7 (1894).

measure be responsible for the continued acceptance of the declaratory theory.

A better explanation of the nature of legal reasoning has been offered by philosopher John Wisdom. Directing himself to the case where there are no issues of fact in dispute, he observes that

> in such cases we notice that the process of argument is not a *chain* of demonstrative reasoning. It is a presenting and representing of those features of the case which *severally co-operate* in favour of the conclusion, in favour of saying what the reasoner wishes said, in favour of calling the situation by the name by which he wishes to call it. The reasons are like the legs of a chair, not the links of a chain. Consequently although the discussion is *a priori* and the steps are not a matter of experience, the procedure resembles scientific argument in that the reasoning is not *vertically* extensive but *horizontally* extensive—it is a matter of the cumulative effect of several independent premises, not of the repeated transformation of one or two.[34]

Wisdom's analysis is helpful to explain the weight of the many factors involved in a decision, and his metaphor of the "legs of a chair" provides a scheme for graphically demonstrating the force of each competing interest in a legal problem or litigation. The prevalent notion of the process of legal reasoning is only a half-truth; it represents only one of the "legs of a chair." Thus, one leg is reliance upon rules of law, another is the possible unsettling effect of new rules of law, a third is the precedents, a fourth is the policy arguments, and so forth. The point is that the nature of legal reasoning, while giving the appearance of being mathematical and syllogistic, is more intricate and less certain than is normally conceived. In addition, it is *sui generis*. Reasoning in law, just as reasoning in morals, suffers from a comparison to, or equation with, either deductive or inductive logic.[35] The myth of mechanistic (declaratory) reasoning clouds a clearer picture of the actual process. A discarding of this myth would prompt the bench and the bar openly to concede and thus more effectively to realize that there are other, and more important, matters to argue before a court than the precedents; and at least there should be several matters argued

---

[34] Wisdom, *Gods,* in PROCEEDINGS OF THE ARISTOTELIAN SOCIETY 185, 194 (1945), reprinted in FLEW, LOGIC AND LANGUAGE 194, 203 (1965).

[35] See HARE, THE LANGUAGE OF MORALS (1952); TOULMIN, REASON IN ETHICS 67-85 (1950). See generally Gottlieb, The Logic of Choice: An Inquiry into the Logic of Judicial Argument, 1961 (unpublished thesis in Harvard Law School Library).

and not *merely* the precedents. Furthermore, the flow of information to a court, as well as its institutional makeup, might be recognized to be in need of re-examination and change.

The cogency of the declaratory theory also rests upon misconstruction of its antithesis. Why should judges be limited in their function to merely "finding" a pre-existing law? What danger is there in allowing a judge to "create" law?[36] The declaratory theory rests in part upon a *reductio ad absurdum* argument which runs as follows: if we allow judges to do more than find the law, we shall be inviting judicial caprice with the result that similar cases will not be decided similarly; the symmetry of the law will be destroyed; personal feelings of the judge rather than law will govern; reliance upon law will become an impossibility. In other words, the only alternative to the declaratory theory is no acceptable system at all, so the theory must be correct, or at least the only one feasible. This conclusion, however, is a *non sequitur*. The alternative to the declaratory theory is not necessarily judicial caprice but rather a restricted from of recognized judicial creativity. To assert that the role of the judge is broader than merely finding the law is not to say that the judge will be entirely free to follow his own predilections. The fallacy involved here is the "all-or-nothing mistake" which assumes "a naked dichotomy where no such simplification is warranted."[37]

Once it is recognized that the rejection of the declaratory theory does not mean the adoption of judicial caprice, a weighty argument for retention of the theory is dissipated. That theory, by postulating a straw enemy, became the answer to what appeared to be a very serious problem: if one did not accept the theory, judges would be uncontrolled and uncontrollable. The only solution was to prevent the subjective element from entering into the decisional process, either in the form of personal bias or innovative ability. This position, carried to its necessary conclusion, would require removing judges and replacing them with logicians since the really important

---

[36] Before the rise of legislatures and codification, which came in the nineteenth century, most law was created by judges. See Wyzanski, *History and Law*, 26 U. CHI. L. REV. 237, 240-42 (1959). In recent years, the notion has spread that only legislatures can "make" law, but the notion is false. Not only courts, but executives and administrators, make law—and at an increasing rate. Even private organizations participate directly in the law making process. *Compare* TRUMAN, THE GOVERNMENTAL PROCESS (1951) *with* McCONNELL, PRIVATE POWER AND AMERICAN DEMOCRACY (1966).

[37] See FEARNSIDE & HOLTHER, FALLACY—THE COUNTERFEIT OF ARGUMENT 30 (1959).

element is the deductive syllogism from the precedents to the instant case.[38] That there is a subjective element in judicial decision-making, and a large one at that, can no longer be doubted.[39] And the unavoidable subjective element in law, coupled with a referential element linking law with society in general, demands a more sophisticated view of the judicial process than the declaratory theory is capable of supplying.

It may be objected that although the alternative to the declaratory theory is not necessarily judicial caprice, nevertheless the door to caprice is opened by removal of the only fetters upon the judges that the legal system imposes. In other words, the declaratory theory may not be completely accurate, but at least it offers a restraint upon judges that is otherwise unavailable. Thus, according to a nineteenth century judge, "Nothing keeps a judge so strictly in the line of his duty, as the feeling and constant realization of the fact, that he is bound by precedents. He knows, that his opinion will be by the legal profession with all its astuteness subjected to the severest criticism, and if he dares to depart on a given question from the well marked line of precedents, either his ability or integrity is in great danger of being impugned."[40] The answer to this assertion is that there are institutional restraints upon the office; the judge is not to act from individual and personal motives but rather he should decide the case according to "law" which may or may not be represented in precedents. It is not a "government of men" to decide outside the doctrine of precedent if it is recognized that "law" means more than precedent and if the case is decided disinterestedly. In an age of legislative and even more of executive dominance, it seems a bit odd to be concerned about "judicial tyranny." The real problem is how to make courts more effective.

Some may object that this discussion is moot since nobody believes in a strict version of the declaratory theory.[41] While few per-

---

[38] See Breitel, *supra* note 23, at 69: "The key numbers in the digests will give you the cases, the black letter in the hornbooks and the Restatements will give you the principles, let the lawyers do the work, and just carry along placidly until the day comes when the computers will make it even easier."

[39] See Miller & Howell, *The Myth of Neutrality in Constitutional Adjudication*, 27 U. CHI. L. REV. 661, 671-83 (1960); Yntema, *The Hornbook Method and the Conflict of Laws*, 37 YALE L.J. 468, 477 (1928).

[40] Clarke & Co. v. Figgins, 27 W. Va. 663, 672 (1886).

[41] *But see* STONE, *op. cit. supra* note 25, at 235. The history of the strict English deference to *stare decisis* is traced in HART & SACKS, THE LEGAL PROCESS: BASIC PROB-

sons accept the theory in full force, such an objection misconceives
the effect of overt removal of the theory, the advantages of which are
varied.   In the first place, removal would give a clearer picture of
how the system operates and thereby make it easier to identify its
deficiencies.   In addition, arguing a case before a judge would be
more purposeful, for the judge and the lawyers would be forced to
see "all" of the legs of the chair, not just some of them.   In each case
the movement of law could be seen as only a part of the larger movement of society.   Moreover, the strained contortions through which
some courts now go to fit a decision into a well-developed line of
authorities could be avoided.[42]   More importantly, however, the
removal of the vestiges of the declaratory theory would provide
a foundation for a different view of the role of the judicial process.
Although these advantages are somewhat less significant with regard
to the Supreme Court, which has tended to be a policy maker on a
grander scale than other courts, nevertheless, it is important to see
that the judicial process, vis-à-vis the other governmental processes
of law making, is basically creative.

However, Professor Mishkin has suggested that public disaffection

---

LEMS IN THE MAKING AND APPLICATION OF LAW 592-95 (Tent. ed. 1958).   Recently,
however, the House of Lords announced that it will no longer consider itself strictly
bound by precedents. See [1966] 1 Weekly L.R. 1234: "Their Lordships regard the use
of precedent as an indispensable foundation upon which to decide what is the law and
its application to individual cases. It provides at least some degree of certainty upon
which individuals can rely in the conduct of their affairs, as well as a basis for orderly
development of legal rules.

"Their Lordships nevertheless recognize that too rigid adherence to precedent may
lead to injustice in a particular case and also unduly restrict the proper development
of the law.   They propose, therefore to modify their present practice and, while
treating former decisions of this House as normally binding, to depart from a previous
decision when it appears right to do so.

"In this connection they will bear in mind the danger of disturbing retrospectively
the basis on which contracts settlements of property, and fiscal arrangements have
been entered into and also the especial need for certainty as to the criminal law."

See Leach, Revisionism in the House of Lords: The Bastion of Rigid Stare Decisis
Falls, 80 HARV. L. REV. 797 (1967). See also Llewellyn, On Warranty of Quality,
and Society, 36 COLUM. L. REV. 699, 737 (1936): "Still, in the main, secret judicial
innovation lends itself lightly to rape which may be unintentional. It is better policy,
though worse manners, for judges to say so, when they change the law. Change it,
to my mind, and by my reading of the books, they not only do, and must, but
should. . . . Still they should see and say what they are doing."

[42] We believe, with Professor Corbin, that "a better brand of justice may be
delivered by a court that is clearly conscious of its own processes, than by one that
states hard-bitten traditional rules and doctrines and then attains an instinctively felt
justice by an avoidance of them that is only half-conscious, accompanied by an extended exegisis worthy of a medieval theologian." 3 CORBIN, CONTRACTS § 561, at 279
(rev. ed. 1960).

would accompany public realization that the United States Supreme Court makes policy.[43]   As Professor R. G. McCloskey has pointed out, and as our modest survey buttresses, the prestige of the Court appears to rest upon factors unrelated to the declaratory theory.[44] The mystique of the Court and the extent to which people agree with the conclusions of Court decisions seem to be far more important to the Court's prestige.[45]   In fact, abandonment of the declaratory theory would enable the Court to articulate more closely the reasons for its decisions and thus provide clearer guides for the people to follow.[46]   Perry Miller has pointed out that at the turn of the nineteenth century there was great antagonism towards the law because it was too sophisticated for the common man who was unable to use it as a guide for his conduct.[47]   With the increased press coverage of the Supreme Court and even lesser tribunals, the public is becoming increasingly aware of the nature and functioning of the judicial process.   Furthermore, public interest has increased as the type of cases with which the Court deals vitally affect every person.   The apportionment cases, the vast area of civil rights and civil liberties, voting rights, and even obscenity, are pervasive enough to draw into their net the concern of the entire community. Using Alexander Pekelis's phrase, the Court has indeed become immersed in the "travail of society,"[48] which means that much more will be demanded of law because the public appears to be expecting much more.

---

[43] Mishkin, *supra* note 13, at 67-70.

[44] McCloskey, *Principles, Powers and Values: The Establishment Clause and the Supreme Court*, in RELIGION AND THE PUBLIC ORDER 3, 29 n.60 (Giannella ed. 1965): "The trouble is that, although we are accustomed to talk loosely about the 'prestige' of the Court, we know very little about its nature or about what causes it to ebb and flow. I would suggest that when we use the term, we usually have two somewhat different things in mind: The pro-judicial opinion that derives from approval of the Court's specific recent policy trends, and the pro-judicial opinion that rests on a belief in the value of the judicial institution, quite apart from the question of how that institution is currently behaving.   Obviously the first variety is less constant and dependable than the second, and it would be useful (though perhaps impossible) for purposes of prediction to know what proportion of the Court's 'prestige' at any given time is to be attributed to each."

[45] See Miller, *Some Pervasive Myths About the United States Supreme Court*, 10 ST. LOUIS U.L.J. 153, 154-56 (1965).

[46] "In a good society bad laws are never happily tolerated, but uncertain law is intolerable."   Wall Street Journal, June 23, 1966, p. 14, col. 1.

[47] MILLER, THE LIFE OF THE MIND IN AMERICA 102-04 (1965).

[48] PEKELIS, *The Case for a Jurisprudence of Welfare*, in LAW AND SOCIAL ACTION 1, 40 (Konvitz ed. 1950).

The core of the problem created by the declaratory theory is reconciling legal change with the notion of certainty. Simply because society is in a period of extremely rapid change, the law cannot stand still; law by and large must reflect the society in which it exists and which it seeks to govern.[49] With change both constant and cataclysmic, there should be little wonder that law moves both legislatively and judicially. The Constitution must, of course, be updated; the responsibility for this function rests largely, although not entirely, with the United States Supreme Court.[50] In its decisions, the Court necessarily must be forward-looking, purposive, teleological, immersed in the travail of society. Otherwise it could scarcely serve its constitutional purpose. This does not sit well with those who yearn for an *elegantia juris,* for a Court that operates in accordance with their own preconcevied notions of propriety.[51]

In the final analysis, what is wanted from the Supreme Court are

---

[49] As Professor M. S. McDougal points out, we are not concerned with a "mere body of rules but with a whole process of decision, and a process of decision making taking place within the context of, and as a response to, a larger community process." McDougal, *Law as a Process of Decision: A Policy-Oriented Approach to Legal Study,* 1 NATURAL L.F. 53, 56 (1956).

[50] The Constitution may be "changed" by any of our instruments of governance. For example, the internal alterations made by the executive and legislative branches work a change in the constitutional order. Similarly, the failure of state governments to assume their responsibilities has contributed heavily to the decline of federalism. In addition, the Constitution can be altered by amendment. Furthermore, long continued usage, as in the rise of political parties, may be said to effect constitutional change.

[51] Those who would restrict the courts to performing exclusively logicians' exercises fail to realize that political theories explain the function of government rather than dictate it. Some statements of Nobel Prize winner in physics, Percy W. Bridgman, seem apposite: "I will not attach as much importance as do apparently a good many professional lawyers to getting all law formulated into a verbally consistent edifice. No one who has been through the experience of modern physics . . . can believe that there can be such an edifice, but it seems to me that nevertheless I can sometimes detect an almost metaphysical belief in the minds of some people in the possibility of such an edifice. If one needs specific details to fortify his conviction that there is no such edifice, plenty can be found. . . . The situation . . . for the lawyer resembles somewhat the general situation for the scientist. We have seen that in the popular view the scientist assumes that nature operates according to certain broad sweeping generalities. This is paraphrased by saying that the scientist must have 'faith' that there are natural laws. We have not accepted this view. It seems to me that a better description of how the scientist operates is to say that he adopts the *program* of finding as much regularity as he can in the operation of nature, without any prior commitment as to how much he will find. So too it seems to me that here the lawyer should and can make no prior commitment about the possibility of erecting a self-contained self-consistent verbal legal edifice, but all that he can strive for is as self-contained and logically consistent an edifice as he can erect." BRIDGMAN, THE WAY THINGS ARE 308-09 (1959). (Emphasis in original.)

wise decisions, wise in the sense of furthering the values of a democratic polity. If with such decisions there may also be obtained opinions which fit within the concept of idealized versions of the judiciary, so much the better. But the Court has never operated in that manner; it has always been content to make its decisions and to "explain" them in opinions most of which any first-year law student can pull apart with ease. The Justices have always been "result oriented" and politically minded. They have been cognizant of the political consequences of their decisions. In their appraisal of these consequences, they have sometimes erred, as in *Dred Scott*,[52] *Pollack*,[53] and *Butler*.[54] More often, they have overruled themselves.[55] Often, perhaps routinely, they have innovated,[56] in the sense that any ruling on the merits has an element of creativity. In any event, the Court in recent years has had to attempt to adapt itself to changing reality, and it is that effort that is the subject of our concern.

A SECOND PROPOSITION

It seems evident that an effort is being made by the Court, silently and with indifferent success thus far, to develop new institutional means of dealing with the questions of public policy which are presented to it. These questions may involve statutory interpretation or constitutional construction. As Tocqueville and others have observed, all questions of public policy do not reach the Court; nevertheless, they appear there with sufficient frequency to make the Court an important organ of American governance. A second proposition, then, may be stated thusly: *The adversary system, as it has developed, is not entirely suitable to the resolution of the important problems of public polciy which the Court is forced to decide.* It seems accurate to assert that the Justices have already recognized the

---

[52] Dred Scott v. Sandford, 60 U.S. (19 How.) 393 (1857) (invalidating Missouri Compromise of 1820).

[53] Pollack v. Farmers' Loan & Trust Co., 157 U.S. 429 (1895) (invalidating federal income tax).

[54] United States v. Butler, 297 U.S. 1 (1936) (invalidating Agricultural Adjustment Act of 1933).

[55] See generally Blaustein & Field, *"Overruling" Opinions in The Supreme Court*, 57 MICH. L. REV. 151 (1958); Ulmer, *An Empirical Analysis of Selected Aspects of Lawmaking of the United States Supreme Court*, 8 J. PUB. L. 414 (1959).

[56] The "prospective" overruling cases appear to represent an innovation which rests heavily upon political and practical "consequence orientation." This device has allowed the Court to change the law without throwing open all the jails of the country. See, *e.g.*, Johnson v. New Jersey, 384 U.S. 719, 726-35 (1966).

validity of this proposition. The recognition that "policy" plays as great a part as doctrine in the decisional process, the growing tendency to use "non-legal" materials to buttress decisions, the widespread employment of the most open and liberal type of judicial notice—all these, and more, tend to show that the principal function of the adversary system is to present a controversy to the Court. The litigants are important because only they can activate the judicial process.

Unlike legislators or executives, the Court must await the commencement of a lawsuit, which of course limits its power to enunciate policy. That power is also limited by the self-restraint of some Justices, who demand that suits be brought by "proper" plaintiffs in cases involving issues considered amenable to judicial treatment. But self-restraint is, as Mr. Justice Stone once remarked, the only restraint upon the Court once a case has been accepted for decision on the merits.[57] In this respect it differs in some degree from the avowedly political branches of government, the officials of which are the butt of the pressures of politics.[58] Of course it is true, or at least seems to be true, that while the Justices are not prey to the day-to-day pulls and tugs of the political process, they nevertheless have their radar rather keenly attuned to what might be called "the art of the possible." Sometimes they have misread the social signals, but usually they have been in tune with the philosophy of the times in which they operated. The point, however, is that the chief function of the adversary system is to trigger a judicial response. Sometimes it is difficult for interest groups desirous of a Supreme Court decision to find "proper" plaintiffs; the Negro movement was to some extent characterized by this difficulty, particularly in the early 1950s. However, Americans are a litigious people, and the Court has not lacked business in recent years.

Once the machinery of the adversary system has been invoked, a number of significant shortcomings become evident. In the first place, the growing attention paid to what are given the generic label of "policy considerations" in judicial decision-making clearly

---

[57] United States v. Butler, 297 U.S. 1, 79 (1936) (dissenting opinion). See MASON, HARLAN FISKE STONE: PILLAR OF THE LAW 405-18 (1956).

[58] Even in the allegedly independent regulatory commissions, policies tend to be the resultant of a parallelogram of conflicting political forces. See BERNSTEIN, REGULATING BUSINESS BY INDEPENDENT COMMISSION (1955) . See also FRIENDLY, THE FEDERAL ADMINISTRATIVE AGENCIES (1962); HORSKY, THE WASHINGTON LAWYER 59-119 (1952).

evidences a breakaway from the traditional adversary system.[59] What are "policy considerations?" Often employed but seldom defined, the term is one of the most loosely used in legal terminology. When it is defined it is in terms of higher level abstractions, which become meaningless in application.[60]

However, when policies are identified, and when they stand in opposition to doctrinal commands, a judge must act as legislator,[61] since weighing considerations of *social* advantage is what legislatures do, subject to judicial vetoes when constitutional limitations are transgressed. But it is also what courts inevitably do. Policy considerations are part of the legal order, not outside of it and not alien to it. The problem is whether the adversary system of constitutional adjudication is adequate to provide relevant data and criteria for the satisfactory resolution of policy questions. The answer that we suggest is "no." We further suggest that considerable evidence is available now to indicate a departure from the system as it was known historically and that further institutional changes must be developed if the Court is to remain vital. These latter suggestions derive from an evaluation of both the adequacy of the flow of information to the Court and the competence of the Justices to rule on complex problems of public policy.

The notion that the Supreme Court depends upon the adversaries to furnish it with the data relevant and necessary to decision is an obvious fiction. As Judge Wyzanski has stated:

> This tendency of a court to inform itself has increased in recent years following the lead of the Supreme Court of the United States. Not merely in constitutional controversies and in statutory interpretation but also in formulation of judge-made rules of

---

[59] The function of the adversary system is to disclose for resolution *factual* disputes within the framework of the declaratory theory of law.

[60] That judges should more forthrightly face the policy considerations behind a rule of law has long been advocated. See, *e.g.*, Holmes, *The Path of the Law*, 10 HARV. L. REV. 457, 467 (1897); Llewellyn, *Some Realism About Realism*, 44 HARV. L. REV. 1222, 1252-53 (1931). However, definitions (or even descriptions) of "policy" considerations are rare. Professors Lasswell and McDougal have offered the following: "*Policy norms.* These are propositions about how values ought to be distributed, including those to which we have given special mention, like power, respect, knowledge, safety and health, comfort and convenience." Lasswell & McDougal, *Legal Education and Public Policy: Professional Training in the Public Interest*, 52 YALE L.J. 203, 241 (1943). (Emphasis in original.)

[61] The Supreme Court also acts as a legislature when it refuses to act. See Harper & Rosenthal, *What the Supreme Court Did Not Do in the 1949 Term—An Appraisal of Certiorari*, 99 U. PA. L. REV. 293 (1950).

law, the justices have resorted, in footnotes and elsewhere, to references drawn from legislative hearings, studies by executive departments, and scholarly monographs.[62]

The object is to inform the judicial mind, and that is done by adversaries in briefs and oral argument and by the Justices who take cognizance of material deemed relevant and helpful to them.[63] The policy function which the Court must perform "can only be successfully carried out if the Court consciously strives to inform itself as fully as possible of the factual setting of each case and the social consequences likely to flow from each decision."[64] In addition, part of an adequate informing process must be directed at assisting the Justices to select the "correct" criteria for evaluating and, at times, choosing from among several relevant policies.[65]

The problem has troubled some of the Justices, who have not found the orthodox means of informing the judicial mind adequate. Mr. Justice Frankfurter once remarked: "Can we not take judicial notice of writing by people who competently deal with these prob-

---

[62] Wyzanski, *A Trial Judge's Freedom and Responsibility*, 65 Harv. L. Rev. 1281, 1295 (1952). The author continued: "Such resort is sometimes defended as an extension of Mr. Brandeis' technique as counsel for the state in *Muller v. Oregon*. In Muller's case, however, Mr. Brandeis' object was to demonstrate that there was a body of informed public opinion which supported the reasonableness of the *legislative* rule of law. But in the cases of which I am speaking these extra-judicial studies are drawn upon to determine what would be a reasonable *judicial* rule of law. Thus the focus of the inquiry becomes not what judgment is permissible, but what judgment is sound. And here it seems to me that the judge, before deriving any conclusions from any extra-judicial document or information, should lay it before the parties for their criticism." *Id.* at 1295-96. (Emphasis in original.)

[63] The signals or inputs a judge receives are usually conflicting; in addition, they are normatively ambiguous. In other words, there is difficulty enough with the "is" but when it comes to the "ought," then any decision-maker, including a judge, is beset with a welter of inconsistent demands. *Cf.* Lasswell & McDougal, *supra* note 60, at 239-43. See also Shklar, Legalism *passim* (1964).

[64] Alfange, *The Relevance of Legislative Facts in Constitutional Law*, 114 U. Pa. L. Rev. 637, 639 (1966).

[65] See Cohen, The Faith of a Liberal 192-93 (1946): "If, however, there are any principles of political science which enlightened experience makes clear, they are (1) that the worst form of government is that which separates power from responsibility, and (2) that the weakest government is that which has relatively little access to the sources of information. And does not the fiction that the courts only follow the words of the Constitution in fact relieve them of the responsibility . . . and is it not also true that this fiction that the courts decide only questions of law prevents us from organizing the courts so that they could have the opportunity of making adequate investigation into the actual facts on which they have to pass? Do we want our judges to be not only irresponsible to any earthly power, but also independent of adequate knowledge of the social consequences of their decisions?"
For a recent exposition of the use of socio-legal data in adjudication, see Green, *Sociology in Court*, Wall Street Journal, April 10, 1967, p. 1, col. 1.

lems? Can I not take judicial notice of Myrdal's book without having him called as a witness? . . . It is better to have witnesses, but I did not know that we could not read the works of competent writers."[66] In this same connection, Mr. Justice Brennan has observed that "the briefs of counsel are always helpful, but each of us is better satisfied when he not only checks but also supplements those materials with independent research."[67] A serious difficulty with this procedure of self-information which goes to the heart of the judicial system is that the adversaries will have no opportunity to know or to meet such information with opposing or contradictory data. A further trouble is that no guidelines exist by which the Justices are to act; each is free to do as little or as much "independent research" as his time (and that of his assistants) will permit. On the other hand, he is not required to do any at all, and can wholly rely upon what counsel brings to him. He is free to be as lazy or energetic as he wishes.

Moreover, to the extent that "independent research" is conducted, there is a breakaway from the orthodox view of the function of the adversary system. The judge himself becomes an active and avowed element in the informing process. Of course he can do this without violating the expectations of the adversary system by relying upon a liberalized and expanded concept of judicial notice. Information can and does flow to the Supreme Court dehors the "normal" paths. Moreover, the same occurrence may be observed throughout the adjudicatory process, whether it is judicial or administrative.[68]

---

[66] Frankfurter, J., quoted from oral argument in MURPHY & PRITCHETT, COURTS, JUDGES, AND POLITICS 318 (1961).

[67] Brennan, *Working at Justice,* in AN AUTOBIOGRAPHY OF THE SUPREME COURT 299, 303 (Westin ed. 1963).

[68] See Wormuth, *The Impact of Economic Legislation upon the Supreme Court,* 6 J. PUB. L. 296, 307-08 (1957). See generally 2 DAVIS, ADMINISTRATIVE LAW TREATISE §§ 15.01-.14 (1958, Supp. 1965) . Put another way, the Supreme Court at times takes "legislative facts" into consideration. See Alfange, *supra* note 61, at 667-79; Karst, *Legislative Facts in Constitutional Litigation,* 1960 SUP. CT. REV. 75.

The expanded use of amicus curiae briefs appears to be an outgrowth of the Court's desire to learn more about the law which they are called upon to make. See Krislov, *The Amicus Curiae Brief: From Friendship to Advocacy,* 72 YALE L.J. 694, 717 (1963). Primary evidence of the use of extra-record facts in constitutional adjudication can be found in Dennis v. United States, 341 U.S. 494 (1952). See also Cascade Natural Gas Corp. v. El Paso Natural Gas. Co., 386 U.S. 129 (1967) (Stewart, J., dissenting): "[T]he Court lays down 'guidelines' with respect to complex issues which will shape the future of an important segment of this Nation's commerce. In so

"The adversary principle," Professor Philip Selznick has observed, ". . . lends legitimacy to partisan advocacy within the legal process, allowing and even encouraging the zealous pursuit of special interest by means of self-serving interpretations of law and evidence."[69]   In constitutional adjudication, however, it is apparent that these self-serving interpretations do not—cannot—carry the weighty task of bringing all of the data and arguments to the attention of the Court.   Even the use of amici curiae briefs and of "Brandeis briefs" fall short of the need.   Independent research, conducted by "judge and company," apparently is considered necessary.   The adversary system is simply not adequate to the need; the parochial and specialized interests of individual litigants, whether natural or corporate persons or unincorporated associations, cannot fully produce all the information which the Justice needs in coming to a decision and in writing his opinion.   As Selznick says, the assumptions behind the adversary principle "have not been fully analyzed or tested," and "there is evidence that partisan advocacy is weakened under conditions that may become increasingly prevalent: [including] the commitment of a tribunal to a positive outcome . . . [and] reliance on experts and investigators who serve the court directly . . . ."[70]   As the Supreme Court in its constitutional decisions becomes more and more purposive or instrumental—that is, pays greater attention to the policy considerations—the need for analysis and testing of the adversary system has become obvious.   The Court is drawing away from it, but has not yet produced a viable alternative means of decision-making.   The Court is still a court, hampered by all of the shortcomings of litigation as a means of developing public policy.

Litigation—the adversary system—is not adequate, for other reasons as well.   In addition to the invalidity of the underlying assumption that the flow of information to the Court is sufficient to

---

doing the Court roams at large, unconfined by anything so mundane as a factual record developed in adversary proceedings."

[69] SELZNICK, SOCIOLOGY OF LAW 16 (1965) (mimeographed; to be published in the forthcoming International Encyclopedia of Social Sciences) (quoted by permission).

Of importance, but of peripheral interest to the inquiry here, is the inadequacy of the adversary system—of judicial review itself—when so-called "low-visibility" administrative decisions are challenged. These small claims are not worth litigating, even though they may be of importance to the individual; accordingly, some other institution, such as the "ombudsman," may well be in order. On this point, see GELLHORN, WHEN AMERICANS COMPLAIN (1966).

[70] *Ibid.*

the need, there is another (also unwarranted) assumption of equal or greater importance: that the Justices have the competence or expertise requisite to make many of the pronouncements on public policy that they issue. A final unfounded assumption is that the Justices have some means of forecasting and evaluating the social consequences of their decisions—which, again, is simply not true. These latter two inadequacies of the adversary system may be treated together.

Supreme Court Justices must rise above the narrow knowledge and analysis presented by the litigants and view the scheme or problem entire. The late Judge Charles Clark said in 1956 that "experience has taught me that only rarely and perhaps fortuitously may an opinion be expected to rise above its sources in the presentations of counsel."[71] One would have to examine all of the data formally presented to the Supreme Court in individual cases to determine whether Judge Clark's assertion is valid for the High Bench. The arguments and information presented often do require the independent research we have mentioned, although that research may be confined (in most, if not all, cases) to the arguments and issues presented by counsel. Professor Lon Fuller has observed that the moral force of a judgment is at a maximum if a judge decides solely on the basis of arguments presented to him. "Because if he goes beyond these he will lack the guidance given him by the parties and may not understand the interests that are affected by a decision rendered outside that framework."[72] But that is often what he must do, for as Woodrow Wilson said, Americans look for "statesmanship" in their judges.[73]

Fuller's statement is helpful so far as it goes, but it fails to take into consideration the growing evidence of the lack of judicial competence or expertise, which is sometimes expressly recognized by members of the Court and sometimes an obvious conclusion from the manner in which opinions are written.[74] Judges, for example,

---

[71] Harmar Drive-in Theater, Inc. v. Warner Bros. Pictures, Inc., 239 F.2d 555, 559 (2d Cir. 1956) (Clark, J., dissenting).

[72] FULLER, THE PROBLEMS OF JURISPRUDENCE 707 (1949).

[73] WILSON, CONSTITUTIONAL GOVERNMENT IN THE UNITED STATES 168 (1908).

[74] See, e.g., Railroad Comm'n v. Rowan & Nichols Oil Co., 310 U.S. 573, 580-82 (1940), and 311 U.S. 570, 575-77 (1941). In administrative law, the point is exemplified in the cases involving the "scope of review" of administrative decisions. See 4 DAVIS, op. cit. supra note 68, §§ 29-.01-.11.

do not receive the type of economic analysis requisite to better decisions. Mr. Justice Frankfurter, in an off-bench statement, made the point in these words:

> Take a problem that has been confronting the Supreme Court, Sherman Law regulation of the movie industry. A number of decisions have been rendered finding violations under the Sherman Law. Does anybody know, when we have a case, as we had one the other day, where we can go to find light on what the practical consequences of these decisions have been? . . . I don't know to what extent these things can be ascertained. I do know that, to the extent that they may be relevant in deciding cases, they ought not to be left to the blind guessing of myself and others only a little less informed than I am.[75]

This passage tells us several things: (a) the bench, at least in antitrust cases, has no particular expertise and must be educated; (b) the bar has not been helpful in this educational process; (c) judges are concerned with the consequences of decision as well as doctrine; and (d) the adversary system may be at fault in that it does not provide a court with the proper institutional means of informing itself. Judges have no way of becoming expert on many matters and must make, as Frankfurter suggests, "blind" guesses. Neither can they forecast the societal impact of their decisions, for the system does not provide a way of feeding back that data to them—assuming that it is available, which assuredly it is not. Furthermore, judges are not "renaissance men"; they cannot be expected to be expert in *all* of the complex problems presented to them.

Paying attention to policy considerations—adhering to a "jurisprudence of consequences"—makes adjudication enormously more complicated. For a judge to weigh considerations of social advantage is far more difficult than to apply rules or announce prin-

---

[75] FRANKFURTER, SOME OBSERVATIONS ON SUPREME COURT LITIGATION AND LEGAL EDUCATION 17 (1954). See General Bronze Corp. v. Ward Prods. Corp., 262 F. Supp. 936, 937 (N.D.N.Y. 1966) (Foley, J.): "Justice Frankfurter wrote in Marconi Wireless Telegraph Co. of America v. United States, 320 U.S. 1, 60, . . . that it is an old observation that the training of Anglo-American judges ill fits them to discharge the duties cast upon them by patent legislation. Although not a complete novice in patent legislation, the prolonged deliberation I found necessary in this instance—interfered with often by the pressures of the routine court work, the nature of much of this in this federal district being undeferable—brought home the truth of this old observation and the senselessness by federal judges untrained in the patent art to pretend otherwise." (Parallel citations omitted.)

ciples in given cases. It calls for a quality of expertise in the legal profession that is rare indeed and for which legal education does little to prepare them. Cardozo noted this many years ago: "Some of the errors of courts have their origin in imperfect knowledge of the economic and social consequences of a decision, or of the economic and social needs to which a decision will respond. In the complexities of modern life there is a constantly increasing need for resort by the judges to some fact-finding agency which will substitute exact knowledge of factual conditions for conjecture and impression."[76] The need still exists—and has become more pressing as society has become more complex.

This fact, if none other, should be sufficient to forego adherence to the declaratory theory of law despite any possible symbolic value it may possess. To insist that judges act like judges in the Blackstone manner, in other words, is to deprive them of the very means which would make them more efficient and expert. The adversary system is not likely to be improved unless and until there is a general recognition of its shortcomings and of the needs of rational policy-making by an appointed bench. The adversary procedure embodies a conflict theory and assumes that when two parties are at odds on constitutional issues and cannot settle their differences, by some magic (the legal counterpart of the classical economist's "invisible hand") the Court's resolution will inure to the general good. This will be true, however, only if the Justices have the requisite competence, both to dispose of the substantive matter at issue and to predict the consequences of alternative decisions. Robert H. Jackson, when Attorney General, recorded the astonishment of Europeans that American monetary policy could be decided in a private law suit involving $15.60.[77] National public policies cannot (and will not) continue to be made judicially, we suggest, unless some better means of making decisions is created. Of course, it is true that the Court has recognized its limitations in a number of matters (including monetary policy) with the possible result that a further diminution of

---

[76] CARDOZO, THE GROWTH OF THE LAW 116-17 (1924).

[77] JACKSON, THE STRUGGLE FOR JUDICIAL SUPREMACY 103 (1941). For a statement that non-adversary procedure is more appropriate in some cases than adversary procedure, see Hyser v. Reed, 318 F.2d 225, 237-38, 246 & n.20, cert. denied, 375 U.S. 957 (1963) (parole board procedures). See also Kaplan, Civil Procedure—Reflections on the Comparison of Systems, 9 BUFFALO L. REV. 409 (1960) (comparing German system with American adversary system).

power in the Supreme Court may take place.   In any event, the conclusion seems valid: the adversary system is inadequate.

A THIRD PROPOSITION

The final proposition may be stated as follows: *If the Supreme Court is to remain a significant and meaningful instrument of governance, then it must react and direct itself to an ever-changing reality.*   What is needed is that the Supreme Court find itself a new role, as well as new institutional characteristics.   When in the late 1930s and 1940s it abdicated its position as an authoritative faculty of political economy and ceded to the political branches of government ultimate control over politico-economic decisions, the need was evident—and pressing—for the creation of a new role.   This was found in the drive for equality—the Negro rights cases, the urban voter cases, the criminal law cases—by Justices deeply concerning themselves with the workings of society and tackling some abrasive problems they (as also the other organs of government) had theretofore avoided.[78]   The spin-off from this activity has been great—in legislation, in executive programs, in state laws.   But the very success of the Warren Court—and, outwardly at least, it has been highly successful, perhaps the most successful Court in history—raises two crucial questions: (1) Has the Court about worked itself out of critical social problems with which to deal?[79] and (2) Why has the Court had this success?

---

[78] In the drive for racial equality, franchise equality and fair treatment of criminal suspects, for political and other reasons, the Court became the only governmental organ that could institute constitutional change.   What it did there, as well as elsewhere, was to open the way to change, which has come with breathtaking speed in reapportionment matters but which has been slow indeed with respect to the position of the Negro.   In this latter regard a report of the Civil Rights Commission issued in February, 1967, indicated that racial isolation in education is increasing, both in the South and North, despite the *Brown* decision. See Washington Post, Feb. 20, 1967, p. A-1, col. 8, and p. A-5, col. 1.

[79] We are aware that merely posing such a question will astonish many students of the Court.   What is said subsequently in the text is in terms of long-range tendencies rather than what may (or may not) occur in the near future.   In brief, our position is predicated on the belief that the activism of the Warren Court is a short-term phenomenon.   In this connection, *compare* Adderley v. Florida, 385 U.S. 39 (1966), *with* Fortson v. Morris, 385 U.S. 231 (1966).   What is being suggested may be characterized as neither a tactical retreat nor a full-scale strategic withdrawal by the Court; rather, it is that the center of governmental gravity is slipping ineluctably toward the political branches of government and that the Court at some time will find itself with little of a fundamental nature on its docket.

See Graham, *Supreme Court Preview: A Quieter Year Ahead*, N.Y. Times, Oct. 2, 1966, p. E-8, col. 1: "The Supreme Court convenes tomorrow for the ceremonial

So far as basic law is concerned, the voting situation is about settled, the Negro now has equality in law if not in fact, and there is little that can be done by way of developing *new* principles in the criminal law area. In each of these doctrinal fields, to be sure, cases will continue to be brought to the Court for settlement; but in large part they will result in resolution and refinement of the details of already established principle.[80] For example, the Court may venture into the areas of juvenile courts[81] and military law. But that development, if it comes, would merely extend its recent criminal law holdings. What may be foreseen, then, is a diminishing role for the Court—unless and until new areas are tackled. Furthermore, it is difficult indeed to discern what these areas might be. Our suggestion is that the Court will soon have to start a search for a new role, or find itself increasingly concerned with the minutiae of public policy.

It is here that the second question obtrudes: Why has the Court been successful in recent years? This success is taken for granted, applauded or disapproved in accordance with the observer's personal values, with little or no effort made to learn the bases for it. It is suggested, inter alia, that the Court has succeeded because it has,

---

opening of its 1966 term, amid indications that the pendulum is swinging back from the high point of its liberalizing impact on American life.

"The shift results not from changes of mind or personnel on the Court, but rather through the steady shrinking of the number of the nation's ills that take the form of unjust laws. . . . [A] review of the Court's upcoming work suggests that fewer of the nation's major problems are coming its way."

[80] The success of the Warren Court in promulgating national norms in the areas of civil rights and civil liberties should not be taken to mean that these norms have been or will be translated into operational reality. The contrary may well be the case. *Cf.* Miller, *Mulkey v. Reitman: A Brave But Futile Gesture?*, 14 U.C.L.A.L. Rev. 51 (1966); Miller, *On the Need for "Impact Analysis" of Supreme Court Decisions*, 53 Geo. L.J. 365, 389-92 (1965); Wells & Grossman, *The Concept of Judicial Policy-Making: A Critique*, 15 J. Pub. L. 286 (1966). The power of the Court to change the behavior patterns of Americans is at best unknown and highly discontinuous. Despite all the Court has done in recent years in rendering decisions having the projected effect of enhancing the dignity of disadvantaged Americans, its history as a protector of the unlettered and weak and of dissenting minorities has been anything but favorable.

Furthermore, with a change in Court personnel, which will come soon, it is possible that the thrust and tenor of recent decisions will be reversed. In addition to Mr. Justice Tom C. Clark, who has already announced his retirement to take place in 1967, there may be two or three other vacancies within the next year or two. A shift in position is even possible in some areas without a change in personnel, as the Court reads the social tea leaves and perceives the white reaction to what some consider to be excesses in the Negro movement and the growing involvement in a war in Asia.

[81] See Paulsen, *Kent v. United States: The Constitutional Context for Juvenile Cases*, 1966 Sup. Ct. Rev. 167.

as Alexander Pekelis suggested twenty years ago, immersed itself in the travail of society.[82]   Since 1940 it has made itself meaningful to the drives and urges of significant segments of the American people and has been able to translate into constitutional command some of the ideals of the Constitution which have long lain dormant. The Justices have recognized that it makes little sense in a unified, if not entirely uniform, nation for the principle of *Barron v. Baltimore*[83] still to apply.   Furthermore, and probably of vastly greater importance, they did not hesitate to grasp the nettle of racial segregation at the very time that the Congress was moribund, the Executive reluctant, and the Negro people on the march; and they recognized that "one malarious peasant" should not be permitted to wield electoral power equal to that of twelve residents of a city.   In so doing, they have made themselves part of a government of affirmative orientation, part, that is, of the Positive State.[84]   They have been creating a teleological jurisprudence in harmony with the politico-economic decisions of Congress and the Executive.

In making these advances, the Court does not appear to have markedly or obviously diminished in public esteem.   Efforts to reverse the Court's reforms have aborted.   In addition, Senator Sam Ervin of North Carolina is, at this writing, striving to have a bill enacted which would *enlarge* the Court's powers.[85]   By its decisions the Court has remained meaningful to the American people and its continued acceptance will not depend upon its adherence to the declaratory theory or whether its decisions are "reasoned" or "principled"—unless the terms "reason" and "principle" are taken to mean, not logical derivations from pre-existing doctrine, but "a process of disciplined observation, coupled with a recognition that

---

[82] See note 45 *supra* and accompanying text. See Miller, *Notes on the Concept of the "Living" Constitution*, 31 GEO. WASH. L. REV. 881, 911 (1963).

[83] 32 U.S. (7 Pet.) 243, 250 (1833) (announcing that the Bill of Rights applies only to the federal government).

[84] The concept of the Positive State is developed in previous articles by the senior author. See Miller, *The Public Interest Undefined*, 10 J. PUB. L. 184 (1961); Miller, *An Affirmative Thrust to Due Process of Law?*, 30 GEO. WASH. L. REV. 399 (1962); Miller, *Constitutional Revolution Consolidated: The Rise of the Positive State*, 35 GEO. WASH. L. REV. 172 (1966).

[85] S. 2097, 89th Cong., 1st Sess. (1965). See *Hearings Before the Subcommittee on Constitutional Rights of the Senate Committee on the Judiciary*, 89th Cong., 2d Sess., pts. 1, 2 (1966). The bill would confer standing to challenge expenditures to sectarian institutions under certain federal aid-to-education statutes.

choices must be made among alternatives and a cognizance of the consequences of the decisions. . . ."[86]

At present, three areas seem possibly ripe for greater judicial development, with the result that the Supreme Court might maintain its position of power and respect.   While other areas might be suggested, Court activity to provide greater review of public administration, clearer recognition of the group basis of society, and adaptation of a domestically oriented Constitution to an interdependent world would be especially propitious.   The passport cases, the criminal law cases, and some recent administrative law decisions all point to a greater interest in the individual *qua* individual in his dealings with the public administration.   So, too, with the group basis of society, although the Court has been reluctant overtly to recognize it.   However, a number of cases at least give a hint of the development toward a constitutional theory of group action.[87]   Furthermore, there is the decision in *Marsh v. Alabama*[88] existing in the United States Reports as a time bomb ticking away, available for use whenever the Court would desire to recognize the governmental character of the huge corporate combines.[89]   While there is some indication that the Court will consider the third area of possible activity, the reluctance to rule in the area of foreign affairs may minimize such a venture.[90]   The extent to which the Supreme Court can successfully assimilate such constitutional tasks cannot, of course, be forecast with precision.   At a time when the docket each year is crowded and when students of the Supreme Court are calling upon the Justices to make fewer decisions, it may seem odd to suggest that

---

[86] Miller & Howell, *The Myth of Neutrality in Constitutional Adjudication*, 27 U. CHI. L. REV. 661, 694 (1960). Another view may be found in BICKEL, THE LEAST DANGEROUS BRANCH (1962). See Wechsler, *Toward Neutral Principles of Constitutional Law*, 73 HARV. L. REV. 1 (1959).

[87] See HORN, GROUPS AND THE CONSTITUTION 152-180 (1956); MILLER, PRIVATE GOVERNMENTS AND THE CONSTITUTION 13 (1959).

[88] 326 U.S. 501, 507 (1946). See Berle, *Constitutional Limitations on Corporate Activity*, 100 U. PA. L. REV. 933, 949-51 (1952).

[89] See PEKELIS, *Private Governments and the Federal Constitution*, in LAW AND SOCIAL ACTION 91 (Konvitz ed. 1950).

[90] See Banco Nacional de Cuba v. Sabbatino, 376 U.S. 398 (1964); Moore, *Federalism and Foreign Relations*, 1965 DUKE L.J. 248. Subsequent to the decision, Congress enacted a statute which will require a Court decision on the merits of the case. Foreign Assistance Act of 1964, 78 Stat. 1013, 22 U.S.C. § 2370 (e) (2) (1964). The statute, upheld in the district court, Banco Nacional de Cuba v. Farr, 243 F. Supp. 957 (S.D.N.Y. 1965), 6 VA. J. INT'L L. 173 (1965), has not yet reached the Supreme Court. See also F. Palacio y Compania v. Brush, 256 F. Supp. 481 (S.D.N.Y. 1966).

the time is fast approaching when a new constitutional role for the High Bench must be carved out. But precisely that is suggested.

Whether the three areas of possible concern will in fact be tackled is not at all certain. Without the institutional means necessary to make "rational" decisions in a nation increasingly dominated by "technocrats," it may well be that none of the areas—nor, for that matter, others that might be mentioned—will receive serious concern. That the social milieu in which the Court operates is ever changing is an obvious truism—but one not sufficiently faced as yet.[91] Dean Don K. Price, in a seminal book,[92] attributes the factor of change, both in extent and in its rapidity, to the scientific revolution.[93] Science (and its by-product, technology) are creating situations which pose fundamental problems to the nature of American democracy.[94] Public policies in the future, according to Dean Price, will be determined more by scientific and technological developments we cannot now foresee than by political (or legal) doctrines that we can now state.[95] The conditions of human existence have been altered more in the past one hundred years than in all of previous human history and the future portends even faster change.[96] Already government has undergone radical alterations from that condition which existed as recently as 1900. The age of administration, of bureaucracy, of planning has come; organizations dominate the polity; the lines between public and private and between foreign and domestic are being blurred.[97] Legislatures and courts are nineteenth century institutions, neither of which has demonstrated any high degree of interest or ability in improving its methods to meet new conditions.

---

[91] *Cf.* Miller, *Technology, Social Change, and the Constitution,* 33 Geo. Wash. L. Rev. 17, 19-20 (1964).

[92] Price, The Scientific Estate (1965), reviewed in Miller, Book Review, 1966 Duke L.J. 622.

[93] *Id.* at 15-20.

[94] The scientific revolution is one of the vital forces "behind institutions, behind constitutional form and modifications" which historian Frederick Jackson Turner maintained called "these organs into life and shaped them to meet changing conditions." Turner, The Frontier in American History 2 (1920). See Landynski, *The Making of Constitutional Law,* 31 Social Research 23 (1964).

[95] Price, *op. cit. supra* note 89, at 186.

[96] See *ibid.*; Commoner, Science and Survival (1966); Lapp, The New Priesthood (1965).

[97] Adumbrated in Miller, *Constitutional Revolution Consolidated: The Rise of the Positive State,* 35 Geo. Wash. L. Rev. 172, 182-84 (1966).

The three areas of possible judicial interest mentioned above all involve, in greater or lesser degree, aspects of the scientific-technological revolution. One may speak normatively and say that the Supreme Court should not shy from the issues presented by them. But we are not hopeful. That is a dour note on which to end this commentary about the power of the Court; nevertheless, it does seem to be justified. To make a prediction: the "activist" Court presided over by Chief Justice Earl Warren will soon taper off into relative desuetude.

By Way of Conclusion

The hypotheses suggested in this article are not to be considered as anything more than tentative formulations. If empirically validated, they would go far toward showing that the symbolic view of the Court and of the orthodox notion of the rule of law are not requirements of a viable legal order. The point we should like to emphasize, however, is not that Professor Mishkin's analysis and conclusions are shaky. Rather it is that further intuiting of conclusions about the Supreme Court, usually based upon nothing more than casuistical exercises on Court opinions, will not serve the needs of scholarship or, of far greater importance, of that greater understanding of adjudication which will at once permit higher levels of attainment by bench and bar and result in maintenance of the Court's position in the power structure of American government.

As matters stand now, we suggest, the Court is on the verge of a considerable diminution of power vis-à-vis the avowedly political branches of government. That would be a tragedy, for it seems clear beyond peradventure that the High Bench, if it seizes the opportunities, could have a role, however immeasurable, to play in helping effect the nexus between a proliferating government and the individual on the one hand and between the pluralistic centers of power in American society and the individual (and also as between those centers of power and government) on the other.

The Court will not be able to accomplish these objectives unless and until is it institutionally buttressed. If law, as Frankfurter said, "presupposes sociological wisdom as well as logical unfolding,"[98] the Court must have the assistance necessary to make sociologically wise

---

[98] Frankfurter, *The Process of Judging in Constitutional Cases,* in An Auto-biography of the Supreme Court 267, 270 (Westin ed. 1963).

decisions in a dynamic social milieu. On this score, one should not be at all optimistic, for the likelihood is that little meaningful will be done. Perhaps incremental improvements will come about, possibly through expanded use of amici curiae briefs but more probably only as individual Justices perceive and act upon the need. But that will not suffice. Just as it has become evident in recent years that Congress must reorganize itself if it is to retain its present power, attenuated though it may be,[99] so too the Supreme Court and commentators must recognize that the adversary system—the product of private-law litigation in an agricultural, even feudal society—and the declaratory theory are simply not adequate in the modern era. What type of improvements or changes should be made we only partially suggest. However, just as there is a vital need for factual studies of the legal order,[100] including constitutional adjudication, a concomitant requirement exists for the invention of new techniques and new aids for the nine men whose fate it is to sit upon the Supreme Court of the United States. The American people by and large do seem still to be willing to permit the Court to make its ostensibly portentous pronouncements upon public policy, and thus to wield some political power. How long this will continue we do not predict.

The new constitutional order which has become so familiar in recent years, following the watershed year of 1937, has produced a government of affirmative responsibility—the Positive State. Exemplified in many legislative and administrative programs, it is the American version of the welfare state. During this period the Supreme Court, without announcement and without fanfare but with considerable controversy, has been engaged in working out an affirmative set of constitutional concepts.[101] The Positive State requires such a positive jurisprudence. If, as Woodrow Wilson said, "constitutions must be Darwinian in structure and practice," so too must the institutions of government. The Supreme Court must be ready and able to meet the challenges of the unknown future.

---

[99] See, e.g., THE CONGRESS AND AMERICA'S FUTURE (Truman ed. 1965).

[100] See, e.g., SCHUBERT (ed.), JUDICIAL BEHAVIOR 4 (1964); Kommers, *Professor Kurland, the Supreme Court, and Political Science*, 15 J. PUB. L. 230 (1966).

[101] Cf. ROSTOW, THE SOVEREIGN PREROGATIVE (1962).

7
ON THE NEED FOR "IMPACT ANALYSIS" OF SUPREME COURT DECISIONS

Those who believe, without empirical evidence, that the Justices have enormous power in American society reach that conclusion by intuition. Very few scholarly studies have been made of what happens when the Supreme Court makes a decision. The principal reason for such a paucity of studies has been stated previously: the operative ideology of American lawyers, and indeed of others who study the Supreme Court, is one of "analytical positivism." This is a view of law, including constitutional law, as a discrete entity, separate and apart from the political economy of the United States.

But it has long been known that the Justices in their decisions usually state juristic theories of politics, and often they display certain value preferences in economics. The question is whether these theories and preferences are acceptable to the people generally. Napoleon once said that the politics of the future would be concerned with moving the masses; the Napoleonic future is here, but scholarship is faulty—at least in the study of the Supreme Court. This essay sets forth the need for a different type of

"On the Need for 'Impact Analysis' of Supreme Court Decisions" was originally published in 53 *Georgetown Law Journal* 365 (1965). Reprinted with permission of the publisher; copyright © 1965 by the *Georgetown Law Journal*.

scholarship, one that would look to the consequences of the decisions of the Supreme Court and determine the extent to which they are translated into the behavior patterns of Americans. If this is done, as it should be, then of necessity those who study the Court must draw upon the insights of such disciplines as political science, economics, sociology, and psychology.

The question of compliance with Supreme Court decisions becomes particularly acute when it is alleged, as it often is, that some decisions have contributed to the increase of crime in the United States. A connection between decisions and the rise in crime has never been demonstrated. The need is obvious — but unfulfilled. In this chapter the question is posed, not answered. It would take a number of scholars and considerable resources to accomplish the tasks necessary to produce verifiable generalizations about the power of the Court. Without such in-depth studies, one should be chary about speaking of the "impact" of the Supreme Court. The question is not whether it has no power — of course, it has some — but how much.

Asserting that those who advocate development of "neutral principles" in constitutional litigation take a too limited view, Professor Miller suggests that critics of the Supreme Court evaluate the "impact," or societal effects, of the Court's decisions, as well as analyze the reasoning used in the Court's opinions. After an extensive analysis of the role of change in our legal structure and the position of the Supreme Court in our social and governmental structure, he calls upon those who comment upon the Court's decisions to take cognizance of the milieu in which the Court operates. Using the 1963 Supreme Court Review as an example, he points to shortcomings of present criticism and emphasizes that only when scholars develop rules about constitutional law, as opposed to rules of constitutional law, will a true understanding of the Supreme Court be attained.

The final cause of law is the welfare of society. The rule that misses its aim cannot permanently justify its existence . . . . Logic and history and custom have their place. We will shape the law to conform to them when we may; but only within bounds. The ends which the law serves will dominate them all.

—*Benjamin Nathan Cardozo*[1]

INTRODUCTION

The Anglo-American legal system is at least 1000 years old—even older if one adds its Roman law history. It is remarkable that in all that time, with the millions of lawyers (and other students of the legal process) who have come and gone, there is no accepted conception of the nature of the judicial process. This is particularly true of that peculiar institution of constitutional adjudication in the United States, but it is also valid for adjudication generally. Neither is there any really satisfactory method of judicial criticism, if by "satisfactory" one means a method which will comprehensively analyze and explicate all aspects of the judicial decision. Courts have been central to the development of law in English and American history, yet much that makes up the conventional wisdom is demonstrably faulty. It was so demonstrated, in part at least, by the intellectual movement during this century which bears the label of "legal realism," the chief exponents of which included Cardozo and Frank, Llewellyn and Arnold, Douglas and the two Cohens, as well as Moore and Bingham. But those idol-smashers did only half

---

[1] THE NATURE OF THE JUDICIAL PROCESS 66 (1921).

a job at best; they ripped the facade off the classical jurisprudential idea that the appellate judge was a passionless vehicle for the application of the law to the facts of the case. However, they have done nothing to replace it.[2] Cardozo's "summons to a better understanding,"[3] issued forty years ago, remains unanswered.

The ancient conception—that the judge did not have a creative role in deciding cases—has not been the same since. The shambles of classical jurisprudence lie in ruin, like ancient Mayan temples, but no one, other than Professor M. S. McDougal,[4] has as yet tackled the rebuilding task. Such a job of reconstruction is necessary if courts are to retain—perhaps "regain" would be a better word, now that the administrative state has arrived—their central position in the legal system. Furthermore, the temples of classical jurisprudence are still peopled; many, perhaps most, who write about law and legal subjects still adhere to its tenets, although in a more sophisticated form. Thus what Morris Raphael Cohen rightly derided as the "phonograph" theory of justice[5] is proving hard to bury and to keep interred. Just as the common-law forms of action, "although buried, still rule us from their graves," so, too, if scholarship in the law reviews is any criterion, the conventional wisdom of yesteryear still abides. The late Karl Llewellyn said in 1960 that legal realism "is tending in modern jurisprudential writing to be treated as an episode to be relegated to history."[6] Some writers even proffer remarks—usually derogatory—about "neorealists"![7]

The hardihood of the former wisdom may be attributed to a number of causes, but whatever the cause, it is clearly to be seen in the commentary upon the Supreme Court of the United States, and the written opinions of its Justices. Since 1803 the Court has been reviewing acts of other organs of government, state and national, but its decisions are still the subject of intense interest and both responsible and irresponsible criticism. There is still debate over what Americans often gratulate them-

---

[2] Legal realism, it should be mentioned, was largely an effort to describe what went on in fact in the process of appellate adjudication. It was never a philosophy and did not purport to be one, and thus left the rebuilding task to others.

[3] CARDOZO, THE GROWTH OF THE LAW 145 (1924).

[4] See, e.g., McDOUGAL, STUDIES IN WORLD PUBLIC ORDER (1960).

[5] M. R. COHEN, LAW AND THE SOCIAL ORDER 380-81 n.86 (1933).

[6] LLEWELLYN, THE COMMON LAW TRADITION 508 (1960).

[7] E.g., BICKEL, THE LEAST DANGEROUS BRANCH: THE SUPREME COURT AT THE BAR OF POLITICS 81 (1962); cf. Gilmore, Legal Realism: Its Cause and Cure, 70 YALE L.J. 1037 (1961).

selves as their unique contribution to the science of government, judicial review: its scope, its role, and the very nature of the constitutional adjudicative process. Much of this debate in recent years has tended to be a call for "principled" decision-making and better opinion-writing. Accordingly, it may be taken to be a sort of counter-revolution to the legal-realist movement, which often scoffed at the idea that legal rules, as such, were the main determinants of appellate court decisions. The counter-revolutionaries may be said to be swinging the pendulum back, at least to the extent of saying that the rules are not irrelevant to the decision-making process.[8] But they offer little more than an *ad hominem* call for "reason" in adjudication or "principled" decisions (sometimes "neutral" principles) or decisions in accord with "the law as it has been received and understood,"[9] and accordingly they have only a limited value. They do not analyze the concept of reason, nor do they set forth which principles they advocate.

Obviously, something more is needed if there is ever to be a truly satisfactory *description* of the adjudicative process. Equally obviously, quite a bit more is needed if there is ever to be an adequate *prescription* of what courts, particularly the Supreme Court, should do in those human disputes which are brought before them for judgment. My purpose in this brief article is to suggest *one* added dimension which should be considered in an evaluation of judicial opinions, namely, "impact analysis" of the societal effects of Supreme Court decisions.

The late Felix Cohen set forth a like suggestion, at far greater length, more than thirty years ago. But that seed fell on barren ground, although some small efforts have been made to fill the gaps Cohen discussed. He was concerned with the uses to which law (and the legal process) were put in society:

> [L]aw has instrumental value in so far as it promotes good human activity, or more briefly, the good life. The good life involves both intrinsic and instrumental values, so that possible non-human goods (e.g., the well-being of domestic animals) which law can attain indirectly by affecting human conduct are not excluded from our valuations, appearing as results which endow human life with instrumental value. And on the other hand, since law is the work of human beings, any intrinsic values which may appear in the legal order will be accounted for in an evaluation of the lives of those directly implicated in this order. Accordingly, the valuation of law is part of that branch of ethics which we

---

[8] See Shapiro, *The Supreme Court and Constitutional Adjudication: Of Politics and Neutral Principles*, 31 GEO. WASH. L. REV. 587 (1963).

[9] Griswold, *Foreword: Of Time and Attitudes—Professor Hart and Judge Arnold*, 74 HARV. L. REV. 81, 91 (1960).

have called moral science, and every legal element can receive a final evaluation in terms of the good life.[10]

In the present discussion, neither the "good life" nor any theory of
evaluation is set forth; the gist of what follows is the suggestion that
adequate legal criticism, at the barest minimum, must look to the consequences of law and of judicial decisions, as well as to the corpus of
doctrine often called precedent. Professor Paul A. Freund once said that
"to understand the Supreme Court . . . is a theme which forces lawyers
to become philosophers"[11]—but, unhappily, very few have; moreover,
if the present suggestion is valid, then lawyers will have to be privy to
the insights of such disciplines as economics and sociology and political
science if they are to be able to comment meaningfully upon Court
decisions.

The Elements of Impact Analysis

Understanding of the Supreme Court and of its role in the American
system will be furthered by systematic and comprehensive attention
paid to the social impact of Court decisions. Impact analysis has at
least two facets: (a) an appreciation by judges of the consequences
of their decisions; and (b) an evaluation by commentators of the
social effect of judicial decisions. It looks to the consequences of judicial
decisions and evaluates them in accordance with the extent to which
they further the attainment of societal goals. It thus involves asking
what the law should be as well as what it is. "[D]emocracy," Frank H.
Knight has said, "has assumed the task, enormously more difficult than
enforcing a law known to all, of deciding what the law ought to be and
making any changes called for."[12] That statement pinpoints the problem
in constitutional adjudication: the need for deciding what the law "ought
to be."

Now, what constitutional law "ought to be" in substantive terms is
a question beyond the scope of this article. It is, nonetheless, meet to
say that we should not forget, as indeed lawyers have often forgotten,
that the Constitution (and the social order it governs) was established
for certain, quite definite purposes. Without going into the question of
what may have been the "real" motivations of the fifty-five men now
revered in America's hagiology as the Founding Fathers, the Preamble

---

[10] F. S. Cohen, Ethical Systems and Legal Ideals 17-18 (1933).

[11] Freund, On Understanding the Supreme Court 7 (1949).

[12] Knight, *On the Meaning of Justice*, in NOMOS VI: Justice 1, 2 (Friedrich & Chapman
eds. 1963).

to the Constitution itself sets forth the objects for which it was written: "to form a more perfect union, establish justice, insure domestic tranquility, provide for the common defense, promote the general welfare, and secure the blessings of liberty . . . ." These familiar words set the tone, and Mr. Chief Justice John Marshall's opinion in *McCulloch*[13] thirty-two years later established the method—by adding the concept of an evolving Constitution—through which American constitutional development has taken place. Constitutional interpretation has proceeded side by side with legislation (and, in the present century, with administrative law-making) to make up a legal system by which the ideals set forth in the Preamble have been and are being furthered.

An essential point here is *change*, which is a primary characteristic of American society (for a number of reasons, not least of which is the scientific-technological revolution) and which may be seen throughout American law, both public and private. Constitutional change, it is submitted, should be evaluated in terms of whether or not it tends to further the ideals of the Preamble. As Knight has said: "The real task faced is that of social progress, definable only as a *direction* of change (in a complex sense, mostly negative) through alleviating some of the grosser *in*justices that a society can agree upon and find remediable."[14] The accomplishment of that task can be helped through impact analysis, for it is only when given decisions are criticized and evaluated in terms of postulated goals that it can be determined whether social progress is being attained, just as initially it is only through attention to consequences that the Court can determine the criteria for particular decisions. Impact analysis cannot set the goals of decision-making—that has to come from elsewhere—but can assist in two ways: (a) in providing a basis for decision and (b) in evaluating the decisions themselves.

THE JUDICIAL PERSPECTIVE

If another dimension is added to the judicial process, so that it encompasses both a conceptual scheme and an appreciation of effects of decisions, the result will be a major alteration in the image of constitutional adjudication. A number of problems will be raised thereby, problems of a complexity that goes far beyond what has hitherto been true. For the judiciary, the new dimension presents somewhat different challenges from that of the observer of the judicial process. Hence, a

---

[13] McCulloch v. Maryland, 17 U.S. (4 Wheat.) 316 (1819).
[14] Knight, *supra* note 12, at 3.

separate exposition will be made. What follows in this subsection is a listing of some of the problems raised by "impact analysis" from the standpoint of the federal judiciary, and more specifically, from the very specialized point of view of the Supreme Court. While, as will be shown below, much of what is said here has a wider application, nevertheless, the narrower concentration seems desirable.

Law as a Process

It is fair to say that law and the legal system in the United States have yet to come to terms with the factor of social change. Commentators, both on and off the bench, have not been able to reconcile the conflicting demands—the "antinomies," as Cardozo called them—of rest and motion, and of the basic social constant of change with its ineluctable concomitant of legal change. The Anglo-American legal system grew out of a relatively static society, a society which got its cosmology in Newtonian mechanics and its philosophy from Descartes, a society which had not yet felt the hurricane forces unleashed by the scientific-technological revolution. Law, when the legal theorists constructed a framework for analyzing it, was viewed as a static system—a closed system of concepts—which made up a "seamless web" of immutable truths. Legislation, which is largely a 19th-century phenomenon, came along later to spoil that vision and to inject the factor of calculated, purposive change in law. The ancient learning was such, however, that even today the center of attention is still the courts and the judges, and there is still a lingering suspicion of legislators.[15]

Social change is one of the commonplaces of the day. As W. Lloyd Warner has put it, "the processes of change are in themselves integral parts of the social system."[16] Brought about by the accelerating impact of scientific and technological development, alterations in the social structure are creating the conditions which produce obvious and continuing legal change. The Anglo-American legal system, as Professor Paul Deising has said, developed "by denying change."[17] This was accomplished through the use of legal fictions and similar techniques which

---

[15] Reflected, for example, in the fact that the law schools have until recent years paid little attention to the legislative process. A similar gap may be found in the almost complete failure to grapple with the administrative process, except in courses on judicial review of administration, i.e., "administrative law."

[16] WARNER, THE CORPORATION IN THE EMERGENT AMERICAN SOCIETY 18 (1962).

[17] DIESING, REASON IN SOCIETY 154 (1962). See generally Miller, *Notes on the Concept of a "Living" Constitution*, 31 GEO. WASH. L. REV. 881 (1963); Miller, *Technology, Social Change, and the Constitution*, 33 GEO. WASH. L. REV. 17 (1964).

permitted the form of older concepts and institutions to remain while the substance changed. However, the time has come—it is, indeed, past— when change must not only not be denied, it must be openly avowed. In terms of the American Constitution, the need is for avowal of the evolutionary character of that document with all that that implies for traditional views of laws and constitutions.

The Principle of Doctrinal Polarity

The adversary system of litigation, at least so far as appellate practice is concerned, is bottomed on the notion of a rather high degree of uncertainty in the law that may be considered relevant and applicable in any given case. That characteristic seems to be valid so far as private-law litigation is concerned; but even if disputed there, it seems to be beyond question with respect to constitutional adjudication. Any case which reaches the Supreme Court, and certainly those upon which the Court rules on the merits, may be said to involve at least two conflicting lines of doctrine. A convenient label for this characteristic is the Principle of Doctrinal Polarity. Litigants in constitutional cases represent conflicting social interests and collide in a clash of opposites when before the Court; for these litigants, as Oliphant and Hewitt maintained thirty-five years ago, "two conflicting major premises can always be formulated, one embodying one set of interests, the other embodying the other."[18]

This, of course, is familiar learning. But what is not familiar are the criteria by which judges choose between the conflicting interests. It is clear enough that if one accepts a certain major premise, then conclusions follow by ineluctable logic.[19] But why are those premises

---

[18] Oliphant & Hewitt, *Foreword* to RUEFF, FROM THE PHYSICAL TO THE SOCIAL SCIENCES at xv (1929); see McDougal, *The Ethics of Applying Systems of Authority: The Balanced Opposites of a Legal System*, in THE ETHICS OF POWER: THE INTERPLAY OF RELIGION, PHILOSOPHY, AND POLITICS 221 (Lasswell & Cleveland eds. 1962). Examples of the "balancing" of these conflicting interests abound in Supreme Court litigation. See, *e.g.*, Dennis v. United States, 341 U.S. 494, 524-25, 542 (1951) (Frankfurter, J., concurring); American Communications Ass'n v. Douds, 339 U.S. 382, 399 (1950). See generally Frantz, *The First Amendment in the Balance*, 71 YALE L.J. 1424 (1962).

[19] The Court's opinion is lengthy, but its thesis is simple: (1) The withdrawal of citizenship which these statutes provide is "punishment." (2) Punishment cannot constitutionally be imposed except after a criminal trial and conviction. (3) The statutes are therefore unconstitutional. As with all syllogisms, the conclusion is inescapable if the premises are correct. But I cannot agree with the Court's major premise—that the divestiture of citizenship which these statutes prescribe is punishment in the constitutional sense of that term.
Kennedy v. Mendoza-Martinez, 372 U.S. 144, 201-02 (1963) (Stewart, J., dissenting).

chosen in the first place? This question is not answered in the cases. Such a failure to explain the bases of choice has led Mr. Justice Black to castigate the interest-balancing approach and, at least in first amendment cases, to proffer an absolutist conception, one in which a literal "plain meaning" is made of the first amendment.[20] Mr. Justice Black may be correct in his criticisms of the Frankfurter approach, but does not himself give much more help in explaining why he accepts certain premises.

A Jurisprudence of Consequences

The clash on the Supreme Court and the Principle of Doctrinal Polarity pose a problem for which no one as yet has supplied a solution. The consequence has been a situation of the mutual exchange of *ipse dixits* and *ad hominem* statements by Justices of the Supreme Court and by commentators. Thousands of words have been written, for example, about the recent voting cases and about the school prayer decisions. But those who approve and those who decry have one common ground: they do not provide readers with any basis for explaining why they accept one premise over another. It is here that "impact analysis" would seem to be of some assistance. The following hypothesis is suggested as a way of thinking about the problem: *Choices are made by Justices from among conflicting principles (or inconsistent interests) not because of compelling law, but because of an evaluation of what the impact of given decisions is thought to be.*[21] As said above, the judicial decision is a law-creating institution; in it, the Justices seek to manage a segment of the future. Rather than engaging solely in retrospection, the Justices are also looking forward—result-oriented, in the non-invidious sense of the term—as much as they are concept-oriented.

Holmes, as usual, noted the situation many years ago when he stated:

---

[20] See, *e.g.*, Black, *The Bill of Rights*, 35 N.Y.U.L. REV. 865 (1960); Cahn, *Justice Black and First Amendment "Absolutes": A Public Interview*, 37 N.Y.U.L. REV. 549 (1962). *But see* Griswold, *Absolute Is in the Dark—A Discussion of the Approach of the Supreme Court to Constitutional Questions*, 8 UTAH L. REV. 167 (1963).

[21] *Cf.* WASSERSTROM, THE JUDICIAL DECISION 172-73 (1961). In discussing the justification of decisions, Professor Wasserstrom maintains that a "two-level" process is involved—first, the decisions "must be shown to be formally deducible from some legal rule," and second, "the rule upon which its justification depends must be shown to be itself desirable." Wasserstrom concludes: "The two-level procedure expressly provides that only those premises, those legal rules, whose implementation has been ascertained to be conducive to the production of socially desirable consequences, can count as good reasons for individual judicial decisions." *Ibid.* (Professor Wasserstrom does not enlighten us to how "socially desirable consequences" can be ascertained.)

I think that the judges themselves have failed adequately to recognize their duty of weighing considerations of social advantage. The duty is inevitable, and the result of the often proclaimed judicial aversion to deal with such considerations is simply to leave the very ground and foundation of judgments inarticulate, and often unconscious, as I have said.

. . . I cannot but believe that if the training of lawyers led them habitually to consider more definitely and explicitly the social advantage on which the rule they lay down must be justified, they sometimes would hesitate where now they are confident, and see that really they were taking sides upon debatable and burning questions.[22]

The Holmesian statement still holds true, at least in part. But it can be extended somewhat: it is submitted that judges normally do weigh "considerations of social advantage"—*i.e.*, take the consequences of their decisions into account—whether or not they articulate those considerations in their opinions. As Holmes said, this is "inevitable" and unavoidable. The question is not: Should a judge take policy considerations into account? Rather it is this: Which policy should he choose? For choose he must, however his opinion may be phrased.

It is in private law as well as public law that a jurisprudence of consequences may be discerned. And it is, as I have said, familiar learning. But it needs repeating because it has not struck home and has not become widely accepted by lawyers generally. The essential point is that the Supreme Court in constitutional adjudications, hearing as it does only a handful of cases each year, deals with a fluid situation, and, accordingly, must look forward as well as back. It must "legislate," at least in part, and determine what the law should be as well as what it is. This is because each case that comes before it, and is decided on the merits, is in basic part unique.

But saying that the Court does "legislate" via impact analysis does not necessarily mean that it should openly avow that it does. Nor does it answer the questions of how much "legislation" and when.

The Need for Expertise

A jurisprudence of consequences poses complex problems. In the first place, impact analysis makes the task of adjudication enormously more complicated. For judges to weigh considerations of social advantage is a far more difficult job than to apply rules or principles in given cases. If done in any systematic and thoroughgoing manner, it calls for a quality of expertise on the part of both judges and lawyers for which

---

22 Holmes, *The Path of the Law*, 10 HARV. L. REV. 457, 467-68 (1897).

their legal education will not have prepared them. As Cardozo said forty years ago:

> Some of the errors of courts have their origin in imperfect knowledge of the economic and social consequences of a decision, or of the economic and social needs to which a decision will respond. In the complexities of modern life there is a constantly increasing need for resort by the judges to some fact-finding agency which will substitute exact knowledge of factual conditions for conjecture and impression.[23]

Reference to one situation may serve to indicate the problem more specifically: antitrust law. The Sherman Act has all the attributes of a constitutional provision. Both in the original statute, which is couched in generalized terms, and in its exegesis by the Court there may be seen a close analogy to "pure" constitutional cases. Writing a decade ago, Mr. Justice Frankfurter made the following statement concerning the judicial task in antitrust cases:

> Take a problem that has been confronting the Supreme Court, Sherman Law regulation of the movie industry. A number of decisions have been rendered finding violations under the Sherman Law. Does anybody know, when we have a case, as we had one the other day, where we can go to find light on what the practical consequences of these decisions have been? . . . I don't know to what extent these things can be ascertained. I do know that, to the extent that they may be relevant in deciding cases, they ought not to be left to the blind guessing of myself and others only a little less uninformed than I am.[24]

What bothered Mr. Justice Frankfurter should trouble his colleagues on the bench, as well as all other members of the legal profession. The decisions of the Supreme Court in Sherman Act cases, since, as John R. Commons said, it acts as "the first authoritative faculty of political economy in the world,"[25] have important consequences for the nature of the American economy and for the government-business relationship. Should the Supreme Court act as blindly as Frankfurter suggests it does? Should it not have greater assistance from members of the bar, plus aid from political economists in making the essentially economic decisions involved in antitrust law? Such a suggestion has in fact been proffered by lawyer-economist Mark S. Massel of The Brookings Institution. In a paper published in 1962, Massel concluded:

> It seems clear that means must be found to alleviate the burden of the judges in order to insure significant application of the public intent behind the anti-

---

23 CARDOZO, op. cit. supra note 3, at 116-17.

24 FRANKFURTER, SOME OBSERVATIONS ON SUPREME COURT LITIGATION AND LEGAL EDUCATION 17 (1954).

25 COMMONS, LEGAL FOUNDATIONS OF CAPITALISM 7 (1924).

trust laws. . . . Obviously, such efforts should not be based on any belief that they would reduce the importance of judicial judgment. . . . Economic advice can be used to help to define the issues, to organize data, to suggest analysis of evidence and precedent, to outline available alternatives for the judicial decision, and to make reasonable predictions about the consequences of such alternatives.[26]

This calls for a level of expertise not often found within the legal profession, on or off the bench, for lawyers must be able to utilize the insights of economists. It is, furthermore, questionable at the present time whether the skills of economists measure up to the need set forth by Massel. But is there any feasible alternative to following up on his suggestion, once one accepts the Frankfurter proposition that the Justices on the Court are milling around in the dark without effective guidance?

One alternative, of course, would be for the Court to remove itself (or be removed) from the task of making antitrust decisions. It is entirely possible that this will eventually take place,[27] for ever increasingly the economic decisions of government are made either administratively, under delegations of power from Congress, or directly by Congress itself. Regardless of whether the Court will at some time cease to make decisions of a politico-economic nature, the situation today approaches absurdity. A Court invested with the power of such decision-making admittedly has little or no expertise in the problem; the Department of Justice, with several hundred lawyers, few if any of whom have any economic learning, does little or nothing to provide assistance for the Court; and the practicing bar only adds to the already dismal picture. At a time when the government-business interface in the United States is undergoing profound change, we still struggle under the myth that Sherman Act questions are legal questions and hence are for

---

[26] Massel, *Economic Analysis in Judicial Antitrust Decisions*, 20 A.B.A. ANTITRUST SECTION 46, 58 (1962). *Compare* Friendly, *Reactions of Lawyer—Newly Become Judge*, 71 YALE L.J. 218, 221-27 (1961), *with* Hyneman, *Free Speech: At What Price?*, 56 AM. POL. SCI. REV. 847 (1962). Hyneman states: "[N]one of the judges to date . . . has so far produced an opinion that stands as proof that his decision rests on a comprehensive, sharply discriminating and systematic scrutiny of the known and probable social consequences of the act under consideration." *Id.* at 851.

[27] It is not likely that fragmentation of economic decision-making among several branches of Government, as well as agencies within the executive branch, will long continue. The imperatives of the scientific-technological era demand centralization. *Cf.* Miller, *Technology, Social Change, and the Constitution*, 33 GEO. WASH. L. REV. 17 (1964). A key statute in this centralization is the Employment Act of 1946, 60 Stat. 23, 15 U.S.C. § 1021 (1958). See ROSTOW, PLANNING FOR FREEDOM: THE PUBLIC LAW OF AMERICAN CAPITALISM (1959); Miller, *An Affirmative Thrust to Due Process of Law?*, 30 GEO. WASH. L. REV. 399 (1962); *Unrecognized Economic Revolution*, 1964 THE ECONOMIST 550.

courts to decide. Either the courts must get out of the act or they must be assisted so as to be able to cope with the basic problems of Sherman Act enforcement.

Assuming the latter alternative is followed, impact analysis would be of some help. But it is an immensely difficult task and one not likely to be followed. It is complex enough for antitrust, which we have used as an example, but if magnified to the range of questions decided by the Supreme Court, then the task becomes one of staggering proportions. If the Justices are to be held, as is suggested above they should be, to the expertise of political economists in Sherman Act cases, and if they are to be held to similar lofty positions of expert knowledge for other complex societal questions, the question immediately arises as to whether or not the problem could be met and resolved in any reasonably satisfactory way. No doubt it was considerations such as these which led to the advent of the "administrative state" and to the abdication of the judiciary from any sustained scrutiny of the substance of economic and social decisions entrusted to the public administration by Congress.[28] The question which now presents itself with increasing persistence is whether those considerations of non-expertise argue for removing the judiciary from all fields of economic regulation.

But if judges are not experts in economics, they also are not particularly expert in many other areas of societal concern in which their decisions have an impact. Can the same argument be made for judicial abdication in such areas as the position of ethnic groups (principally, the Negroes) in this country, the administration of criminal law, the separation of church and state, and representation in legislatures? All of these decisional areas have found the Supreme Court under attack from one source or another.

There are other aspects to the difficult problem facing the Supreme Court if it should ever systematically and comprehensively undertake to gauge its decisions in the light of their consequences, as well as justify them doctrinally. One of these is the flow of information to the Court. What data are relevant for use in the judicial decision-making process? And how should these data be relayed to the Justices? We have heard

---

[28] Lawyers, with invincible parochialism, still overemphasize the importance of the judiciary in the governmental process. This is particularly true of the legal practitioner, who keeps asserting that administrators should act more like judges act (or are supposed to act). *Compare* Friendly, *The Federal Administrative Agencies: The Need for Better Definition of Standards*, 75 HARV. L. REV. 863 (1962), *with* Benjamin, *A Lawyer's View of Administrative Procedure—The American Bar Association Program*, 26 LAW & CONTEMP. PROB. 203 (1961).

much in recent years about the employment of assertedly "nonlegal" data in *Brown v. Board of Educ.*[29] Some social scientists have hailed the famous footnote eleven of that case as a landmark in the Court's recognition that sociologists and psychologists, and the like, have something to say of relevance to constitutional adjudication. Others—for example, the late Professor Edmund Cahn—have disagreed,[30] and have tended to question such data. But of course the "Brandeis brief" has been in operation since 1908,[31] and the Court has long used "nonlegal" matter, such as statistics and political theory, in its decisions.[32] One need only refer to such well-known decisions as the *Social Security Cases*,[33] *Lochner v. New York*,[34] particularly the dissenting opinion by Mr. Justice Holmes,[35] and *Dennis v. United States*[36] to indicate this.

Nevertheless, it is one thing to say that the Justices have often employed "nonlegal" data in their opinions, but it is quite another to maintain that they have used it properly. If it be granted that it is at least the lesson of history that such data are relevant to constitutional adjudication, how should it be relayed to the Court? Furthermore, how are the Justices to determine the validity of the learning from such disciplines as economics, political science and sociology?[37] Is there such agreement among the practitioners of these esoteric pursuits that a lawyer may without fear accept the statements of any of them? The answer to that, quite obviously, is no. Accordingly, there is the further problem of evaluating the conflicting propositions advanced by equally respected members of the nonlegal professions. The flow of information to the Court, according to the orthodox notion, is via the briefs and argument of counsel, the record of the trial court and the concept of judicial notice. This must be augmented, either through the invention of new techniques or by improving present methods, if that flow is to provide the Justices with the valid insights of disciplines other than law. It will

---

[29] 347 U.S. 483 (1954).

[30] See Cahn, *Jurisprudence*, 30 N.Y.U.L. REV. 150 (1955); *cf.* Greenberg, *Social Scientists Take the Stand: A Review and Appraisal of Their Testimony in Litigation*, 54 MICH. L. REV. 953 (1956).

[31] Muller v. Oregon, 208 U.S. 412, 419 n.1 (1908).

[32] See Wormuth, *The Impact of Economic Legislation Upon the Supreme Court*, 6 J. PUB. L. 296 (1957).

[33] Carmichael v. Southern Coal & Coke Co., 301 U.S. 495 (1937); Steward Mach. Co. v. Davis, 301 U.S. 548 (1937); Helvering v. Davis, 301 U.S. 619 (1937).

[34] 198 U.S. 45 (1905).

[35] *Id.* at 74.

[36] 341 U.S. 494 (1951).

[37] See Frank, *The Lawyer's Role in Modern Society*, 4 J. PUB. L. 8 (1955).

do little good, and perhaps much harm, if all that is furnished is the competing "wisdom" of experts for both sides of the case, experts who may be expected to testify in accordance with the desires of the party retaining them. The "fallacy of the impartial expert" should be recognized, if not exploded. The problem that this poses is of major proportions: the Justices can and do take the consequences of their decisions into account; should they continue to operate on the basis of assumptions and untested hypotheses? If not, then how is the situation to be improved?[38]

The Demand for Predictability

The question of the extent to which the Court *should* be forward-looking must also be posed. What is the proper balance between principle and result, between preexisting concept and an evaluation of the consequences of a decision? That the Justices on the Court do look prospectively (*i.e.*, legislate) seems to be beyond argument. But how much of this should they do?[39] That judges can and do "legislate" has been recognized by many members of the bench. Holmes, for example, did not deny this, but said that the judge was confined from "molar to molecular" motion.[40]

The question of how much is too much judicial norm-setting cannot be more than posed here. An adequate answer to it would entail an inquiry beyond the scope of the article. Nevertheless, it may be said that one important facet of the question is the extent to which predictability—*i.e.*, certainty—should be striven for and is attainable in the constitutional

---

[38] Judge Charles Wyzanski met this problem by appointing an economist as one of his "law" clerks when he had an important case before him. See KAYSEN, UNITED STATES V. UNITED SHOE MACHINERY CORPORATION: AN ECONOMIC ANALYSIS OF AN ANTITRUST CASE (1956).

[39] This problem—how much is too much?—seems to be at the center of the difficulty of those academic lawyers who decry the Court's recent reapportionment decisions. None deny the law-making proclivities of the Court, but want it sharply circumscribed—although they never tell us, save in response to specific decisions, how much is too much. See, *e.g.*, Neal, *Baker v. Carr: Politics in Search of Law*, in THE SUPREME COURT REVIEW 252 (Kurland ed. 1962). In this regard, the academicians join the politicians whose "ox is being gored" by the reapportionment decisions. Strange bed-fellows! One can understand the dismay of the politicians, who may soon be out of office, but it is difficult to discern just what it is that academic critics want. Dean Eugene V. Rostow may have put his finger on the core of the matter when he said that critics (academic and otherwise) "are uttering a protest which they find . . . hard to reduce to logical form. It is not so much a protest against the Court as against the tide of social change reflected in the Court's opinions." ROSTOW, THE SOVEREIGN PREROGATIVE 111 (1962).

[40] Southern Pac. Co. v. Jensen, 244 U.S. 205, 221 (1917) (Holmes, J., dissenting).

adjudicative process. This is a question of exceeding complexity, calling for a reconciliation of the great antinomies of rest and motion, of a static order and a dynamic flux, of stability and progress. Whitehead asserted that:

> There are two principles inherent in the very nature of things, recurring in some particular embodiments whatever field we explore—the spirit of change, and the spirit of conservation. There can be nothing real without both. Mere change without conservation is a passage from nothing to nothing. Its final integration yields mere transient non-entity. Mere conservation without change cannot conserve. For after all, there is a flux of circumstance, and the freshness of being evaporates under mere repetition.[41]

If it be granted that change is the law of life and that constitutional law is an evolving system[42]—and who can deny it?—then the question of predictability must be seen as subordinate to, or at least on the same level as, the attainment of desirable social ends—in short, the realization of justice in the particular case. Predictability, or certainty, accordingly, is not the only goal of the constitutional adjudicative process. And that is so, even though one may sympathize with the plaintive cry of the late Mr. Justice Owen Roberts who, in the 1940's, asserted that Supreme Court decisions were like "a restricted railroad ticket, good for this day and train only."[43] How the Court might rule on a given case thus becomes, for the observer, not an evaluation of precedent, but an intuitive feeling a close observer of the high bench gets from long continued study of particular Justices and the trends of their decisions.

This means that on the present Court one can foresee without too much possibility of error how Justices Black, Douglas, Goldberg and Mr. Chief Justice Warren are likely to rule in certain cases. In other words, in some cases, *e.g.*, civil rights, F.E.L.A., regulation of business, there is a fairly high degree of predictability (certainty) for a number of the Justices. And this, oddly enough, is decried by some commentators for a number of reasons, such as wrong reasoning, "result-oriented," and so on.[44] These observers are willing to forego this type of certainty, while plumping for better judicial method.

What, then, is the *proper* method? There is no accepted model of the judicial process in the sense of a conception which both fully ex-

---

[41] WHITEHEAD, SCIENCE AND THE MODERN WORLD 281 (1925).

[42] See Miller, *Notes on the Concept of the "Living" Constitution*, 31 GEO. WASH. L. REV. 881 (1963).

[43] Smith v. Allwright, 321 U.S. 649, 669 (1944) (Roberts, J., dissenting).

[44] *E.g.*, Griswold, *supra* note 9; see Miller, *A Note on the Criticism of Supreme Court Decisions*, 10 J. PUB. L. 139 (1961).

plains what takes place and also projects what should occur. The Supreme Court is forward-looking in its decision-making; it does take into consideration the impact its decisions will have. But it is also interested in stare decisis and in as much stability as can be attained. In its decisions it reconciles these two polar opposites and compromises—perhaps "makeshift compromise,"[45] in Cardozo's term—between a desire for certainty and a search for justice. "The goal of juridical effort, says Demogue, is not logical synthesis, but compromise."[46] But how know where to strike the balance, to effect the compromise? The task for the judge is one thing, for the lawyer or commentator upon the Court another.

The Reality of Judicial Bargaining

Reference to what is perhaps the most revealing exposition of the Supreme Court in action lends support to this "compromise" view of the judicial process. In Alpheus Thomas Mason's biography of Mr. Chief Justice Harlan Fiske Stone[47] there are recounted a number of examples of this type of decision-making. A clear example is *Ex parte Quirin*,[48] the case of the Nazi saboteurs. Eight German nationals had been caught soon after they landed on the eastern shore of the United States in 1942. They were tried by a special military commission established by the President. Convicted by the commission, their counsel sought review by habeas corpus in the Supreme Court. The issue was the jurisdiction of the commission to try the Germans, particularly in light of *Ex parte Milligan*,[49] a Civil War case holding that a military tribunal had no jurisdiction over a civilian defendant where civil courts were in operation. The Supreme Court, on summer recess, was specially convened on July 29, 1942, to hear the question. The Court upheld the power of the President. As Mason puts it: "The decision itself, a cryptic *per curiam*, upheld the jurisdiction of the Military Commission to try the Germans and announced that an opinion would be filed later."[50] The ensuing pages of the biography are a fascinating account of how Mr. Chief Justice Stone conducted a diligent search to find precedent to justify the previously reached decision. The question, in Stone's mind, was what was "good judicial diplomacy" in the circumstances. One of

---

45 CARDOZO, THE PARADOXES OF LEGAL SCIENCE 6 (1928).

46 *Id.* at 5.

47 MASON, HARLAN FISKE STONE: PILLAR OF THE LAW (1956).

48 317 U.S. 1 (1942).

49 71 U.S. (4 Wall.) 2 (1866).

50 MASON, *op. cit. supra* note 47, at 657.

those circumstances, it may be noted, was that six of the Germans were put to death soon after the Court's decision and before its opinion had been released. This factor caused the Chief Justice and his colleagues, to use his term, certain "embarrassments."[51] The opinion finally was released on October 29, 1942. The times were difficult; the nation was at war; the President was insistent that the eight Germans be killed; congressional sentiment was summarized as follows:

> Our people are of the opinion that the eight Nazi saboteurs should be executed with all possible dispatch. . . . They are confident that the military tribunal will decree their death. Any interference with that trial by civil court would strike a severe blow to public morale.[52]

The Supreme Court thus faced enormous pressure, and it may be that the Justices did as well as could be asked of anyone in the situation. Nonetheless Mason comments:

> However one looks at it, approval of presidential and commission action after the fact, in ignorance of what had taken place, was stiff medicine. To Stone's chagrin, perhaps, the judiciary was in danger of becoming part of the executive juggernaut.[53]

That aside, the interesting point in *Quirin* is the "decide first, opine afterwards" procedure. How often this characterizes the Supreme Court's operations is not known; the legal profession is not often favored with such a candid exposition as that contained in Stone's biography. Nevertheless, as a recent study documents, "leadership" and "bargaining" do take place in the Court's deliberations.[54] There is considerable give-and-take on the Court. Opinions are rewritten and even votes are changed on the basis of a complex interchange among the nine men. "To bargain collectively," moreover, "one must have something to trade and also a sanction to apply if the offer is rejected or if there is a renege on the bargain. The personal honor of the Justices minimizes the possibility of a renege in the usual sense of the term, though under existing Supreme Court practice a Justice is free to change his vote up to the minute the decision is announced in the courtroom."[55] What a Justice has to offer in the bargaining process are his vote and his concurrence in an

---

[51] *Id.* at 661.

[52] N.Y. Times, July 29, 1942, p. 11, col. 2 (statement by Representative Celler).

[53] MASON, *op. cit. supra* note 47, at 666.

[54] Murphy, *Marshaling the Court: Leadership, Bargaining, and the Judicial Process,* 29 U. CHI. L. REV. 640 (1962).

[55] *Id.* at 657.

opinion; on the other hand, the sanction which might be used against a Justice is the threat of a dissenting or concurring opinion.

The question, then, of "how much is too much?" by way of forward-looking depends in large part upon the caliber of the personnel of the Court and the extent to which leadership is possible and bargaining takes place. It depends as well upon an evaluation of the social milieu in which the Court operates and the social context (impact) of the decision. As I have said in a previous paper:

> How and when [do] changes in constitutional interpretation come about[?] A fundamental hypothesis, and a corollary thereto, may be suggested. *The hypothesis is this: A change in constitutional interpretation is feasible (perhaps even necessary) when the positive law of the Constitution is not in consonance with the living law of society and an attempt is being made to bring the two into coincidence. The corollary is this: A Court decision may itself operate so as to help create the favorable social milieu—by acting as a catalytic agent to precipitate a change in an unsteady equilibrium.*[56]

Mr. Dooley once opined that the Supreme Court tended to follow the election returns, but what seems more accurate is that the Court has its antenna keenly tuned to the prevailing climate of opinion and to the direction in which the political winds are blowing. In this respect, both elections *and* Court opinions may be said to reflect the same sort of consensus that is operating at any one time within the American polity. Judges, then, are not necessarily confined from "molar to molecular" motion; immersed in the "travail of society," at times they must be willing to break loose, to "experiment, which always involves a leap into the dark future."[57]

Such leaps—as in the recent reapportionment cases—are not improper in and of themselves, even though obloquy has been heaped upon them by some academic commentators. The position of these commentators, when one reflects upon it, is a most astonishing proposition: that there is a certain, prescribed, undeviating way for the Court to operate. There is none, of course, although the conventional academic wisdom would have us believe that such a model of judicial propriety does exist. The conventional wisdom is based on a faulty view of history, an erroneous conception of modern society, and a lack of appreciation of the niceties of American government.[58] This is not, it may be noted, necessarily to

---

[56] Miller, *supra* note 42, at 915-16.

[57] M. R. Cohen, *The Place of Logic in the Law*, 29 Harv. L. Rev. 622, 638 (1916).

[58] See Wilson, Constitutional Government in the United States 157 (1908). "The Constitution," says Wilson, "is not a mere lawyers' document," but rather "the vehicle of a nation's life." *Ibid*. It is noteworthy that most, if not all, of the contemporary academic

defend the decisions in the reapportionment cases, but merely to suggest that they are less out of line with the century-and-three-quarters of Supreme Court review of other governmental action than many critics are willing to admit. To cite but one example, the Court's decision in the *Steel Seizure Case*[59] in 1952 is fully as open to the shrill criticism that the reapportionment decisions have elicited; oddly, however, the academic commentators apparently find nothing in that strange case to criticize.

THE CHANGING ROLE OF THE SUPREME COURT

The Image of the Court

Would it be better if there were a conscious avowal by judges of the ends sought to be served in adjudication? Would a frank recognition of the two elements produce a more satisfactory picture of the judicial process? One commentator, Father Albert Broderick of the Catholic University School of Law, so believes; he maintains that the

> constitutional judge . . . is a legislator constantly revising and adapting. There is undoubtedly some difference from legislation: whereas on-again, off-again of a particular law or course of legislation at successive legislative sessions would be acceptable, in a Court it would not. But with this obvious qualification, might the Supreme Court not frankly avow that its decisional development in broad areas committed to its care is directed towards orderly achievement of currently accepted social goals?[60]

Whether Father Broderick's suggestion should be followed depends in large part upon the "image" of the Supreme Court and whether such frankness would impair its position in the value hierarchy of the American people. A number of reactions to this question may be discerned. On the one hand, there are some who admit that the Court can and does "legislate," *i.e.*, does look forward and take social consequences into consideration, but who stoutly maintain that this should not be revealed to the laity else they will suffer emotional shock and that will cause

---

critics of the Court fail to point out the period in history when, in their judgment, the Court acted properly, fail to take into consideration the socio-economic changes which have characterized this nation since 1787, particularly since 1900, and fail to analyze the Court as an integral part of a government of a fundamentally different nature than was the government of, say, 1850.

59 Youngstown Sheet & Tube Co. v. Sawyer, 343 U.S. 579 (1952).

60 Broderick, *Evolving Due Process and the French Institutionalists: Reflections on the Right to Counsel and the Adamson Dissent*, 13 CATHOLIC U.L. REV. 95, 135 (1964).

them to think less of the Court.[61] It is not at all clear how this school of opinion knows just what the American people think of the Court, if indeed they think of it at all, or how they would react to the notion that the facade should be ripped off the judicial process. That aside, the fact that the American people are legalistic and litigious, as Dicey and de Tocqueville long ago noted, does not mean that they also have the same view of the Court and its process as do lawyers. (For that matter, as noted above, lawyers themselves still argue, and bitterly, about judicial method.) Those who think that the mystery should be kept about the Court's process may be said to belong to the school of "squid jurisprudence," the major tenet of which is to keep the truth from all except the priesthood of the law. These observers believe that they themselves have the intellectual stamina to withstand the trauma of knowing that decisions are not brought by judicial storks, but fear the effect of that knowledge on the populace at large. They wish, accordingly, to hide the facts of judicial government from the people behind a cloud of impenetrable ink.

Now, it may well be, as General Charles de Gaulle has said, that leadership and prestige require mystery. "There can be no prestige without mystery. In the designs, the demeanor, and the mental operations of a leader, there must always be a 'something' which others cannot altogether fathom, which puzzles them, stirs them, and rivets their attention."[62] Hence, possibly the Supreme Court will suffer institutionally from both taking on too much (not exercising self-restraint, as Justices Frankfurter and Harlan would have them do) and from a candid avowal of the mysteries of the decisional process on the Court. Frankfurter's views are well known; their last, and perhaps most effective statement, came in 1962 in his impassioned dissenting opinion in

---

[61] E.g., HAYEK, THE CONSTITUTION OF LIBERTY 206 (1960); Cooperrider, *The Rule of Law and the Judicial Process*, 59 MICH. L. REV. 501 (1961); *cf.* M. R. COHEN, LAW AND THE SOCIAL ORDER 380-81 n.86 (1933). Cohen states:

> When I first published the foregoing views [on judicial legislation] in 1914, the deans of some of our law schools wrote me that while the contention that judges do have a share in making the law is unanswerable, it is still advisable to keep the fiction of the phonograph theory to prevent the law from becoming more fluid than it already is. But I have an abiding conviction that to recognize the truth and adjust oneself to it is in the end the easiest and most advisable course. The phonograph theory has bred the mistaken view that the law is a closed, independent system having nothing to do with economic, political, social, or philosophical science. If, however, we recognize that courts are constantly remaking the law, then it becomes of the utmost social importance that the law should be made in accordance with the best available information, which it is the object of science to supply.

Ibid.

[62] Quoted by James Reston, N.Y. Times, Aug. 21, 1964, p. 28, col. 3.

Baker v. Carr.[63] Harlan echoed this in 1964 and added a touch of his own while dissenting in *Reynolds v. Sims.*[64] In that case, extending the "one man-one vote" doctrine to both houses of state legislatures, Mr. Justice Harlan asserted that such decisions sapped the vitality of the American political system, weakened the fabric of federalism, and reflected a mistaken view of the function of the Supreme Court:

> [T]hese decisions give support to a current mistaken view of the Constitution and the constitutional function of this Court. This view, in a nutshell, is that every major social ill in this country can find its cure in some constitutional "principle," and that this Court should "take the lead" in promoting reform when other branches of government fail to act. The Constitution is not a panacea for every blot upon the public welfare, nor should this Court, ordained as a judicial body, be thought of as a general haven for reform movements.[65]

The learned Justice, it may be noted, cited no evidence for these statements. Just who, it may be asked, believes the Court is the "haven" he mentions or that the Constitution will cure every major social ill? Mr. Justice Harlan sets up and knocks down the flimsiest of straw men in that statement. But it is a clear statement of concern for the impact or the consequences of judicial decisions. In some respects it recalls to mind a not dissimilar blast of outrage uttered thirty years ago by Mr. Justice McReynolds in his dissenting opinion in the *Gold Clause Cases*:[66] "Loss of reputation for honorable dealing will bring us unending humiliation; the impending legal and moral chaos is appalling." The concern for purported adverse social consequences is, as we have previously noted, not atypical of the judicial process. However, it is not often that we are favored with such classic statements, which, in both instances, appear to be based entirely upon what Mr. Justice Harlan calls his "conviction" and not upon any evaluation of empirical data. This is not to say that the members of the Court's majority in *Reynolds* offer any better delineations of the reason for their conclusions; these conclusions seem, in final analysis, to be *ipse dixits*. Neither do they display any concern for or appreciation of the social consequences of their decisions. Both the majority and the dissenters in *Reynolds* wrote opinions which are noteworthy for their conclusions but not for their "reasoning." Neither is different in any essential way from the way Justices have been writing opinions since the Court was first established.

---

63 369 U.S. 186, 266 (1962).
64 377 U.S. 533, 589 (1964).
65 *Id.* at 624-25.
66 294 U.S. 240, 381 (1934).

What this may mean is that the Justices feel that a frank avowal of the decisional process, along the lines that Father Broderick has suggested, is not desirable. They may be right. It is possibly the prudential way for the Court to follow in the enunciation of rules *of* constitutional law.

A second viewpoint on the image of the Court is to deny that there is any validity to the notion of the living Constitution or to law as an evolutionary phenomenon. This, too, has its adherents; they belong to the school of what Pound called "mechanical jurisprudence." To them, the Constitution is a static, unchanging instrument and the task of the Court is to keep it so. It is difficult to see how this viewpoint has any basis at all; it can hardly be taken seriously at this date.[67]

Another group pays lip service to the idea of change—not denying it but not really accepting it, either—and maintains that Court opinions, whatever the result may be, should be "reasoned" or "principled."[68] A number of these also believe that the Court should have an essentially quietistic role in government—exercise "judicial self-restraint" in the manner that Mr. Justice Frankfurter was alleged to do—and should not intrude into "political thickets" or other abrasive areas which might ultimately jeopardize the high position of the Court in the value hierarchy of Americans. But these commentators seldom explain what they mean by "reason" or "principle" or suggest any guidelines which might be used as bases for knowing when to restrain. Members of this group fear that by trying to do too much, the Court will lose status and not do anything. They seem to believe that either the Court should be preeminent in position and power or that it will plummet to the other extreme. But even if the Court should lose esteem, as it has in some quarters, and even if it should be subjected to pressure or attempted loss of jurisdiction by congressional statute, surely one need not suppose that the Court will be eliminated from the American scene.

The fundamental question involved in this discussion is the role of the Supreme Court in a society characterized by rapid social change. This in turn means fitting the Court into a governmental structure which has assumed the responsibility of "managing" change. In a well-known

---

[67] This is what Dean Griswold had called, in another context, the "fundamentalist theological" approach. Griswold, *supra* note 20, at 172. See, *e.g.*, Pittman, *The Law of the Land*, 6 J. Pub. L. 444 (1957); 102 Cong. Rec. 6821 (1956) (extension of remarks of Representative John Bell Williams).

[68] See, *e.g.*, Bickel, The Least Dangerous Branch: The Supreme Court at the Bar of Politics (1962).

passage, Sir Henry Maine once stated that change in law (and thus in social institutions) comes in three ways: through legal fictions employed by judges, through judges taking "equity" into consideration, and through legislation.[69] His remarks related for the most part to the common law and to the categories of private law. But what about constitutional law, American variety?

The Governmental Posture of the Court

Whatever may have been the intention of the Founding Fathers, the American government has during this century taken on a fundamentally new posture. The "Positive State" has come into being, characterized by massive governmental interventions into socio-economic affairs. This has been discussed elsewhere and requires no present restatement.[70] The question for present purposes is not the extent and nature of this intervention, or of its constitutionality; rather, it is the governmental posture of the Supreme Court of the United States.

It is doubtless accurate to maintain that each of the branches of the national government has been undergoing an evolution, not only with greater rapidity in recent years, but also throughout American history. Thus it is that Congress by and large has found its role changing as new problems face the nation.[71] It has reacted to these new problems in varying ways; what they are need not be recounted at this time. This is equally true of the Executive: there is no question that this branch is the recipient of slowly accreting powers. The United States is becoming—perhaps has become—an "administrative state," one in which the locus of effective power is in the executive-administrative branch.[72] If that be granted, and there would seem to be a consensus among informed observers on the point of both Congress and the Executive, where does that leave the Court?

In many respects, the judicial task has changed markedly in the past three decades. In the first place, the judiciary has long since given up

---

[69] MAINE, ANCIENT LAW 15-20 (1931).

[70] See ROSTOW, PLANNING FOR FREEDOM: THE PUBLIC LAW OF AMERICAN CAPITALISM (1959); Miller, An Affirmative Thrust to Due Process of Law?, 30 GEO. WASH. L. REV. 399 (1962); Miller, The Public Interest Undefined, 10 J. PUB. L. 184 (1961); Unrecognized Economic Revolution, 1964 THE ECONOMIST 550.

[71] See Miller, The Changing Role of Congress, 50 A.B.A.J. 687 (1964); Symposium—The Changing Role of Congress, 32 GEO. WASH. L. REV. 929 (1964).

[72] See CORWIN, THE PRESIDENT: OFFICE AND POWERS, 1787–1957 (4th rev. ed. 1957); NEUSTADT, PRESIDENTIAL POWER (1960); Symposium—The Presidential Office, 21 LAW & CONTEMP. PROB. 607 (1956); cf. CATER, POWER IN WASHINGTON (1964).

any sustained constitutional scrutiny of the economic decisions of the political branches of government. For those, the Court acts in the role of the interpreter of statutory programs. This does not mean that the creative task of the judge in such matters has been eliminated. Far from it. It merely means that it operates in a different milieu. All statutes require interpretation and, as Bishop Hoadly long ago said, this is a key law-making position.[73]

Second, the Supreme Court has in its constitutional adjudications tended to concentrate upon the field of civil rights and civil liberties. Some of these "constitutional" decisions have come in what are really statutory interpretation matters; for example, in *Greene v. McElroy*[74] and *Kent v. Dulles*,[75] the Court made what may be termed constitutional decisions without actually doing so in fact. With respect to "pure" constitutional decisions (those based upon an interpretation of the fundamental law itself), the areas of principal concern have been the administration of the criminal law, the church-state position, the position of the Negro in American society, patterns of voting for legislatures, and loyalty-security problems. All of these have raised storms of controversy and have enmeshed the Supreme Court deeply in the governmental process—but in a way different from the 1890-1937 heyday of nay-saying by the Court.

This is the third—and most important—change in the judicial task: Rather than being a negative censor of programs proposed by the political branches of government, as it was during the 1890-1937 period, the Court now has an *affirmative* posture. This is best seen in the several series of cases concerning the Negro, the administration of the criminal law and the apportionment of legislatures. This tendency has been discussed elsewhere, so there is no present need to develop it in full.[76] The change from an aristocratic censor of the legislature to an institution which sets affirmative norms is both a subtle and a profound one in the

---

[73] Benjamin Hoadly, Bishop of Bangor, Sermon Before the King, 1717, p. 12, as quoted in GRAY, THE NATURE AND SOURCES OF THE LAW 102 (2d ed. 1927).

[74] 360 U.S. 474 (1958) (validity of the industrial security program of the Department of Defense).

[75] 357 U.S. 116 (1958) (passport procedure of the Department of State).

[76] Miller, *An Affirmative Thrust to Due Process of Law?*, 30 GEO. WASH. L. REV. 399 (1962); see ROSTOW, THE SOVEREIGN PREROGATIVE (1962), who states:

The powers of the Court are a vital and altogether legitimate part of the American Constitution. They should be used positively and affirmatively to help improve the public law of a free society capable of fulfilling the democratic dream of its Constitution in the turbulent second half of the twentieth century.

Id. at xxxiv.

jurisprudence of the Supreme Court. It has not come through any announced shift, but it may be seen through an evaluation of what the Court has done during the past quarter-century. It is, accordingly, a fundamentally different Court—at least in part—which sits now in Washington; and it is as an altered institution, operating within the facade of its older function, that it should be evaluated and discussed.

Cooperation as the Norm

The "affirmative" jurisprudence of the Court means that its relationships to the other branches of Government, and to the state governments, have also changed. In brief, this change places an emphasis upon *cooperation* between the branches, rather than conflict, and *cooperation* between the central and parochial governments of the federal system, rather than aloofness. As to the former, it is a long road from President Jackson's perhaps apocryphal sneer ("Chief Justice Marshall has made his decision, now let him enforce it") to the use of armed force by two modern Presidents in the enforcement of judicial decrees against recalcitrant state governments.[77] So, too, in the relationships between the judiciary and Congress: there is at least a tacit, perhaps an express, recognition in the national legislature that Court decisions must be accorded a very high degree of deference. Attempts during the past twenty-five years to change such decisions, by amendment or by statute, have not been successful. While it is true that legislation has followed the tidelands decisions,[78] decisions on state taxation of interstate commerce[79] and *Jencks*,[80] nevertheless, many far-reaching judicial decisions have remained law. The effort to amend the Constitution to "overrule" the *Pink* and *Belmont* cases failed,[81] as apparently has the more recent effort to overturn the

---

[77] See Pollitt, *The President's Powers in Areas of Race Relations: An Exploration*, 39 N.C.L. REV. 238 (1961).

[78] United States v. Louisiana, 339 U.S. 699 (1950); United States v. Texas, 339 U.S. 707 (1950); United States v. California, 332 U.S. 19 (1947). These three cases were nullified by Submerged Lands Act of 1953, 67 Stat. 29, 43 U.S.C. § 1301 (1958). See KAUPER, CONSTITUTIONAL LAW: CASES AND MATERIALS 261-62 (2d ed. 1960).

[79] Northwestern States Portland Cement Co. v. Minnesota, 358 U.S. 450 (1959); see 73 Stat. 555 (1959), 15 U.S.C. §§ 381-84 (Supp. V, 1964) (relating to the power of the states to impose net income taxes on income derived from interstate commerce). For a discussion of congressional action following Northwest Airlines v. Minnesota, 322 U.S. 292 (1944) (state taxation of airlines), see KAUPER, *op. cit. supra* note 78, at 490-91.

[80] Jencks v. United States, 353 U.S. 657 (1957) (production of government documents in criminal actions); see Jencks Act, 71 Stat. 595 (1957), 18 U.S.C. § 3500 (1958), passed in response to this decision. For a brief discussion, see KAUPER, *op. cit. supra* note 78, 893-94.

[81] United States v. Pink, 315 U.S. 203 (1942); United States v. Belmont, 301 U.S. 324

School Prayer Cases.[82] Perhaps the best-publicized recent attempt to vitiate a Supreme Court ruling was the vain effort in 1964 by both houses of Congress to avoid the effects of legislative apportionment, which was put on a "one man-one vote" basis by the decision in *Reynolds v. Sims.*[83] And it may be said that the Civil Rights Act of 1964[84] is a (belated) legislative recognition of the need to cooperate with the Court (and the Executive) in the massive realignment of the status of the Negro now under way. Cooperation, not conflict, is by slow accretion becoming the norm within the rubric of "separation of powers."

Similarly, cooperative actions may be seen growing within the units of the federal system. Obvious in the many grant-in-aid and other financial programs annually enacted by Congress, and placed in the hands of the states for localized administration, it can also be seen in the impact which Court decisions have upon the states. Of course, this tendency runs as far back as *Martin v. Hunter's Lessee*[85] and *Cohens v. Virginia,*[86] which established the power of the Supreme Court to review decisions of state courts on federal questions, and includes the decades of commerce clause and due process decisions relating to state legislation. Just as Supreme Court decisions, to bring the discussion up to the present day, have had a higher degree of cooperation from the other branches of the national government, so it may be said that they are receiving cooperation from the states. As such, they are a reflection of the growing unity, if not uniformity, of the American people. The picture of course is not an even one. Some decisions, as in racial segregation, have been systematically ignored by some states; however, even here almost every state is beginning the adjustments which must be made if the Negro is to attain first-class citizenship, adjustments which have become necessary because of national governmental decisions. Other decisions, as in school prayers, may have fallen on barren soil, in that it is likely that they are seldom followed anywhere.[87] The reapportionment decisions, it would seem, have

---

(1937). The controversy in the early 1950's over the treaty and agreement-making power of the federal government reflected a reaction to the Supreme Court's opinions in such cases as *Pink* and *Belmont*, which upheld the independent power of the President to conclude international agreements. An attempt to amend the Constitution, by the so-called "Bricker Amendment," failed by one vote in the Senate. See KAUPER, *op. cit. supra* note 78, at 310-12.

[82] Engel v. Vitale, 370 U.S. 421 (1962); Abington School Dist. v. Schempp, 374 U.S. 203 (1963); see Note, *School Prayer and the Becker Amendment*, 53 GEO. L.J. 192 (1964).

[83] 377 U.S. 533 (1964).

[84] 78 Stat. 241, 42 U.S.C.A. § 2000 (Supp. 1964).

[85] 14 U.S. (1 Wheat.) 304 (1816).

[86] 19 U.S. (6 Wheat.) 264 (1821).

[87] For example, in Kentucky it seems that most school districts will not adhere to the

been accepted by an appreciable number of American people[88] and a thorough readjustment of legislative districts on both the state and the national level would seem to be coming. In this instance, the affirmative jurisprudence of the Court has found ready allies and cooperation in many, if not all, states.

The Popular Reaction

It is submitted that the American people, speaking broadly, do not disapprove of the new jurisprudence of the Supreme Court. Despite certain obvious evidence to the contrary, the decisions in the past twenty-five years appear to have touched responsive chords in the nation. The swirl of controversy engulfs the Marble Palace, it is true, but nevertheless it is difficult to discern a nation-wide groundswell of opinion which would either overturn particular decisions or which would basically alter the Court's power. Instructive testimony on this score may be found in the decisions on the *School Prayer Cases*.[89] When those decisions were enunciated, cries of outrage went up from many parts of the country, but principally, it would seem, from those who had not taken time to read what the Court had said or to understand its decision. The tide of opposition peaked in early 1964 in the effort to get an amendment through Congress on the issue.[90] However, this attempt appears to have foundered, because of widespread efforts to explain the decisions and also to support them. The Court has not been treated well by the bar, practicing or academic, in explaining decisions to the American people. Even so, what passes for public opinion in this nation has looked upon the Court and the Constitution as symbols of awe and reverence.[91]

Oddly enough, as mentioned above, other than the politicians, it is the scholars and commentators upon the Supreme Court who have felt most outraged by decisions in sensitive areas, or who have at least felt sufficiently uneasy to put their opinions into print. For some of them, the

---

decisions. See N.Y. Times, Aug. 30, 1964, § 1, p. 36, col. 1. The earlier decisions on the church-state question, such as McCollum v. Board of Educ., 333 U.S. 203 (1948), apparently had little effect. See Patric, *The Impact of a Court Decision: Aftermath of the McCollum Case*, 6 J. Pub. L. 455 (1957), one of the few attempts to apply impact analysis to a Court decision.

[88] According to a Gallup Poll, 47% of the people approve of the decisions, 30% disapprove, and 23% have no opinion. Washington Post, Aug. 19, 1964, § A, p. 7, col. 2.

[89] Cases cited note 82 *supra*.

[90] See *Hearings Before the House Committee on the Judiciary*, 88th Cong., 2d Sess., ser. 9 (1964); Note, *School Prayer and the Becker Amendment*, 53 Geo. L.J. 192 (1964).

[91] See Lerner, *Constitution and Court as Symbols*, 46 Yale L.J. 1290 (1937).

image of the Court has been tarnished. But for them, the question of the Court's methodology and of whether its mysteries should be divulged to the laity, is predicated upon unexamined views of the entire governmental process, in particular that of the Supreme Court. That Court is to be studied and understood, it is submitted, only as an organ in a government of affirmative responsibility, one which has undertaken obligations far beyond those of yesteryear, a government toward which the American people look for guidance and for succor. The Court, accordingly, as a *constitutional* tribunal is not to be evaluated as a court deciding only the routine disputes of *meum* and *tuum*, but as an organ which has great public-policy influence.

THE PERSPECTIVE OF THE "DISINTERESTED" OBSERVER

The main task of the commentator upon the Supreme Court and its jurisprudence is to contribute to the understanding of that peculiar American institution. An important secondary task is to provide a flow of informed commentary which will serve the purpose of constructive criticism of the Court and its work, and thus assist in keeping the Justices within proper bounds. These are no mean jobs. On the contrary, they call for a combination of insight and judgment which requires meticulous attention to detail as well as a grasp of the theory and philosophy of judicial action. Moreover, the products of this effort have a definite, albeit unmeasurable, impact upon the decisional process. Commentators upon the Supreme Court form a part of the law-making process of the Court.[92] Constitutional law is not a completed, but a growing and self-correcting, system. It grows by what Morris Raphael Cohen called "the interaction between social usage and the work of legislatures, courts, and administrative officials, and even legal text writers."[93] The growing incidence of law review material cited in Supreme Court opinions is testimony of the extent to which legal writers have influence upon the Justices[94] (or, at the very least, of the extent to which Justices consider such writings helpful in buttressing their previously made decisions).

Contribution to the understanding of the Supreme Court and its product will come about when the commentators develop valid descriptive or

---

[92] *Compare* Newland, *Press Coverage of the United States Supreme Court,* 17 WESTERN POLITICAL Q. 15 (1964), *with* Newland, *The Supreme Court and Legal Writing: Learned Journals as Vehicles of an Anti-antitrust Lobby?,* 48 GEO. L.J. 105 (1959).

[93] M. R. COHEN, REASON AND LAW 76 (1950).

[94] Reynolds v. Sims, 377 U.S. 533 (1964), is particularly noteworthy in this respect.

predictive rules *about* constitutional law and its creation and operation as distinguished from rules *of* constitutional law. As Cohen put it, we should not forget that

> law is essentially concerned with norms that regulate, rather than with uniformities that describe, human conduct. The laws that natural science seeks to discover . . . are uniformities which if valid at all cannot be violated. . . . But it is of the very essence of legal rules that they are violable and that penalties or sanctions are provided for their various violations. They do not state what always is, but attempt to decide what ought to be.[95]

The difference is between the "scientific validity of real rules *about* law . . . [and] the legal validity of rules *of* law . . . ."[96] Impact analysis permits insight to be attained into the operative rules *about* law, the rules of how law acts in the social milieu.[97]

Ignored Areas of Inquiry

Constitutional law degenerates into theology and barren exegeses upon the sacred text of the Constitution unless and until it is tested by its consequences. But for such testing to be accomplished attention must be accorded at least three matters, each of which has received little attention in scholarly commentary upon the Supreme Court: (a) an appreciation of the ends sought to be served by the process called constitutional law (and, accordingly, of the ends of American society itself); (b) a method of ascertaining the causal connection between judicial decision and social change, by no means a self-evident proposition; and (c) knowledge of what may broadly be called the political economy of American constitutionalism (the political science, the economics, the psychology, the sociology).

Merely listing these indicates the poverty of knowledge about the constitutional adjudicative process that is the unhappy present fact. Not only do most commentators fail to take the ends or purposes of law and society into account, some even go so far as to deny vehemently that it is a proper inquiry. The most that can be said for that point-of-view is that it tends to relegate discussion of the Supreme Court and its jurisprudence to the same sort of sterile exercises that characterized theological literature during the Middle Ages: endless discussion about mi-

---

[95] M. R. COHEN, LAW AND THE SOCIAL ORDER 205 (1933).

[96] Rumble, *American Legal Realism and the Reduction of Uncertainty*, 13 J. PUB. L. 45, 75 (1964).

[97] See McDougal, *The Ethics of Applying Systems of Authority: The Balanced Opposites of a Legal System*, in THE ETHICS OF POWER: THE INTERPLAY OF RELIGION, PHILOSOPHY, AND POLITICS 231 (Lasswell & Cleveland eds. 1962).

nute doctrinal points. To be sure, there is some value in doctrinal clarification. To quote Cohen again:

> [W]ithout the use of concepts and general principles we can have no science, or intelligible systematic account, of the law or of any other field. And the demand for system in the law is urgent not only on theoretical but also on practical grounds. Without general ideas, human experience is dumb as well as blind.[98]

The point, however, is that more is needed than concepts and general principles. That "more" is the three matters listed above: the ends of law, the causal connection, the political economy of American constitutionalism.

Just as there is an absence of systematic attention paid to the ends of law, so too is there a paucity of knowledge about the relationship between judicial decision and social change. Many observers make statements of an a priori nature. Others proceed on assumptions, acting as if there were causal connections between Court decisions and social change without examination of the bases of those assumptions. Typical are those who have been called "police-prosecution oriented critics of the Courts"— those who assert that judicial decisions have had the consequence of antisocial behavior. Professor Yale Kamisar in a recent article has effectively shown the untenable factual foundation of such criticism.[99] Another example is a former president of the American Bar Association, Mr. John C. Satterfield, who maintained in 1962 that "fundamental changes are being made in our form of government by judicial decisions."[100] But if anything is known about social change, it is that it is not unilinear; changes in societal institutions are brought about by a process of multiple causation, one of which at times may be Court decisions—but only one. There is a poverty of knowledge about the relationship between law and social change.[101] However, that does not mean that students of the Court should not make the effort to develop insights along such lines.

The ends of society may be considered to be an aspect of ethics or of moral and political philosophy; the causal relationship between law and social change may be said to concern sociology. Lawyers, then, who comment upon Supreme Court decisions must perforce be aware of the mysteries of those intellectual pursuits. So it is with the third requirement of developing rules *about* law—knowledge of the political economy of American constitutionalism. Here, again, it is obvious that the bulk

---

[98] M. R. COHEN, *op. cit. supra* note 93, at 63.

[99] Kamisar, *On the Tactics of Police-Prosecution Oriented Critics of the Court*, 49 CORNELL L.Q. 436 (1964).

[100] Satterfield, *The President's Page*, 48 A.B.A.J. 595 (1962).

[101] See HAGEN, ON THE THEORY OF SOCIAL CHANGE (1962).

of the commentary makes little or no reference to the insights of the political science or of the economics of given decisions. Writers have busied themselves with the niceties of procedure or with the refinement of doctrine. For example, as Judge Henry J. Friendly has noted, in the field of administrative law there is an almost complete failure to note and criticize the substantive aspects of the public administration.[102] What Mr. Justice Frankfurter[103] and Mr. Massel[104] stated with respect to antitrust decisions is further evidence of the void. The gap may be seen with particular clarity in the plethora of law journal articles which have been produced discussing *Baker v. Carr*[105] and its aftermath. In this commentary there is an almost complete lack of reference to the manner in which the political system of this nation operates.[106] Some critics line up on one side, in full bay in their denunciation of the decisions; while on the other side, the defenders stand in measured array, stoutly affirming the Court in the apportionment cases.[107] For both sides it may be said that they have made little factual inquiry whatever as to the meaning for the political structure of the cases.[108]

---

[102] Friendly, *The Federal Administrative Agencies: The Need for Better Definition of Standards*, 75 HARV. L. REV. 863, 868 (1962).

[103] FRANKFURTER, SOME OBSERVATIONS ON SUPREME COURT LITIGATION AND LEGAL EDUCATION 17 (1954).

[104] Massel, *Economic Analysis in Judicial Antitrust Decisions*, 20 A.B.A. ANTITRUST SECTION 46, 58 (1962).

[105] 369 U.S. 186 (1962).

[106] See, *e.g.*, Friedelbaum, *Baker v. Carr: The New Doctrine of Judicial Intervention and Its Implications for American Federalism*, 29 U. CHI. L. REV. 673 (1962); Lucas, *Legislative Apportionment and Representative Government: The Meaning of Baker v. Carr*, 61 MICH. L. REV. 711 (1963); McCloskey, *Foreword: The Reapportionment Case*, 76 HARV. L. REV. 54 (1962); McKay, *Political Thickets and Crazy Quilts: Reapportionment and Equal Protection*, 61 MICH. L. REV. 645 (1963); Neal, *Baker v. Carr: Politics in Search of Law*, in THE SUPREME COURT REVIEW 252 (Kurland ed. 1962). *But see* Goldberg, *The Statistics of Malapportionment*, 72 YALE L.J. 90 (1962); Schattschneider, *Urbanization and Reapportionment*, 72 YALE L.J. 13 (1962); Sindler, *Baker v. Carr: How to "Sear the Conscience" of Legislators*, 72 YALE L.J. 23 (1962).

[107] The commentators upon the reapportionment decisions seem to proceed by what Holmes once called the "inspirational" method. "I sometimes tell students," Holmes said in 1899, "that the law schools pursue an inspirational combined with a logical method, that is, the postulates are taken for granted upon authority without inquiry into their worth, and then logic is used as the only tool to develop the results." Holmes, *Law in Science and Science in Law*, in COLLECTED LEGAL PAPERS 210, 238 (1920). But the question in the reapportionment decisions is not so much the logic as the worth of the postulates from which both the Justices and the commentators proceed.

[108] *But see* Goldberg, *supra* note 106; Schattschneider, *supra* note 106; Sindler, *supra* note 106.

State of Scholarly Commentary Today

The 1963 *Supreme Court Review*[109] is illustrative, by and large, of the state of scholarly commentary today. Operating under an editorial policy illustrated by quotations from Mr. Justice Frankfurter and Judge Learned Hand, which calls for critical but responsible discussions of the judicial process, the editor, Professor Philip B. Kurland, presents the following: (a) a Harvard Law School professor, Ernest J. Brown, on the *School Prayer Cases*; (b) an assistant professor of law at the University of Chicago, David P. Currie, on the extension of American labor disputes to ships flying "flags of convenience"; (c) a University of Kentucky law professor, Thomas P. Lewis, on the "sit-in" cases; (d) a University of Chicago economist, George J. Stigler, on "block-booking" of motion pictures; (e) the Dean of the University of Wyoming Law School, Frank J. Trelease, on the Arizona-California water hassle; (f) an assistant professor of law at the University of Michigan, Jerold H. Israel, on the right to counsel in state criminal trials; (g) a professor of law at the University of Chicago, Stanley A. Kaplan, on "insider trading" on the stock market; (h) a professor of political science at Brandeis University, John P. Roche, on the expatriation cases; and (i) extracts from correspondence between Mr. Justice Frankfurter and Professor Nathaniel L. Nathanson of Northwestern University regarding the assertion the Justice once made about the nonexistence of a common law of judicial review of administrative action. Let us turn to an analysis of these papers as leading examples of Supreme Court commentary today. What sort of theory of the judicial process do they reflect? Are they coherent statements of what the Court should do as well as what it has done? In attempting a brief answer to these questions the essays will be considered collectively, with references now and then to specific statements.

By and large, the authors appear to believe that what is important about a judicial decision is the manner in which the judgment is justified in the opinion(s) of the Court. Put another way—and with some exceptions—their main inquiry is whether the authors think the Justices have adequately explained the bases for their decisions. Adequacy of explanation, in turn, seems to be predicated upon whether the opinions are phrased in the methodology and terminology familiar to lawyers.

---

[109] This is the fourth in an annual hard-cover series of the University of Chicago Press, edited by Professor Philip B. Kurland of that university.

Thus we have Professors Currie and Israel opining, in the time-honored style of law-review editors, that the Court was "right" but for the "wrong" reasons. Professor Currie suggests "the Court may quite possibly have reached the correct result in *McCulloch* and *Incres*, but certainly not for any of the reasons it considered important";[110] and Professor Israel, while approving the result in *Gideon v. Wainwright*,[111] believes that "the Court might have framed an opinion . . . consistent with the accepted image of judicial review."[112] On the other hand, Professor Brown appears to feel that the Court not only used the wrong reasons in the 1963 *School Prayer Cases*, but also reached the wrong result. He bids us to "look to the Constitution"[113] and to find that the plaintiffs in those cases did not have the requisite standing to challenge the validity of the school prayers.

Such analyses overemphasize one aspect of the case and slight other equally important features. By concentrating upon the reasoning of the Justices as displayed in their opinions, the commentators have almost completely neglected both the substantive decision itself and the analysis of its importance in the manner in which values are shaped and shared within the nation. Professor Brown, however, does note that we "cannot explore the minds of Justices, and what they do not put on paper we do not know."[114] There is no impact analysis here, save in the brief note by Professor George J. Stigler, who as an economist presumably has not had the benefits of a legal education, and to some extent in Dean Frank J. Trelease's discussion of the Arizona-California water controversy. The tacit assumption seems to be that if the Justice writing the Court's opinion has phrased it in a manner sufficient to make lawyers feel comfortable, the inquiry can then stop. But is this so? I suggest that it is not even half the job necessary, if such commentary is to further understanding of the constitutional adjudicative process. A part of the additional task is an evaluation of the consequences of the decision. As Roscoe Pound observed in 1908:

> Scientific law is a reasoned body of principles for the administration of justice, and its antithesis is a system of enforcing magisterial caprice, however honest,

---

[110] *Flags of Convenience, American Labor, and The Conflict of Laws*, in THE SUPREME COURT REVIEW 34, 99 (Kurland ed. 1963).

[111] 372 U.S. 335 (1963).

[112] *Gideon v. Wainwright: The "Art" of Overruling*, in THE SUPREME COURT REVIEW 211, 270 (Kurland ed. 1963).

[113] *Quis Custodiet Ipsos Custodes?—The School-Prayer Cases*, in *id.* at 1, 32.

[114] *Ibid.*

and however much disguised under the name of justice or equity or natural law. But this scientific character of the law is a means, —a means toward the end of law, which is the administration of justice. . . . Law is not scientific for the sake of science. Being scientific as a means toward an end, it must be judged by the results it achieves, not by the niceties of its internal structure; it must be valued by the extent to which it meets its end, not by the beauty of its logical processes or the strictness with which its rules proceed from the dogmas it takes for its foundation.[115]

Of the papers in the 1963 volume of the *Supreme Court Review*, only that of the economist (Professor Stigler) makes any attempt to evaluate a Court decision "by the results it achieves, not by the niceties of its internal structure." Quite obviously, this paucity of impact analysis will not do, if ever students of constitutional adjudication are to attain an adequate understanding of that process. That task of understanding, it is to be emphasized, involves something different from the task of advocacy. It is one thing to present legal doctrine so as to achieve a desired end for a client; that, I take it, is the essence of an attorney's job before an appellate court. But it is quite another thing to ask the question of the nature of the adjudicatory process when the goal is that of scholarly understanding, without any interest other than that of furthering human knowledge.[116]

What may be seen in the commentary upon the Supreme Court is what may be termed "absolutistic legalism."[117] In brief, this is the fallacy which maintains that the Court and its jurisprudence is to be equated with an ordinary court of law. Believers in the fallacy parse Supreme Court decisions in much the same way as they would the decisions of, say, the Supreme Court of Missouri in a case involving the formation of a contract or the imposition of tort liability. Without going into the question of whether even *those* issues require more than "pure" legalistic lore to understand them (I believe they do), "we cannot pretend that the United States Supreme Court is simply a court of law."[118] The issues before it depend upon the evaluation of facts of all types, their consequences, and the values which are attached to those consequences. "These are questions of economics, politics and social policy which legal

---

[115] Pound, *Mechanical Jurisprudence*, 8 COLUM. L. REV. 605 (1908).

[116] *Compare* Professor Herbert Wechsler's demand for neutral principles from Supreme Court Justices, *Toward Neutral Principles of Constitutional Law*, 73 HARV. L. REV. 1 (1959) (Wechsler as professor), *with* the same gentleman's advocacy in Brief for Petitioner, New York Times Co. v. Sullivan, 376 U.S. 254 (1964) (Wechsler as practicing attorney).

[117] See M. R. COHEN, *op. cit. supra* note 93, at 88.

[118] *Id.* at 73.

training cannot solve unless law includes all social knowledge."[119] Adherence to the fallacy of legalism will never produce meaningful insights into the role of law in society or of predictive or descriptive rules *about* law.

If ever we are to be able to slough off the sterilities of legalism in commentary upon the Court, legal educators, it would seem, must take the lead. And that means that the role and function of the law school must be reexamined. Its position within a university structure is larger than the mere production of specialists who will man the nation's law offices in the practice of the law. That is, of course, an indispensable element in the task of the law school. But there is more. Without developing the topic fully, it may be said that scrutiny of the questions posed in this subsection is also the responsibility of the law schools. They are not doing it now. But they should. There is no reason to have a law school as part of a university unless it devotes itself to more than turning out legal technicians.[120]

Personal Values of the Commentator

This section is headed by reference to the "disinterested" observer. The word "disinterested" was put in quotes in order to indicate that in scholarly and other commentary upon the jurisprudence of the Supreme Court (or of any other area, for that matter), no one can be wholly impartial or disinterested or neutral. Everyone, that is to say, brings in to his scrutiny of a problem area a set of values which unavoidably colors his research or study—or, in the case of the judge, his decision. The idea of value-free research is a myth; it is unattainable in spite of the best intentions. "Values are an integral part of personality and as long as we are human," a political scientist has said, "we can assume that these mental sets and preferences will be with us."[121] That there can be a value-free social science is chimerical. Even when a researcher claims impartiality, "there can be no doubt that he has simply driven his moral views so far underground that even he himself may no longer be aware of them."[122]

---

[119] *Id.* at 74.

[120] At the very least the requirement is for continuing and meaningful relationships with other parts of the university structure. This has become particularly important with the advent of public law as the principal basis of the legal system. See Miller, *The Impact of Public Law on Legal Education*, 12 J. LEGAL ED. 483 (1960).

[121] EASTON, THE POLITICAL SYSTEM: AN INQUIRY INTO THE STATE OF POLITICAL SCIENCE 225 (1953).

[122] *Ibid.*

The idea that personal values inevitably accompany—and color—research in human affairs (including law) is widely accepted by leading social scientists of the era.[123] In like manner, a "disinterested legal science," including that part of it which is devoted to analysis and explication of the role of the Supreme Court, is nonsense. It is unattainable. What this requires, accordingly, is avowedly "facing the valuations" which are present in all commentary upon the Court. And that requirement, which unhappily is present in almost none of the commentary, has two aspects. It is important, in the first place, in order to permit readers of exegeses upon Supreme Court texts to be able to evaluate them in the light of the admitted value preferences of the writers. And secondly, it is necessary in order for social (and legal) data to be managed—to be organized into a coherent presentation. The first facet is of particular significance in the subject matter of this article, for only when a writer's value premises are set forth expressly and carefully is it possible to determine the validity of conclusions which are reached. The ends of intelligible comment upon such an important societal institution as the Supreme Court are not served by hiding, or by ignoring, the value preferences which are brought to the exposition by all commentators (including, of course, the present writer).

The task of delineating such value premises will not be easy, just as it will be difficult, as noted above, for commentators to set forth with particularity and comprehensiveness the goals of the constitutional adjudicative process. But both jobs are necessary and must be tackled if a full understanding of the Court is to be attained, if valid rules *about* constitutional law are to be developed.

CONCLUSION

Speaking in 1881, Oliver Wendell Holmes stated that

the philosophical habit of the day, the frequency of legislation, and the ease with which the law may be changed to meet the opinions and wishes of the public, all make it natural and unavoidable that judges as well as others should openly discuss the legislative principles upon which their decisions must always rest in the end . . . .[124]

Thus the idea that what has herein been called "impact analysis" would be useful in the analysis and explication of the jurisprudence of the Supreme Court is far from novel. In fact, it was not novel even to

---

[123] See Miller & Howell, *The Myth of Neutrality in Constitutional Adjudication*, 27 U. CHI. L. REV. 661 (1960).

[124] HOLMES, THE COMMON LAW 78 (1881).

Holmes, for Jeremy Bentham said much the same thing earlier in the 19th century.[125] The two Cohens, among others, said it in the 1920's and '30's; writing as important figures in the movement since called "legal realism," Morris Raphael Cohen and his son, Felix, emphasized the need for looking to the ends and purposes of law and the adjudicative process.[126] Others have made similar pleas.

The present article is an effort to update the discussion, to reaffirm the need for more than conceptual analyses, if ever an understanding of the Supreme Court is to be attained, and to point out some of the difficulties of such an undertaking.[127] It will not be an easy task, for it calls for a level of competence and expertise on the part of both judge and commentator that is rare indeed. But it is necessary. One may be pardoned the hope that the on-going discussion of the role and jurisprudence of the Supreme Court will soon encompass deeper and broader studies, studies which will produce the needed rules *about* constitutional law and the Court, as well as analytical expositions of the Court's doctrine.

---

[125] See FRIEDMANN, LEGAL THEORY 266-75 (4th ed. 1960).

[126] See M. R. COHEN, *op. cit. supra* note 93; F. S. COHEN, THE LEGAL CONSCIENCE (L. K. Cohen ed. 1960).

[127] See Mayo & Jones, *Legal-Policy Decision Process: Alternative Thinking and the Predictive Function*, 33 GEO. WASH. L. REV. 318 (1964).

8

THE SUPREME COURT, THE ADVERSARY SYSTEM, AND THE FLOW OF INFORMATION TO THE JUSTICES

(Coauthor: Jerome A. Barron)

Central to an understanding of the Supreme Court is its method of operation. The Court is much like any other court in this respect: it operates through the "adversary system." Hence, courts are not self-starters; they must await some litigant or litigants to bring them into operation. Once begun, however, the adversary system operates in ways not contemplated in the orthodox model, particularly in the ways that judges inform themselves.

We have already seen (in Chapter 3) that Supreme Court Justices bring their intellectual "can't-helps" with them. That, however, is only a small part of the ways in which judges inform themselves or approach the resolution of constitutional law issues. Under the orthodoxy, the Justices must rely, with little exception, on the litigants — the adversaries — to inform them about the problem to be decided. That is the pretense; the facts are otherwise. Informing the judicial mind is a complex matter, one in which the Justices themselves (and their law clerks) are important parts. Members of the High Bench have never been reluctant to move outside what the

"The Supreme Court, the Adversary System, and the Flow of Information to the Justices" was originally published in 61 *Virginia Law Review* 1187 (1975). Reprinted with permission of the *Virginia Law Review* and of Fred B. Rothman & Co.

lawyers for the litigants bring to them. One reason for this is the realization that what the Supreme Court decides involves great governmental affairs, as Chief Justice Earl Warren once said. The lawsuits may appear to deal with the litigants only, but people throughout the nation have an interest in the outcomes.

That the legal profession, both the lawyers and judges, are not sufficient to the need of adequate development of all the aspects of a given case is fast becoming self-evident. It calls, at the very least, for a thoroughgoing reexamination of the premises of the adversary system as a means of setting public policy. This essay is a preliminary inquiry into this question. Admittedly, it is one of great complexity, but it needs airing, and soon, if the courts are to continue in their task of saying what the law is. For that unavoidably also involves saying what the law should be—a job of far greater and more portentous proportions.

I

"How to inform the judicial mind . . . is one of the most complicated problems."[1] That assertion by Justice Felix Frankfurter succinctly states the essence of the inquiry under study here. The pretense is otherwise: As reflected in judicial opinions and textual commentary alike, it is widely assumed—possibly even believed—that
the traditional method of informing the judicial mind through the
"normal" operations of the adversary system is sufficient to the
need.

The traditional or "Blackstonian" conception of the judicial process clearly defines the formal system of information flow to the
court. Under this conception, an appellate judge refers to briefs and
the record, to answers gleaned from questions asked during oral
argument, and to "strict" judicial notice. The judge finds and applies the law in a "principled" way, accepting the facts as found by
the trial court. Little lawmaking is permissible.

This study was undertaken with the assistance of a grant from the National Science
Foundation, and was conducted under the auspices of the Program of Policy Studies in
Science and Technology of The George Washington University. The article should not in any
way be attributed to the National Science Foundation in particular, or to the federal govern-
ment in general; neither should it be attributed to the Program of Policy Studies in Science
and Technology or to The George Washington University. The help of Dr. Charles Lamb,
Research Political Scientist at the Program of Policy Studies, is gratefully acknowledged.
Professor Miller wishes to thank Joseph L. Tasker for his research assistance.

[1] Oral Argument, Briggs v. Elliott, Brown v. Board of Educ., 347 U.S. 483 (1954), reproduced in L. FRIEDMAN, ARGUMENT 63 (1969).

Forty years ago, Professor Edmund M. Morgan described several important premises of the Blackstonian model:

> (1) Our courts are agencies of society for the adjustment of disputes between litigants. The disputes must be real, not moot. Litigants cannot call upon courts to decide hypothetical controversies. (2) Our trial courts of common law are bipartite. Each consists of a judge and a jury. Our courts of equity have no juries. The division of functions between judge and jury in courts of common law has set the pattern for the conduct of the judge in dealing with questions of law and fact in courts of equity. (3) The judge has exclusive authority to determine the tenor and applicability of rules of law. Neither the judge nor the jury begins a trial with knowledge of any disputed and disputable matter of fact; disputes as to disputable matters of fact must be resolved on the basis of material presented at the trial. (4) The court, whether consisting of judge and jury or of judge alone, has no machinery for discovering, without the aid of the parties, matters of fact which are disputable and disputed. Consequently, the court must apportion between the parties the burdens of making the facts appear in an orderly and reasonable manner. It is the function of the judge to allocate these burdens. (5) The system is designed to produce, so far as practicable, a rational investigation and rational adjustment of disputes as to both law and fact. It necessarily posits a tribunal capable of reasoning rationally.[2]

To those premises there may be added at least five other premises concerning the Supreme Court. (1) Lawyers appearing before the Court are assumed to be sufficiently capable of dealing with complex socio-economic and technological matters. At the very least, the assumption is that counsel are roughly equal in competence. (2) The Justices, too, are competent to handle the immensely complicated matters that come before them. They are believed capable of resolving public-policy problems that the peculiarities of the American constitutional order cast before them for decision; their resolution furthers the common good. (3) The Justices act as justice blindfolded, with strict impartiality and without any personal preferences or predilections affecting the decisions. They have no pre-existing biases. (4) The Justices rule in accordance with "the law," which is considered to be, in Jhering's terminology, "a heaven of

---

[2] Morgan, *Judicial Notice*, 57 HARV. L. REV. 269 (1944). *See also* Roberts, *Preliminary Notes Toward a Study of Judicial Notice*, 52 CORNELL L.Q. 210 (1967).

legal concepts" from which the one principle most appropriate may be unerringly identified and applied. The law, thus, is not created anew in each constitutional decision, but pre-exists. Furthermore, the Justices are interested only in applying "the law," not in the personalities of the litigants or in the social consequence of their decisions. (5) Truth in the judicial sense comes from the clash of opposites, in the arena of the courtroom. In a limited yet nonetheless clearly valid way the Court acts as a minature "marketplace of ideas," which Justice Holmes told us was the way in which society determined the "truth."[3]

So stated, it may readily be seen that several of the ten premises of the adversary system do not comport with reality. Adherence to this formal system has been under attack, particularly during recent years when the Supreme Court has shown a marked tendency to "legislate" by stating, and thus trying to promulgate, norms of general applicability. An analysis of the *Abortion Cases, Roe v. Wade*[4] and *Doe v. Bolton,*[5] and of *New York Times Co. v. Sullivan*[6] and its progeny reveals an "informal" pattern of decisionmaking, one far more complicated than the orthodox model. Indeed the process is of such complexity that, as one appellate judge, quite seriously, said when told of our study, "let me know when you find out." Our analysis was less directed to the reasoning employed by the Justices in reaching their conclusions, than an attempt to determine the data considered relevant, the sources from which the data were obtained, and the principles enunciated by the Court as they relate to what the adversaries provided. We have explored the extent to which these data and principles were brought to the attention of the Court by lawyers for the parties directly involved, the role, if any, played by amici curiae, and the extent to which indepenent research was employed by the Justices, if at all.

Three problems arise when the information informally flows to the Supreme Court so as to become a major factor in the Court's ultimate decision. First, the development of such an extra-formal information flow may sap the integrity and morale of the formal adversary system. Second, if information critical to decision has not been disclosed to counsel prior to decision for their reaction, funda-

---

[3] First enunciated in Abrams v. United States, 250 U.S. 616 (1929)(dissenting opinion).

[4] 410 U.S. 113 (1973).

[5] *Id.* at 179 (1973).

[6] 376 U.S. 254 (1964).

mental questions of fairness concerning notice and hearing are raised. Third, if the "true" information flow to the Supreme Court is not the formal Blackstonian model, then perhaps we should overtly re-structure the formal means of informing the Court.

If it can be shown that the operating assumption of constitutional lawyers is that the formal Blackstonian model is simply inadequate to provide a sufficient information base for decision, the question of how best to provide the materials necessary for Supreme Court decision should be publicly debated for suggestions for change. That decision can begin with recognition that the decisionmaking process should comport with four objectives:

(1) *Openness.* The process should be as open as possible because openness in an institution which speaks for all of the judiciary is no less to be sought when judges are the principal governmental actors than when legislators and Presidents are concerned.

(2) *Relevance of the adversary system.* If the formal model for informing the Court by the briefs and argument of the lawyers on review plus the record below endures, that model requires restructuring to make it relevant and responsive to the true ways the Supreme Court informs itself rather than merely to the received wisdom concerning the Court. If the Court requires material information from the social or natural sciences which the record below simply does not provide and which counsel before the Court do not offer, then the inadequacy of the formal model should be frankly recognized. The pretense that the formal model works when it does not should not be maintained.

(3) *Obligation for Court to know what may be knowable.* If the "informal" information flow to the Court is, in cases of great social impact, the decisive information base for the Court, the difficulty is that the data which the Court has obtained without benefit of counsel may not be sufficiently authoritative. More relevant data may exist. But because the "informal" information flow is not open, and is in fact almost impregnable to external scrutiny, the Court denies itself information which it might have regarded as crucial had that information only been formally made known to it during its deliberations or at some time prior to final rendering of decision.

(4) *Fairness.* If the real information base for decision is not revealed to counsel and to litigants, the Court is deprived of the reaction of counsel to that information. Moreover, the opportunity for litigants to discuss the relevance of data basic to their success in the

litigation would appear to be demanded by even a minimal conception of fairness. If the Court makes an assessment of data central to the merits of a decision on an extended conception of judicial notice, *i.e.*, on the basis of data arising from the "informal" information flow, do we not have a problem of profound proportion?

These four objectives provided the background for our study. Our goal was to enlarge understanding about the Supreme Court, rather than to contribute to the predictability of future decisions. We tested some of the assumptions about the adversary system, limited, however, to the "inputs" to the system.[7] To aid our inquiry, we circulated a questionnaire to 175 law and political science professors whose academic specialty is constitutional law.[8] Their

---

[7] There are very few studies of the flow of information to the Justices. Furthermore, none of the established casebooks used in constitutional law classes devotes any attention to the question.

[8] The content of the questionnaire was as follows:

1. What have been, to your knowledge, the principal ways in which justices of the Supreme Court have *typically* informed themselves on issues brought before them for decisions? More specifically, what have been the ordinary sources of information and the usual means whereby it has been communicated?

2. What illustrative cases are you aware of where Supreme Court justices have gained, through *atypical* means, information pertaining (directly or indirectly) to cases decided by the Court?

3. Our major objectives include: (a) the identification and analysis of information flow in six prominent lines of Supreme Court decisions; (b) the development of the early stages of descriptive models of information flow to the Court; and (c) the generation of information flow hypotheses for future research. Which of these themes would you consider to be the most fruitful lines of inquiry? What other objectives would be useful to pursue?

4. At this time, we are weighing the possibilities of utilizing such approaches as systems theory, communication/information models, and "schema theory" (see Axelrod, "Schema Theory: An Information Processing Model of Perception and Cognition," 67 *Am. Pol. Sci. Rev.* 1248 (1973)) in developing models of judicial information flow. Of these models or bodies of theory, which would you consider to be most suitable for describing the flow of information to the Supreme Court? Why? What other models or theories might be worth exploring in this project?

5. With regard to the flow of information, how should or could the adversary system be modified to improve its functioning and to facilitate the fulfillment of its purposes in constitutional adjudication at the Supreme Court level? What should be the role of social science data at the Supreme Court level? What revisions in Supreme Court practice would be necessary to integrate the social science factor into the work of the Court?

6. Please make any additional comments on any aspect of this project.

7. Finally, in this study it is obvious that we are focusing on cases which illustrate major revisions in the law which have been accomplished by the Supreme Court. What, if any, differences are there in the way the Court informs itself when it decides cases which result in fundamental social change and when it makes less controversial interpretive decisions?

responses significantly influenced the course of the study.

Some limits to the study should be identified at the outset. First, the judicial opinion is at best an imperfect instrument for revealing the data and premises considered by judges to have been important in reaching their decisions.[9] The office of the opinion purportedly is to explain the thinking processes of judges, to give reasons in the language and logic familiar to lawyers for the decisions reached. About all one has is what the judges choose to tell us in their opinions, and to compare what is said and cited there with what was said and cited by counsel. Opinions in important constitutional cases, it merits iteration for emphasis, are likely to be more the products of a complex process of internal bargaining on the Supreme Court than exercises in logic or the articulation of reasons untarnished by either that system of internal give-and-take or the unstated premises of the opinion writer.[10] Second, we do not suggest that the development of the premises described here are perforce duplicated in all, or even most, Supreme Court cases. We do suggest, however, that the self-generated role of the Court in moving the direction of a case beyond the "adjudicative" facts involved appears clear in the transcript of the oral argument in *New York Times Co. v. Sullivan* and may be duplicated in cases of similar significance. It is also clear that the particular facts of the abortion cases before the Court in *Roe v. Wade* and *Doe v. Bolton* were a matter of almost no concern to counsel for the litigants, amici, and to the Justices. Counsel for all parties, and for the amici in both cases, recognized quite early that these cases were going to stimulate rules of law far beyond those necessary to decision. The record, briefs and argument do not in themselves reveal why the facts of either set of cases produced, in *Times*, a rule which revolutionized the traditional law of libel and, in the *Abortion Cases*, a legislative doctrine that purportedly invalidated the abortion laws throughout the country. Third, this study is preliminary in nature; only hypotheses are proffered, rather than definitive conclusions. One problem that inheres in such a pilot study is the extremely small number of cases thoroughly scrutinized. It will have to be left to other times and other persons to test the hypotheses that will be set forth below.

---

[9] *See* Miller, *On the Choice of Major Premises in Supreme Court Opinions,* 14 J. Pub. L. 251, 255-59 (1965).

[10] *See generally* W. Murphy, Elements of Judicial Strategy (1964).

With such broad questions as these in mind, we now turn to the several hypotheses developed in the study.

II

Proposition No. 1

The Supreme Court tends to ignore narrow "adjudicative" facts and to focus on larger, more general problems.

Since the earliest days of the republic the Court has steadfastly refused to issue advisory opinions at the request of other branches of government.[11] Professor Felix Frankfurter spelled out the reasons for this in a paper written fifty years ago.[12] The essence of that paper is that advisory opinions are not desirable because the Justices do not have the advantage of factual situations in which the legal principles may be seen. But what the Court will not do openly, or by invitation from Congress or the President, it will do by going far beyond the facts of a case to attempt to settle cases not then before the Court. "Backdoor" advisory opinions of that type are neither novel nor frequent.[13] But they are employed often enough to raise serious questions.

In the *Abortion Cases,* the Court treated the cases as open invitations to write broad, "advisory" opinions setting forth a legislative prescription to cover not only the particular litigants and other members of their class, but all women who become pregnant. Since the plaintiffs had both succeeded in three-judge district courts in having the Texas and Georgia statutes invalidated, their appeals had to be on the narrow grounds of the courts' refusal to issue injunctions barring future enforcement of the statutes. Nevertheless, the parties asked the Court to decide all of the constitutional issues involved.

In the *Roe* decision, Justice Blackmun's "advisory" opinion established a set of three trimesters dealing with the abortion decision

---

[11] *See* Flast v. Cohen, 392 U.S. 83, 96 (1968); Hayburn's Case, 2 U.S. (2 Dall.) 409 (1792); 3 CORRESPONDENCE AND PUBLIC PAPERS OF JOHN JAY 486-89 (H. Johnston ed. 1890) (concerning the Supreme Court's refusal to render, at President Jefferson's request, its advice on the scope of U.S. treaties with France).

[12] Frankfurter, *A Note on Advisory Opinions,* 37 HARV. L. REV. 1002 (1924).

[13] A well-known recent example of this phenomenon is Miranda v. Arizona, 384 U.S. 436 (1966).

and the power of a state to intervene. During the first three months, "the abortion decision and its effectuation must be left to the medical judgment of the pregnant woman's attending physician."[14] During the second trimester, the state may promote the interest of the health of the mother, "if it chooses," by regulating the abortion procedure "in ways reasonably related to maternal health."[15] During the final trimester, after the fetus has "quickened" to viability, "the State in promoting its interest in the potentiality of human life may, *if it chooses,* regulate, and even proscribe, abortion except where it is necessary . . . for the preservation of the life or health of the mother."[16] All of this was done in the name of privacy and of due process of law and of a steadily increasing "compelling interest" in the states in the matter of live births.

In *Roe,* a class action, the classes were represented by three very different plaintiffs: a childless married couple, with the wife having a neural-chemical disorder making a pregnancy a threat to her physical and mental health; an unmarried pregnant woman; and a physician. Even assuming that these were proper classes,[17] it is difficult to ascertain just how the Court got from that set of factual situations to the trimester system established in its opinion. The Court's opinion, larded with historical data not in the record, pays little attention to Ms. Roe or other appellants or other members of their "classes." Nowhere in the Court's opinion is there an indication of how long Ms. Roe had been pregnant; it accepted "as true" both that she existed and was pregnant when the suit was brought to test the Texas anti-abortion statute, and that she was unmarried and unable lawfully to secure an abortion. According to the Texas brief, "[n]either the Appellants nor the Appellee offered any evidence" at the hearing before a three-judge federal court convened to adjudge the constitutionality of the Texas statute.[18] Since the Court did not know the status of the appellants, the opinion could not be limited to one of the trimesters of pregnancy.

The conclusion is inescapable: Narrow "adjudicative" facts in the *Roe* case were not considered important insofar as they dealt with

---

[14] 410 U.S. 113, 164 (1973).

[15] *Id.*

[16] *Id.* at 164-65 (emphasis added).

[17] The Court did not address this question in the *Abortion Cases,* but the subsequent case of Eisen v. Carlisle & Jacquelin, 417 U.S. 156 (1974), makes the question critical.

[18] Brief for Appellee at 4, Roe v. Wade, 410 U.S. 113 (1973).

the status of the person seeking to invalidate the Texas law. The Court went even further: It slid over an argument of mootness, because "our law should not be . . . [so] rigid" as to proscribe adjudication because of the normal 266-day human gestation period.[19] Ms. Roe, in other words, was important to the trimester decision only because a pregnant woman was necessary to bring the action; once brought, the details of her condition became irrelevant.[20]

In *Doe v. Bolton*, there were two class representatives: a married, 22-year old woman who was pregnant, whose marriage was unstable and whose husband had abandoned her; and second, a group of physicians who wished to perform abortions. In its brief,‚ Georgia challenged this class configuration:

> *The use of this unwieldy group of plaintiffs for important constitutional litigation was never justified by the plaintiffs or discussed by the court below.* In the complaint . . . plaintiffs alleged that a class action . . . was appropriate to the circumstances. Rule 23 [of the Federal Rules of Civil Procedure] provides three clearly delineated alternatives . . . . [T]he plaintiffs [did not] state facts to meet the prerequisites set forth in Rule 23(a).
>
> The most serious defect resulting from this approach is that the class which "Mary Doe" claimed to represent was described in ambulatory terms which changed its complexion at various times. Different issues arise according to the limits of the definition of the class . . .
>
> Without a limitation and description of the class, the case is necessarily filled with numerous issues which are merely amorphous and hypothetical. A description of the class is absolutely necessary because the judgment is effective only on those found to be mem-

---

[19] 410 U.S. 113, 125 (1973).

[20] The oral argument in the district court demonstrates much the same willingness to ignore the facts of Ms. Roe's pregnancy:

Jay Floyd [Assistant Attorney General of Texas]: As to the unmarried, pregnant female, a unique situation arises: Is her action now moot? Of course, if moot, there is no case or controversy.

Q. It's a class action, wasn't it?

Floyd: It was a class action.

Q. Surely, you would—*I suppose we could almost take judicial notice of the fact that there are, at any given time, unmarried, pregnant females in the State of Texas.*

[Laughter]

Couldn't we?

Floyd: *Yes, your honor.*

Oral argument at 30, Roe v. Wade, 314 F. Supp. 1217 (N.D. Tex. 1970) (emphasis added).

bers. . . . The effect of the judgment is unpredictable and incalcula-
ble unless the court has specified those whose rights have been adju-
dicated.[21]

The Court rejected this argument and went even further in *Doe*
than in *Roe*. The conclusions of *Roe* were accepted, but then the
Court went on to say that "the medical judgment [about abortion]
may be exercised in the light of all factors—physical, emotional,
psychological, familial, and the woman's age—relevant to the well-
being of the patient." The attending physician is "to make his best
medical judgment"—to act "for the benefit, not the disadvantage,
of the pregnant woman."[22] In this connection, the abortion need not
be performed in a hospital accredited by the Joint Commission on
Accreditation of Hospitals; the attending physician need not get
advance approval of the abortion committees established by hospitals; and, finally, a requirement that there be confirmation of the
need for abortion by two Georgia-licensed physicians was declared
invalid.

Contrary to *Roe,* the Court in *Doe* was content merely to cite no
history or other "authority"; it did not set forth precisely why the
Georgia statutory provisions were invalid. We are left to assume
that the "compelling interest"/due process rationale in *Roe* covers
the different situations in *Doe*. As Justice Rehnquist asserted in his
dissenting opinion, the Court used equal protection analysis to cover
a due process decision—something new under the constitutional
sun.[23]

These cases suggest that the recently relaxed rules of standing
mean that a casual litigant[24] can at times do what Congress and the
President cannot: he can obtain an advisory opinion. The Court is
neither required to take such cases, nor, if it does, to issue such
opinions. The power is there, but it is discretionary. And that is so
whether the cases come by writ of certiorari or by direct appeal.[25]

---

[21] Brief for Appellees at 29-31, Doe v. Bolton, 410 U.S. 179 (1973)(emphasis added).

[22] 410 U.S. 179, 192 (1973).

[23] *Id.*

[24] Even a transient group of law students has been given standing to challenge agency
action. United States v. SCRAP, 412 U.S. 669 (1973). *But see* United States v. Richardson,
418 U.S. 166 (1974); Schlesinger v. Reservists Committee to Stop The War, 418 U.S. 208
(1974).

[25] Although technically appeals to the Supreme Court are not discretionary, they are in fact
handled much like petitions for certiorari. *Cf.* R. STERN & E. GRESSMAN, SUPREME COURT
PRACTICE §§ 4.28, 4.29 (4th ed. 1969).

The *Abortion Cases* were appeals from three-judge courts; but those appeals could easily have been dismissed because of mootness or other grounds of nonjusticiability. It is obvious that the Court wanted to rule on abortion, and further, to rule broadly, and that it found in Ms. Roe and Ms. Doe two parties who, although they had won declaratory relief in the lower courts, nonetheless were permitted to appeal because they did not get everything they had asked for. That they did not get that specific relief from the Supreme Court either is wryly amusing—but they did obtain a sweeping advisory opinion.

As in the *Abortion Cases,* the statement of law and policy in *New York Times Co. v. Sullivan* was far broader than the facts of the case required. While this in itself may not be surprising, it is significant that the briefs for the Times make it clear that it was not its expectation that the rule promulgated in *Times* would be far broader than was required under the facts.[26] Professor Herbert Wechsler, like a careful advocate, wrote his brief for the New York Times to allow the Supreme Court to hold simply that the first amendment does not permit a conclusion that libel per se has occurred when the plaintiff, a government official, has not been named and there was no intent to injure him. Indeed, any inhibition to first amendment values that might result by permitting Commissioner Sullivan to sue could have been corrected by simply holding that the first amendment forbids the application of the law of libel per quod to an unnamed public official. Or to put it even more plainly, where a public official is not mentioned in an alleged libel that reflects on his official duties, the first amendment will prevent a recovery.

To a limited extent the breadth of the principle formulated by the Court was suggested by Wechsler's argument in his brief that the Alabama court had greatly overstated the traditional common law of libel in a determined effort to hold that Commissioner Sullivan,

---

[26] Nevertheless, some of the briefs submitted to the Court were clearly directed to intertwining civil rights issues with the question of the constitutionality of a civil defamation recovery by a public official against a newspaper. For example, the brief submitted by counsel for co-petitioner Abernathy emphasized that "their trial below was a 'race trial' in which they were from first to last placed in a patently inferior position because of the color of their skins." Brief for Petitioner Abernathy in Reply to Respondent's Brief in Opposition to the Petition for a Writ of Certiorari at 52, New York Times Co. v. Sullivan, 376 U.S. 254 (1964). Much of this brief recounts the history of the struggle for black civil rights. It is impossible to guess the extent to which this influenced the Court, but the racial bias associated with Sullivan may have played a part in the establishment of a new doctrine designed to affect libel cases not involving race at all.

although unnamed in the offending editorial, had in fact been defamed by the Times:

> It need not be shown, as the Sedition Act required, that the defen-
> dant's purpose was to bring the official "into contempt or disrepute";
> a statement adjudged libelous *per se* is *presumed* to be "false and
> malicious" as the trial court instructed here. (R. 824) . . . .
>
> It should be added that the principle of liability, as formulated by
> the Supreme Court of Alabama, goes even further than to punish
> statements critical of the official conduct of individual officials; it
> condemns the critique of government as such. This is accomplished
> by the declaration that it is sufficient to sustain the verdict that in
> "measuring the performance or deficiencies" of governmental bodies,
> "praise or criticism is usually attached to the official in complete
> control of the body" (R. 1157). On this thesis it becomes irrelevant
> that the official is not named or referred to in the publication. The
> most impersonal denunciation of an agency of government may be
> treated, in the discretion of the jury, as a defamation of the hierarchy
> of officials having such "complete control." A charge, for example,
> of "police brutality," instead of calling for investigation and report
> by supervising officers, gives them a cause of action against the com-
> plainant, putting him to proof that will persuade the jury of the truth
> of his assertion. *Such a concept transforms the law of defamation
> from a method of protecting private reputation to a device for insulat-
> ing government against attack.*[27]

This passage is significant because it asks for the creation of a first
amendment-based privilege for the benefit of the media with respect to suits by public officials not named in the publication alleged to be defamatory. Wechsler's brief took a very limited and
cautious approach to the reincarnation of the seditious libel argument. Libel of named elected public officials need never have been
dealt with by the Court in *Times,* so limited and precise was Wechsler's analysis. The Times brief did not seek the extension of first
amendment protection against libel to all elected public officials,
whether named or unnamed. But the brief did introduce the powerful idea that allowing Sullivan to recover would in fact revive the
law of seditious libel, in a manner sufficient to cause the Court to
give wider protection than the Times sought.

In *Roe* and *Times,* therefore, the Supreme Court (a) ignored

---

[27] Brief for Petitioner at 49-50, New York Times Co. v. Sullivan, 376 U.S. 254 (1964).

adjudicative facts; (b) was not interested in the litigants *qua* litigants, but only as a means to an end; (c) stated a general, as distinguished from a specific, norm; and (d) thus became in fact a "self starter."

Proposition No. 2

The bar treats the Court much like a legislative committee. A variety of major premises are offered on the basis of their virtue as policy rather than of their authoritative character as law.

In response to our questionnaire, Professor L.H. Mayo asked, "Can we legitimately accept the proposition that some of the most critical Supreme Court decisions require very little data—only a strong ethical idea?" This is an important question. To understand its true significance, however, it is necessary to focus on the extent to which in cases like the *Abortion Cases* and *New York Times Co. v. Sullivan* the Supreme Court actively sought and was offered a choice among ethical ideas, or doctrinal choices, and nothing else.

The *Abortion Cases* present another example of what has long been known about the Supreme Court—that there is a wide disparity in the quality of the attorneys who practice before the Court. Those who follow the Court closely, and who periodically witness oral arguments there, know this as a matter of course. Again, however, the pretense is otherwise: the operational assumption of the adversary system presumably is that lawyers are of roughly equal competence.[28]

Roe v. Wade reveals the difference in approach between the sophisticated treatment of the issues by counsel and amici curiae seeking to invalidate the Texas statute as compared with the relatively routine approach to the problem by the Attorney General of Texas. Although the Attorney General did submit data concerning the viability of the fetus, nowhere in the briefs or argument is there found a statement similar to the following excerpt from appellants' brief:

---

[28] That this is not so was vividly shown in Gideon v. Wainwright, 372 U.S. 335 (1963), the case in which Court-appointed counsel Abe Fortas overwhelmed the opposition. *See* A. Lewis, Gideon's Trumpet (1964). It was also shown in many of the legislative reapportionment cases, such as Baker v. Carr, 369 U.S. 186 (1962). As the Freund Report of 1972 noted, "[t]he average level of oral advocacy in the Court is . . . disappointingly low." Federal Judicial Center, Report of the Study Group on the Caseload of the Supreme Court 42 (1972).

This Supplementary Appendix consists of offset reproductions of particularly relevant legal, medical, and social science publications, all of which are in the public domain.

Legal materials and commentary include a table showing in simplified form the types of statutes regulating the medical procedure of induced abortion in the United States. . . .

Similarly included, for the Court's convenience, are offset copies of all major court decisions, both state and federal, which passed upon significant substantive and procedural points in cases which questioned the validity of restrictions on medical abortion.

Finally, the principal medical and social science publications concerning relevant aspects of medical abortion incidence, safety, and need, have also been offset and included in this Appendix. None of the materials are highly technical, and several have been *noticed judicially* in support of state and federal decisions. . . . *These materials are included to ensure that the Court will not be without what Judge Learned Hand denominated as "the aid of unpartisan and authoritative scientific assistance in the administration of justice" in this case. Parke-Davis & Co. v. H. K. Mulford Co.*, 189 Fed. 95, 115 (C.C.S.D.N.Y. 1911).

The subject matter of this case—restrictions on the medical procedure of abortion—is particularly *susceptible to predisposition*. What in scientific circles is accepted fact may in other circles be heresy. The folklore on abortion, contraception, and human fertility in general is not likely to rest on firm scientific foundations. Only a few short years ago, an examination of texts used in medical schools revealed that "[t]wo thirds of the texts (25 texts) contained either no mention of contraception or only isolated reference to it, with no complete discussion." Tietze, et al, Teaching of Fertility Regulation in Medical Schools, 196 J. American Medical Ass'n 20, 23 (1966). If the medical profession only recently began to examine and understand contraception, with abortion lagging years behind, it is not to be expected that lawyers, judges, and the public at large would be fully knowledgeable in either or both fields.

As indicated above, *the lower state and federal courts have taken judicial notice of non-record scientific materials needed for a full understanding of the subject matter of abortion*. This practice has firm foundations in decisions dating back throughout this century. . . .

All of what is included has been carefully sifted in order to present the most directly relevant materials. *It is the hope of the parties that these materials will be of use to the Court in reaching an informed and just decision.*[29]

If the Supreme Court were a congressional committee, submission of such data would be routine. However, submission of this data to the Supreme Court in a constitutional case is not routine. Cognizant of other times when the Court judicially noticed extra-record facts, the attorneys for Ms. Roe brought to the Justices a mass of information relevant only to the larger, more general questions of the case—those that applied to women generally, rather than Ms. Roe specifically. By acting like counsel before a legislative committee, counsel were, in effect, asking the Supreme Court to make new social policy, rather than to rule in accordance with "the law."

Counsel also sought to influence what they admitted were "predispositions" prevalent about abortion. The pro-abortion amici briefs are replete with data on public and professional attitudes toward abortion, and may in some respects be considered a primitive public-opinion poll. For example, the Supplemental Brief for the Planned Parenthood Federation of America, Inc., and the American Association of Planned Parenthood Physicians contains the following statements:

> This supplemental brief is submitted for the purpose of bringing the prior brief up to date as of September 15, 1972 with reference to factual information *to which the judicial notice of this Court is respectfully invited,* with reference to developments in the applicable law in the past year, and with reference to the arguments as to the rights of the fetus advanced by appellees and various *amici* in their support subsequent to the filing of our brief.
>
> The facts set forth in Point I relate to the experience under the recent statutes which permit abortion on request in the early stages of pregnancy. These facts support the conclusion reached in the majority of the relevant cases decided in the past year (Point II), that no compelling state interest justifies statutes, like those of Texas and Georgia, which infringe the rights of women and doctors in relation to the obtaining and furnishing of abortion services. Indeed, it appears from these facts that compelling state interests require that such restrictions on the performance of abortion be removed.[30]

---

[29] Appendix to Jurisdictional Statement at 2, Roe v. Wade, 410 U.S. 113 (1973) (emphasis added).

[30] Supplemental Brief for the Planned Parenthood Federation of America, Inc., and the

The factual data indicates: an increase in the number of abortions from 1970 to 1971; that legal abortions are safer than childbirth; that availability of abortion reduces the infant mortality rate; and that discrimination against the poor and the non-white is substantially eliminated by permitting abortion. The brief also provides data on professional and public support for abortion:

> . . . the effect of the new permissive state statute[s] on public health and welfare has been salutary and the substantive position they reflect is supported by the general public as well as by national spokesmen for the medical profession, the legal profession and many other professional and lay groups throughout the country.[31]

This is really lobbying the Court, and if believed by the Justices, might be taken to show that the public was ready for the abortion decisions. The data were submitted with the request that judicial notice be taken of them. That means "retrial" at the Supreme Court level, without benefit of adversarial presentations.

Illustrative of the legislative-type arguments presented in the *Abortion Cases* is the following statement in the amicus brief of the Planned Parenthood Federation of America, Inc. and the American Association of Planned Parenthood Physicians: "[PPFA] and the [AAPPP] believe that they can provide the Court *facts* about contraceptive failure, unwanted births, and abortion which will not otherwise be presented."[32] The responsibility for determining the validity of facts is, at least as a matter of first instance, for the trial court, and even then, facts may be received by the trial court only insofar as those facts bear on the issues of the case as they affect the litigants. The brief of PPFA and AAPPP is innocent of any suggestion that the facts they presented to the Supreme Court were first presented to the district court, or that if they had been, such "facts" could successfully have been introduced into evidence. PPFA and AAPPP summarized the reasons they presented "facts" to the Supreme Court about contraception, abortion, and unwanted births:

American Association of Planned Parenthood Physicians as Amici Curiae at 2, Roe v. Wade, 410 U.S. 113 (1973).

[31] *Id.* at 3-13.

[32] Brief for Planned Parenthood Federation of America, Inc. and American Association of Planned Parenthood Physicians as Amici Curiae at 8, Roe v. Wade, 410 U.S. 113 (1973) (emphasis added).

In this brief *amici* have presented factual material, as well as legal arguments, to demonstrate that the Texas and Georgia abortion statutes, by prohibiting all abortions other than those performed for the specific reasons set forth in the statutes, violate fundamental constitutional rights of women and their physicians.

The facts on contraception, abortion and unwanted births which *amici* discuss . . . demonstrate the compelling need for a decision on the merits of these cases. Contraception, which provides the first line of defense against compulsory pregnancy and childbearing, is neither available to all nor fully effective when used. Literally millions of individuals have no access to the most effective, or indeed, any contraceptives because of their economic situation or because of inadequate medical or pharmaceutical services. In addition, many women for medical or other reasons, cannot avail themselves of the most effective techniques of contraception.[33]

The reference to "facts" in these excerpts is obviously not to adjudicative facts as they emerge after being introduced at trial under the rules of evidence. Rather, they are legislative facts, often presented at a level of flat assertion unaccompanied by supporting data.

The amicus brief filed in *Roe v. Wade* on behalf of New Women Lawyers, Women's Health and Abortion Project, Inc., and the National Abortion Action Coalition is entirely a legislative-fact argument. No attempt was made to focus upon the specific individuals involved:

Nearly ten years ago a medical expert reported that "the risk to life from an abortion, performed by an experienced physician in a hospital on a healthy woman in the first trimester of pregnancy is far smaller than the risk ordinarily associated with pregnancy and childbirth." (Dr. Christopher Tietze, Legal Abortion in Eastern Europe *J.A.M.A.* 175: 1149 (1961, April). A recent study of the death rate from childbirth in the United States revealed that there are still 20 deaths per 100,000 pregnancies among American women. *Studies in Family Planning*, 34:6-8 September 1969, Population Council, New York. The same study reported that the death rate due to legalized abortion performed in hospitals in Eastern Europe is 3 per 100,000 pregnancies. And so, in the United States today, giving birth is nearly 7 times more dangerous than a therapeutic abortion.[34]

---

[33] *Id.* at 9-10.

[34] Brief for New Women Lawyers *et al.* as Amici Curiae at 10, Roe v. Wade, 410 U.S. 113 (1973).

Amici here are comparing deaths from abortion in Eastern Europe to deaths from pregnancy in the United States. The problems of relevance and validity of the evidence are not even mentioned, much less analyzed. Another example of legislative fact is the following passage from the same brief:

> It is *common knowledge* that an abortion no longer entails the danger it did in the mid 1800's and early 1900's when the Texas and Georgia abortion laws as well as the laws of nearly all the other states were first enacted. In fact, as pointed out above, there is considerable evidence that abortion now carries about the same, if not lesser risks than childbirth. . . . Therefore the medical rationalization to sustain abortion restrictions can be easily dispensed with.[35]

These passages seem to be an example of using the amicus brief as a tactic for pressure group activity before the Supreme Court. The brief provides the reason for wanting a broad ruling, presenting mainly legislative facts.

To properly evaluate the interplay between the Court and a sophisticated constitutional lawyer that occurred in *New York Times Co. v. Sullivan* one must remember that if the libel were held to apply to the plaintiff and if the statements complained of were untrue, damage to the plaintiff's reputation was presumed under Alabama libel law. Therefore, a holding that due respect for first amendment values required proof of actual injury to reputation would easily have sufficed to remove the seditious libel aspect from the facts of the *Times* case. Traditional state libel rules would have been left intact.

In his brief for the New York Times, Professor Wechsler did not take the position that the first amendment should be interpreted to create an absolute privilege against permitting recovery by public officials for defamation. As he phrased the matter, the scope for first amendment limitations on the traditional law of libel was quite limited: "If there is room for protection of official reputation against criticism of official conduct, measures of liability far less destructive of freedom of expression are available and adequate to serve that end."[36] Wechsler suggested, as examples of less destructive measures of liability, requirements that the "official prove special

---

[35] *Id.* at 45-46.
[36] Brief for Petitioner at 31, New York Times Co. v. Sullivan, 376 U.S. 254 (1964).

damages, actual malice, or both."[37]

At oral argument Professor Wechsler apparently sensed the Court's willingness to fashion a first amendment rule broader than the rule he had suggested in his brief. His subtle change of position from brief to argument is shown in the following exchange:

> MR. JUSTICE GOLDBERG: Mr. Wechsler, your basic position, if I understand it correctly, is that under the First and Fourteenth Amendments no public official can sue for libel constitutionally and get a verdict with respect to any type of false or malicious statement made concerning conduct, his official conduct?
>
> MR. WECHSLER: That is the broadest statement that I make. But I wish in my remaining time to indicate what the lesser submissions are, because there are many that must produce a reversal in this case.[38]

This interchange indicates that there is at least a tacit agreement among the Justices and members of the sophisticated Supreme Court bar to treat the Court much like a legislative committee. In sum, a process of subtle and sophisticated joint policy-making is engaged in by counsel and the Justices.

Many possible policy choices were open to the Court in *Times*. One such choice was to establish an absolute first amendment privilege to defame an elected public official if the defamation does not specifically name the official and the defamation arises only by implication because a governmental unit under the care of the official has been criticized. Another policy choice was to compensate the official for the loss of the damage remedy by a right of reply which is absolutely privileged on the part of the public official. Neither of these alternatives was adopted by the Court, although both were discussed at oral argument. Less expansive incursions into traditional libel law were also suggested, either explicitly or implicitly, by Professor Wechsler. For example, Wechsler urged that a qualified rather than an absolute privilege should be conferred on the citizen who falsely and maliciously libels a public official. A qualified privilege would, according to Wechsler, accommodate the conflicting interests of official reputation and of freedom of discussion. Another policy choice offered by Wechsler was a rule which

---

[37] *Id.*

[38] Oral Argument at 38, New York Times Co. v. Sullivan, 376 U.S. 254 (1964).

would limit the action by a public official to proof of damage. As a corollary proposition, Wechsler suggested a first amendment ban on punitive damages.[39]

Another choice, related to the first policy choice, was a holding that there was no evidence in the record to support a finding that the particular statements in the advertisement published by the Times had any tangible adverse effect on the reputation of Sullivan.[40] This choice involved a suggested rule that in a libel case, where a first amendment interest is alleged to be infringed, the Supreme Court can review the facts which justify the infringement. In such a case, there is a question of fact which also presents a constitutional issue. In those circumstances, the Supreme Court is freed from the notion that as an appellate court it cannot independently review facts. Since the Supreme Court can constitutionalize a field of law, when it expands constitutional doctrine it also expands its powers beyond functions associated with the normal appellate model. In oral argument, Wechsler mentioned two cases where the Court had done this in the past.[41]

The sixth choice involved a ruling which would place limits on the power of the jury to set damages in libel cases where the injury to reputation is presumed and not proved. After an exchange between Justice Brennan and Professor Wechsler, both agreed that this option, the objectives of which might be satisfied by adoption of some of the other choices, was an independent submission.[42]

A seventh choice—that the Times' contacts with Alabama were too slight or minimal to authorize valid service of process over the Times in Alabama as a matter of fourteenth amendment due process—was mentioned only in passing by Wechsler during oral argument. The Justices did not question him concerning it. Wechsler, however, had extensively briefed the point. The Court in a footnote in its opinion rejected this jurisdictional argument, claiming that the Times under Alabama law had waived the issue and that it would not inquire into it since it was decided upon an independent and adequate state ground.[43]

---

[39] *Id.* at 39.

[40] *Id.* at 40.

[41] *See* Thompson v. Louisville, 362 U.S. 199 (1960); Bridges v. California, 314 U.S. 252 (1941).

[42] Oral Argument at 41, New York Times Co. v. Sullivan, 376 U.S. 254 (1964).

[43] 376 U.S. at 264 n.4.

The extent to which some of the lawyers in the *Times* case perceived that the case was going to provide an opportunity for the creation of new law is illustrated by the candid presentation of doctrinal choices in the amicus brief for the American Civil Liberties Union:

> In recognition of the problems raised by alleged libels about public officials, many courts have evolved specific modifications of the general law of libel to meet the realities of the public official situation and to protect First Amendment rights. They have done this on a variety of different theories: some have defined the substantive law as calling for more extreme accusations to justify a holding of libel per se as to a public official; some have obliterated the extremely tenuous distinction between fact and comment and permitted "fair comment" on public officials whether based on facts truly stated or not; some have held the presumptions of damage and malice inoperative as to public officials; some have in effect shifted the burden of proof to the plaintiff; and some have tended to exonerate by a finding of "substantial truth."[44]

In a sense these statements do coincide with the Blackstonian model of the lawyer's function at the bar, since they are a description of what other courts have done. However, these submissions were not presented on the basis of their authoritative legal character, but rather reflected adherence to a basic philosophical or political goal—safeguarding the "right of the American people to speak their minds about those whom they elect or appoint to public office."[45]

In terms of what is necessary to encourage criticism of government, not a single question was directed from the bench to the lawyers in the *Times* case as to what the experience had been in states having a liberal fair comment rule, as compared to those that did not, with regard to the impact on vigorous debate and political commentary in the press. The submissions of doctrinal choices in *Times* were offered in a vacuum so far as empirical data were concerned. Moreover, in *Times* empirical information was neither mentioned nor sought. The calculus for selection of the "winning" ethical ideal is not indicated.

From the foregoing discussion of the approach of counsel to the

---

[44] Brief for the ACLU and New York Civil Liberties Union as Amici Curiae at 25, New York Times Co. v. Sullivan, 376 U.S. 254 (1964).

[45] *Id.*

Court in the *Abortion Cases* and *New York Times Co. v. Sullivan*, we suggest that the function of briefs and argument in formative Supreme Court decisions is not to inform the Court as to what rule of "law" in any traditional sense the Court is compelled to apply. Rather, it is to offer some empirical data or law-policy hypothesis which counsel anticipate the Court already has a predisposition to accept.

Proposition No. 3

*New doctrine at times is urged on counsel
by the Court, rather than the reverse; as a
result a shift may occur from a limited position in the briefs to a broad position during
oral argument.*

The reason, on the facts of the *Times* case, that the defense of truth was inadequate to free the Times from damages was not that truth was too heavy a standard of care for the press. Rather it was the fact that the plaintiff had not been specifically defamed. The following colloquy between Professor Wechsler and Justice Stewart illustrates this point:

> MR. JUSTICE STEWART: Putting it bluntly, the reason you couldn't meet that defense is that some of thse statements were not true?
> MR. WECHSLER: But beyond that, the point I am trying to make, Mr. Justice Stewart, is that the plaintiff was contending that the statement said that Sullivan had bombed King's home. It was true that King's home was bombed. But it was not true that Sullivan bombed his home, or that we conceived that anybody in the world in his right mind could read this to say that Sullivan had bombed his home. That was the difficulty.[46]

Minimally, Wechsler asked as a first amendment matter that libel by innuendo should not be available to a public official who was in fact not named by the libel. Justice Stewart, however, was more interested in talking about the inadequacy of the defense of truth to protect the press from oppressive libel judgments. Little interest was shown in Wechsler's much more careful approach to the defense of truth in this specific context. Wechsler had contended

---

[46] Oral Argument at 35, New York Times Co. v. Sullivan, 376 U.S. 254 (1964).

that the defense was inadequate not because it could not protect the Times under the facts but because it was irrelevant to the main defense: Sullivan was not libelled because he was never contemplated or mentioned in the allegedly libelous statements in the advertisement. Therefore, the veracity of the statements was irrelevant to Sullivan's suit against the Times.

Thus, the Court was led to change the common law of libel in the states in which truth was a defense to defamation because the peculiar facts in *Times* made truth an irrelevant defense. In Wechsler's view, the Times could not plead or prove truth with regard to the alleged defamation because in the Times' view the defamation should never have been interpreted as the plaintiff construed it. For present purposes, our conclusion is that a desire by the Justices to create a new social policy may tempt them to state the arguments they would like a petitioner to make when counsel, acting cautiously and conventionally, have proffered more limited arguments.

Doubtless reacting to the vibrations implicit in the Court's question to him in oral argument, Professor Wechsler broadened his statement of the rule announced by the Supreme Court of Alabama:

> [A] public official is entitled to recover presumed and punitive damages subject to no legal limit in amount for the publication of a statement critical of his official action of an agency under his general supervision, if the court finds that the statement tends to injure reputation—which the court did find here—and the jury finds that the statement makes a reference to him.[47]

Wechsler thus seems to have changed position in oral argument from that taken in the briefs, with his effort to get the Court to announce a new rule of law being much more candid in argument. When speaking to the Justices, his basic position was that the first amendment prevented *any* libel recovery for criticism of official conduct. When Justice Brennan asked whether there were any limits to criticism of official conduct which would fall outside the protection of the first amendment,[48] Wechsler replied by emphasizing the opportunity the case presented to the Court to state a new rule. He conceded that his position in the briefs that an award of damages for defamation concerning official conduct to a public official was

---

[47] *Id.* at 29.
[48] *Id.* at 30-31.

equivalent to seditious libel was, legally and historically, not impregnable, and that the constitutionality of the Sedition Act of 1798 had never been specifically ruled on by the Court. But he used the ambiguity in the law as a springboard for the formulation of new doctrine:

> MR. WECHSLER: We are talking about the full ambit of the First Amendment. I realize the weight of this argument at this time. The Sedition Act was never passed on. But on the other hand as I see our case we are in the same position that the contempt cases were in in 1940, when the scope of the contempt power had never been considered by this Court. When obscenity was here, that issue had never been considered. In short, this is a field of constitutional interpretation which is 35 years old. That is a fact of life. And this is the first time that we have had the opportunity—that the opportunity has arisen to make this submission in this Court. But I believe that if James Madison were alive today, so far as anything I can see, anything that he wrote, particularly in the report on the Virginia Resolutions, that the submission that I am making is the submission he would make.[49]

These illustrations from the oral argument in the *Times* case indicate that the Court can subtly steer counsel beyond the frontiers of traditional doctrine. The Justices by implication and by the substantive content of their questions, suggest to counsel their willingness to venture into new questions and to chart new constitutional doctrine.

The difficulty with this process is that it is too subtle. The implications and suggestions of Justices may be easily grasped when the advocate at the bar is a constitutional law professor from Columbia University Law School. But the subtle cues may not be as readily discovered when the advocate is an able Alabama lawyer whose life work is not absorbed with every raised eyebrow at Supreme Court oral argument and every nuance in Supreme Court decisions. If the Court wanted to establish a new first amendment privilege to protect the media against libel suits by elected public officials, that intention should have been communicated to the parties. The Justices should have assured that all parties would be able to respond fully and fairly to this novel and fundamental issue. That, surely,

---

[49] *Id.* at 31-32.

would have been a more direct, even more honest, way of proceeding. And it would have comported with the essence of the adversary system.

Proposition No. 4

The integrity of non-legal (and other) data
is frequently not subject to test or challenge
by the losing party.

The problem of untested data is crucial; it challenges the validity of the adversary system as a means of setting public policy. Edmond Cahn's criticism of the Court's decision in *Brown v. Board of Education*[50] points up the problem. Though a strong believer in the justness of the result reached in the case, Professor Cahn was troubled by the use of the data and wrote in a well-known essay that the materials cited by the Chief Justice simply did not support the proposition for which they were listed.[51] That is indeed a critical insight, which, if true, casts into doubt the employment of social science data by judges, quite often without having been brought to the attention of the Court by counsel. One is reminded of Judge Jerome Frank's pungent remark in 1956: "I think it is a mistake for my colleagues needlessly to embark—without a pilot, rudder, compass or radar—on an amateur's voyage on the fog-enshrouded sea of psychiatry."[52] Judges should exercise "vigilance, critical examination, and searching inquiry"[53] when dealing with social and behavioral science materials.

In the *Abortion Cases*, Justice Blackmun thought it necessary to determine the reason for enactment of the 19th-century state laws making abortion a crime. He accepted the idea that the laws were for the protection of the health of women, as against the argument that they were to protect unborn children. Modern medicine, Blackmun said, has reduced the problem of infection and death in

---

[50] 347 U.S. 483 (1954).

[51] *See* Cahn, *Jurisprudence*, 30 N.Y.U.L. Rev. 150 (1955), 31 N.Y.U.L. Rev. 182 (1956). Cahn's criticism differs from the widespread, often uninformed allegations that the Court in *Brown* had relied on "sociological" rather than "legal" data. *See, e.g.*, N.Y. Times, July 17, 1955, at 37, col. 3 (views of Senator Thurmond). This latter comment displays a depressing lack of knowledge of how courts, including the Supreme Court have always acted.

[52] United States v. Flores-Rodriguez, 237 F.2d 405, 412 (2d Cir. 1956)(concurring opinion).

[53] Cahn, *Jurisprudence*, in 1957 Annual Survey of American Law 575, 586 (R. Collings ed. 1958).

abortion, and thus undercut the reason for the statutes.[54] Black-mun's point was that medically supervised abortions were harmful to the woman at the time that the statutes became law. In so con-cluding he rejected the view that the laws were "the product of a Victorian social concern to discourage illicit sexual con-duct"—saying that "no court or commentator has taken the argu-ment seriously."[55] Faced then with a choice between protection of prenatal life and prevention of harm to women as a basis for the state laws, Blackmun opted for the latter.[56]

By summarily rejecting the argument that these laws were en-acted for the purpose of protecting the fetus, Blackmun made it necessary that the authorities he cited for his conclusions be tested in order to determine whether they in fact support that result.

Justice Blackmun said, "[w]hen criminal abortion statutes were first enacted, the procedure was a hazardous one for the woman," citing page 19 of C. Haagensen and W. Lloyd, *A Hundred Years of Medicine* (1943).[57] The difficulty with Blackmun's opinion is that he

---

[54] 410 U.S. 113, 149 (1973). It should be noted that this is the opposite of the orthodox rationale for due process limitations, which requires only that a reasonable basis be shown for a statute. *See* Woods, Housing Expediter v. Cloyd W. Miller Co., 333 U.S. 138 (1948); Marcus Brown Co. v. Feldman, 256 U.S. 170 (1921); Block v. Hirsch, 256 U.S. 135 (1921). Blackmun's analysis implies that when that "reasonable basis" is eliminated, a formerly permissible statute may become unconstitutional.

[55] 410 U.S. 113, 148 (1973).

[56] *Id.* at 151:

Parties challenging state abortion laws have sharply disputed in some courts the con-tention that a purpose of these laws, when enacted, was to protect prenatal life [citing *Abele v. Markle*, a 1972 federal district court decision]. Pointing to the absence of legislative history to support the contention, they claim that most state laws were designed solely to protect the woman. Because medical advances have lessened this concern, at least with respect to abortion in early pregnancy, they argue that with respect to such abortions the laws can no longer be justified by any state interest. There is some scholarly support for this view of original purpose [citing two articles by Professor Cyril Means of New York Law School]. The few state courts called upon to interpret their laws in the late 19th and early 20th centuries did focus on the State's interest in protecting the women's health rather than in preserving the embryo and fetus [citing *State v. Murphy*, an 1858 New Jersey case].

[57] All operations during the 19th century were both painful and subject to almost certain infection. As the authors say in the book cited in the text —

the greatest handicap of the surgeons of a hundred years ago and before was infection. Almost every accidental wound brought to a hospital for treatment, and every opera-tive wound made in a hospital, became infected. A high percentage of these infections were serious ones. Under these circumstances surgery was limited to minor procedures on the surface of the body, and to opening abesses and amputating limbs that had to be dealt with. The surgeons dared not invade the great cavities of the body, the chest, the head, and the abdomen.

C. Haagensen & W. Lloyd, A Hundred Years of Medicine 19 (1943).

states conclusions about medicine with a certitude the data does not support. For example, he observed that viability of a fetus usually occurs at 28 weeks but may occur as early as 24 weeks; however, the source he cites for this statement actually says that viability can vary between fetal weights of 400 grams (20 weeks gestation) and 1000 grams (28 weeks gestation). But that source maintains that survival even at 700 or 800 grams is unusual.[58] The importance of establishing fetal viability, according to Justice Blackmun, is that this is the point where the state has a "compelling interest" in the protection of potential life.

Justice Blackmun, moreover, relied extensively on two law review articles published by a source with a definite point of view on the abortion controversy—Professor Cyril Means of the New York Law School, who had been a member of Governor Rockefeller's commission to review New York's abortion laws.[59] In his second article, published in 1971, Means not only commented on pending cases before the Court; he also analyzed the arguments of counsel and amici. The judicial procedure here is questionable:[60] If the articles were written from a particular point of view, then they should be treated more as briefs than as dispassionate disquisitions of a topic.[61]

In *Times,* a stunning alteration of the American law of libel was generated, at least in part, by Professor Wechsler's stimulating

---

[58] L. HELLMAN & J. PRITCHARD, WILLIAMS OBSTETRICS 493 (14th ed. 1971). *See also* STEDMAN'S MEDICAL DICTIONARY 1388 (22d ed. 1972), in which it is said that "viability" usually connotes a fetus that has reached 20 gestational weeks and 500 grams in weight.

[59] Means, *The Law of New York Concerning Abortion and the Status of the Foetus, 1664-1968: A Case of Cessation of Constitutionality,* 14 N.Y.L.F. 411 (1968); Means, *The Phoenix of Abortional Freedom: Is a Penumbral or Ninth-Amendment Right About to Arise From the Nineteenth-Century Legislative Ashes of a Fourteenth-Century Common-Law Liberty?,* 17 N.Y.L.F. 335 (1971).

[60] The decision in the *Abortion Cases* has been unsuccessfully challenged on the grounds that the Court took judicial notice of inaccurate material on this issue. The case is Ernest v. Miller, File No. 7103, (Circuit Court of the City of Richmond, Virginia, September 10, 1974). The case was dismissed by Judge R. L. Williams and was unreported.

[61] *See* Miller, *The Myth of Objectivity in Legal Research and Writing,* 18 CATH. U.L. REV. 290 (1969).

Justice Blackmun is not unique in his use of legal periodicals; Justice Black apparently relied on a law review article by John Frank, a former clerk and government lawyer in the Interior Department, in writing his opinion in Duncan v. Kahanamoku, 327 U.S. 304 (1946). The article is Frank, Ex Parte Milligan v. The Five Companies: *Martial Law in Hawaii,* 44 COLUM. L. REV. 639 (1944). *See generally* Newland, *Legal Periodicals and the United States Supreme Court,* 7 U. KAN. L. REV. 477, 486 (1959).

analogy between the civil action for libel damages brought by Sullivan against the New York Times to the criminal prosecutions for libel by the federal government against political antagonists under the short-lived Alien and Sedition Law. In *New York Times*, Wechsler's brief made particular use of historical works on the history of freedom of the press. The strength of the historical parallel in terms of the 18th-century consequences on freedom of expression of a seditious libel prosecution, as compared with the 20th-century consequences on freedom of expression of a civil defamation suit for damages, is examined at no place in the briefs, argument, or record with any rigorous comparative historical perspective. Furthermore, the authenticity of the historical texts discussing the Alien and Sedition Law cited by the Times' counsel is nowhere subjected to critical examination by opposing counsel. Historical texts which might not be permitted to be introduced in evidence at trial for any purpose thus are permitted to create an illusion of authority and authenticity before the Supreme Court by virtue merely of citation and quotations in the brief.[62]

The core of the problem is how a judge can validly choose from among conflicting social scientists.[63] That problem is exacerbated

---

[62] On oral argument, Justice Goldberg apparently tried to test the strength of Wechsler's analogy of Sullivan's civil recovery for damages to a criminal prosecution for seditious libel by asking this question concerning the ruling of the Alabama Supreme Court:

> MR. JUSTICE GOLDBERG: . . . Would there be encompassed in the Court's ruling that since this, in the language of Mr. Sullivan's testimony, reflected upon the community as well as upon himself, and since the ad refers to southern violators, did the Court mean that any member of the community was libeled by this?
>
> MR. WECHSLER: I can't say that the Court went that far, Mr. Justice. I think that emphasis must be placed on the official position of Commissioner Sullivan.

Oral Argument at 26, New York Times Co. v. Sullivan, 376 U.S. 254 (1964).

It is interesting that the respondent's brief did not challenge the analogy of civil defamation suits for damages to criminal prosecutions for seditious libel. After all, the latter were brought by the state to punish an alleged offense against the state. Sullivan, if he had prevailed, would have won civil damages.

[63] The "empirical" data which counsel cites and asks the Court to accept may at times be very fragmentary and impressionistic, as the following excerpt from oral argument before the district court in *Doe v. Bolton* clearly indicates:

> MRS. HAMES [Counsel for Appellant]: There was an article in Sunday's *New York Times* which reported the substantial number of abortions in New York; but more significantly, it found that there were only 4.6 deaths per 100,000 live births the first year, and 3.5 the second year.
>
> So that the New York clinical experience has proved to be successful.
>
> Q. Mrs. Hames, *is there any limit to the judicial notice we can take? I mean, is last Sunday's newspaper a perfectly permissible thing for us to rely on in deciding a case like this?*

when within the workings of the adversary system judges take judicial notice of data not subject to the test of the courtroom. "Independent research"[64]—the term is Justice William Brennan's—makes the judge an active, third-party participant in the informing process.

The members of the Court simply do not believe they can rely upon counsel to bring before them all relevant data, however labelled. So they conduct, as Brennan said, independent research; they send their law clerks scurrying through the libraries and elsewhere, as did Justice Louis Brandeis,[65] to add to the totality of knowledge about the social issues that they must decide as

---

H. . . . I think that this study is a published document. It is a very recent published document, but it is something that does receive wide circulation as a Public Health Department Report. I do not have a copy of it, because it is such a recent report. There are similar reports by the U.S. Public Health Department. We have previously furnished reports to the Court's library, and will be happy to do so on the statistical information.

I do recognize—

Q. Well, aren't such things something that go to legislative judgment rather than constitutional evaluation?

H. I think it is important that the legislature not encumber a fundamental constitutional right with so many procedures as to effectively manipulate it out of existence. . . . I think that that is not properly a legislative judgment.

Q. Well, you were just talking about statistics, however, in recent reports, and this kind of thing. . . .

H. Well, I would also, instead of the *New York Times*, which I recognize is not a very widely accepted source for judicial notice, however, a higly recognized newspaper, I would cite a study by Dr. Christopher Teitze, who is the recognized medical authority in the area of statistics, in which he finds that complications are lower—

Q. When you say "the" recognized authority, you mean there are no others?

H. Well, I—

Q. "a."

H. —"a," excuse me.

Q. All right.

H. He finds that complications are lower in clinics than in hospitals, and were lower for hospital outpatients than for inpatients. And that study is found—

Q. But don't you think there are other factors there, that more complicated cases go into hospitals, that the more complicated cases are in-patients rather than outpatients?

H. He took that into consideration in arriving at his statistics. I'm sorry, I should have pointed that out.

Oral Argument at 14-15, Doe v. Bolton, 319 F. Supp. 1048 (N.D. Ga. 1970) (emphasis added).

[64] *See* Brennan, *Working at Justice,* in AN AUTOBIOGRAPHY OF THE SUPREME COURT 300, 303 (A. Westin ed. 1963).

[65] *See* A. BICKEL, THE UNPUBLISHED OPINIONS OF MR. JUSTICE BRANDEIS 216-18 (1957). This judgment (of Professor Bickel) is an evaluation of all of the Brandeis papers now at the Harvard Law School.

lawyers.[66] Thus when facts are freely found at the appellate level through an expansive use of judicial notice, the lawsuit is in fact retried in the appellate court but without benefit of counsel. Consider the following argument from the petition for rehearing in *Doe v. Bolton*:

> The point is that the Appellees had no opportunity at any stage in this case to present evidence which would show that the State's regulatory scheme regarding abortion is reasonably related to, and even demanded by hazards to, maternal health in the first trimester . . . .
>
> . . . .
>
> The Court has taken judicial notice of innumerable facts and factors, some which are expressly referred to in the Court's decision and some which are unknown to the parties but which apparently were extricated from various sources by the Court's diligent research, which facts nevertheless should be subject to refutation and counterevidence since they form the foundation for the Court's opinion and compromising dichotomy of constitutional stages of fetal growth. With no opportunity for Appellees to demonstrate the factual basis, in terms of current medical science, that its interest attaches at a particular point in the natural development of a human fetus, the Court has seized upon the convenient point of "viability" and crystallized constitutional command which bars state action.[67]

Bentham once said that decisions were not made by judges alone but by "judge and company."[68] "Judge and company" may refer not only to the Justices, their clerks, and counsel for the parties, but to the *zeitgeist*. The *Abortion Cases* provide ready illustration. Perhaps, Justice Blackmun and his colleagues in the majority knew intuitively that 1973 was a propitious time for enunciation of the sweeping conclusions in those cases. The intuitions of the Court probably reflected the views of the majority of the people at the time.[69] If that be so, then that intuitive knowledge is an

---

[66] In one instance, two Justices directed that a room in the Supreme Court building be set aside and the admiralty books from the Library of Congress assembled there, so their law clerks could extract from the collection any material that might bear upon the case at hand. J. FRANK, THE MARBLE PALACE 114 (1958).

[67] Petition for Rehearing at 2-4, Doe v. Bolton, 410 U.S. 179 (1973).

[68] Quoted in P. FREUND, ON UNDERSTANDING THE SUPREME COURT (1949).

[69] *But see A Review of State Abortion Laws Enacted Since January 1973*, 3 FAMILY PLANNING/POPULATION REP. 88, 92-3 (1974):

> While a number of states have attempted to enact abortion laws which conform to the Supreme Court decisions, some states have taken a more hostile attitude and have

immeasurable aspect of the informing process of the judicial mind.[70]

There is no way that judicial guesses about public receptivity of decisions can be subjected to test or challenge through the usual workings of the adversary system—unless, possibly, each party employs a sophisticated polling device to determine the views of the public. But if polls are relevant—and the Supreme Court has yet to make a poll a criterion of decision—it would only be because the Justices know that they are stating general norms, and further know that in this country for such norms to be accepted they must be in accord with the deepest drives and instincts of at least a majority of the people. Just as trial judges do not like to be reversed on appeal, neither do Supreme Court Justices like to be reversed by public opinion. So their intuitions about public response must, speaking generally, be correct. As Cardozo put it, ". . . judges ought to be in sympathy with the spirit of their times."[71] The deeper problem, however, comes when the spirit of the age is really merely the spirit of the group "in which the accidents of birth or education or occupation or fellowship"[72] have placed a judge.

---

adopted laws which seem to be unconstitutional, either in whole or in part. It is clear that state legislators have frequently interpreted the Supreme Court decisions as narrowly as possible and have sought to restrict abortions by enacting collateral requirements which will have a deterrent effect on a woman's decision, made together with her physician, to have an abortion.

[70] In *Roe,* the Court received information on the opinions of Americans concerning abortion:

An opinion survey conducted in 1971 for the Commission on Population Growth and the American Future indicated that half of all Americans believed that abortion should be a matter decided solely between the individuals and their physicians. An additional 40 percent would have permitted abortion under certain circumstances and only 6 percent flatly opposed abortion under any circumstances. *Report of the Commission on Population Growth and the American Future,* at 103. In a national Gallup Poll in January, 1972, 57 percent of those questioned agreed that the "decision to have an abortion should be made solely by a woman and her physician." 37 percent disagreed and six percent had no opinion. For the first time in such national polls a majority of the Roman Catholics interviewed, 54 percent, expressed support of general abortion reform. *The New York Abortion Story,* Planned Parenthood Federation of America, Inc. (1972). The latest Gallup Poll conducted in June, 1972, the results of which were published by *The New York Times* on August 25, 1972, show that 64 percent of the public (including a majority of Roman Catholics) now believe that the decision to have an abortion should be left solely to the woman and her doctor.

Supplemental Brief for the Planned Parenthood Federation of America, Inc., and the American Association of Planned Parenthood Physicians as Amici Curiae at 11, Roe v. Wade, 410 U.S. 113 (1973).

[71] B. CARDOZO, THE NATURE OF THE JUDICIAL PROCESS 174 (1921).

[72] *Id.*

In final analysis, this decisional process involves retrying the case at the highest level, where the Justices are the sole participants in the informing process. This process provides no hearing, no right to counsel or cross-examination, no opportunity to present contrary arguments. These procedures are not required for the pronouncements of a legislature. But even as the Supreme Court moves to become a third legislative chamber by issuing general norms, it still remains a court. It looks like a court and acts like a court. Thus, there are certain institutional requirements that should be honored.[73]

Proposition No. 5

New doctrine enunciated by the Supreme Court may emanate partly from within and partly from without the Court's institutionalized information process.

Neither the litigants nor the amici argued or suggested the extraordinarily broad sweep of the opinions in *Roe* and *Doe*. Nowhere in the briefs or oral argument can there be found the "trimester" code of permissible abortions. That legislative scheme arose from the Justices themselves. Blackmun took the material brought by counsel and by adding to it, he greatly loosened concepts of judicial notice. Rather than waiting for other cases to spell out what the Constitution allows in given situations where women wish to have abortions, the Court sought to settle all of the questions at one time.[74]

It thus seems to be clear beyond question that the Court was an active participant — a third party — in the litigation of the two abortion cases. It was not content to follow the guidance of counsel as to the issues to be decided or the constitutional base upon which they should be placed.

The use of the "actual malice" test for enforcing the *New York Times Co. v. Sullivan* doctrine also appears to have been entirely a Court-developed doctrine. The briefs and arguments of counsel never referred to it. There is nothing in the briefs in *Times* to suggest

---

[73] That the Court has acted unconstitutionally was implied by Justice Brandeis in Erie R.R. v. Tompkins, 304 U.S. 64, 79 (1938).

[74] Not all questions were decided in the *Abortion Cases;* the rights of the would-be father were not decided.

that anything is meant by "actual malice" other than what the private law of libel had always meant, *i.e.*, an actual intent to inflict harm on another. Yet "actual malice" was chosen by the Court as the title for a new doctrine to adjudicate defamation cases where public officials were involved. As the Court used the "actual malice" term, it refers to a standard of care which would hold the publisher harmless against the public official plaintiff unless it could be shown that the publisher acted in knowing or reckless disregard of the truth or falsity of what was said.

Because of his first amendment seditious libel point, Wechsler suggested no damages accrued to Sullivan unless actual malice by the Times against Sullivan could be shown. The Court responded with a rule saying the Times would not be liable in defamation to a public official unless it could be shown that it had published either in knowing or in reckless disregard of the truth or falsity of what was said. The petitioner had not sought such a rule.

The primary thrust of Wechsler's argument was that the Times editorial which had not mentioned Sullivan had not libelled him. As a common law matter, Wechsler apparently believed that a case in libel by innuendo had not been made out against the Times under the facts of the *Times* case:

> . . . [M]ost courts would rule that the document could not be libelous under the common law of the United States because the only references here that could be taken to refer to respondent are references to police; that that is too large a group in the setting of this evidence to permit the statement to be read to mean either all policemen or to mean not all policemen but just the commissioner in charge.[75]

Similarly, neither amici nor counsel for Sullivan specifically developed the new "actual malice" definition providing privilege to defame the public official for everything but "calculated falsehood." In a way, however, the comments by Mr. Nachman, counsel for Sullivan, on truth or falsity by a kind of osmosis generated the "actual malice" doctrine on the part of the Court:

> MR. JUSTICE WHITE: But if it were held that a newspaper can publish a falsehood which it thought to be true, that would still not save the *Times* here?

---

[75] Oral Argument at 47, New York Times Co. v. Sullivan, 376 U.S. 254 (1964).

MR. NACHMAN: You mean a reasonable belief in truth?

MR. JUSTICE WHITE: Yes.

MR. NACHMAN: No, sir, not under Alabama law. It would have to be true.

MR. JUSTICE WHITE: But on the facts of this case you say they knew it was false or essentially false?

MR. NACHMAN: Yes, sir, we say on the facts of this case there was ample evidence from which a jury could find that there was the kind of recklessness and abandon and inability to look at facts at the beginning before publication, which could be the equivalent of intent.[76]

It was Nachman who talked about "recklessness [that was] the legal equivalent of intent,"[77] and who also clarified the policy-making aspect of the basic distinction urged by Wechsler: "We submit that this and no other Court has ever made a distinction between libel of public officials and libel of private persons."[78]

As a factor in deliberateness or intent Nachman emphasized that the Times had retracted insofar as Governor Patterson was concerned but had refused to do so for Sullivan. Nachman argued that if the defendant refused to retract after a showing of falsity which merited retraction, that constituted a recklessness that should justify a conclusion of malice. Even conceding that the Times refused to retract because the paper did not believe that the ad had even mentioned Sullivan, the Nachman suggestion indicated a sensible option for the Court. "Actual malice" would be determined by refusal to retract after proof of falsity. Yet the rule enunciated in *Times* is that the focal point of whether the material published was published with reckless disregard of truth or falsity is the time of publication rather than the time at which retraction was asked. We are not told why the Court made the time of publication rather than the time of retraction dispositive. The Court easily could have devised an "actual malice" test which could have predicated liability upon failure to retract after proof of falsity. In fact, Nachman suggested this.[79]

---

[76] *Id.* at 76-77.

[77] *Id.* at 76.

[78] *Id.* at 78.

[79] On the question of malice and deliberateness, to get to a matter that Mr. Justice White raised earlier in the argument, we submit, sir, that there was plenty from which the jury could find deliberateness. We think that the inconsistent treatment of

Harriet Pilpel has given us the following information concerning the origins of the actual malice test in the *Times* case:

> To the best of my recollection, the precise point on which the decision in *New York Times* against Sullivan rested, namely, the requirement of knowing falsity or reckless disregard of the truth as a prerequisite to a successful suit for libel by a public official, was not specifically urged on the court in the briefs. This is what both Judge Nanette Dembitz and my partner, Nancy F. Wechsler, both of whom worked on the case with me, also recollect in this connection.[80]

The Justices were content to make a broad ruling, without regard to details. As a result, ten years after the new definition of "actual malice" became the law, state courts still have difficulty understanding it. An example is *Branch No. 496, Letter Carriers v. Austin*,[81] where the Supreme Court was presented with the question of the applicability of state libel law and the *New York Times* doctrine to a labor dispute governed by federal labor law. In *Letter Carriers*, Justice Marshall addressed the confusion about the meaning of "actual malice" under *New York Times:*

> [B]oth courts [below] thought that instructions which defined malice in the common law sense — as "hatred, personal spite, ill will, or desire to injure" — were adequate under [Linn v. Plant Guard Workers of America, Local 114, 383 U.S. 53 (1966)].
>
> This reflects a fundamental misunderstanding of the Court's holding in *Linn*. The *Linn* court explicitly adopted the standards of *New York Times v. Sullivan* . . . and the heart of the *New York Times* test is the requirement that recovery can be permitted only if the defamatory publication was made "with knowledge that it was false or with reckless disregard of whether it was false or not."
>
> Of course, the Court [in *Linn*] also said that recovery would be permitted if the defamatory statements were shown to have been made with malice. But the Court was obviously using "malice" in the special sense it was used in *New York Times*—as a shorthand

---

Governor Patterson and this plaintiff, the treatment of this plaintiff after investigation showing falsity, the treatment of this plaintiff by the testimony of the Secretary telling the jury that it was not substantially incorrect, after his own lawyers couldn't even plead truth, the failure of the *Times* to apply a very rigorous set of advertising acceptability standards as they call it . . . .

Oral Argument at 75, New York Times Co. v. Sullivan, 376 U.S. 264 (1964).

[80] Used by permission.

[81] 418 U.S. 264 (1974).

expression of the "knowledge of a falsity or reckless disregard of the truth" standard. Instructions which permit a jury to impose liability on the basis of the defendant's hatred, spite, ill will, or desire to injure are "clearly impermissible." . . . "[I]ll will toward the plaintiff or bad motives, are not elements of the *New York Times* standard." *Rosenbloom v. Metromedia, Inc.*, 403 U.S. 29 n.18 (1971) (Opinion of BRENNAN, J.).[82]

If counsel had been given the benefits of the direction of the Justices' thinking during the formative stage of decision in *Times*, then perhaps the Court might have formulated a standard which at least would have given the operative term for the *New York Times* standard a different name. The experienced constitutional lawyers who were on the brief, if asked about the merits of a new definition, might have predicted the confusion that would result from the formulation of a new test, bearing the same name in libel law, malice, as an old doctrine having an entirely different meaning. If the Court had asked counsel for briefs on its intention to re-define malice, the lower courts and the media might have been spared ten years of confusion. Compliance with law can be frustrated when access to the information upon which a decision is based is needlessly restricted.

Proposition No. 6

The Justices bring certain predilections,
sometimes known and sometimes unknown,
to the decisional process.

Professor Paul Wieler described the adversary process as a process

which satisfies, more or less, this factual description: as a prelude to the dispute being solved, the interested parties have the opportunity of adducing evidence (or proof) and making arguments to a disinterested and impartial arbiter who decides the cases on the basis of this evidence and these arguments.[83]

We have already shown that deciding "on the basis of this evidence

---

[82] 418 U.S. 264, 281 (1974).

[83] Wieler, *Two Models of Judicial Decision-Making*, 48 CAN. B. REV. 406, 412 (1968). *See also* Neef & Nagel, *The Adversary Nature of the American Legal System from a Historical Perspective*, 20 N.Y.L.F. 123 (1974).

and these arguments" was simply not true with respect to the cases under study — and by inference to other important constitutional (and perhaps other) cases. The "disinterested and impartial arbiter" is now the subject of attention.

Under the orthodox conception of the judicial process, a judge, sitting with black robes in an impressive chamber, embodies justice blindfolded. In this role, he is not a political actor. Consequently, adversary adjudication does not permit counsel, speaking generally, to furnish public opinion data to the courts. Public opinion not only is irrelevant to considerations of the "rule of law"; it could, if followed, become that "tyranny of the majority" against which the Constitution protects. Further, lawyers have little or no competence — neither, for that matter, do behavioral scientists — to furnish such data to the Court at such times as the Justices are receptive to it. A lawyer would be ill advised to tell the Court that its decree would be disobeyed.

In 1908, President Theodore Roosevelt attacked the myth:

> The chief lawmakers in our country may be, and often are, the judges, because they are the final seat of authority. Every time they interpret contract, property, vested rights, due process of law, liberty, they necessarily enact into law parts of a system of social philosophy; and as such interpretation is fundamental, they give direction to all lawmaking. The decisions of the courts on economic and social questions depend upon their economic and social philosophy. . . .[84]

And in 1921, Judge Benjamin Cardozo stated in a famous series of lectures:

> I have spoken of the forces of which judges avowedly avail to shape the form and content of their judgments. Even these forces are seldom fully in consciousness. They lie so near the surface, however, that their existence and influence are not likely to be disclaimed. But the subject is not exhausted with the recognition of their power. Deep below consciousness are other forces, the likes and the dislikes, the predilections and the prejudices, the complex of instincts and emotions and habits and convictions, which make the man, whether he be litigant or judge.[85]

---

[84] 43 Cong. Rec. 21 (1908) (annual message to Congress).
[85] B. Cardozo, *supra* note 71, at 167.

More recently, Justice Douglas has said:

> Judges are not fungible; they cover the constitutional spectrum; and
> a particular judge's emphasis may make a world of difference . . . .
> Lawyers recognize this when they talk about "shopping" for a judge.[86]

The Justices, as sentient beings, are not intellectual eunuchs; they must be considered to know what others know or perceive. They are aware of the trends of social and political development. And they know, by intuition at least, when the social climate is ready or ripe for a certain decision. For example, in 1956 the Court rejected, for unpersuasive reasons,[87] a clear opportunity to invalidate miscegenation laws—an invitation that was accepted eleven years later.[88] As political actors, the Justices knew that outlawing miscegenation two years after *Brown* would probably have been too much of a blow to established mores — and thus would have enmeshed the Court in a maelstrom of criticism that would harm both its own prestige and power and the civil rights movement itself. In 1967, the decision came without fanfare and with no harm to either value.

Perceptive Americans have known, or should have known, since the earliest days of the republic that the Court's constitutional decisions are statements of juristic theories of politics. Fifty years ago, John R. Commons called the Supreme Court "the first authoritative faculty of political economy in the world's history."[89] The Justices have for three decades foresworn making ultimate economic policy decisions (save in the area of state taxation and regulation of interstate commerce) and have, instead, become a faculty of social ethics.

Professor Martin Shapiro said in 1964:

> The political jurist begins with what any fool could plainly see if his
> eyes were not beclouded by centuries of legal learning, that judges

---

[86] Chandler v. Judicial Council of the Tenth Circuit, 398 U.S. 74, 137 (1970)(dissenting opinion). *See generally* M. SHAPIRO, LAW AND POLITICS IN THE SUPREME COURT: NEW APPROACHES TO POLITICAL JURISPRUDENCE (1964); Deutsch, *Neutrality, Legitimacy, and the Supreme Court: Some Intersections Between Law and Political Science*, 20 STAN. L. REV. 169 (1968); Wechsler, *Toward Neutral Principles of Constitutional Law*, 75 HARV. L. REV. 1 (1959).

[87] Naim v. Naim, 350 U.S. 891 (1955) (per curiam).

[88] Loving v. Virginia, 388 U.S. 1 (1967).

[89] J. COMMONS, LEGAL FOUNDATIONS OF CAPITALISM 7 (1924).

and courts are an integral part of government and politics, would be meaningless and functionless outside of government and politics and are, therefore, first and foremost, political actors and agencies.[90]

Roe v. Wade provides recent illustration. There, Justice Blackmun found that a fetus is not a "constitutional person," a conclusion central to the final result in the case. To support his ruling, he cited several constitutional provisions dealing with persons, some lower court cases, some medical literature, and some law journal articles. He concluded: "In short, the unborn have never been recognized in the law as persons in the whole sense."[91] A clue to the meaning of this statement may be found in Blackmun's earlier statement:

> We need not resolve the difficult question of when life begins. When those trained in the respective disciplines of medicine, philosophy, and theology are unable to arrive at any consensus, the judiciary, at this point in the development of man's knowledge, is not in a position to speculate as to the answer.[92]

But if, as Blackmun says, there is a wide divergence of thinking on the question, by saying the judiciary could not provide the answer, in fact he did provide the answer. Like the maid in Byron who, "whispering 'I will ne'er consent' — consented,"[93] Justice Blackmun, saying "we cannot do it," did it. The constitutional concept of a person that encompasses corporations[94] now excludes unborn children. That is a matter of philosophy, not of logic.

If, as suggested above, the Justices, when deciding important constitutional cases, are active participants in the informing function of the Supreme Court, the manner in which they select the data through independent research becomes of critical importance. Quite possibly, the Justices are not only active participants; they are the most important of the participants. They can and do roam far afield, apparently selecting facts and law to buttress their pre-existing positions. When this information is incorporated into

---

[90] Shapiro, *Political Jurisprudence,* 52 Ky. L.J. 294, 297 (1964).

[91] 410 U.S. 113, 162 (1973).

[92] *Id.* at 159.

[93] BYRON, DON JUAN, Canto I, Stanza 117.

[94] *See, e.g.,* Louis K. Liggett Co. v. Lee, 288 U.S. 517 (1933); Pierce v. Society of Sisters, 268 U.S. 510 (1925).

opinions through expanded judicial notice, without critical examination and testing, the legitimacy of the Court's decision may be
undermined.

III

"How many lawyers have any real awareness of how courts arrive
at a decision?"[95] When Chief Justice Roger J. Traynor made that
inquiry, he concluded that not enough members of the profession
have such an awareness. This study has attempted to fill part of the
gap that Traynor noted; we have suggested several propositions
that, if validated by further research, can contribute to a larger
understanding of the decisional process of the Supreme Court.

If Supreme Court Justices have indeed become, in some important constitutional cases, the most important fact-finders in the
decisional process, what does this portend for the adversary system?
Several conclusions seem appropriate.

Most fundamental, perhaps, is the question of procedural fairness. If the rights and duties of uncounted Americans are being
affected or influenced, if not controlled, by Supreme Court decisions
often based on independent research conducted *sua sponte* by the
Justices, then the products of those researches, to the extent that
they are significant in the final decisions, are not tested by contrary
argument. Those who lose, whether they are the particular litigants
before the bar of the Court or those in the general public whose
values run counter to the decisions, are not accorded their "day in
court" that is basic to fairness. At times, as in *Erie Railroad Co. v.
Tompkins*[96] and *Terminiello v. Chicago*,[97] the situation worsens,
with the Court rendering decisions on *issues* not briefed or argued
by either party. In such instances, the Court completely disregards,
in the formulation of its decision, the information brought to it by
counsel. More often, though, the Justices use (or discard) data
brought by the parties, and supplement it with their own research
to which the parties cannot respond.

Not having an opportunity to contest the factual data judicially noticed and otherwise employed, whether or not stated in the

---

[95] Traynor, *Badlands in an Appellate Judge's Realm of Reason*, 7 Utah L. Rev. 157, 158
(1960).

[96] 304 U.S. 64 (1938).

[97] 337 U.S. 1 (1949).

opinions, would make little difference, save to the immediate parties, were the Court to confine itself to cases involving only the parties before the Court. Society, that often-used but never defined judicial construct, would not be harmed. But since its 1958 decision in *Cooper v. Aaron*,[98] the Little Rock school segregation case, the Court has sought to expand the operative impact of its decisions to cover more and more people. Choosing their cases because of the general importance of the issues, rather than because of the litigants, they have become a third legislative chamber in fact, at once superior to Congress (in that the Court can overrule Congress on constitutional matters) and inferior (in that Congress can overrule the Court on questions of statutory interpretation). They seek to state and thus to update "the law of the land," and consider their pronouncements on constitutional issues to be controlling.

But in so doing the Justices have found it necessary to expand their factual research to determine, to their satisfaction, data beyond the immediate litigants. Sophisticated members of the Supreme Court bar are, to be sure, fully aware of the propensity of the Court to state general norms, and construct their briefs and arguments accordingly, larding them with wide-ranging socio-economic data. These lawyers are not disturbed, as are some academic commentators, about the Court "re-trying" a case at Supreme Court level through a greatly expanded use of judicial notice or about the Court stating general norms — so long as the results comport with their values.

Professor John Ely takes a stricter view: He argues that the Court in *Roe v. Wade* is "indulging in sheer acts of will," asserting that the *Roe* decision "is bad because it is bad constitutional law, or rather it is *not* constitutional law and gives almost no sense of an obligation to try to be."[99]

Ely calls *Roe* another "Lochner" decision — and, on one level, this is quite right. It will be recalled that Justice Holmes, in one of his most ringing dissents, said that the majority had decided the *Lochner*[100] case on an economic theory to which the majority of the

---

[98] 358 U.S. 1 (1958).

[99] Ely, *The Wages of Crying Wolf—A Comment on* Roe v. Wade, 82 YALE L.J. 920 (1973). It is difficult to reconcile Professor Ely's assertion that the *Roe* decision "is *not* constitutional law" with the development of constitutional law by the Supreme Court since the earliest days of the republic. Whatever its wisdom, the Court's decision in *Roe is* law until overruled. *Compare* note 106 *infra*.

[100] Lochner v. New York, 198 U.S. 45 (1905).

country did not adhere. Holmes could find nothing in the Constitution to invalidate the New York maximum-hour law, so he would have upheld it. On the surface that brings to mind the majority and dissenting opinions in *Roe* and *Doe* — save for one critical factor, the relevance of which has not yet been established in our jurisprudence: the fact, as established by polls, that the majority of Americans favored abortion. Hence Justice Blackmun did not emulate Justice Peckham; he did not substitute his philosophy for that of the people. Rather he put the will of the people into effect — as he understood it. But in so doing he illustrated a complaint Cardozo made in 1924:

> Some of the errors of courts have their origin in imperfect knowledge of the economic and social consequences of a decision, or of the economic and social needs to which a decision will respond. In the complexities of modern life there is a constantly increasing need for resort by the judges to some fact-finding agency which will substitute exact knowledge of factual conditions for conjecture and impression.[101]

The Court did not have that "exact knowledge" about which Cardozo spoke.

The lack of a sound factual base in promulgating general norms raises the question of legitimacy. Speaking generally, legitimacy refers to the right or title to rule — that is, to set the norms by which people are governed. In a nation that considers itself democratic, this right comes from the people, who through their ballots elect their rulers. Ever since *Marbury v. Madison*[102] controversy has swirled around the propriety of an appointed group of lifetime judges, making ultimate decisions. History and long-continued practice have, however, now settled the question insofar as it concerns the rights and duties of persons, natural or artificial, either against each other or against the state.[103] But what is still controversial, and has not yet received any systematic scholarly attention, is the legitimacy of the Supreme Court's stating norms of general

---

[101] B. CARDOZO, THE GROWTH OF THE LAW 116-17 (1924). *See also* F. FRANKFURTER, SOME OBSERVATIONS ON SUPREME COURT LITIGATION AND LEGAL EDUCATION 17 (1954) (speaking of the Justices left to "blind guessing" about the "practical consequences" of Sherman Act decisions).

[102] 5 U.S. (1 Cranch) 137 (1803).

[103] Evidence of this fact is found in United States v. Nixon, 418 U.S. 683 (1974); Gravel v. United States, 408 U.S. 606 (1972); Powell v. McCormack, 395 U.S. 486 (1969).

applicability. This is a question that demands the attention of legal scholars,[104] for it is the problem that lies at the heart of both the *Abortion Cases* and *New York Times* decision.

It is one thing to make law interstitially, as Holmes said,[105] but quite another to make law wholesale. One may readily agree with Chief Justices Marshall and Burger that it is "emphatically the province and duty of the judicial department to say what the law is,"[106] but on the historical record the "law" so stated referred, prior to *Cooper* v. *Aaron,* only to the parties before the bar of the Court. All that a Supreme Court decision did historically was to delegate power to lower court judges, federal and state, to put the decision into operative effect in subsequent litigation.[107] It can be said that the legitimacy the Supreme Court has attained since 1803 is based in large part on its image as an impartial arbiter in the disputes between individuals or between individuals and the State. That image, in turn, is predicated upon two bedrock conceptions: first, that the Court merely finds but does not make the law; and second, that the Court is confined to the facts as found by the trial court or as found through a rigidly restricted use of judicial notice. The first conception has been smashed — Supreme Court Justices themselves admit the creative nature of their task.[108] The critical question

---

[104] P. KURLAND, POLITICS, THE CONSTITUTION AND THE WARREN COURT 170-206 (1970) is one of the few preliminary intellectual forays into this area.

[105] Southern Pacific Co. v. Jensen, 244 U.S. 205, 221 (1917) (dissenting opinion).

[106] United States v. Nixon, 418 U.S. 683, 703 (1974) (Burger, C.J., quoting from Marbury v. Madison, 5 U.S. (1 Cranch) 137, 177 (1803)).

[107] In somewhat different terms, Professor Walter Murphy observed in 1959:

The Supreme Court typically formulates general policy. Lower courts apply that policy, and working in its interstices, inferior judges may materially modify the High Court's determinations.

Murphy, *Lower Court Checks on Supreme Court Power,* 3 AM. POL. SCI. REV. 1015, 1018 (1959). In our judgment, Murphy was wrong in stating that the Court "formulates general policy," if by that he means a norm binding on all others similarly situated to those in the case at bar.

[108] *E.g.,* Justice White, dissenting in Miranda v. Arizona, 384 U.S. 436, 531-32 (1966), said:

That the Court's holding today is neither compelled nor even strongly suggested by the language of the Fifth Amendment, is at odds with American and English legal history, and involves a departure from a long line of precedent does not prove either that the Court has exceeded its powers or that the Court is wrong or unwise in its present reinterpretation of the Fifth Amendment. It does, however, underscore the obvious—that the Court has not discovered or found the law in making today's decision, nor has it derived it from some irrefutable sources; what it has done is to make new law and new public policy in much the same way that it has done in the course of interpreting other great clauses of the Constitution. This is what the Court historically

has become whether the moral force of their judgments is dependent upon adherence to as much as possible of the Blackstonian model of the appellate process. By issuing "legislative" judgments, the Court, it is believed, risks its prestige and eventually its power. In short, the Blackstonian model as symbol of impartial justice is itself of surpassing importance.[109]

The problem of the Court's moral force can perhaps best be seen from the perspective of a discussion of the evolution of the *New York Times* doctrine. The case law evolving from *Times* demonstrates an allegiance by the Court to a tentative generalized policy pronouncement and to candid recognition of trial and error. In *Rosenbloom v. Metromedia, Inc.*,[110] Justice Brennan conceded that the Court had assumed in *Times* that public persons would be able to "command media attention to counter criticism." The Court then noted that this assumption was unproved.[111]

Significantly, the proposition that public persons would be able

---

has done. Indeed, it is what it must do and will continue to do until and unless there is some fundamental change in the constitutional distribution of governmental powers.

But if the Court is here and now to announce new and fundamental policy to govern certain aspects of our affairs, it is wholly legitimate to examine the mode of this or any other constitutional decision in this Court and to inquire as to the advisability of its end product in terms of the long-range interest of the country. At the very least the Court's text and reasoning should withstand analysis and be a fair exposition of the constitutional provision which its opinion interprets. Decisions like these cannot rest alone on syllogism, metaphysics or some ill-defined notions of natural justice, although each will perhaps play its part. In proceeding to such constructions as it now announces, the Court should also duly consider all the factors and interests bearing upon the case, at least insofar as the relevant materials are available; and if the necessary considerations are not treated in the record or obtainable from some other reliable source, the Court should not proceed to formulate fundamental policies based on speculation alone. (Footnote omitted.)

[109] Compare Mishkin, *Foreword: The High Court, the Great Writ, and the Due Process of Time and Law*, 79 HARV. L. REV. 56, 62-70 (1965) *with* Miller & Scheflin, *The Power of the Supreme Court in the Age of the Positive State: A Preliminary Excursus*, 1967 DUKE L.J. 273, 522 (1967). *See also* L. LEVY, AGAINST THE LAW: THE NIXON COURT AND CRIMINAL JUSTICE xiv (1974):

My bias is in favor of well-wrought opinions that demand respect even from doubters who prefer different results. Regrettably, the judicial crusaders exert a greater influence than the judicial craftsmen. *The public cares about results and has little patience for reasons.* (Italics added.)

Professor Levy fails to cite any examples of "well-wrought opinions."

[110] 403 U.S. 29 (1971).

[111] Thus the unproved, and highly improbable generalization that an as yet undefined class of "public figures" involved in matters of public concern will be better able to respond through the media than private individuals also involved in such matters seems too insubstantial a reed on which to rest a constitutional distinction.

403 U.S. 29 at 46-47 (1971).

to attract media attention to counter criticism and thus would not suffer if their libel remedies were restricted appeared for the first time in the Court's opinion in *Times*—it was never presented to counsel for briefing and argument. The clear implication is that from the beginning the assumption was untested and unproven.

In *Gertz v. Robert Welch, Inc.*,[112] the Court's latest modification of the *New York Times* doctrine, at least four major pronouncements with respect to the impact of the first amendment generally, and the *New York Times* doctrine specifically, on state libel law were made: (1) The Court repudiated the extension of the *Times* privilege to defamation situations which involved public issues, or matters of public interest, even though the plaintiff was neither a governmental official nor a public figure. The extension of the *Times* doctrine to defamations involving matters "of public interest" had been approved only three years before in *Rosenbloom*. (2) The Court held that the traditional state law of libel was unaffected by the first amendment except where liability was imposed without fault. In other words, the Court ruled that, except in situations where the *New York Times* standard applies, the ordinary state libel law will apply. Typically, this would mean that liability for defamation can be imposed in such circumstances for actual injury caused by negligent misstatement. (3) The Court held that it was inconsistent with the first amendment to permit the imposition of punitive damages in any libel case unless the *Times* standard of actual malice for "reckless disregard for the truth or falsity of what was said" was met. (4) The Court cleaved to the rule of *Curtis Publishing Co. v. Butts* and *Associated Press v. Walker*[113] that "a 'public figure' who is not a public official may also recover damages for a defamatory falsehood whose substance makes substantial danger to reputation apparent." But in *Gertz*, the definition of "a public figure" was contracted by the Court's holding that a well-known attorney "who has achieved no general fame or notoriety in the community" is not necessarily a public figure by virtue of substantial community activities. In such circumstances, inquiry must be directed to the nature and extent of the plaintiff's participation in the particular controversy which occasioned the defamation.

This "experimental" approach to legislative fact by the Court in

---

[112] 418 U.S. 323 (1974).
[113] 388 U.S. 130 (1967).

Gertz was caustically criticized by Justice White in his dissent. He characterized the two new and fundamental holdings concerning the impact of the first amendment on state libel law set forth in *Gertz* in this way:

> I do not suggest that the decision is illegitimate or beyond the bounds of judicial review, but it is an ill-considered exercise of the power entrusted to this Court, particularly when the Court has not had the benefit of briefs and argument addressed to most of the major issues which the Court now decides. I respectfully dissent.[114]

White summarized the circumstances behind the decision and its consequences:

> Except where public officials and public figures are concerned, the Court now repudiates the plurality opinion in *Rosenbloom* and appears to espouse the liability standard set forth by three other Justices in that case. The States must now struggle to discern the meaning of such ill-defined concepts as "liability without fault" and to fashion novel rules for the recovery of damages. These matters have not been briefed or argued by the parties and their workability has not been seriously explored. Nevertheless, yielding to the apparently irresistible impulse to announce a new and different interpretation of the First Amendment, the Court discards history and precedent in its rush to refashion defamation law in accordance with the inclinations of a perhaps evanescent majority of the Justices.[115]

Further, the lack of data to support fundamental assumptions in *Gertz* about experience is particularly emphasized in Justice White's dissent. The Court said that the first amendment precluded imposition of punitive damages in the absence of actual malice as that term was defined in *New York Times*. Justice White challenged the basis for that holding, stating:

> I note also the questionable premise that "juries assess punitive damages in wholly unpredictable amounts bearing no necessary relation to the actual harm caused." . . .
>   The Court points to absolutely no empirical evidence to substantiate its premise. For my part, I would require something more substantial than an undifferentiated fear of unduly burdensome punitive

---

[114] 418 U.S. 323, 370-71 (1974) (dissenting opinion).
[115] *Id.* at 378-80.

damage awards before retooling the established common law rule and depriving the States of the opportunity to experiment with different methods for guarding against abuses.[116]

Justice White further complained that "[t]here has been no demonstration that state libel laws as they relate to punitive damages necessitate the majority's extreme response."

The progression of the *Times* doctrine shows an ethical leap in the dark[117] followed by extension[118] and then by revision[119]—in short, an impressionistic trial and error approach. A full decade after the pronouncement in the *Times* case, the same technique employed in *Times* with the same type of results, leading to complete confusion in the courts and the media, is still being employed. In *Times,* as we have seen, the Court created a new "actual malice" standard for libels of public officials, a standard which had, prior to its announcement, never been made known to counsel for briefing and argument. Similarly, the doctrine of the *Times* case was, subsequently, extended to a far wider class than that represented by the plaintiff. The Court reached out to give protection to the media, with little regard to contrary arguments.

IV

Several suggestions can be made for improving the method of dealing with the independent development of legislative fact and legal doctrine by the Supreme Court.

(1) *Remand for Trial Court Adjudication of Legislative Fact*

One method would be to suggest that the Court remand the issue of the taking of judicial notice of a particular issue of legislative fact

---

[116] *Id.* at 396-97. The lack of substantiation for the fundamental main premise in the Court's opinion in *Gertz* has recently been commented on elsewhere:

Justice Powell concluded that a private individual deserves a greater degree of protection than does a public figure. He claimed that public figures will usually have greater access to the media in order to rebut defamatory charges, but he produced no substantiation for this assertion and, indeed, seemed unsure of it. Rather, he relied primarily on what he termed a "compelling normative consideration": the public figure, typically, has chosen to run "the risk of closer public scrutiny" while the private person has made no such choice [footnotes omitted].

The Supreme Court, 1973 Term, 88 HARV. L. REV. 41 at 143-44 (1974).

[117] *See* New York Times Co. v. Sullivan, 376 U.S. 254 (1964).

[118] *See* Rosenbloom v. Metromedia, Inc., 403 U.S. 29 (1971).

[119] *See* Gertz v. Robert Welch, Inc., 418 U.S. 323 (1974).

to the trial court. This remand would be more consistent with the orthodox model of the appellate process. It is doubtful, however, whether the Supreme Court will be eager to have questions of legislative fact in matters of vital social policy decided by federal district judges.[120] Professor Alfange writes of legislative fact as if such material came to the Court solely through the efforts of counsel.[121] Our

---

[120] Although we use the distinction between adjudicative facts and legislative facts, we, unlike the new Federal Rules of Evidence, do so without any affection for that distinction. We note also the criticism we received from one of our respondents, Professor Chester Antieau of Georgetown University Law Center, on the point: "Don't use adjudicative v. legislative facts. Use *determinative* facts. Make the Court take a view that they shall not take notice of a determinative fact; nor shall they overturn a jury-decided determinative fact."

The need for prior resolution by the trial court of factual and legal issues fundamental to the resolution of a case before the Supreme Court has only recently been highlighted by the Court itself.

In Roe v. Doe, 420 U.S. 307 (1975) (per curiam), the Supreme Court dismissed a writ on the ground that it had been improvidently granted. The case involved an attempt by a psychiatric patient to prevent the publication of an anonymous case history of her treatment. An amicus brief filed by the American Psychiatric Association, the American Psychoanalytical Association and the American Orthopsychiatric Association urged the Court not to review the case until a more adequate record was before it. In the opinion of the amici, trial court determination on a number of factual and legal issues was indispensable. *See* New York Times, February 20, 1975, at 34, col. 1.

[121] Writing in 1966, Professor Alfange defended the use of the appellate brief to bring social science findings and empirical data to the attention of the Court. The Brandeis brief, in Alfange's view, is still indispensable in constitutional litigation because the "importance of questions of fact in the adjudication of constitutional claims has not been the least diminished" since Louis Brandeis filed his famous brief for Oregon in Muller v. Oregon, 208 U.S. 412 (1908). Alfange responded to criticism which has been lodged against the Brandeis brief.

> First [it has been said that] the form of the brief and the reply brief is not always the best means of making data available for accurate appraisal by the courts. But the use of the brief surely ought not to preclude a trial of the legislative facts, if only because fuller examination would be preferable. The important factor is that courts be as fully appraised as possible of pertinent legislative fact; the ingenuity of advocates and the stimulation of advocacy may well be able to overcome technical difficulties. Where an adequate trial of the facts is not held, however, and the appellate courts find it necessary to be more fully informed on factual questions, a remand to the lower court for a more thorough trial would be entirely in order.

Alfange, *The Relevance of Legislative Facts in Constitutional Law,* 114 U. PA. L. REV. 637, 667-68 (1966).

Alfange does not suggest specific ways for counsel to get a "trial of the legislative facts" in a case that comes to the Supreme Court in the exercise of its appellate jurisdiction.

Brandeis developed his brief to show the rationality of a legislative decision dealing with labor conditions. As Professor Paul Freund has cogently pointed out, "a court that relies on the presumption [of validity] in sustaining a statute does so more confidently and more comfortably if some factual foundation has been established for the validity of the law." P. FREUND, SUPREME COURT OF THE UNITED STATES: ITS BUSINESS, PURPOSES, AND PERFORMANCE 152 (1963). The situation is much more difficult, however, when a Brandeis brief is used to

study of *Times* and the *Abortion Cases* suggests the contrary—that legislative facts often come to the Court through its independent efforts.

A former Supreme Court clerk, now a law professor, in replying to our information flow questionnaire made a response which comports with our hypothesis that fundamental empirical assumptions flow from deeply held value judgments that dwell in a different universe of discourse than information which is presented and tested within the structure of the adversary process:

> I would say most important information is gleaned through a long-term socialization process involving the Justice's education and experience, that of his law clerks, and the persons and media that impinge upon him—contrast Douglas with Powell. To take your libel cases,

---

attack legislation, for then the social science data take on a new significance: the issue is *not* whether such data exist but their *validity*—an entirely different matter. Furthermore, as Professor Paul Rosen has said, Brandeis's "curious argument that the Court only needed to note the existence and not the validity of facts was legally sound because it rested on the traditional principle of presumptive constitutionality." P. ROSEN, THE SUPREME COURT AND SOCIAL SCIENCE 181 (1972). The Justices, however, *must* make such an evaluation, both when they do independent research and when counsel present data from social scientists with opposing views. Facts, in other words and despite the cliche to the contrary, do *not* "speak for themselves." Facts do not exist, in any case before the Court, without a theory; they do not, as Whitehead put it, exist in "non-entity."

In replying to a question as to how the adversary system could be improved at the Supreme Court level, and what revisions in Supreme Court practice would be necessary to integrate the social science factor with the work of the Court, Professor Edward Barrett said:

> Given the inherent limitations (and frequent unreliability) of social science data some adequate process for challenge is essential. If the data is used only in the Brandeis brief—to show that there is a reasonable body of information which supports a finding of reasonableness—then the problem is minimal. But if social science data is used to establish facts upon which legislation may be held unconstitutional, then there is a major problem. If the data is used at trial, mechanisms for testing do exist. If it comes in only later, we have no adequate basis yet for testing and critiquing. Worst of all is where the Court comes up with the data based on its own research and counsel have no opportunity to challenge it. (Used by permission.)

The problem is that the "actual malice" standard of *Times*, and the decision invalidating the imposition of libel damages without fault in *Gertz*, were announced *ex cathedra*. Each decision was based on untested empirical assumptions, *i.e.*, the assumed ability of public officials to be able to secure a forum in the media, and the detriment punitive damages were assumed to present to vigorous media expression.

In light of these considerations, a fundamental question arises: Has the Brandeis brief become a means for circumventing the rules of evidence at trial? Can social "facts" which could never successfully be introduced at trial be freely entered and accepted at the appellate stage? Is, in other words, litigation at the Supreme Court level in fact sometimes a trial *de novo*?

for example, it seems unlikely that any specific source provided information on the effect of libel laws on first amendment values.[122]

When asked to comment on what should be the role of the Supreme
Court with respect to social science data and how Supreme Court
practice should be revised to integrate that factor into the work of
the Court, the same scholar said:

> [W]hat ought to be the Court's role, say, in constitutional adjudi-
> cation? For example, if definitions of "cruel and unusual" ought to
> change with the times, then surely sophisticated public opinion polls
> (choose your strata—educated, or noneducated) are preferable to the
> Justices' inferences from their individual experiences and readings.
> Such data should not be introduced, however, through appellate
> briefs, appendices, amicus briefs, or citations to secondary sources
> where it is not subjected to rigorous scrutiny. A fortiori, it (or assump-
> tions without benefit of data) should not be used in opinions when
> the sources have not even been raised in the course of argument. If it
> is appropriate, it deserves to be introduced in the trial court record
> and subject to scrutiny, criticism, challenge, etc. To be sure, cross-
> examination and the adversary system won't determine scientific va-
> lidity, but they seem preferable to casual introduction of such evi-
> dence on appeal without opportunity to examine it.[123]

Remand to the trial court for findings of legislative fact is within
the power of the Supreme Court, although the Court cannot control
state courts in that regard. If routinely done, it would go far toward
obviating the disquietude expressed by those who feel that a free-
wheeling employment of judicial notice at the Supreme Court level
leaves much to be desired.

(2) Adoption of Rules for Judicial Notice of Legislative Facts

The problem of grappling with judicial notice of legislative facts
is underscored in the new Federal Rules of Evidence. Rule 201 is
entitled "Judicial Notice of Adjudicative Facts."[124] In its comment

---

[122] Used by permission.

[123] Used by permission.

[124] Rule 201 provides:

(a) Scope of Rule. This rule governs only judicial notice of adjudicative facts.

(b) Kinds of facts. A judicially noticed fact must be one not subject to reasonable
dispute in that it is either (1) generally known within the territorial jurisdiction of the
trial court or (2) capable of accurate and ready determination by resort to sources
whose accuracy cannot reasonably be questioned.

on Rule 201, the Advisory Committee justified its failure to deal with judicial notice of legislative facts by quoting with approval from Professor Morgan's praise of the unrestricted power of a judge to determine the content or applicability of a rule of domestic law. Morgan wrote that in such circumstances "the judge is unrestricted in his investigation and conclusion." Further, the Advisory Committee quoted the following statement from Morgan: "He [the judge] may make an independent search for persuasive data or rest content with what he has or what the parties present."[125] The Advisory Committee then says of these views:

> This is the view which should govern judicial access to legislative facts. It renders inappropriate any limitation in the form of indisputability, any formal requirements of notice other than those already inherent in affording opportunity to hear and be heard and exchanging briefs, and any requirement of formal findings at any level. It should, however, leave open the possibility of introducing evidence through regular channels in appropriate situations.[126]

The view expressed above reflects the current Supreme Court practice with respect to legislative facts. One difficulty with this practice is that the competence of lawyers who appear before the Court varies.[127] Therefore, concern has been expressed that resort to the proposed rule would be uneven and would be unlikely to assure full exposure by the Court to relevant legislative facts. Yet full exposure to all the data upon which a particular legislative determination is based should be the desideratum for any ideal model of the

---

(c)   When discretionary. A court may take judicial notice, whether requested or not.

(d)   When mandatory. A court shall take judicial notice if requested by a party and supplied with the necessary information.

(e)   Opportunity to be heard. A party is entitled upon timely request to an opportunity to be heard as to the propriety of taking judicial notice and the tenor of the matter noticed. In the absence of prior notification, the request may be made after judicial notice has been taken.

(f)   Time of taking notice. Judicial notice may be taken at any stage of the proceeding.

(g)   Instructing jury. In a civil action or proceeding, the court shall instruct the jury to accept as conclusive any fact judicially noticed. In a criminal case, the court shall instruct the jury that it may, but is not required to, accept as conclusive any fact judicially noticed.

[125] Morgan, *Judicial Notice,* 57 HARV. L. REV. 269, 270 (1944).

[126] FED. R. EV. 201 (Advisory Committee Note).

[127] Experienced Supreme Court counsel with whom we have discussed this matter suggest that some lawyers will not be aware of the dependency of the resolution of a particular issue on a question of legislative fact.

information flow to the Supreme Court.

In the past, inquiry into legislative facts in constitutional litigation has focused on the validity or invalidity of existing legislation. But the use of an assumption about experience, unsupported by any disclosed recitation of legislative fact, as the necessary premise for establishing a new rule of constitutional law has been a major part of the focus of our study. These assumptions about experience include such debatable assumptions as: (a) abortion is a safer procedure than childbirth; (b) low-income people would not travel to a jurisidiction where an abortion would be permissible; (c) vigorous debate is the operating premise of the first amendment; (d) public officials do not need a libel remedy to give them a remedy against media attack because their very status equips them to respond to their defamers in the forum where the attack occurred; and (e) the consequence of an attack by the press against a public official will inevitably be debate.

Recitation of these premises may be considered in the light of Professor Kenneth Karst's comments on the necessity for giving counsel an opportunity to contest the legislative fact determinations made by courts:

> When the court makes law, however, it does so, if not for "generations of litigants yet unborn," at least for a great many others who are not in court. A minimum requirement is some statement of the legislative facts (other than those facts on which everyone plainly agrees) that affect the decision. Furthermore, our forced reliance on the litigants to help represent broad social interests demands that the parties be given a chance to contest such assertions of legislative fact. This opportunity to challenge should be given whenever the determination of an issue of legislative fact affects the ultimate decision, even though the legislative fact be a "background fact," and even though it may be necessary to reopen the trial for this purpose.[128]

It is not clear whether Karst's plea for an opportunity to challenge a judicial determination of legislative fact is directed to the Supreme Court as well as the trial courts. Certainly the case for such a procedure in the Supreme Court, in the light of this study, is strong—particularly in situations like the *Abortion Cases* and the *Times* line of cases, because the dependence of newly developed

---

[128] Karst, *Legislative Facts in Constitutional Litigation*, 1960 SUP. CT. REV. 75, 109 (1960).

principles of constitutional law on *ex cathedra* experiential assumptions by the Supreme Court in those cases obscures the necessity for the objective and fair resolution of basic legislative fact determinations. The problem doubtless varies from case to case. For example, it is apparent, in assessing whether a state law requiring truckers to use contour mudguards unreasonably burdens interstate commerce, that the "cost of the mudguards to the regulated truckers" is rather obviously going to be a matter of fundamental importance.[129] But the assumption in *Times*, on the other hand, that restricting libel laws will stimulate "vigorous and robust" debate is at base merely an unsubstantiated judicial impression of experience. The oscillating path of libel law in the Supreme Court since the *Times* case in 1964 illustrates that the Court has itself come to question its own assumptions in this area.

A rule providing for a hearing on legislative facts is by no means the only possibility for changing Supreme Court practice to deal more fully and fairly with judicial notice of legislative facts.[130] One of our respondents' comments has stimulated us to suggest a modified pre-trial conference procedure: With respect to how the adversary process could be improved at the Supreme Court level, Professor Henry Abraham responded as follows:

> A cynic might say by abolishing it! Not such a bad idea. But since that isn't likely, I'd suggest compulsory providing of all pertinent data at pretrial via the good office of the judge.[131]

An interesting feature of this observation is that it appears to assume that a pre-trial conference is a feature of Supreme Court practice. This, of course, is not so.[132] Yet the exchange of information by counsel with a Justice or officer of the court prior to oral argument in the Supreme Court might help to expose social science materials

---

[129] Bibb v. Navajo Freight Lines, Inc., 359 U.S. 520 (1959).

[130] There is, of course, a question of whether such procedure would be consistent with the Court's statutory grants of appellate jurisdiction. But this problem aside, even under present Supreme Court practice, the Court could recommend the appointment of a master for the purpose of making findings of fact that are fundamental to the resolution of a pending constitutional case before the Court. For a discussion of the Court's use of masters in original jurisdiction cases see R. STERN & E. GRESSMAN, SUPREME COURT PRACTICE § 10.13 (4th ed. 1969).

[131] Used by permission.

[132] But the Second Circuit has adopted a similar procedure. *See* Kaufman, *The Pre-Argument Conference: An Appellate Procedural Reform*, 74 COLUM. L. REV. 1094 (1974).

which the Court has already uncovered or has an interest in, thereby giving those materials a scrutiny and a testing they do not now receive.[133]

Our conclusion is that the present approach to social science at the Supreme Court level is inadequate. It is haphazard, inherently underinclusive, and it fails to meet the requirements for authentication and scrutiny that respect for the integrity of social science data demands. A rule such as proposed above appears to be in order. The advantage of this suggestion over the first is that it does not require remand to the trial court; it permits the Supreme Court to control the process, while allowing the adversaries to have their "day in court."

(3) Appointment of a Panel of Resident Social Scientists

The Court could appoint a panel of resident social scientists, who would be requested to investigate matters of legislative fact which appear to the Court to require further study. The obvious difficulty with this proposal lies in the inherent subjectivity that social science unavoidably involves, and the consequent lack of agreement among social scientists on the controversial issues presented to the Court for resolution. A political scientist responding to our questionnaire stressed the need for establishing the objectivity and complete assessment of social science data by the Supreme Court. But where the constitutional law professors urged the submission of such data to the testing and scrutiny of the adversary process insofar as that is provided by the requirements of notice and hearing, the political scientists suggested an incompatibility with social science data and the adversary method:

> Any scientific approach requires an objective assessment of all the evidence that can be obtained. In that respect, incompatibilities with the art of advocacy may be encountered. Emphasis on arguments

---

[133] With respect to considering the integration of social science into the work of the Supreme Court, some difference in viewpoint concerning the difficulties in validating social science materials can be perceived as between the lawyer and political scientist respondents to the questionnaire. Thus one political scientist writes:

> Social science data is something the Justices should know about, but it should not be determinative. . . .
>
> If the clerks are trained to look in the right places for social science material, and lawyers are discouraged to submit social science materials, perhaps no revisions in Supreme Court practice would be necessary.

(Used by permission).

that support one party and a disregard or a deliberate de-emphasis of arguments supporting the opposing party would be unacceptable to a scientific appraisal of a situation. Should a social science approach become more dominant in the adjudication of disputes, attorneys for the respective parties would have to resolve the conflict in the framework of a dispassionate joint research endeavor.[134]

When we speak of authenticating "social science" data at the Supreme Court level, it is appropriate to ask how such authentication is to be accomplished. One respondent to our questionnaire, who is both a political scientist and a law professor, made the following suggestion:

> But on a more modest and practical level, I think that the Court should appoint a social scientist to help take the opposite side to any argument that relies heavily upon social science data, since in my experience the use of such data by one side is usually not met evenly by the other side but rather the other side attempts to bury it with cliches. More "clash" regarding the accuracy and verifiability of such data might itself help educate the Supreme Court. In the longer run, I think that such data is immensely important to the Court's role in interpreting a "living" Constitution.[135]

Another suggestion made by one of our respondents that appears quite workable, but which might be controversial, is the following: "Perhaps the Solicitor General might be routinely charged, in cases where the government is not a party, to intervene and to present a brief dealing with the broad public aspects of the controversy."[136] This has much to be said for it. The amicus brief of Solicitor General Archibald Cox in *Baker v. Carr*[137] is considered by some commentators to have been extremely influential. As an officer of the national government, the head of a first-class group of lawyers who are adept by experience in viewing litigation broadly, the Solicitor General could accordingly become an evaluator of relevant social science data and routinely present it to the Court. That could mean that social scientists could be used by the Solicitor General on a "when needed" basis. The amicus brief of the Solicitor General would in

---

[134] Used by permission.
[135] Used by permission.
[136] Used by permission.
[137] 369 U.S. 186 (1962).

effect present the social and behavioral science learning on particular issues, leaving to the Justices the choices to be made when the social and behavioral scientists disagree (as they usually will).

A problem with this proposal is that the Solicitor General is not necessarily an "objective" advocate or amicus, as was shown in the spring of 1975 when Robert Bork submitted an unpublished manuscript to the Court, purporting to show that capital punishment reduced the incidence of homicide. That study has since been severely criticized.[138] Bork's submission to the Justices is questionable simply because no apparent effort was made to present a rounded assessment of capital punishment from the social science viewpoint. In other words, the line between Bork as amicus and Bork as advocate was blurred.

(4) *Licensing the Supreme Court Bar*

A certification or licensure system could be developed to improve the quality of the Supreme Court Bar. Chief Justice Burger has recently spoken out about the quality of advocacy in criminal law cases; and the Freund Report on the workload of the Court has stated, as has been previously mentioned, that the quality of oral advocacy before the Supreme Court is quite low. Perhaps this argues for a corps of lawyers, with special competence in Supreme Court litigation, who would be the only lawyers allowed to act as adversaries before the Court. If a litigant in, say, New York or Illinois or Rhode Island or Alabama wanted to take a case to the Court, his counsel would then have to act rather like a British solicitor and identify a "Supreme Court barrister" to take the case to the Court. That could be done by the Court rigidly limiting those admitted to practice before it.

The benefits of such a suggestion are obvious. Lawyers are not fungible; they bring varying degrees of competence to the Supreme Court. A small cadre of highly trained, experienced Supreme Court advocates would go far toward eliminating some of the present inadequacies in advocacy.

---

[138] The Washington Post, April 1, 1975, § A, at 1, col. 1. Yet Bork's memo does underscore an observation made to the authors by Professor Chester Antieau suggesting the need, on the civil side, for "public control of public issues." In other words, perhaps public issues should not be entirely resolved by lawyer-judges in a private lawsuit. Surely, there is room for the required participation of governmental representatives in cases involving the most fundamental questions of public policy. *See also* R. JACKSON, THE STRUGGLE FOR JUDICIAL SUPREMACY 101, 103-04 (1941).

Recently, Professor Freedman has asked some pertinent questions about such certification: why, he asks, should it be limited to trial lawyers? After all, the litigator, unlike the office lawyer, operates in the open, in the court room, not in the insulation of his offices. Professor Freedman also points out that no certification can be fair if it has a grandfather clause. Further, he contends that the courts should do far more to take affirmative steps against counsel whom they perceive to be incompetent than they do presently.[139]

In sum, licensure could tend to produce an elitist corps of lawyers who would not reflect the divergent interests of a pluralistic society. Nonetheless, as matters now stand, lawyers like Archibald Cox, Eugene Gressman, and Anthony Amsterdam illustrate that establishment of a group of Supreme Court "barristers" is possible; the problem is how to expand such a group to include representatives of the varied interests in the nation.

(5) *Requests by the Supreme Court for Further Information on Questions of Legislative Fact*

As the relevance of legislative facts to the resolution of a particular case becomes clear to the Court as a result of deliberations during conference, or during oral argument, or after reading the briefs, the Court could ask counsel for further briefs on a particular point. The Court does so on occasion now. The Court should strive to determine the views of counsel where a case appears to involve an assessment of data never considered by the trial court or which does not appear plainly in the briefs submitted to the Supreme Court.

As with most of the other suggestions presented here, this would mean that the Court would cede some of its present freedom in determining, as Chief Justice Warren once said, what is best for the American people. "We, of course, venerate the past," said Warren, "but our focus is on the problems of the day and of the future as far as we can foresee it." He went on to say that in one sense the Court was similar to the President, for it had the awesome responsibility of at times speaking the last word "in great governmental affairs" and of speaking for the public generally. "It is a responsibility that is made more difficult in this Court because we have no constituency. We serve no majority. We serve no minority. We serve only the public interest as we see it, guided only by the Constitution

---

[139] M. FREEDMAN, LAWYERS' ETHICS IN AN ADVERSARY SYSTEM 99-103 (1975).

and our own consciences."[140]

In many respects, the problem now being considered is how far the public wishes the Justices to be guided by their consciences, the Constitution providing only a point of departure for, rather than the answer to, constitutional questions. When the focus of judicial attention becomes "great governmental affairs" rather than merely the rights and duties of individuals or of individuals and the State, conscience may not be sufficient to the need. It is incumbent upon the Justices not to resort to blind guesses about the effect of their decisions or to an uncritical acceptance of data. The Justices should do their best to inform themselves about all relevant data concerning a given issue of great public interest.

The Justices should not pretend that the Supreme Court of the United States is like any other court. It is not; it is, as Frankfurter said, a very special type of court, one that, to cite but one example, was so different to Benjamin Cardozo when he moved from New York's Court of Appeals to the Supreme Court that he found his prior judicial experience to be of little help.[141] In a famous passage, Learned Hand once said:

> I venture to believe that it is as important to a judge called upon to pass on a question of constitutional law, to have at least a bowing acquaintance with Acton and Maitland, with Thucydides, Gibbon and Carlyle, with Homer, Dante, Shakespeare and Milton, with Machiavelli, Montaigne and Rabelais, with Plato, Bacon, Hume and Kant, as with the books which have been specifically written on the subject. For in such matters everything turns upon the spirit in which he approaches the questions before him. The words he must construe are empty vessels into which he can pour nearly anything he will. . . . [Judges] must be aware that there are before them more than verbal problems; more than final solutions cast in generalizations of universal applicability. They must be aware of the changing social tensions in every society which make it an organism; which demand new schemata of adaptation; which will disrupt it, if rigidly confined.[142]

If that is valid, then it is readily discernible what a great distance must be travelled before the Court itself, and members of the bar

---

[140] 395 U.S. vii, x-xi (1969) (remarks upon retirement from the Court).

[141] R. JACKSON, THE SUPREME COURT AS A POLITICAL INSTITUTION 53-54 (1955).

[142] Hand, *Sources of Tolerance*, 79 U. PA. L. REV. 1, 12-13 (1930).

who practice before it, have reached that degree of intellectual attainment and attitude.

There can be little question of the need for adaptation of Supreme Court methodology in deciding issues in which their decisions set general norms designed for applicability throughout the nation. Equally, there can be little question that no attention is being paid to that critical problem; rather, the judges and the bar are presently caught up in a pursuit of cutting down the caseload of the Court.[143] But that pursuit is a bootless quest and will not solve the more important problem of how the Supreme Court should go about its policymaking task. That much we hope we have demonstrated in this preliminary inquiry. The need is for institutional invention adequate to permit the Justices to reach for, if not attain, the goal set by Learned Hand.

9
PUBLIC CONFIDENCE IN THE JUDICIARY

Recent years have brought a literal explosion of litigation. More and more, Americans are turning to the courts for the redress of grievances, real or imagined. Accordingly, judges, not excluding the Supreme Court, are routinely called upon to do much more than they did in the past.

One consequence of the increased litigation has been a diminution in the confidence people have in judges. The growth of an educated populace, taught through application of the scientific method to have questioning minds, has produced a skepticism, whether merited or not, about the quality of American judges. In the long run, there can be no guarantee of justice except whatever confidence the personality of the judge inspires. Hence, it is important that the reasons for popular dissatisfaction with the judiciary be subjected to deep and continuing scrutiny. That such scrutiny is not accomplished, save in small part, is one of the conclusions of the following essay.

"Public Confidence in the Judiciary" is reprinted, with permission, from a symposium on Judicial Ethics appearing in *Law and Contemporary Problems,* Volume 35, No.1, Winter 1970, published by the Duke University School of Law, Durham, N.C. Copyright, 1970, by Duke University.

When it is realized that the rights of Americans rest ultimately in the hands of some 7,000 men and women who are the judges on our state and federal courts, and it is further realized how very little we know in fact both about them in person and how they operate on the bench, then it becomes imperative that the quality of our judges, as well as the quality of the justice they dispense, be thoroughly understood. We mistrust the judiciary, including the Supreme Court, at our peril. But the judges, including the Justices on the Supreme Court, must earn the confidence of thoughtful Americans. This essay, then, presents ways of thinking about the continuing problem of public confidence in the judiciary.

To distrust the judiciary marks the beginning of the end of society. Smash the present patterns of the institution, rebuild it on a different basis . . . but don't stop believing in it.

—Honore Balzac, *quoted in* O. KIRCHHEIMER, POLITICAL JUSTICE 175 (1961).

I

INTRODUCTION

Discontent, popular and professional, with the operations of American courts and the legal system is not a new phenomenon. In the formative decades of American constitutional history antagonism to law and lawyers was prevalent, in large part because the inherited English common law was considered to be too sophisticated and abstruse for the common man, who was unable to use it as a guide for his conduct.[1] Lawyers were held in such low repute that some states—for example, Indiana—by statute permitted anyone to practice law. During modern times that latent popular disaffection has spread to the legal profession itself, manifested by, among other things, a spate of publications criticizing a lack of "craftsmanship" by Justices of the Supreme Court.[2] The discontent is based upon both fact and fancy; taken together, its various forms add up to an endemic lack of confidence in the judiciary.

"Public confidence in the judiciary" is a term that is often used but never defined. It is one of those concepts that everyone thinks he understands but which does not have a hard core of solid content upon which all agree. As such, it may be analogized to such other undefined terms as "public policy" or the "public interest"[3] or to Justice Potter Stewart's remarkable burst of candor in the *Jacobellis* case that while he could not define hard-core obscenity, he knew it when he saw it.[4] Some useful purpose may be served by adhering to the obvious fiction that high-level legal abstractions such as "policy" or "public interest" have a definite meaning (although surely a persuasive case for putting more content into them can be made), and obscenity may be merely in the eyes of the beholder, as Justice Stewart implied; but there can be no excuse for not attempting to supply substance to the concept of public confidence in the judiciary. It is not enough to say that one knows it when he sees it. In this paper, I should like to proffer some preliminary observations on that theme. An effort will

---

[1] *See* P. MILLER, THE LIFE OF THE MIND IN AMERICA 102-04 (1965).

[2] *E.g.*, A. BICKEL, THE SUPREME COURT AND THE IDEA OF PROGRESS (1970).

[3] *See* Miller, *The Public Interest Undefined*, 10 J. PUB. L. 184 (1961).

[4] Jacobellis v. Ohio, 378 U.S. 184 (1963).

be made not to poach on the preserves of the other authors in this symposium on judicial ethics, although of necessity some overlap will be discernible. The main focus will be on the federal bench, although some mention of state courts will be made.

In a widely heralded speech in 1906, Roscoe Pound called attention to the "causes of popular dissatisfaction with the administration of justice."[5] Pound's address may be considered to be the point of departure for administrative reform of the courts. Delay was the principal factor that he singled out as a cause of discontent, a theme echoed by Chief Justice Warren E. Burger in his first public utterance as Chief Justice. Burger underscored a complaint of millions of Americans in their question, "Why does American justice take so long?" and answered that it is in large part "a lack of up-to-date procedures and standards for administration or management and especially the lack of trained administrators." He also said: "Only by the adoption of sound administrative practices will the courts be able to meet the increased and increasing burdens placed on them. The time has passed when the court system will carry its load 'if each judge does his job.' There must also be organization and system so as to leave the judge to his job of judging." It is evident that Pound's complaint in 1906 requires continuing attention. Leaving a judge "to his job of judging," however, is affected by factors other than the administrative impediments that concern the Chief Justice. To some extent, no doubt highly discontinuous and probably immeasurable, that task is also influenced by "non-judicial" activities of judges. Other matters bear upon the manner in which the complex and intricate art of judging their fellow humans is performed—and in the way in which it is received by its "constituency," the public. There is no higher calling in the American constitutional order than that of sitting in judgment of and assessing liability for the peccadilloes and derelictions of others. That is so even though many of the parties brought before the bench are artificial persons (corporations, for example); in final analysis, the actions of collective organizations are those of identifiable human beings. To pronounce judgment upon them is an awesome duty, requiring attributes of character and personality of the highest order. That some judges—however few in number is beside the point, for even one rotten judicial apple can go far toward spoiling the entire judicial barrel—fall short of the requisite standards of integrity and propriety (nebulous and ill-defined though they may be) creates a large part of the problem of public confidence.

That problem is merely an aspect of a much larger problem of the operations of the entire legal system, and should be viewed in that context. However, what exists in the microcosm of the judiciary is reflective of the macrocosm of the legal system; hence, what is said here about judges and courts may be extrapolated to the entire sweep of American law. It is relevant, nonetheless, to note *en passant* that concentration on *judicial* ethics, important as they are, tends to distort reality.

---

[5] Pound, *The Causes of Popular Dissatisfaction with the Administration of Justice*, 40 AM. L. REV. 729 (1906).

American law in the modern era, whatever it may have been in the past, is neither court-dominated nor even court-oriented. This is the age of administration, and American government is ever increasingly influenced and controlled by huge bureaucracies, both public and private.[6] The ethical problems of law emanate as much or more from *administrative* shortcomings as from the bench (historically in the common law countries, the center of legal power). We have not yet assimilated that fact into the curricula of American law schools, but do it we must, as Dean Levi has said, if legal education is to attain currency with the unceasing demands of a changing society.[7]

"The place of justice is a hallowed place," said Bacon in his essay *Of Judicature,* "and therefore not only the Bench, but the foot pace and precincts and purprise thereof ought to be preserved without scandal and corruption."[8] No one would dissent from that proposition—the judiciary, in all its activities, must be free from 'scandal and corruption." But the problem of public confidence is larger; it mainly involves the lack of a set of standards adequate to enable federal judges to guide their behavior, both on and off the bench. The most that is available for them are the Canons of Judicial Ethics, issued in 1924 by the American Bar Association, plus the constitutional requirement of holding office during "good behavior" and two statutes —one of which makes it a felony for a judge to peddle influence and the other a misdemeanor to practice law while a judge.

That is not enough. Joseph Borkin, author of *The Corrupt Judge,* said in an interview about the ABA's canons: they are simply a compilation of "biblical injunction, custom, common sense, and 'Caesar's wife' admonitions to be above reproach." The ABA has recognized the inadequacy of the canons. Under way at this writing is a serious effort to update and modernize them.[9] But whether the task of establishing a "code of good conduct" for federal judges should be left to a private association of lawyers is itself a difficult question. If a code is to be developed, the task is either that of Congress, operating, of course, within the boundaries of constitutional restraints, or that of the judiciary itself, acting perhaps through the existing structure of the Judicial Conference of the United States and the Judicial Councils and Conferences of the several circuits.[10] Another difficulty is that norms of conduct of federal judges are enforceable in law only by the extraordinary remedy of impeachment, although the action of the Judicial Council of the Tenth Circuit in Judge Chandler's case may point to increased powers in the Judicial Councils—"may" because the Supreme Court refused to reach the merits of Chandler's petition.[11]

---

[6] *See* Miller, *Toward the "Techno-Corporate" State? An Essay in American Constitutionalism,* 14 VILL. L. REV. 1 (1968).

[7] Levi, *Law Schools and the Universities,* 7 J. LEGAL ED. 243 (1965).

[8] 1 F. BACON, WORKS OF LORD BACON 59 (M. Murphy ed. 1876).

[9] The ABA's Special Committee on Standards of Judicial Conduct issued a Preliminary Statement and Interim Report in June 1970; this was debated at the annual ABA meeting in August 1970.

[10] The powers of these bodies are set forth in 28 U.S.C. §§ 331-33 (1964).

[11] Chandler v. Judicial Council of the Tenth Circuit of the United States, 398 U.S. 74 (1970) (deny-

Cumbersome and seldom used, impeachment is a technique of last resort, necessarily so if the independence of the judiciary is to be preserved. As Lord Bryce said in *The American Commonwealth*, it is "the heaviest piece of artillery in the congressional arsenal, but because it is so heavy it is unfit for ordinary use. It is like a hundred-ton gun which needs complex machinery to bring it into position, an enormous charge of powder to fire it, and a large mark to aim at."[12] Impeachment has been invoked a mere eight times for federal judges; in only four cases were convictions obtained. Thomas Jefferson called it a "bungling" way of removing a judge: "experience has already shown," he wrote to Judge Spencer Roane of Virginia, "that the impeachment the Constitution has provided is not even a scarecrow."

Even so, that is all that is now permitted under the statutes and the Constitution. Current attempts to define "good behavior" legislatively are not certain to survive foundering on constitutional shoals.[13] The guidelines issued in 1969 by the Judicial Conference of the United States in an effort to limit off-bench activity of federal judges have since been rescinded, mainly, it seems, because of the change in Chief Justices in 1969 and because the anxiety occasioned by the revelations that led to the unprecedented Fortas resignation had ebbed. Those guidelines have now been replaced by the operation of an "interim advisory committee" established by the Conference to counsel judges on questions of ethics, including non-judicial activities. In any event, the guidelines (as well as the counsel of the advisory committee) carry no formal suasion. Nor do the ABA canons. Informal sanction no doubt occurs, mainly from the Chief Judges of the circuits and districts, under which judges may be persuaded or encouraged to do their job better.[14] But that is hardly an adequate remedy.

As with any institution, the judiciary unquestionably prefers self-policing over promulgation of externally established norms of behavior. Judges may be counted on to resist strenuously any attempt by Congress to legislate specific rules. There are solid reasons for this, other than a natural reluctance against airing one's dirty laundry in public. For instance, the notion of an independent judiciary is crucial to the American constitutional order. We know too much about other countries, such as Nazi Germany, where the courts became arms of the state, not to place judicial independence high in the scale of values to be preserved. And judges must be independent insofar as the demands of the state are concerned and also from influences external to government. That does not mean that federal judge

---

ing Judge Chandler's motion for leave to file petition for writ of mandamus or prohibition against the Council).

[12] 1 J. BRYCE, THE AMERICAN COMMONWEALTH 208 (2d ed. rev. 1891).

[13] *Compare* Kurland, *Constitution and the Tenure of Federal Judges: Some Notes from History,* 3 U. CHI. L. REV. 665 (1969), *with* Kramer & Barron, *Constitutionality of Removal and Mandatory Retirement Procedures for the Federal Judiciary; the Meaning of "During Good Behavior,"* 35 GEO. WASH. L. REV. 455 (1967).

[14] Testimony, as yet unpublished, in hearings held by the Senate Subcommittee on Separation of Powers in 1970 revealed that chief judges so act.

are or should be wholly free to roam at will; they have not been since the Judiciary Act of 1789, for the state can set certain parameters of judicial power. Furthermore, there are arguments, persuasive to some, about the symbolic position of the courts that militate toward keeping their internal operations secret—and thus leaving what policing may be necessary to the judges themselves, acting *in camera*.[15]

II

THE CONTEXT, HISTORICAL AND CONTEMPORANEOUS

To pose the question, "Is there a lack of public confidence in the federal judiciary?," is to put the problem in a way that is difficult, perhaps impossible, to answer. It is far too abstract and ambiguous. The manner in which questions are put usually determines their answer; or as Justice Frankfurter said, in law, as elsewhere, correct answers are predicated on asking the correct questions.[16]

What, then, are the "correct" questions about public confidence in the judiciary? That in itself is not susceptible of easy reply.[17] There is no such thing as "the" public; rather, a series of publics exist within the American polity. The basic societal unit is the pluralistic social group, not the individual as the myth (and the Constitution) imply. The question of public confidence, accordingly, can be broken down into at least the following components: (a) *which groups* (or the leaders thereof) within the nation hold (b) *how much esteem* (or respect) for (c) the *courts* (trial and appellate, state and federal) through (d) *selected periods of time?* Put that way, certain assumptions may be discerned: that groups vary in their estimation of the performance of the judiciary; that group leaders are the key individuals, not the mass; that certain factors may be identified as accounting for greater or lesser esteem in which courts are held; that there may be a variance between the confidence accorded trial judges as compared with the appellate bench; that an analogous variance may be identified with respect to the state and federal courts; and that the degree of esteem will differ for individuals and groups through time.

These questions and assumptions demand carefully refined analyses based on solid empirical evidence. Little data exist that are sufficient to the need. In the brief compass of this article, therefore, attention will be concentrated mainly on isolating some of the factors that seem to account for confidence in the courts, although of necessity reference will have to be made to the other assumptions and the other segments of the problem as posed. First, however, a brief glance at history and the contemporary social context.

---

[15] *Cf.* Mishkin, *The High Court, the Great Writ, and the Due Process of Time and Law*, 79 HARV. L. REV. 56, 62-70 (1965), *criticized in* Miller & Scheflin, *The Power of the Supreme Court in the Age of the Positive State: A Preliminary Excursus*, 1967 DUKE L.J. 273, 522.

[16] Estate of Rogers v. Comm'r, 320 U.S. 410, 413 (1943); Priebe & Sons v. United States, 332 U.S. 407, 420 (1947).

[17] *Compare* F. COHEN, THE LEGAL CONSCIENCE: SELECTED PAPERS OF FELIX S. COHEN 3 (L. Cohen ed. 1960), *with* Mayo & Jones, *Legal-Policy Decision Process: Alternative Thinking and the Predictive Function*, 33 GEO. WASH. L. REV. 318 (1964), on the problem of identifying problems.

Speaking very broadly, public confidence in American courts involves a belief in the fairness and impartiality of the tribunal, with the judge dispensing speedy decisions in accordance with "the law" considered, as Holmes said, as a set of external standards applied in a neutral way. So defined, it may be said that a lack of confidence in the judiciary has been at least endemic throughout American Constitutional history. One can go back at least as far as President John Adams's last-gasp appointment of John Marshall to be Chief Justice, and the latter's opinion in *Marbury v. Madison* (in which he should have recused himself) nullifying some "midnight" appointments of the President while simultaneously asserting judicial supremacy, to discover harsh indictments of the Supreme Court of the United States. As is well known, the new President, Thomas Jefferson, got the decision he desired but for the wrong reasons—and was thoroughly incensed. Jefferson was not bemused or deluded by notions of "neutral principles" or an impossible posture of judicial objectivity, as have been some modern commentators. He knew, by experience or intuitively, that the judges' black robes often hid feet of clay; and that it is folly compounded to ask them to do the intellectually impossible. What he wanted was that they act to further values important to him, rather than those important to his political enemies. That sentiment was echoed by, for example, Judge Spencer Roane of Virginia, who called Marshall's decision in *Cohens v. Virginia* "monstrous," mainly, it would appear, because it enhanced national power at the expense of the states.[18] Then, as now, there is but one truly basic principle governing assessment of the courts: that of the "gored ox." In other words, people seem to like or dislike judges and courts in direct proportion to the way in which judicial decisions affect, or appear to affect, values considered of fundamental importance to themselves.[19] For example, *Brown v. Board of Education* and its aftermath for a time greatly enhanced the confidence of black Americans in the Supreme Court, while simultaneously causing many white Americans to criticize it severely. Despite some fervent assertions to the contrary, it was the *impact* of *Brown*, not the reasoning in the Court's opinion, that irritated white America.

Quite possibly, although this is not susceptible of exact proof because history is an art, not a science, judges were held in less esteem in the past than they are today. One reason for that may be the fact that most law in Anglo-American legal history was judge-made, and law, all too often, was considered by many to be an enemy, not a protector. We tend to forget during modern times of the ostensible

[18] Note, *Judge Spencer Roane of Virginia: Champion of States' Rights—Foe of John Marshall*, 66 HARV. L. REV. 1242 (1963). *See also* Wechsler, *Toward Neutral Principles of Constitutional Law*, 73 HARV. L. REV. 1 (1959); Christie, *Objectivity in the Law*, 78 YALE L.J. 1311 (1969). Professors Wechsler and Christie state the conventional wisdom about adjudication; they seem to believe in an idealized model of how judges operate. They ought to pay more attention to what judges *do* than to what judges *say they do*—often two quite different things. Their criticisms of judges, furthermore, tend to be quaint anachronisms, exuding a musty air of having been brought down from the attic of obsolete concepts.

[19] *Compare* Miller & Scheflin, *supra* note 15, *with* Miller, *The Myth of Objectivity in Legal Research and Writing*, 18 CATH. U.L. REV. 290 (1969).

sovereignty of the legislature—enunciated, for example, in the *Steel Seizure Case* in 1952—that legislatures are by and large latter-day institutions insofar as law-making is concerned.[20] The movement toward codification, which got major impetus in the late nineteenth century, may be taken as a highlight of a trend toward legislative supremacy. For whatever reason, much but not all law-making was taken from the judges by legislators—who in turn in the twentieth century have ceded much of it to the bureaucracy, with the willing acquiescence of the judges.

Just why the law-making power was taken over by the elected representatives of the people cannot be determined with any exactitude.[21] One little explored factor may be the fact—at least, it appears to be a fact—that judges, even when elected, tend to come from one stratum of society; or if not that, to reflect the values of one stratum. We live in America, now and in the past, under the myth of a class-less society. The rise of new power groups—for example, the unions and the farmers —led them at times to conquer the legislatures. (This nation has always had its classes, no doubt not so rigid and stratified as in other countries, the myth being nurtured by the core of truth of upward social mobility. Intelligent, promising young men and women have long been co-opted by the "upper" or "ruling" class(es) in the United States, that stratum of society not being able to produce by itself the intellectual manpower requisite to fulfillment of its goals.[22]) Law, whether created judicially or legislatively, has by and large tended to mirror the values of the dominant ruling groups in America. Historical contract law, for instance, was the legal counterpart of a laissez-faire economy, one in which bargain supposedly prevailed over command in the agreements Americans made. But contracts, Sir Henry Maine's false aphorism to the contrary notwithstanding, have always displayed a disparity in bargaining power, particularly in the "agreements" under which a man sold his labor during the early stages of the industrial revolution. Legislative attempts, produced by the trend toward equality early noted by Alexis de Tocqueville, and the rise of new social groups, to rectify those disparities were aborted by the judges in a classic confrontation between the aristocratic institution of the courts and the more democratic legislatures. The judges not only invalidated imposition of legislative norms in wage-and-hour matters on constitutional grounds,[23] they also asserted inherent power to issue injunctions to stave off strikes and other exercises of the burgeoning union movement. So, too, with tort law: judge-made doctrines of contributory negligence, assumption of risk, and the fellow-servant rule tended to aid the industrial structure (the business class) at the expense of the workers. These judicial actions may surely be taken to reflect on the confidence that segments

---

[20] *See* Wyzanski, *History and Law*, 26 U. Chi. L. Rev. 237 (1959).

[21] On the question of the "problem of proof" of social science propositions, see E. Nagel, The Structure of Science (1961); Miller, *Corporate Gigantism and Technological Imperatives*, 18 J. Pub. L. 256 (1969).

[22] *See* J. Weinstein, The Corporate Ideal in the Liberal State (1968); G. Domhoff, Who Rules America? (1967).

[23] The early classic account may be found in J. Commons, Legal Foundations of Capitalism (1924).

of the public have in the basic impartiality of judges. Such legislative reactions as workmen's compensation laws and the Norris-LaGuardia Act evidence that lack of confidence. The former removed industrial accidents from the courts and placed jurisdiction over them in administrative boards; and the latter sharply curtailed judicial power to issue injunctions in labor disputes.[24]

Historically, American judges have always been under attack by some groups—and simultaneously defended by others. Through time, moreover, one person (for example, newspaper columnist David Lawrence) or one group (for example, what Justice Jackson once called a little cult of judicial activists) display contradictory attitudes: in the 1930s Lawrence was a staunch defender of the "nine old men" during President Roosevelt's "court-packing" fight, but the years of the tenure of Chief Justice Warren made him one of the Supreme Court's most vociferous and bitter critics; Jackson's "little cult" are those who tended to attack the Court during the 1930s but who applauded the activism of the Warren Court.[25] Those, of course, are merely two examples of the principle of the gored ox in operation, restated only to indicate some of the historical perspective necessary for the present inquiry. Another bit of evidence to buttress the point is the way the businessman no longer considers the Supreme Court as ultimate guardian of his interests; instead he (and other groups), have, as Grant McConnell has shown in his *Private Power and American Democracy*, co-opted both Congress and the bureaucracy.

Two other factors merit mention: the judiciary today is required to act at a time when polarization is occurring over a number of fundamental goals of the American people, and second, it must operate during a period of the most rapid social change in history. These obviously overlap. The judicial system, a product of the relatively static feudal society, performs best in a period of social quiescence. Put in constitutional terms, this means, as Yves Simon has said, that due process of law—the core concept of the American legal order—really works only when there is no basic conflict over goals and values.[26] When, as today, there is such a controversy—for example, in the position of the Negro in America—serious difficulties arise. In other words, the judicial process (and the adversary system) are predicated on underlying agreement on base values or goals, the task of the process and the system being that of settling the details of reaching those ends. Said in still another (military) way, the process assumes acquiescence on strategy, and makes provision for ironing out disagreements on tactics to achieve accepted strategic ends.

---

[24] There is a current movement to re-judicialize unfair labor practice cases by removing trial of them from the National Labor Relations Board and placing them under the jurisdiction of the federal district courts. S. 3671, 91st Cong., 1st Sess. (1970) (introduced by Senator Tower, R. Texas). This may be considered to reveal a lack of confidence in the NLRB on the part of Senator Tower and his constituency. *See Hearings on Congressional Oversight of Administrative Agencies (National Labor Relations Board) Before the Subcomm. on Separation of Powers of the Senate Comm. on the Judiciary*, 91st Cong., 1st Sess. (1970).

[25] R. JACKSON, THE SUPREME COURT IN THE AMERICAN SYSTEM OF GOVERNMENT (1954).

[26] Y. SIMON, PHILOSOPHY OF A DEMOCRATIC GOVERNMENT 123 (1951); *see* Miller, *An Affirmative Thrust to Due Process of Law?*, 30 GEO. WASH. L. REV. 399 (1962).

Modern America is characterized, *malheureusement*, both by polarizing attitudes toward societal goals and by social change that is awesome and rapid almost
beyond measure. The consequence is not only a crisis in authority, now truistic in
the United States, but also that the legal system is subjected to almost unbearable
tensions. Law and courts (and other institutions) are asked to do much more than
in the past. Justice in the sense of fairness and decency of treatment must be meted
out to individuals and groups which by and large have never had a fair shake of
the dice—Negroes, for example, and those caught in the grip of administration of
the criminal law. Further, social change is to a major extent caused by the scientific-
technological revolution. We are now able to observe the impact of Whitehead's
insight that the most important invention of the nineteenth century was the invention of the art of invention. The result is that the main lines of public policy
are now determined and will continue so to be, more by scientific and technological
developments not now known than by existing political and legal doctrines.[27] What
this means is clear: Law and courts must be avowedly "instrumental" as well as
"interdictory"—a large order, for neither legal institutions nor the profession itself is
prepared for the task.[28]

III

SOME FACTORS BEARING ON PUBLIC CONFIDENCE IN THE JUDICIARY

The foregoing introduction, it is hoped, will serve to give some perspective to a
discussion of some of the factors involved in the people's confidence in judges and
also to adumbrate several matters more fully explored below. A preliminary identification and evaluation, such as the present article, of the characteristics of public
confidence must perforce be sketched in broad strokes and be intuitive rather than
empirical. Social scientists and lawyers have simply not been interested in producing
data sufficient to validate hypotheses or to reach firm conclusions.[29] Why that is so
would itself be an interesting question; the United States, the most legalistic of
nations, has at best a primitive knowledge about the sociology of law. What passes
for scholarship in legal circles has been and still is, with some notable exceptions,
mainly concerned with chopping logic with judges and parsing their opinions—not
unnecessary, to be sure, but far from being productive of the information needed for
a full understanding of law and the legal system. Tentatively, however, the following
questions may be posed as a means of emphasizing the need for empirical data as well
as indicating the perimeter of the problem. In addition, the discussion following each
question will suggest a possible remedy for judicial (and other) shortcomings and at

---

[27] *Compare* D. PRICE, THE SCIENTIFIC ESTATE (1965), *with* R. LAPP, THE NEW PRIESTHOOD: THE
SCIENTIFIC ELITE AND THE USE OF POWER (1965).

[28] *See* Miller & Scheflin, *supra* note 15; Miller, *Public Law and the Obsolescence of the Lawyer*, 19
U. FLA. L. REV. 514 (1967).

[29] *But see* S. WASBY, THE IMPACT OF THE UNITED STATES SUPREME COURT (1970); Dolbeare, *The
Public Views the Supreme Court*, in LAW AND POLITICS IN THE SUPREME COURT (Jacob ed. 1967).

times will also indicate examples where judicial jurisdiction or the actions of judges have been curtailed in the past (and possibly in the future).

1. *To what extent do non-judicial activities of judges contribute to a diminution of public confidence in the judiciary?* This question, of course, assumes that the norm is a high degree of confidence in American courts, an assumption which, as has been noted above, may be more fancy than fact. Nevertheless, degrees of esteem or prestige or confidence may be postulated, and it is in that sense that the question is asked.

However immeasurable it may be, little doubt exists that a few highly publicized off-bench actions of judges have contributed to muddying the ideal image of the courts. The point is so well known that it requires little documentation. One need refer only to such matters as: (a) receiving outside income, whether from investments (as in the case of Judge Clement F. Haynsworth) or from lectureships (former Justice Fortas) or from association with non-profit corporations (Justice William O. Douglas); much of this becomes known only in exceptional circumstances (for example, the revelation that Chief Justice Taft was the beneficiary of a $10,000 annual annuity from Andrew Carnegie, who wished to give financial help to former Presidents—or so he said in his will; Taft's case is the closest factual analogy to the Wolfson annuity that led to the resignation of Justice Fortas); (b) performing other official acts, such as being a close presidential adviser (Taft, Frankfurter, Vinson, Fortas, and Brandeis, to name but five)[30] or acting as a representative of the Chief Executive in negotiating a treaty (Chief Justice Jay) or heading presidential commissions (Justice Roberts on the Pearl Harbor investigation and Chief Justice Warren on the assassination of President Kennedy are examples) or acting as prosecutor in the Nuremberg war crimes trials, as did Justice Jackson; for Jay, Roberts, Warren, and Jackson the acts were well known and widely publicized but the presidential advisers by and large operated in secret (at most, their activity was known to only a few, with the range and extent of it often becoming known only long after death of the judges); (c) making public speeches on controversial matters (examples include Judge Henry J. Friendly's call for change in the privilege of self-incrimination and Judge Skelly Wright's New York University address on *de facto* segregation);[31] (d) acting as executor of estates or directors of banks or corporations; (e) helping to legislate rules of procedure;[32] (f) acting as "silent head" of the Zionist movement

---

[30] *Cf.* Jaffe, *Professors and Judges as Advisors to Government: Reflections on the Roosevelt-Frankfurter Relationship*, 83 HARV. L. REV. 366 (1969).

[31] Friendly, *The Fifth Amendment Tomorrow: The Case for Constitutional Change*, 37 U. CINN. L. REV. 671 (1968); Wright, *Public School Desegregation: Legal Remedies for De Facto Segregation*, 40 N.Y.U.L. REV. 285 (1965). The Madison Lectures, given at New York University Law School by Chief Justice Warren and Justices Black, Brennan, Clark, Douglas, Fortas, and Marshall, are published annually in *New York University Law Review* 1960 to present. The Madison Lecturers often commented on matters in controversy or that easily could come before the Court.

[32] 383 U.S. 1032 (1966) (Black and Douglas, JJ., dissenting to the newly promulgated federal rules of civil procedure).

in the United States (Justice Brandeis);[33] (g) assisting the military services in renovation of their court-martial systems (Judges Mathew McGuire and Alexander Holtzoff); (h) legal adviser to the United States Military Governor of Germany in 1945 (Judge Joseph W. Madden of the Court of Claims); (i) Supreme Court Justices attending, garbed in their judicial robes, a joint session of Congress and hearing (and applauding) President Johnson's call for legislation sure to be litigated on constitutional grounds (the Voting Rights Act of 1965); (j) serving as arbitrator in the Bering Sea controversy (the first Justice Harlan); and (k) discussing with others cases pending decision (the most notorious known example of this was Justice Murphy's habit of talking over cases with his good friend, Edward Kemp).[34]

Enough now is known about non-judicial activities of judges that the Judicial Conference of the United States and the American Bar Association are actively engaged in trying to draft new norms of a much more specific nature.[35] How successful this effort will be is problematical. The commitment to and history of an independent judiciary militates strongly against any formal sanctions being invoked. There is, furthermore, substantial disagreement over limiting anything except the most egregious extra-judicial actions.[36] Different rules may well be advisable for each of the several types listed above. The general principle, however, should be clear and unmistakable: Judges should be judges. Period. Justice must be done by our courts, in the words of the old aphorism, and "it must also be seen to be done." To the extent that off-bench activities contribute to the public's believing that justice is not in fact done, they should be curtailed. The point is *not* whether justice is in fact done; that is important, but only half the picture. Also necessary is a belief—read confidence—that judges are rendering justice. It is to be noted that, of course, the word "justice" is one of multiple referents; often the necessary careful distinction is not made between justice as the output of a court, whatever that substantive result may be, and justice in the sense of that output adhering to some other external norm. In the latter meaning, the term is highly abstract, seldom defined, and may often refer to natural law concepts in a way similar to that which the Supreme Court puts content into due process of law. As we have defined public confidence above, it refers to justice as the outputs of courts that coincide, at least roughly, with those fundamental principles of decency that Supreme Court Justices so often invoke but seldom analyze.[37]

Not all commentators believe in the purist notion of judicial activity. Justice

---

[33] *See* E. Rabinowitz, Justice Louis D. Brandeis, the Zionist Chapter of His Life (1968).

[34] *See* J. Howard, Mr. Justice Murphy; A Political Biography (1968).

[35] The ABA took no action at its August 1970 meeting on the revised Canons.

[36] I should make it clear that I am not arguing that the bench generally is suspect. Perhaps we get those judges that we, as a people, deserve, just as we likely get the type of government we deserve. The hard-rock principle of an independent judiciary is stated with force and fervor by Justices Black and Douglas in *Chandler, supra* note 11.

[37] *See, e.g.,* the classic debate between Black and Frankfurter, JJ., in Adamson v. California, 332 U.S. 46 (1947).

Abe Fortas, during the hearings on his nomination to be Chief Justice, defended his counsel to the President by citing a number of examples where others had acted in rather similar fashion. (Left unstated by the former Justice is how past conduct of others which may in itself have gone beyond propriety can justify present activity. The question is otherwise: Whether *both* Fortas's and other judges' actions fell short of the desirable standards of probity.[38]) Perhaps the most eloquent defense of extra-judicial assignments by judges came from the late Judge John J. Parker:

> I am not one of those who thinks that a man ceases to be a man and a citizen when he becomes a judge and would have him retire from life as though he were entering a monastery. . . . To him much has been entrusted by the people. They have a right to expect much of him, not only in the performance of his judicial duty, but also in the way of intellectual leadership. A judge will be a better judge if he is a good citizen and takes his full part in bettering the life of the community in which he lives. While he should not enter into political contests, there is no reason why he should not make his voice heard and his influence felt in any movement for the betterment of the race or the improvement of the community. In the work of bar associations, on the boards of educational, charitable and religious organizations, on public occasions where his wisdom and guidance are needed by the people, there is no reason why he should not play a full part of a leader in our democracy.[39]

Judge Parker also defended acceptance of what he called "unusual tasks" by judges, saying that "when a call comes for a judge to do something for his country, which no one but a judge can do so well, he should not hesitate to undertake it." In accordance with that position, Parker justified the extra-judicial activities of Jay, Harlan, Roberts, and Jackson mentioned above.

Surely, however, Judge Parker assumed the answer in the way that he stated the question. Surely, too, there is enough qualified brainpower in this nation of 200 million people not to have to call upon judges to perform extracurricular jobs. However important those tasks may be and however laudatory the motives of the participants, such a practice subtly erodes the indispensable confidence of people in the impartiality and integrity of the judiciary. Those off-bench actions of judges listed above, unavoidably, *are* political actions; it demeans the judiciary and diminishes its dignity for it to be used as a source of manpower for political trouble-shooting.

It follows, if that be valid, that the other types of nonjudicial activities are improper a fortiori. Under no circumstances can they be justified. Justice Douglas's dissenting opinion in the *Chandler* case states a different view; to him, "Federal judges are entitled, like other people, to the full freedom of the First Amendment."[40]

---

[38] As a former law professor, Fortas would hardly have accepted in the classroom such an argument as he put forth in his attempt to justify his continuing to be personal counsellor to the President after becoming a Justice.

[39] Parker, *The Judicial Office of the United States*, 23 N.Y.U.L.Q. REV. 225 (1948).

[40] What Justice Douglas also left unsaid was that the first amendment is not an absolute—at least in the eyes of the majority of the Court—and that certain people having a special status may find their "full freedom" curtailed at times. Perhaps the as yet unsettled analogy is the extent to which members

That is an interesting sentiment, faintly reminiscent, albeit in a different way, of Holmes's famous utterance about the right of Boston policemen to strike, but hardly dispositive of the question. Justice Douglas's chief point is the value he places on an independent judiciary; but certainly that independence is not lessened if judges are held to high standards of conduct in their off-bench activities. Independence of the judiciary, that is to say, can only refer to the ability of judges to operate *in their official duties* on the bench without fear or favor; and being called to account, if they are judges of lower courts, by the appellate review process, or if they are Supreme Court Justices, by constitutional amendment (or by statute in the growing number of cases that involve interpretation of statutes). Accountability, of course, is also effected by impeachment—and apparently—by the informal suasion of chief judges.[41] Justice Black's fear, stated in his dissenting opinion in *Chandler*, that "the hope for an independent judiciary will prove to have been no more than an evanescent dream" may be dismissed as mere hyperbole, insofar as it refers to extra-judicial activities of judges. Black and Douglas consider the act of the Judicial Council of the Tenth Circuit concerning Judge Chandler to be unconstitutional; in other words, they believe that judges cannot formally police themselves, even when aided by statute.[42] The majority of the Court thought otherwise and thus apparently made it possible for the judiciary to govern itself—"apparently" because the majority opinion by Chief Justice Burger is noteworthy for being circumspect.

2. *How, if at all, does delay in the courts lead to lessened confidence in their operations?* The question, of course, refers to the operations of *courts*, rather than of *judges*; but the two are inseparable. That the American system of justice (in the sense of producing decisions, without regard to their substantive content) is little better than in the days when Pound spoke (1906) has already been mentioned. Chief Justice Burger's concern reflects a deplorable situation, both in criminal and civil matters. It is common knowledge that persons accused of crimes are often not brought to trial for months, sometimes years; this, it would seem, is one of the motivations behind the "preventive detention" part of the newly enacted crime control bill for the District of Columbia.[43] Often, furthermore, the accused is per-

---

of the military services, "like other people," are entitled to "the full freedom of the first amendment." Judges accept certain limitations on their freedom when they ascend to the bench. It could scarcely be otherwise. Not even Justice Douglas, I would surmise, would go so far as to say that judges have a first amendment right to take part in public partisan political activities. If judges do not like being limited, they can always resign; after all, the 13th amendment is still on the books.

[41] *Hearings of the Subcomm. on Separation of Powers, supra* note 14.

[42] Of course it is true that 28 U.S.C. § 332 is ambiguous, and the legislative history inconclusive as to its meaning; but as with many statutes, it is subject to growth and extension through interpretation. *Cf.* Miller, *Statutory Language and the Purposive Use of Ambiguity*, 42 VA. L. REV. 23 (1956).

[43] In a peculiar bit of logic, Congress, in its infinite wisdom, has concluded that if because of crowded dockets, suspected criminals cannot quickly be brought to trial, then at times they should be incarcerated until trial. In other words, Congress by not increasing the number of courts or streamlining the system, makes it impossible to get a speedy trial; and then decrees that suspects should be jailed until the slow pace of criminal law enforcement reaches the particular defendant's case. This may make sense to the

mitted to "cop a plea" as a way of speeding up the dispensation of "justice" and getting dockets cleared, for as the Chief Justice noted in his "state of the judiciary" speech in August 1970, the only way in which the system works at all is because most defendants confess. A diminution of just ten per cent in the number of confessions would, according to Burger, throw the courts into complete confusion.[44] In civil litigation, the situation is far worse. In some states, tort cases are three or four years in arrears, and suits in contract are hopelessly bogged down. Conditions in the settlement of estates, as in the New York surrogate courts, are also critically deficient.

Delay, of course, is not necessarily attributable to judges alone, although the lazy judge is not uncommon, and there are some who seem to be unable to reach decisions after a trial has been held, possibly because the issues and evidence are so complex. The bar must also bear much of the deserved opprobrium heaped upon courts; lawyers constantly requesting, and being granted, continuances do not engender respect for the profession. Legislatures, too, may be faulted, principally because they have failed to keep abreast of rapid growths in population and increasing demands placed upon the judicial system.

Whatever the cause, however, there can be little doubt that public confidence is diminished by delay in the administration of justice. The remedy, in general, is clear: Speed the process. That justice delayed is justice denied is not an empty truism; as with all such propositions, it is solidly based on fact. How to accelerate the flow of decisions is a much harder problem. Increasing the number of courts would help, as would improving the performance of the profession.

If something like that is not done, a further diminution in the tasks of courts may well eventuate. Already much of commercial law has been removed, *sub silentio*, from the judiciary, the businessman not being able to wait for the tortuous path of litigation to end. Resort to the courts is practically unknown in international business; in domestic commerce, arbitration is ever more the norm. In other words, private judiciaries have been created to dispense justice in the disputes of businessmen. Furthermore, we seem to be on the verge of placing automobile accident cases, perhaps the bulk of tort litigation, in the hands of some sort of administrative tribunal. The analogy here is workmen's compensation, which for different reasons was de-judicialized several decades ago.

3. *To what extent does the competence of judges to handle complex social problems contribute to a lack of confidence?* This question shades off into the fourth (on the nature of the adversary system), but will be discussed separately. The problem is mainly one of comparative expertise. Are other tribunals (that is, administrative agencies) more competent in handling the immensely intricate problems of the modern day?

---

legislative (and bureaucratic) mind, but it seems so wildly nonsensical (and probably unconstitutional) that it must have come from Kafka or perhaps Orwell.

[44] The Chief Justice's "state of the judiciary" message was made before the annual ABA meeting in August 1970 (mimeo.).

Three decades ago the answer, for many issues, was clear, admitted even by Supreme Court Justices:[45] the personnel of the agencies were said to be more competent. A large part of what has been given the generic label of administrative law in American law schools, particularly "scope of review," "standing," and the "substantial evidence" rule, is testimony to a desire, at times avid, on the part of judges to dodge ruling on complicated questions over which the bureaucracy had first—and, as it has turned out, usually the last—opportunity to decide. James M. Landis's lectures, *The Administrative Process*, published in 1938, were a benchmark of the intellectual approbation accorded to administrators. Congress established and delegated power to the agencies; and judges without reluctance recognized their own lack of technical expertise. That some evidence exists tending to show a present-day reversal of that posture of excessive deference to the putative competence of the expert does not mean that people generally, or litigants specifically, have any more confidence in judges than was shown in the past when the massive transfer of power to the bureaucracy occurred. The most that can be concluded is that there is also an increasing lack of public confidence in the bureaucracy; people turn to the courts, and even to Congress, as the only institutions extant that *may* be able to curb the bureaucrats.[46] The businessman, it should be noted, tends to try to trigger Congress, not the federal courts, when he is dissatisfied with decisions reached within the public administration—a phenomenon that has been little noted by administrative law scholars, but which should be, simply because it has resulted in Congress becoming, in part, a "super court of appeals." That is valid even for Supreme Court decisions, which because of the rise of administration tend to be statutory and thus "reviewable" by Congress, as the recently enacted "newspaper preservation act" indicates.[47]

Is there a remedy for the lack of competence in judges? It is difficult to discover one. If the judges themselves admit personal incapacity to understand complicated questions—as did Chief Justice Taft, who said that he never wanted to decide "radio" questions, and Justice Frankfurter, who in *Roman & Nichols* expressly stated a belief in the superior ability of administrators[48]—it is likely that they will be believed. When, they (or Congress, for that matter) try to retrieve power ceded to the

---

[45] *E.g.*, Railroad Comm'n v. Rowan & Nichols Oil Co., 310 U.S. 573, 580-82 (1940) and 311 U.S. 570, 575-77 (1941). *See* K. DAVIS, ADMINISTRATIVE LAW TREATISE *passim* (1958, Supp. 1965) for an exhaustive listing of the cases. *See also* F. FRANKFURTER, SOME OBSERVATIONS ON SUPREME COURT LITIGATION AND LEGAL EDUCATION (1954); General Bronze Corp. v. Ward Products Corp., 262 F. Supp. 936, 937 (M.D.N.Y. 1966) (Foley, J., speaking of the "senselessness of federal judges untrained in the patent art to pretend otherwise").

[46] *Compare* K. DAVIS, DISCRETIONARY JUSTICE (1968) *with* T. LOWI, THE END OF LIBERALISM (1969).

[47] Newspaper Preservation Act, Pub. L. No. 91-353, 84 Stat. 466 (*U.S. Code Congressional and Administrative News*, Aug. 20, 1970). Passed in the summer of 1970, this statute permits newspapers to be excluded at times from operation of the antitrust laws. It is one more instance—two or three dozen can be counted in recent decades—where Congress overrules the Supreme Court. At times the businessman goes directly to Congress from the administrative agency, without even bothering to try to get judicial review of an agency decision; for example, when the FCC a few years ago proposed to put into administrative rule the "code of ethics" on commercials of the National Association of Broadcasters.

[48] *Rowan & Nichols, supra* note 45.

bureaucracy, it will be difficult and perhaps impossible. One thing that could be done would be to improve the way in which the adversary system operates; discussion of that will be deferred to Question 4, below. An obvious suggestion would be to upgrade the quality of our judges, state and federal, trial and appellate. But, here again, major difficulties obtrude.

One is the way in which judges are chosen. Whether elected or appointed, they tend to be drawn from those close to the politicians then in office (those politicians may, of course, be mere surrogates for those who wield real power in the American polity). Federal judges other than Supreme Court nominees must be cleared by the Senator(s) of the state from which they come, a system that has grown extra-constitutionally and that permits the Senate, through its power to consent to nominations, to exercise much control over who gets on the bench. At times nominations are so blatantly partisan or are of such inferior lawyers that they cannot be stomached even by the Senate, an institution that has never been known to be overly squeamish. In any event, Democrats appoint Democrats for the most part and Republicans are adept at finding qualified Republicans, all the while talking about the rule of law! Within each party, of course, there is a wide spectrum of philosophy and opinion; but it is no accident that judges seem to represent, speaking very generally and with some obvious exceptions, a "conservative" viewpoint. Perhaps this is because the profession itself is largely conservative or that law is, in essence, a conserving force within society or—possibly—because the American Bar Association, which tends to be a pillar of baroque orthodoxy, has become a part of the appointing process.[49] Even so, there are wide variances between judges, as Justice Douglas observed in *Chandler*: "Judges are not fungible; they cover the constitutional spectrum; and a particular judge's emphasis may make a world of difference when it comes to rulings on evidence, the temper of the courtroom, the tolerance for a proffered defense, and the like. Lawyers recognize this when they talk about 'shopping' for a judge; Senators recognize this when they are asked to give their 'advice and consent' to judicial appointments; laymen recognize this when they appraise the quality and image of the judiciary in their own community." Justice Douglas's views will be adverted to again below; at present, the point is the simple but hard fact that judges vary in their handling of cases and (what Douglas did not say) in their intellectual capacity. More, they are distinctly not renaissance men, and by no criterion can be expected to have expertise in all of the issues that come before them for decision

---

[49] In the summer of 1970 the Attorney General announced that, contrary to the past, the ABA would be used to screen prospective Supreme Court nominees as well as judges for lower courts. N.Y. Times July 15, 1970, at 16, col. 8. This informal system of making the bar a part of the appointing process tends, among other things, to break down the line between public and private in the American constitutional order. *Cf.* Miller, *supra* note 6. It may seriously be doubted that lawyers alone should have that power and responsibility; if screening of nominees is to be done, surely it would be better if the reviewing body were made up of a representative sampling of the citizenry, not just the fat-cats of the ABA. Once it openly recognized that judges do make law (see text at Point No. 6, below), certainly others than members of the legal guild have an interest in who makes the laws.

Better quality judges would, in short, be a boon, but one should not expect that their appointment would be a panacea (even if they can be identified and get by the political process of elevation to the bench).

But if judges cannot be widely competent, perhaps the judicial institution can be altered to provide them with a higher grade of assistance. At the present time, judges must rely on antiquated machinery and inadequate "internal" personnel to provide them with the data necessary for decision. "External" personnel—*i.e.*, the lawyers—aside, the system which allows a judge to have merely a law clerk or two—and then usually neophytes whose main claim to expertise is law review experience at some relatively adequate law school—is so obviously short of what is needed that only that built-in inertia that is epidemic within the legal profession could tolerate it. Judge Charles Wyzanski recognized this several years ago in the *United Shoe* case,[50] an antitrust decision, when he named economist Carl Kaysen to be his temporary "law" clerk to advise him on the economics of the problem—an experiment that, to my knowledge, has not been repeated. Justice Frank Murphy, whose intellectual talents were minor at best and who was a reluctant member of the High Bench, solved his problem by keeping law clerks for as long as five years and, as noted above, by talking over pending cases with his lawyer-friend, Edward Kemp.[51] The former practice has much in its favor, but the latter strays far over the boundary of propriety. Perhaps law clerks should be drawn from lawyers with at least ten years of practice or from the academic community. Moreover, they could well be augmented by behavioral science experts.

Such a "solution" is not very promising. Possibly it would be preferable, as Professor Louis Schwartz has argued,[52] to recognize that judges cannot be expert in everything, but that they, as social generalists, can be considered to have special talents in the ordering of priorities and values within the community. But if so, this would mean that the bureaucracy would be firmly in command and that the sporadic judicial decision overturning the public administration is not likely to make much difference in the way that the bureaucrats operate. In other words, the day-to-day routine governing power in the United States is now in the hands of the executive-administrative branch, and neither the judiciary nor Congress seem able to do much to alter the pattern. Nor is there much evidence of a real desire to do so—by judges, by members of Congress, by lawyers, by important interest groups, or by the people generally.

4. *Does the adversary system contribute to a diminution of confidence in the judiciary?* During the 1930s much was made by the legal realists of "trial by combat" in American courts, a theme echoed by Eldridge Cleaver in *Soul on Ice*:

---

[50] United States v. United Shoe Machinery Corp., 110 F. Supp. 295 (D. Mass. 1953). *See* C. KAYSEN, UNITED STATES V. UNITED SHOE MACHINERY CORPORATION; AN ECONOMIC ANALYSIS OF AN ANTI-TRUST CASE (1956).

[51] Discussed in HOWARD, *supra* note 34.

[52] Schwartz, *Legal Restriction of Competition in the Regulated Industries, An Abdication of Judicial Responsibility*, 67 HARV. L. REV. 436 (1954).

"In a culture that secretly subscribes to the piratical ethic of 'every man for himself'—the social Darwinism of 'survival of the fittest' being far from dead, manifesting itself in our ratrace political system of competing parties, in our dog-eat-dog economic system of profit and loss, and in our adversary system of justice wherein truth is secondary to the skill and connections of the advocate—the logical culmination of this ethic, on a person-to-person level, is that the weak are seen as the natural and just prey of the strong."[53] Whether or not one subscribes to that sentiment, there can be little question about certain basic shortcomings of the adversary system of dispensing justice in American courts; they include (a) the lack of judicial expertise discussed above; (b) a similar shortcoming in the bar generally; this is manifested *inter alia* by a failure of lawyers properly to argue cases (antitrust is one example); the "external" personnel of the judiciary, on the whole, are badly educated and indifferent practitioners; (c) the hit-and-miss character of litigation, which must await the coming of a proper plaintiff before the system can get into operation; (d) the high cost of litigation, which subtly but obviously tips the scales of justice in favor of those with wealth sufficient to bear those costs; (e) an inability of judges to forecast the impact of their decisions, to weigh, as Holmes said, considerations of social advantage; (f) the tendency of judges to go outside the briefs, record, and argument of counsel to inform themselves about the case at bar; and (g) intellectual adherence to the long-exploded theory of judicial decision-making, often attributed to Blackstone—the so-called "declaratory" theory under which the judge ostensibly has no creative role.

Much of this has been discussed elsewhere,[54] so that no present elaboration is required, and the last factor will constitute Proposition 6 in this listing. It is not to be denied that the adversary system rewards those who can retain the most competent counsel; and further that litigation often is simply too expensive for any except the rich or the government to pursue. My conclusion, admittedly intuitive, is that this contributes in large degree to lessening confidence in the judiciary, a situation not enhanced by the continuing failure of bench and bar to do much to improve such obvious inadequacies.

Is there a remedy? In general terms, yes: the entire system requires thorough study and revamping, so as to make it a more useful and (dare I use the term?) just instrument. This will not be done by merely pecking around at the edges, such as rewriting procedural rules, important though those reforms may be; it will be accomplished only when there is a commitment to complete re-examination. First, however, there must be wide recognition that a problem exists, and by no means is it certain that lawyers or judges or laymen would agree on that. The adversary system is a product of the pre-scientific age, of feudal days, and is best suited for the settlement of the penny-ante disputes of *meum* and *tuum* that once were the main concern of private law. Today, however, law is either all public law or is dominated by public

---

[53] E. CLEAVER, SOUL ON ICE 85 (paperback ed. 1968).

[54] Miller & Scheflin, *supra* note 15; Miller, *Toward a Concept of Constitutional Duty*, 1968 SUP. CT. REV. 199.

law—a fact that American legal theorists have, with some notable exceptions, ignored —and the system is employed in contexts and situations far different from that for which it was originally designed or developed. So, change there should be, deep and thoroughgoing—but let no one be sanguine that it will occur.

5. *To what extent do "dual standards of justice" lead to diminished respect for the judiciary?* Carved deeply on the facade of the Supreme Court building in Washington is the phrase "Equal Justice Under Law," a concept written into the Constitution in the equal protection clause of the fourteenth amendment (which, by a process of reverse incorporation is at times applied against the national as well as state governments).[55] How valid is it? To some, even to pose the question is heretical. But the history of American law furnishes a number of examples in which equality is more mythical than real. Some have been mentioned above—the manner in which tort law during the nineteenth century tended to favor the businessman at the expense of the workers (which led to workmen's compensation, a system by which the legislatures deprived courts of their jurisdiction) and second, the way in which judges were so notoriously anti-labor in issuing injunctions and also in striking down social legislation that numerous statutes were enacted, statutes finally upheld in the constitutional revolution of the 1930s. Such a history is not likely to make the unions revere the courts. Judges are not fungible, as Justice Douglas said; he could have gone on to state that law, when it comes to litigation, is far from certain and that judges are accorded a far greater degree of discretion than what Jerome Frank called the "basic myth" allows.[56] The art of judging is that of making choices from between inconsistent principles or standards. In exercising that "sovereign prerogative of choice" judges are distinctly not guided by adherence to "neutral principles," nor are they wholly objective. Being human, they tend to pursue a set of values deemed important to themselves and to the peer group(s) with whom they identify.[57]

Nowhere is this better seen than in the way in which Negroes are treated in the administration of the criminal law. Wolfgang and Cohen, in their recent careful study, *Crime and Race*, conclude: "In striking ways, the administration of justice appears to fail in affording equality of treatment, so fundamental to a democratic society."[58] Blacks tend to be treated more harshly than whites by the police (although other non-whites, such as Mexican-Americans, also receive like treatment, as do disadvantaged whites); blacks are more often convicted after indictment, get harsher penalties (including the death sentence), and receive fewer commutations of sentence, releases on parole, particularly when inter-racial crimes are concerned. On the other hand, Negro crimes committed on other Negroes are often treated with marked

---

[55] Bolling v. Sharpe, 348 U.S. 886 (1954) is a leading case.
[56] J. FRANK, LAW AND THE MODERN MIND (1931). To Frank, the basic myth was the Blackstone theory.
[57] *Cf.* Miller & Howell, *The Myth of Neutrality in Constitutional Adjudication*, 27 U. CHI. L. REV. 661 (1960).
[58] M. WOLFGANG & B. COHEN, CRIME AND RACE: CONCEPTIONS AND MISCONCEPTIONS 100 (1970).

indulgence, as John Dollard pointed out in his classic account of social life in a small southern town:

> [T]here are different standards of justice for the two castes. While persons are held much more strictly to the formal legal code; Negroes are dealt with more indulgently. It is not a question of different formal codes for Negro and whites, but rather of differences in severity and rigor of application of the code that does exist. This is true only under one condition, however—when Negro crimes are committed on Negroes; when they are done on whites, the penalties assessed may rather be excessively strict. . . . Indeed, this differential application of the white law is often referred to as a merit by Southern white persons; one will be asked to notice that they are lenient and indulgent with Negroes and that Negroes are not nearly so severely punished as whites would be for the same crimes. It is clear that this differential application of the law amounts to a condoning of Negro violence and gives immunity to Negroes to commit small or large crimes so long as they are on Negroes.[59]

Differences in treatment lead to negative attitudes toward the law and the legal system, which are held in either silent contempt or outright derision.

Can a black get a fair trial in the United States? The question is seriously posed. Haywood Burns, national director of the newly formed National Conference of Black Lawyers, answers it flatly: "If by fair one means free of bias, the answer has to be generally NO." Burns asserts that the law discriminates against blacks (and poor people). His principal concern, of course, is with Negroes: "It is folly to say that ours is a government of laws, not men. Laws are made, interpreted and applied by men—and in America's case by men in a racist society. Ultimately, there is the simple and obvious truth that the judicial system is run by people, mostly by white people and that most white people are racially biased."[60] Whether or not one agrees with that, it cannot be gainsaid that ours is a Jim Crow society—sixteen years after *Brown v. Board of Education* and more than a century after the Emancipation Proclamation. (It should be remembered, of course, that the original Constitution made express provision for human slavery.) The conclusions of the Kerner Commission[61] that America is moving toward two nations—one white and one black—may be said to have been anticipated in the manner in which the legal system has operated in the past and still operates throughout the country. This, it should be emphasized, is *not* a regional (southern) phenomenon; it is nation-wide. "Daily," maintains Burns, "in courts throughout the country, black and poor defendants suffer the humiliations of a legal system which refuses to accord them full recognition their dignity as human beings."

I happen to believe that Burns's assertions are valid—and not only in the criminal

[59] J. DOLLARD, CASTE AND CLASS IN A SOUTHERN TOWN 279-80 (1937).

[60] Burns, *Can a Black Man Get a Fair Trial in This Country?*, N.Y. Times, July 12, 1970, at (Magazine). *See* Mapes, *Unequal Justice: A Growing Disparity in Criminal Sentences Troubles Le Experts*, Wall St. J., Sept. 9, 1970, at 1, col. 1.

[61] *See* REPORT OF THE NATIONAL ADVISORY COMMISSION ON CIVIL DISORDERS (1968).

law, but in such other areas as creditors' rights, landlord-tenant law, commercial transactions, and in the way in which administrative agencies, state and federal, deal with the poor and non-white. Kingman Brewster was on the mark, in my judgment, when he said: "I am appalled and ashamed that things should have come to such a pass that I am skeptical of the ability of black revolutionaries to achieve a fair trial anywhere in the United States."[62] More important, however, than whether Burns and Brewster are correct, in the sense that hard evidence can be produced to validate their positions, is the fact that many non-whites and poor people think that dual systems of justice prevail in the United States. Surely the ineluctable consequence is diminished respect for law and for the judiciary. Perhaps I should make it clear that the position taken is general, not specific; I am not passing judgment on, for example, the trial of the Black Panthers in New Haven. What I am saying is this: Given the totality of impacts of the legal system on members of the black (and other underprivileged) communities, it is at least an open question, and probably a working hypothesis, that justice in the sense of fairness and equity of treatment is simply often not available to those segments of American society. The situation may be changing, at least in part, as a result of recent legislation—such as the Office of Economic Opportunity programs—but the very fact such legislation could be enacted is impressive testimony of the proposition advanced.

The picture is not all gloomy. For example, during recent years the Supreme Court has attempted to make the scales of justice balance more evenly; and civil rights legislation, state and federal, is on the books. But the Court, the myth to the contrary, is a relatively feeble instrument of governance,[63] and it is by no means certain that the civil servants in the bureaucracy, as well as their counterparts in the private bureaucracies of business and labor, have any deep-felt commitment to putting legislative norms of legal equality into operational reality. As another example, blacks and others are at times using the courts in efforts to further their own goals— "working within the system," in current jargon, to turn American society around. Environmentalists, for instance, are employing law (and inventing new legal theories) to try to get courts and agencies to act against the polluters[64]—a monumental task, to be sure, but one necessary to try even through ultimate victory is difficult to foresee.

These are exceptions, however. The growing belief, particularly among blacks, that the system's rules discriminate against them is ever more the pattern. It is a dangerous view, one with ominous portents for the United States. As someone said at the time of the trial of the "Chicago Seven," "Who wants to live in a country where he is forced to choose between Abbie Hoffman and Judge Julius Hoffman?" That choice is no choice at all, and if that is all we have, then we are in for it—and

---

[62] Quoted in Burns, *supra* note 60.

[63] *See* Miller & Scheflin, *supra* note 15; and compare BICKEL, *supra* note 2.

[64] *See*, *e.g.*, Sax, *The Public Trust Doctrine in Natural Resource Law: Effective Judicial Intervention*, 68 MICH. L. REV. 473 (1970).

we had better realize it soon. There is no easy or simple way out of such a morass.

The problem is complicated by the backlash of the know-nothings against the courts, especially the Supreme Court and former Chief Justice Earl Warren. Whether from ignorance, the extent of which is boundless, or from partisan political motives, the majority of the Justices of the Warren Court have been accused of such "derelictions" as "coddling criminals" and "protecting subversives"—in other words, of applying some dual standard of justice. Similar reactions were evident concerning racial segregation and the school prayer cases. One Congressman accused the Court of "legislating—they never adjudicate—with one eye on the Kremlin and the other on the National Association for the Advancement of Colored People."[65] The know-nothings have received powerful intellectual support from a little cult of law and political science professors, most of whom are apparently disciples of the late Justice Frankfurter, who decry the product of the Warren Court as being "unprincipled" or not in accord with the law "as it has been received and understood." That these professorial attacks on the High Bench are aimed more at the reasoning of the Justices than, as with the know-nothings, the results, is beside the point. Both believe that the Court acted improperly—and as such, both may be said to lack confidence in at least that important segment of the judiciary. That neither group contributes to a fuller understanding of constitutional adjudication is also irrelevant. They do not, save to serve as examples of what should *not* be done in commenting on judicial activity.

A further aspect of the problem of dual standards of justice exists—that of selective enforcement of the law by officials in the executive-administrative branch. Surely it does not contribute to respect for law and its administrators to see, for instance, an 1899 anti-pollution statute systematically ignored by the bureaucracy, while simultaneously other statutes are at times harshly enforced by other agencies— as in the case of midnight searches of the homes of people on welfare. An aspect of selective enforcement is the manner in which some groups can trigger Congress to overrule the courts of agencies, as in the above mentioned Newspaper Preservation Act of 1970. As Professor Stephen R. Barnett put it in *The New Republic* (July 18, 1970, at 11, 12), that statute presents "a nice lesson in law and order. When powerful publishers break the law—a criminal law at that—they are not even compelled to obey it in the future. They telephone their congressmen, hire some lobbyists, and get Congress to change the law for them." Can there be any wonder when others sneer at law and law enforcement?

6. *Do misconceptions of the public on the nature of the judicial process result in less confidence in the courts?* In other words, is there symbolic value in adherence to the Blackstone declaratory theory of adjudication, which, as Professor Paul Mishkin has said, may be "in part myth" but "which can be sacrificed only at sub-

---

[65] Pollak, *W.B.R.: Some Reflections*, 71 YALE L.J. 1451, 1455 n.17 (1962).

stantial cost?"[66] That cost, to Mishkin, is public disrespect for and lack of confidence in the Justices of the Supreme Court. That is to say, if it became generally believed that the Justices are not rigidly bound by these external principles called law, but can and do read some of their own valuations into their decisions, would that blackened image of the judiciary contribute to lessened esteem?

These three ways of asking the same question all founder on the same rock: The well-nigh complete lack of verified empirical data upon which one can base conclusions about the role of the declaratory theory. I have discussed the matter elsewhere, so that there is no present need to repeat what was said there—save to quote conclusions gleaned from a questionnaire sent to experts on the Supreme Court:

> The results of the survey, admittedly sparse and by no means unanimous, seem to indicate that experts hold the following *beliefs* about the Supreme Court and the symbolic value of the declaratory theory: (1) the American people generally have little or no knowledge about how the Court operates; (2) they probably do not care and would not take the trouble to find out; and (3) they are probably more interested in *what* the Court has done in a substantive sense, rather than how it accomplishes the result.[67]

As a working hypothesis, then, the American people tend to accord a high degree of respect to courts when there is agreement with the results that are reached in decisions. The reasoning of judges, mainly appellate, is important principally to a small coterie of commentators on judicial activity—they who look for neatly phrased and logically coherent explications of the results. They articulate a desire for an *elegantia juris*, seeking aesthetic satisfaction in what they consider to be properly written opinions. As such, they fail to see that judicial decisions must, in any ideal model, be both logically consistent *and* sociologically non-arbitrary.

With the spread of mass higher education and dissemination of the teachings of the legal realists, more and more laymen are beginning to understand, at least partially, some of the heretofore locked-up mysteries of the nature of the judicial process. They also realize the shortcomings of the human mind, both on and off the bench. While not asking the impossible of judges, they do request that judges take part, as Alexander Pekelis once put it, in "the travail of society"[68]—to be, that is, avowedly instrumental as well as interdictory in their decision-making, to espouse a set of values fit for a polity that considers itself democratic in the age of science and technology. Knowing more about courts, they ask more of judges, possibly because, as in the segregation cases, they are the only public officials not deeply immersed (outwardly at least) in the political process. To continue to insist upon calling a judge a neutral automaton, when all human experience refutes that notion, is to be wilfully blind. If judges are to take a more important part in the governance of

---

[66] Mishkin, *supra* note 15.

[67] Miller & Scheflin, *supra* note 15.

[68] A. Pekelis, *The Case for a Jurisprudence of Welfare*, in LAW AND SOCIAL ACTION 1, 40 (M. Konvitz ed. 1950).

America—a proposition which, although fraught with danger, may be vital to the protection of constitutional liberties—then there must be frank and open recognition of the facts of adjudication. The secrecy that has in large part surrounded the internal operations of courts should be eliminated. Good government is open government: Is there any reason why the spirit of the "freedom of information" act should not be rigidly applied to all organs of government, including courts? Once it is conceded that judges can and do make law—and that, indeed, they cannot avoid doing so—then a compelling case can be made for opening up their activities to the full scrutiny of the public.[69] After all, if the Swiss Supreme Court can conduct its affairs openly, why not the American—even though it is doubtless more important in a comparative way?

The mass media generally have not been of help in explaining how courts operate. In the main, they have contented themselves with reporting the bare facts of what courts do, and what others say about judges, not with analyzing and explicating their role in American government. Accordingly, the media have contributed little to a greater understanding of adjudication so necessary in a democratic polity. American scholars have not done much more. They have failed to see the burgeoning need of helping, in small part, to attain the rule of law which might be accomplished by writing for the layman (as Dean E. N. Griswold once advocated)[70] about the legal process generally or by subjecting present and proposed public policies to thorough analysis and criticism.[71]

IV

Conclusions

American judges are custodians of law, insofar as any such exist in the nation; as Chief Justice Marshall said in *Marbury*, it is "emphatically the province" of the judiciary to say what the law is. But if that be so (and it is at most a half-truth), then the ancient question, *Quis Custodiet Ipsos Custodes?*, immediately arises. Who, indeed, should put the judiciary's house in order?

The question, as with all such matters, is not simply answered. Several alternatives may be suggested, no one of which seems entirely adequate: (a) the judges themselves, in a self-policing effort; (b) Congress, either directly or by setting up some agency to do it; and (c) the legal profession, acting through bar associations and with the assistance of the academic branch of lawyerdom. Perhaps it will take

---

[69] Justice Frankfurter, in an off-bench statement, asserted: "The fact is that pitifully little of significance has been contributed by judges regarding the nature of their endeavor, and I might add, that which is written by those who are not judges is too often a confident caricature rather than a seer's version of the judicial process of the Supreme Court." F. Frankfurter, Of Law and Men 32 (Elman ed. 1956). Even lawyers, according to Chief Justice Roger Traynor, are not knowledgeable about how appellate judges reach decisions. *See* Traynor, *Badlands in an Appellate Judge's Realm of Reason*, 7 Utah L. Rev. 158 (1960).

[70] Griswold, *Some Thoughts About Legal Education Today*, 11 Harv. L.S. Bull. 4 (1959).

[71] *See* Miller, *The Law School as a Center for Policy Analysis* (forthcoming).

a cooperative endeavor of all together, with a further leg-up from the Executive (at least in the appointing process). The principle of an independent judiciary is too fundamental to be lightly dealt with. But complete independence, free from all checks, has never been true. Trial judges are subject to review and all judges are subject to legislative review, save in constitutional matters—and in those instances amendment is possible. No doubt the answer, if and when it comes, will be after long discussion, hammered out on the anvil of political compromise. Whether it will be adequate cannot be predicted.

This essay has posed some of the questions involved when considering the concept of public confidence in the judiciary. Enough has perhaps been said to show that a problem does exist, one that is difficult to state with precision because it has many facets and because its exact dimensions are unknown.[72] It will not be easily resolved, for it is a segment of a larger lack of confidence in the American institutions of authority, both public and private.

A final note: much of what has been said in this paper is not based on compilations of factual data, simply because none are available. A great need exists for scholars, legal and otherwise, to make empirical studies of the questions posed in Section III and simultaneously to give rigorous thought to possible ways and means to rectify observed shortcomings in the judiciary. In so doing, much of the mythology enveloping the bench should be dissipated: if we are governed (at least in part) by judges, surely we are entitled, pursuant to democratic theory, to know not only who governs but how they do it. Greater knowledge *could* lead to greater confidence. That, I admit, is an article of personal faith. I cannot prove it; I simply believe it.[73]

---

[72] Since the text was written I have read Judge Skelly Wright's *Poverty, Minorities, and Respect for Law*, 1970 DUKE L.J. 425, and find much in it with which I can agree.

[73] Another question that bears upon the confidence some members of the public have in the judiciary concerns the extent to which it is thought that the courts are too lenient on suspected criminals. Many people so believe; they also believe that there is a direct correlation between judicial cognizance of the constitutional rights of criminal defendants and the rising crime rate in the United States. Whether that belief is valid has not been documented by empirical proof. *See* Miller, *Some Pervasive Myths About the United States Supreme Court*, 10 ST. LOUIS U.L.J. 153, 181-83 (1965). Its validity, however, is not the point; rather, it is that it is believed to be true. An analogue of this might be the way in which the judicial system may have been used for "political" trials, as in the case of Dr. Benjamin Spock. *Cf.* O. KIRCHHEIMER, POLITICAL JURISPRUDENCE (2d ed. 1970). Again, there are some who believe that the system is being used for "political" ends, a proposition that is at once controversial and unproved, simply because no data exist to show what motivates prosecutors, including the Attorney General of the United States.

10
PRIVACY IN THE MODERN CORPORATE STATE

To what extent is privacy protected by the Supreme Court? The word "privacy" is not mentioned in the Constitution, but a right of privacy has been identified by the Justices in recent years. One of the most noteworthy instances is the recognition that the constitutional provision of due process of law includes privacy; in turn, this privacy protects the right of a pregnant woman to an abortion.

Despite considerable literature to the contrary, privacy is by no means highest among the values favored by Americans. This chapter discusses the lack of empirical knowledge of the extent to which Americans value privacy, and then indicates that privacy is protected only when the fundamental interests of the State are not jeopardized. That such a position runs counter to the accepted notions of privacy and of constitutional law is obvious, but it is the only tenable conclusion that can be reached. That conclusion may not be popular, but it cannot be gainsaid.

"Privacy in the Modern Corporate State" was originally published in 25 *Administrative Law Review* 231 (1973). Reprinted with permission of the American Bar Association and its Section of Administrative Law.

The larger lesson is implicit: the Supreme Court is not the staunch guardian of our rights and liberties that many think it is. For its treatment of privacy is paralleled by its treatment of other issues that come before it. In sum, we are ill advised to rely upon the courts, including the Supreme Court, to protect us either from our own follies or from governmental deprivations. At times, yes, but usually, no.

(A brief commentary on this essay by Professor David Weisstub of York University has been deleted.)

I. INTRODUCTION

This essay is speculative in nature; it is concerned with the role that privacy plays in modern industrialized nations and the protection that the law gives to it. To understand privacy one must see it in social and historical context. A search of the nonlegal literature, however, reveals much by way of *a priori* assumptions but little by way of empirically tested hypotheses. In many respects, privacy is a concept that is often discussed but seldom adequately defined; it is somewhat analogous to other legal concepts of high-level abstraction—we know it (or its absence) when we see it, somewhat like Justice Potter Stewart, in a remarkable burst of candor a few years ago, said that he could not define obscenity but he knew it when he saw it.[1] Perhaps this is because it is a label for a response to certain situations, rather than a full-blown legal concept. I am inclined to believe, although admittedly the conclusion is reached intuitively rather than by hard evidence,

---

*Access to government information and an individual's right to privacy may be viewed as different sides of the same coin. Professor Miller discusses the underlying values providing for both rights. His paper was delivered as one of the Annual Lectures before the Osgoode Hall Law School, York University, Toronto, Canada. Professor David Weisstub of that school's Law Faculty commented on Professor Miller's paper.... The Editors.

†Professor, National Law Center, George Washington University.

[1]Jacobellis v. Ohio, 378 U.S. 184 (1964).

that privacy is a value—a preference, if you will—mainly of the middle-class and upper middle-class—of, that is, the societal group roughly labelled as the "elite" or the "establishment." In saying that, I realize that I run counter to a good deal of conventional wisdom, which seems to suggest that most people seek privacy, desire it, value it, and otherwise hold it in high esteem. Put briefly, I simply do not think that such a proposition has been or, much more importantly, can be validated.

Personal privacy, thus, is like freedom: Both are 18th- and 19th-century values of diminishing significance in the modern age—if, indeed, they ever had any substantial basis in social attitudes and behavior. Emphasis on privacy and freedom in law and legal literature, furthermore, comes at precisely the time that the demands of the State for ever increasing amounts of data and the closing of the frontier make their realization, in any reasonably substantial manner, unlikely at best. The thrust of this paper is a discussion of privacy, but surely it must be seen in the context of freedom as well: The "right to know" (as an aspect of freedom) collides with the "right to be let alone" (the constitutional notion of privacy). In the ensuing discussion, attention will be accorded mainly to what has happened, is happening, and may happen in that highly industrialized, bureaucratically organized nation to the south of Canada—the United States of America. This is done in the interests of parsimony of effort and because it appears that lawyers there have published more about privacy than elsewhere; and also because the U.S.A. purports to be a polity that values privacy and freedom and places them high in the hierarchy of constitutional values. Like it or not, furthermore, what happens south of the Canadian border may well point the direction of things to come in other industrialized nations.

My main theme is that privacy—however defined, itself not an easy task—collides not only with the freedoms of others but with the requirements of State planning in an age of corporativism. Privacy, moreover, is to be seen as one thread of social thought that has had prominence during this century but that is basically inconsistent with another thread—that of loneliness and of *anomie*. Man does exist "all alone and afraid/ In a world he never made." Or as Thoreau put it in *Walden*: ". . . it is easier to sail many thousand miles through cold and storm and cannibals, in a government ship, with 500 men and boys to assist one, than it is to explore the private sea, the Atlantic and Pacific of one's being alone." I am not trying to make that sort of exploration here; it is mentioned simply to provide some basis for thinking about privacy. Private man, in short, confronts and in all probability gives way to lonely man—and *anomic* man, too.

Were time to permit such a digression, it would be interesting to ponder the reasons why no systematic social or behavioral science studies of privacy have been made.[2] That seems to me to be a cause for concern and for wondering why—and also for asking how legal norms about privacy can be adequately discussed without some data from the social sciences. For I maintain, and this discussion is so predicated, that law and legal norms must be seen as a part of the total social process. Contrary to the belief systems of the legal profession, law is not "there," as a discrete entity. So to believe is to engage in what Judith Shklar aptly termed "legalism," which is, as she says, the prevailing ideology of lawyers[3] (and of legal educators, be it said). If we in law have learned anything in the past several decades, it is that legalism is an invalid way of approaching that type of social phenomenon known as "the law."

Most discussions of privacy in the legal literature sooner or later cite the seminal article by Warren and Brandeis.[4] I, too, mention it— but for a somewhat different purpose: I consider it of more than passing interest, perhaps it is of surpassing significance, that publication of that article, which is the first important discussion of an emergent common-law right of privacy, came at precisely the time that the eminent American historian, Frederick Jackson Turner, said that the American frontier had closed. Suddenly an open society, in a geographical sense, became a closed society, knowing finite bounds. A subcontinent had been subdued; and even if there was much yet to be exploited by way of resources, terrestrially there was little left to

---

[2]Inquiry made to several behavioral scientists brought a uniformly negative response. One article, on an anthropological view of privacy, was not helpful. *See* Lundsgaarde, *Privacy: An Anthropological Perspective on the Right to be Let Alone,* 8 HOUSTON L. REV. 858 (1971). In Haiman, *Speech v. Privacy: Is There A Right Not to be Spoken To?,* 67 NW. U. L. REV. 153 (1972), it is suggested that "class biases may affect our thinking" on privacy; but the evidence to support the statement is too scanty to be persuasive. *Cf.,* Lusky, *Invasion of Privacy: A Clarification of Concepts,* 72 COLUM. L. REV. 693 (1972). In WESTIN, PRIVACY AND FREEDOM (1967), there are brief references to the social-science aspects of privacy, but these are far from adequate.

[3]SHKLAR, LEGALISM (1964)

[4]Warren & Brandeis, *The Right To Privacy,* 4 HARV. L. REV. 193 (1890). It has been suggested that the article would never have been written, and perhaps recognition of the "right to privacy" delayed had not the sensationalist press of Boston over-publicized (in Warren's view) the social activities of Warren. *See* MISHKIN & MORRIS, ON LAW IN COURTS 98 (1965) (calling the article "a work of advocacy").

explore. Since then—the turn of the century—what Turner saw for the U.S.A. was extended to the entire North Atlantic "community" by Walter Prescott Webb, whose book, *The Great Frontier*,[5] surely deserves early resurrection. There is much in it that should be considered by those who worry about privacy and freedom and the other secular values of a secular state.

Ponder, too, the implications of "spaceship earth"—the "global village" notion espoused by McLuhan—and its impact, immeasurable and subtle, on the human psyche. In its long-range implications it may have as much influence upon the way we perceive ourselves as some of the other major events in the past 2000 years of human history—the Copernican revolution that forever destroyed the Ptolemaic notion of geocentric universe; the Darwinian theory that erased any validity to the idea of the special creation of man; the Freudian view of the irrational side of the mind of man, that convincingly showed the (partial) invalidity of the notions of rational man espoused by the 18th-century Enlightment philosphers; and Einstein's relativity, plus Heisenberg's principle of uncertainty. (God may not play dice with the universe, as Einstein averred, but so to believe takes a stalwart act of faith). Now we see a single luminous ball, stark and beautiful, floating in an eternity of space—and suddenly we feel, deep down inside, really alone and really afraid. There is nothing quite like the impact on a sentient being of a television picture or a color photograph on the cover of a magazine, depicting this insignificant planet in an insignificant constellation perched on the edge of the galaxy we call the Milky Way—itself only one of an untold number of galaxies. What had to be perceived intellectually, from the time of Copernicus, is now brutally thrust into the consciousness of all including those whose main pastime seems to be to sit glued before the boob tube. The consequences we know not yet, but one would be foolish to ignore the phenomenon. Surely now, even more than in John Donne's time, we can say that our intellectual heritage is "all in peeces, all cohaerence gone."

II. THE CONTEXT

No useful purpose would be served to delineate in detail all of the characteristics of the modern advanced nation-state. Some may be

---

[5]*See* Turner, The Frontier In American History (1920). Webb's book was published in 1952.

singled out for special mention, however, for they bear upon the thesis of this paper. First, and perhaps most apparent, is the scientific-technological revolution with its concomitant of rapid, even cataclysmic social change. Surely it ranks with the agricultural revolution, which occurred about the time of the Neolithic period, during which man first began his tortuous path towards domestication. Through most of human history, known and unknown, man rested in the bosom of agriculture as the basis of wealth and tangible property as the basis of power. That began to change with the beginnings of modern science, not so long ago as we should count time (it may be dated from Francis Bacon in the 17th century, although that selection of course is arbitrary) but really eons ago when life-styles and belief-systems are compared. The scientific-technological revolution began slowly, but accelerated to a pace that now is rapid beyond historical measure and also continues to increase. The net result, brought about, as Whitehead said, by that most important of all inventions, "the invention of the art of invention," not only is that man's perception of the world is changing, his environment is rapidly being altered, and he is slowly beginning to realize that his institutions—social and political, economic and legal—will, as Dean Don K. Price put it, be determined more by scientific discoveries as yet unknown than by presently known legal and political doctrines.[6] We are aboard a train careening madly along a track, physicist Ralph Lapp has said, with no one in the engine and with most of the human race in the caboose, looking backwards.[7] Small wonder, then, that a well-nigh overwhelming sense of nostalgia seems to be sweeping the United States, accompanied by a turning away from rational thought. The "Jesus freaks" are only the latest of a growing phenomenon of a rejection of what science and technology have wrought. I do not find it astonishing for a mammal, however sentient, that has spent untold eons close to the soil to reject the chrome and steel, the glass and aluminum of the contemporary nation-state.[8] What is astonishing is the fact that it has taken so long to develop and that it is still a tiny minority who want to stop the world of "overskill" and get off.

Other social factors may be briefly mentioned, not because they are unimportant but because they in part are corollaries to the funda-

---

[6]PRICE, THE SCIENTIFIC ESTATE (1965).

[7]LAPP, THE NEW PRIESTHOOD: THE SCIENTIFIC ELITE AND THE USE OF POWER (1965).

[8]*Cf.*, Von Eckardt, *The New Urban Vision* (Mimeographed address before Am. Ass'n for Adv. of Science) (Dec. 1972).

mental idea that science and technology have had and are having an enormous impact upon the way that humans order their affairs. Included are at least the following: the industrialization of ever-increasing areas of the world; the growth of cities; and an exponential growth in population. The Industrial Revolution is now rightly seen as merely the first beginnings of the scientific revolution. Relatively recent in origin, it roughly parallels the rise of the nation-state as the characteristic form of political order. After beginning in the West, it is now spreading the planet over. Modern man is industrialized man—or soon will be, as Clark Kerr and Associates pointed out several years ago.[9] With the rise of industry came the movement to cities, to megalopoli that now may be seen as the most prominent form of local government (even though in the United States a given megacity is "governed" by multiple jurisdictions—some 1400 in the case of New York City). The 1970 census showed that the middle of the United States was being emptied, as people moved off the farms (which became corporate in nature) and from the small towns to more salubrious climates or to places where they could enjoy what are called amenities in today's world. Jammed together in sprawling antheaps, they pursue their *anomic* lives as members of the "lonely crowd," *fantasizing* about a mythical golden age of unlimited opportunity and unlimited space. Finally, the number of people alive today is greater by far than ever before in history, and even with the recently noted lessened birth rates in the United States (and perhaps elsewhere) that number will be significantly larger in the next 50 years. In many respects, population growth is attributable to efficient death-control measures, which keep more people alive longer (albeit often without their mental faculties) than ever before. That there is a direct correlation between size and density of population and the conditions of freedom (and of privacy) seems obvious to me.[10] That more control measures will come is about as certain a forecast as can be made. Their beginnings already are apparent, as will be shown below.

The growing trend toward more social controls on individual behavior is, in large part, a resultant of the pressure of people on resources. We have heard much in recent months, since publication of a book with that title, about "the limits to growth"[11]—to economic

---

[9]KERR *et al.*, INDUSTRIALISM AND INDUSTRIAL MAN (1964).

[10]*See* Miller, *Some Observations on the Political Economy of Population Growth*, 25 LAW & COMTEMP. PROB. 614 (1960).

[11]MEADOWS *et al.*, THE LIMITS TO GROWTH (1972). For criticism, see PASSELL & ROSS, THE RETREAT FROM RICHES (1973)

growth, that is. And surely that is one of the pressing problems of the day. I recognize that it ill becomes a citizen of the wealthiest nation in history to advocate that the time has come for serious thought to be given to limiting growth—but that is precisely what is being suggested. The first halting beginnings of a movement in that direction may now be seen in the United States. The major illustration is the National Environmental Policy Act of 1969, a statute which, as is becoming more and more evident, is basically inconsistent in its commitment to the "quality of life" with the Commitment of the Employment Act of 1946 to the "quantity of life."[12] Limiting growth means, for present purposes, more social controls, and it is that hard fact that I now emphasize.

The modern state is the interventionist state—the "positive state," one with affirmative obligations toward the populace. It involves a societal shouldering of a duty of constitutional dimensions, a duty to take action to create and maintain within the economy minimal conditions of employment opportunities and of the basic necessities of life. Exemplified in a broad range of programs, it is the American version of the welfare state. Its charter is the Employment Act of 1946, which, although a statute, in its importance may be said to have made constitutional law. Under its terms, it is "the continuing policy and responsibility" of the United States Government "to use all practicable means consistent with its needs and obligations and other essential considerations of national policy, with the assistance and cooperation of industry, agriculture, labor, and state and local governments" to create and maintain conditions "under which there will be afforded useful employment opportunities . . . and to promote maximum employment, production and purchasing power." It is, in short, a commitment to promote economic growth as a Good Thing. As has been said, this statute conflicts with the National Environmental Policy Act of 1969. But inconsistency in policy often is The American Way. I do not criticize it, but merely point out that at some future time some hard choices will have to be made between the conflicting goals of the two statutes.

There are at least five characteristics of the Positive State that are worth mention.

---

[12]The Employment Act may be found in 15 U.S.C. § 1021 *et seq.* (1970). The environmental act may be found 42 U.S.C. § 4321 *et seq.* (1970). *Cf.,* Miller & Davidson, *Observations on Population Policymaking and the Constitution*, 40 GEO. WASH. L. REV. 618 (1972).

1. *The change from a Constitution of "limitations" to one of "powers."* No longer do we believe in the Jeffersonian idea that "that government is best that governs least"; the prevailing notion, in the words of Robert Hutchins, is that "that government is best that governs best." The turning point to a new type of government came in 1937 in Chief Justice Hughes' opinion in *West Coast Hotel Co.* v. *Parrish,*[13] a minimum-wage case in which a statute was attacked as a deprivation of freedom of contract under the due process clause of the Fourteenth Amendment. Said Hughes: "The liberty safeguarded [by the Fourteenth Amendment] is *liberty in a social organization* which requires the protection of law against the evils which menace the health, safety, morals, and welfare of the people. Liberty under the Constitution is thus necessarily subject to the restraints of due process, and regulation which is reasonable in relation to its subject and is adopted in the interests of the community is due process." (Italics added.)

Consider that for a moment. Note that Hughes speaks of "liberty in a social organization" and also that due process, in addition to being a protector of human liberty, can now be used to restrain liberty. We have not seen the last of that new view of what historically had been called "constitutional limitations." Liberty in a social organization means that the individual *qua* individual will have to give way to societal or, at least, group "rights." And that, I put it to you, is what the Supreme Court has been doing in the past three or four decades.[14] Whether they realize it or not, the Justices have been articulating a modern version of Thomas Hill Green's concept of "positive freedom" and of collective well-being.[15] The notion of positive freedom, according to Green, reflected the rediscovery of the community as a corporate body of which both institutions and individuals are a part; the net result is that a concept of collective well-being or the common good underlies claims to private rights. The duty of government, under this conception, is not so much to maximize opportunities for individual freedom per se; it is "to insure the conditions for at least a minimum of well-being—a standard of living, of education, and of security below which good policy requires that no considerable part of the population shall be allowed to fall."[16]

---

[13]300 U.S. 379 (1937).

[14]*Cf.,* HORN, GROUPS AND THE CONSTITUTION (1956).

[15]*See* Miller, *Toward A Concept of Constitutional Duty,* 1968 SUP. CT. REV. 299, for a brief discussion of this.

[16]SABINE, A HISTORY OF POLITICAL THEORY 674 (1937).

Freedom, in other words, has become a social right as well as something of value for the individual. Green wanted to reunite the individual with the social order of which he is a member and without which his existence has no meaning. Individual freedom, as a social phenomenon, can be protected only by the legal and other institutions that the community can provide. "When we speak of freedom as something to be highly prized," asserted Green, "we mean a positive capacity of doing or enjoying something worth doing or enjoying, and that, too, something that we do or enjoy in common with others. We mean by it a power which each man exercises through the help or security given him by his fellow men, and which he in turn helps to secure for them."[17] I am not suggesting that the Supreme Court has openly embraced Green, but, rather, that his views that freedom can only be seen in the total social context are finding affirmation in judicial decisions nevertheless. Green, furthermore, does not speak of privacy as such; but there is much that is relevant on that concept in his views of human liberty.

2. *The advent of a system of overt economic planning.* To speak of planning in a market capitalist system is to speak in contradictions; by definition, that system is "unplanned." But "the choice of society today," Andreas Papandreou has recently argued, "is not between planning and no planning."[18] Rather, he goes on to say, "the choice is only among kinds of planned societies"—given "modern technology, and the quest for a rational order where man will control rather than be at the mercy of his social environment." He might have added what has been shown immediately above—that overt economic planning is now recognized in law, whether by legislative enactment or constitutional interpretation.

If that be so, then it follows inexorably that the State—as, in Gierke's terminology, a "group-person,"[19] or as Papandreou put it, "organicist . . . [with the] image of society as a purposive, willful whole rather than as an assemblage of individuals"—will of necessity require ever increasing amounts of data concerning all aspects of national (and planetary) life in order to be able to plan with at least minimum efficiency. I do not suggest that effective planning is now being done— President Nixon's confident assertion in his first inaugural address

---

17 3 GREEN, WORKS: MISCELLANIES AND MEMOIRS 371 (3d ed. 1891) . *See* RICHTER, THE POLITICS OF CONSCIENCE: T. H. GREEN AND HIS AGE (1964) .

18PAPANDREOU, PATERNALISTIC CAPITALISM 175, (1972).

19*See* GIERKE, NATURAL LAW AND THE THEORY OF SOCIETY, 1500–1800 (paperback ed. 1957) .

that "we have learned to manage the economy" to the contrary not-withstanding. Far from it. The evidence is only too clear that there is much that must yet be learned about techniques of social engineering. The point is that modern nation-states inevitably, unavoidably engage in such activities; and further, that there are definite consequences for ideas of privacy.

The need of the State for data coincides in time with the advent of a technological capacity to store it in computers after it has been gathered by increasingly sophisticated social and behavioral science techniques.[20] There is a compulsion to acquire more and more infor-mation about more and more matters, individual and institutional; but there is no concomitant means by which acquisition, storage, and use of those data can be limited to the absolutely necessary. At the same time, it is relevant to note the guiding principles of the present technological system. According to Erich Fromm, they include: (a) " . . . the principle . . . that something *ought* to be done because it is technically *possible* to do it";[21] if this principle is accepted, says Fromm, then "all other values are dethroned, and technological de-velopment becomes the foundation of ethics"; in other words, "feasi-bility, which is a strategic concept, becomes elevated into a normative concept, with the result that whatever technological reality indicates we *can* do is taken as implying that we *must* do it."; and (b) "the prin-ciple of maximal efficiency and output." Man is de-individualized and de-humanized. An industrialized society, the *summum bonum* of the modern era, makes man the servant, not the master, of what Lewis Mumford calls the "megamachine." Or as Zbigniew Brzezinski put it: "The largely humanist-oriented, occasionally ideologically minded in-tellectual-dissenter . . . is rapidly being replaced either by experts or specialists . . . or by the generalists-integrators, who become in effect house-ideologues for those in power, providing overall intellectual integration for disparate actions."[22]

3. *The alteration of the framework of government.* Federalism and the separation of powers have, by and large, become obsolescent con-cepts. Economic planning, Karl Loewenstein once said, is the DDT of

---

[20]See A. R. MILLER, THE ASSAULT ON PRIVACY (1971).

[21]FROMM, THE REVOLUTION OF HOPE: TOWARD A HUMANIZED TECHNOLOGY 32–3 (1968).

[22]Brzezinski, *The Technotronic Society*, 30 Encounter No. 1, p. 19 (Jan. 1968). *See also* BRZEZINSKI, BETWEEN TWO AGES (1970).

federalism;[23] and so it seems to be (despite plaintive calls for "participatory democracy" and "creative federalism"). Planning by government generates a need for unified and probably uniform economic policies throughout the nation. That requirement is antagonistic to the diversity inherent in federalism; it is also contrary to the fragmentation of power within the national government itself. The fifty states of the U.S.A. are anachronisms, a source of Senators rather than a repository of real governing power, on the way to becoming little more than those vestigial remnants of an agricultural society, the county governments. Within the national government itself, it is truistic indeed in 1973 that power has flowed to the Executive. No matter which party is in power, Democrat or Republican, the President is becoming a monarchical figure—a Charles de Gaulle, if you will. Until very recent times, Chief Executives have been aided in that raw power grab by a more than willing Congress, most of the members of which are quite happy to draw their paychecks and to act as ombudsmen for the constituents. Some contrary movement is visible in early 1973, but it is too early to predict that Congress has either the will or the staying power, or both, to stem the tide toward executive hegemony in government. And the judiciary, despite the American mythology to the contrary, simply does not have the power to do more than strike an occasional blow for human dignity—and with the advent of a Supreme Court dominated by Nixon appointees, it also does not have the will. Having long ago given up making ultimate economic decisions, it has more a ceremonial role than a position of power in the political arena. During Chief Justice Earl Warren's tenure, it tried to become an authoritative faculty of social ethics for the nation;[24] but Warren has retired, Black is dead, Douglas is old, Brennan is aging, and the bulk of the other Justices appear to agree, either tacitly or expressly, with Chief Justice Burger's tart observation in *Laird* v. *Tatum*,[25] the army-surveillance case, that the Court did not sit to review each and every example of Executive activity.

Roscoe Pound once suggested that a nation of continental size could be ruled in but one of two ways—either it had to be a federal union or

---

[23]Loewenstein, *Reflections on the Value of Constitutions in Our Revolutionary Age*, in Zurcher (ed.) , CONSTITUTIONS AND CONSTITUTIONAL TRENDS SINCE WORLD WAR II 191 (rev. ed. 1955) .

[24]*See* Miller, *Toward A Concept of Constitutional Duty*, 1968 SUP. CT. REV. 299.

[25]92 Sup. Ct. 2318 (1972) .

it had to be a despotism. With the decline and fall of traditional federalism, will Pound's observation become the scenario of the future? My answer is yes; and further, that the American form of despotism will not necessarily be viewed with alarm by Americans generally. Of course it will not be called despotism, for as George Orwell and, even earlier, Huey Long have told us, the human propensity for "double-speak" or "new-speak" will mean that it will be called "freedom." That in all probability it will meet little internal resistance is evidenced by the ready acceptance of wage-price controls in 1971[26] (something unheard of as late as 1936) and the relatively small public outcry at the terror bombing of North Vietnam ordered by Nixon in December 1972.

4. *The politicization of law and legal process.* Law, in the sense of interdictory rules, has little role to play in the higher reaches of American bureaucracies, both public and private. With public law becoming the dominant aspect of the legal system, law has become purposive and instrumental. The net result, as the well-known Washington lawyer Charles Horsky said in 1952, is that America is emphatically a "government of men, not of laws."[27] Kenneth Culp Davis, the guru of American academic administrative-law specialists, thoroughly documented the point in his 1969 volume, *Discretionary Justice.*[28] And Theodore Lowi, in *The End of Liberalism* and *The Politics of Disorder,*[29] has spelled out the same point from the perspective of the political scientist.

As a consequence, power rests in the bureaucrats, whether they exist in Galbraith's "technostructures"[30] or Meynaud's "technocracy";[31] and power is becoming increasingly centralized within the expanding bounds of the executive offices of the President. Lawyers abound in Washington, to be sure, but as *apparatchiks* rather than as professionals.

---

[26]*See, e.g., Comment, Administration and Judicial Review of Economic Controls,* 39 U. Chi. L. Rev. 566 (1972).

[27]Horsky, The Washington Lawyer 68 (1952).

[28]With the publication of the Davis book, attention in administrative law took a major turning point—from excessive attention to judicial review of the public administration to the manner in which the bureaucracy carried out its functions, usually in the absence of any court scrutiny. This is not to say that Davis has exhausted the subject, but he does point up a new dimension. *See* Wright, *Beyond Discretionary Justice,* 81 Yale L. J. 575 (1972).

[29]These books by Lowi, published in 1969 and 1971, spell out the shortcomings of "interest-group liberalism" as a way of settling public-policy questions.

[30]Set out in Galbraith, The New Industrial State (1967).

[31]Meynaud, Technocracy (1968) (first published in France in 1964).

Law has been politicized both in its making and in its enforcement —in what might be called the inputs and outputs of the legal system. Although not entirely true, there is enough of it to indicate clearly an emergent pattern. Bargaining among interest groups tends to make public policy (that is, law) the resultant of a parallelogram of conflicting political forces. At the other end of the pipeline, a similar process of bargaining often is evident in law enforcement. In criminal law administration, plea bargaining is now so widespread that it is necessary for the continuing viability of the system; at least that is what Chief Justice Burger recently asserted. He did not put it quite that way, to be sure; what he said was that if only 10 percent fewer suspects pleaded not guilty and demanded a jury trial, the process would break down. In any event, all too often bargaining takes place in law enforcement—in, for example, the consent-decree practice in antitrust litigation. That is plea bargaining in the executive suites, in the area of white-collar crime. Trade-offs are made and bargains are struck. Other examples include such matters as the guaranteed loan to Lockheed and rewriting its C5-A contract, and the way in which the government caved in several months ago to allow retroactivity in previously negotiated wage contracts. Much the same can be said when new policies are announced, as, for example, in "Phase III" of the new Nixonomics; according to the New York Times (January 13, 1973) that policy was a bargain struck between Nixon and George Meany, head of AFL-CIO. I do not wish to press this point too far, but do suggest that not only law-making but law enforcement, which is outwardly the clearest instance between business and the state, becomes merely an internal dialogue—a family squabble, so to speak—to the extent that bargaining exists in the outputs of the system (particularly in business matters).

5. *The blurring of the line between public and private.* That there has never been as sharp a line between what is purportedly public and what is private as the orthodoxy asserts is now becoming obvious. The point may be particularly seen in government-business relationships. As Robin Marris expressed it: "The industrial capital of western democracies is no longer divided into two classes, 'public,' and 'private,' but rather into three, 'public,' 'private,' and 'corporate.' The corporate sector likes to be described as 'private,' but this may represent no more than a desire to conceal."[32] That is not a new observation. As long ago as 1913 Woodrow Wilson said in *The New Freedom*: "One of the most

---

[32]MARRIS, THE ECONOMIC THEORY OF 'MANAGERIAL' CAPITALISM 13 (1964).

alarming phenomena of the time . . . is the degree to which government has become associated with business. I speak, for the moment, of
the control over the government exercised by Big Business. Behind
the whole subject, of course, is the truth that . . . government and
business must be associated closely."[33] So they must be and so they are,
then and more so now.

That business is government, furthermore, is a proposition that an
increasing number of observers are making. Insofar as American constitutional doctrine is concerned, a couple of Supreme Court cases,
plus a scattering of dicta in other cases and some decisions in state
courts, have held corporations amenable to constitutional norms.[34]
The trend, if that it is, tends to be more incipient than actual—although Alexander Pekelis' assertion in the 1940s that the next generation of constitutional lawyers will ever increasingly be concerned with
the dimension of private governments may well be on the way to being
validated.[35] Pluralistic groups are being recognized in constitutional
theory; a leading example is the clutch of decisions called the *White
Primary Cases*[36] dealing with the right to vote in primary elections of
the Democratic Party. Those cases involved the black Americans, and
stand as landmarks in the history of constitutional evolution—illustrat-
ing how a drive for increased recognition of group rights not only can
further individual dignity but also can have some important ramifications in other areas. They also involved the political parties; and
might be said to have "constitutionalized" them, for they are not mentioned in the fundamental law.

The Resulting Synthesis

The emerging politico-economic order that is being produced is
corporatist in nature; an indigenous form of American corporativism
is being created. As yet, there is no finished theory about the corporate
state, or, indeed, even a consensus that it exists. I do not wish to attempt an adumbration of such a theory as this time, but do suggest

---

33Wilson's book, which was a compilation of his campaign speeches in 1912,
should not be taken as meaning that anything substantial was done to curb the
power of the corporations. *See, e.g.*, WEINSTEIN, THE CORPORATE IDEAL IN THE
LIBERAL STATE: 1900–1918 (1968).

34Marsh v. Alabama, 326 U.S. 501 (1946) is the leading case. *See* Miller, *Legal
Foundations of the Corporate State*, 6 J. ECONOMIC ISSUES No. 1, p. 59 (March 1972).

35PEKELIS, LAW AND SOCIAL ACTION 94–127 (Konvitz ed. 1950).

36The leading cases are Smith v. Allwright, 321 U.S. 649 (1944) and Terry v.
Adams, 345 U.S. 461 (1953).

that a careful study of Eugen Ehrlich's *The Fundamental Principles of the Sociology of Law*,[37] and an application of Ehrlichian jurisprudence to the modern industrialized social orders would go far toward demonstrating the validity of the hypothesis of the corporate state, American style. Suffice it now merely to note that Ehrlich insisted, above all else, that attention must be paid not only to the positive law but to the "living law"—which, he maintained, is to be seen in contrast to that which is in force merely in the courts and with the officials. "The living law is that law which is not imprisoned in rules of law, but which dominates life itself."

Law, then, including constitutional and administrative law, is much more than the command of the sovereign or a corpus of rules. It is what important societal decision-makers actually do, a flow of decisions or a process rather than a static system. The black-letter rules are important and necessary, but only part of the picture. The living law provides the necessary legal nexus between state and social group necessary to support a theory of corporativism.

The corporate state, furthermore, is a collectivity—a "group-person," in Gierke's terminology—that is larger than the arithmetical sum of the individuals (natural and artificial) that comprise it.[38] In addition, government has drives and interests of its own to further; and since it has a monopoly on the legitimate use of force and on the peaceful settlement of disputes, it does further them. Despite the original conception of the American Constitution, we now have a government of powers rather than of limitations. And we have created a monarchical presidency.

Some of the implications of viewing the State as a group-person were stated by Ernest Barker in 1913:[39]

> If we make groups real persons, we shall make the national State a real person. If we make the State a real person, with a real will, we make it indeed a Leviathan—a Leviathan which is not an automaton, like the Leviathan of Hobbes, but a living reality. When its will collides with other wills, it may claim that, being the greatest, it must and shall carry the day; and its supreme will may thus become a supreme force. If and when that happens, not only may the State become the one real person and the one true

---

[37]First published in 1912 in Austria; translated by W. Moll and published in the United States in 1936.

[38]The concept has been recognized, perhaps inadvertently, by President John F. Kennedy, when in 1952 he said: "The public interest is the sum of the private interests and perhaps it's even a little more. In fàct, it is a little more." New York Times, March 8, 1972, p. 18.

[39]Barker, *Introduction*, in Gierke, *supra* note 19 at lxxxv.

group, which eliminates or assimilates others: it may also become a mere personal power which eliminates its own true nature as a specific purpose directed to Law or Right.

Six decades later, Barker's observations bear an uncanny similarity to much of constitutional law and politics in the United States. The State in the modern era has become an anthropomorphic superperson whose reality is as real as that of human beings—and surely as real as those incorporeal constitutional persons, the corporations. That is being recognized in governmental policies emanating from all branches of government. And the Supreme Court, even when it is making its rulings that appear to further individual rights and liberties, has really often been speaking about individuals as members of groups. Finally, as Barker has said, ". . . the State . . . [has] become a mere personal power." One has only to contemplate the theory of the office as enunciated in recent months by President Nixon to note that Barker was indeed prescient.

So much for prologue—over-long, to be sure, yet far too short to do justice to the complexity of the social context in which privacy as a legal norm should be viewed.

III. THE POVERTY OF THEORY

That American law—judge-made or statutory—has not evolved a complete or satisfactory resolution of the privacy question is obvious. True, there is a developing common law of privacy, mainly created by state courts in tort actions. True, also, the Supreme Court in recent years has discovered within the interstices of the Constitution a right of privacy that at times is protected. True, furthermore, the Fourth Amendment's provision against unreasonable searches and seizures is a type of constitutional commitment to privacy insofar as enforcement of the criminal law is concerned.

These are not small developments, and we shall have occasion in a moment to examine the latter two in greater detail. The point now is more basic: Despite this discernible movement in the law, there is a poverty of legal theory (and doctrine) about privacy in the United States. The further point is that it is only when the State itself does not feel threatened by assertions of privacy that constitutional law reflects a judicial desire to protect it. The word "threatened" is used broadly, as indicating something more than a danger to the peace and security of the nation but also to the economic health of the nation. It is with that in mind that I have selected several cases for consideration—*Laird* v. *Tatum*, the army surveillance case;[40] *Wyman* v. *James*, on the permissibility of a warrantless search of a welfare recipient's home;[41] the recent decisions loosening the curbs on abortion;[42] the *Walling* case, on the allowability of "fishing expeditions" into internal corporate records by government officers;[43] the *Reynolds* case, on the use of "executive privilege" in courts (a form of secrecy or government privacy);[44] *NAACP* v. *Alabama*, on the right of some groups to keep their activities from public disclosure;[45] and the 1972 case on wire-tapping.[46]

Although each dealt with a separate situation, I think there is a thread—admittedly dimly seen—uniting them. Thus we see seven situations: (a) protected privacy to abort oneself, coming at a time when official recognition of population pressures is escalating; (b) privacy of one's home not protected despite the Fourth Amendment, when the State's treasure was the issue; (c) refusal to allow a war protestor a ruling on the merits when admittedly he had been the object, as a part of a group, of army spying; (d) a corporation, despite being a constitutional person, being lawfully subjected to "fishing expeditions" by administrative officials; (e) the State keeping its records secret in a tort action against the government, in an exercise of executive privilege; (f) associational privacy for groups not considered to endanger the fabric of society or otherwise to threaten societal values; and (g) a freedom from wire-tapping that is more ostensible than real. I put it to you that the common thread tying these cases together is that privacy receives protection when it is perceived to further, admittedly often in an inchoate manner, the values of the State as a group-person.

So, if there is a theory, it seems to me that it should be constructed around a hypothesis such as that just suggested. There may be other ways to draw disparate judicial rulings on constitutional matters together, but none that seems as valid. Seen in this way, then, privacy becomes a concept much broader and much more complex than it is under such orthodox definitions as that of Professor Arthur R. Miller, who, after declaring that privacy is "difficult to define because it is ex-

---

40 92 Sup. Ct. 2318 (1972).

41 400 U.S. 309 (1971). For discussion and other cases, see Davis, Administrative Law Text 62 (1972).

42 93 Sup. Ct. 705 (1973).

43 Oklahoma Press Co. v. Walling, 32 U.S. 186 (1946).

44 345 U.S. 1 (1953).

45 357 U.S. 449 (1958).

46 United States v. U.S. District Court, 407 U.S.— (1972).

asperatingly vague and evanescent," then says that "the basic attribute
of an effective right of privacy is the individual's ability to control the
circulation of information relating to him."[47] To Alan Westin, the
leading American student of privacy, it is "the claim of individuals,
groups, or institutions to determine for themselves when, how, and to
what extent information about them is communicated to others."[48]
You will note that neither definition—they are essentially variations on
a single theme—is sufficient to encompass the breadth of problems suggested by the cases we have selected for review. Under neither would
abortion be recognized as a "right of privacy"; nor is there any recognition of the government's right of privacy or of the fact that corporations (surely a "group" or an "institution") may be treated differently
from natural persons. Finally, in choosing a handful of cases I am not
suggesting that they represent all the legal thought on privacy. The
cases were selected as illustrations, rather than exhaustive expositions
of a complex subject. I do think, however, that they are sufficiently
representative to form the germ of a theory.

Let us, then, repair to the cases, to the expressions by the Supreme
Court of the United States of its varying views on privacy. We begin
with the most recent—the abortion cases, *Roe* v. *Wade* and *Doe* v.
Bolton. Decided together on January 22, 1973, they are interesting examples of judicial decision-making, both in the way that status to
challenge a state's abortion laws was accorded without much published
argument and because the Court, as it is increasingly wont to do in
recent years, rendered a decision that went far beyond the immediate
litigants (and thus became a sort of "back-door" advisory opinion).[49]
But interest in judicial methodology is not ours; rather, it is in what
was decided and why and how. In as latitudinarian an opinion as the
Court has ever produced, one of President Nixon's "strict constructionists," Justice Harry Blackmun, joined by two other Nixon appointees
and all members of the bench save Justices White and Rehnquist,
sweepingly invalidated the criminal abortion laws of Texas and
Georgia (and, inferentially, all other state laws similar in content).
Why? Because, Justice Blackmun says, of an implied constitutionally
protected right of privacy:

---

[47] A. R. MILLER, THE ASSAULT ON PRIVACY 25 (1971).

[48] WESTIN, PRIVACY AND FREEDOM 7 (1967).

[49] The Court, throughout its history, has refused to issue formal advisory opinions; in recent years, however, it has tended to do so by making pronouncements
on issues and questions not before the Court in a given case. *The Abortion Cases*,
93 Sup. Ct. 705 (1973), provide one illustration; Miranda v. Arizona, 384 U.S. 436
(1966) is another.

The Constitution does not explicitly mention any right of privacy. In a line of decisions, however, . . . the Court has recognized that a right of personal privacy, or a guarantee of certain areas or zones of privacy, does exist under the Constitution. In varying contexts the Court or individual Justices have indeed found at least the roots of that right in the First Amendment; . . . in the Fourth and Fifth Amendments; . . . in the penumbras of the Bill of Rights; . . . in the Ninth Amendment . . . ; or in the concept of liberty guaranteed by the First Section of the Fourteenth Amendment. . . .

Then, after inexplicitly stating that those decisions "make it clear that only personal rights that can be deemed 'fundamental' or 'implicit in the concept of ordered liberty' " are included "in this guarantee of personal privacy," Blackmun goes on to say that it is to be found in the Fourteenth Amendment's concept of personal liberty and is thus "broad enough to encompass a woman's decision whether or not to terminate her pregnancy." Borrowing from equal-protection law (as Justice Rehnquist noted in dissent), Justice Blackmun then set up a set of "trimesters" when abortions may be obtained; it is only in the last trimester (the 6–9 month period) that the state's interest is sufficiently "compelling" to permit it to proscribe abortions. Finally, the Court held in the *Doe* case that the "privileges and immunities" clause protected persons travelling from another state who wanted an abortion in Georgia—again, an extension of previous law.[50]

Of interest also is Justice Douglas' concurring opinion, in which he set out several categories of rights he considers protected by the due process clause of the Fourteenth Amendment. He drew, *inter alia*, on *Griswold* v. *Connecticut*,[51] in which a right of "marital privacy" was found sufficient to strike down Connecticut's anti-contraceptive laws and on *Eisenstadt* v. *Baird*,[52] which said that "If the right of privacy means anything, it is the right of the *individual*, married or single, to be free from unwarranted government intrusion into matters so fundamentally affecting a person as the decision whether to bear or beget a child." This opinion is noteworthy for the attempt to delineate some of the contours of the constitutional right of privacy, something that Justice Blackmun left undefined.

What, then, is to be made of the abortion cases? What lessons can be drawn? First and most obvious is the propensity of a tribunal made

---

[50]Justice Blackmun's opinion interpreted the privileges and immunities clause of Article IV of the Constitution, rather than that of the 14th Amendment. 93 Sup. Ct. at 751.

[51]381 U.S. 479 (1965).

[52]405 U.S. 438 (1972).

up, in large part, of strict constructionists, to expand the Fourteenth Amendment quite beyond anything in recent years. Privacy is liberty from state interference, "the right to be let alone" absent a compelling governmental interest. But that right to be let alone in terminating pregnancies is a decision of one part of the duo that produced the fetus—nowhere is the would-be father mentioned[53]—and it is also in final analysis a decision to be made by the doctors. The potential mother is the one who is protected.

Why did this decision come when it did and in the way it did? Justice Blackmun's lengthy opinion gives few clues as to the reasoning from facts to conclusion; he neatly bridges the chasm by taking a mental leap. I have no objection to that as such, for it is in the grand tradition of opinion writing by the Supreme Court, but I do find it of more than passing puzzlement to dredge up sound reasons for the conclusion. Others may dispute this, but I see the decisions as being based on the "zeitgeist"; abortion is an idea "whose time has come," something that seven Justices recognized and then clothed their conclusion in the turgid language with which lawyers are familiar, language larded with history and other data. Just how privacy became a part of liberty is really not explained; nor indeed are the criteria set forth by which the Court finds new rights, hitherto undiscovered, in the interstices of the spare, lean prose of the Constitution. I applaud the decision; I find difficulty with the "reasoning." But more importantly, it seems to me to support the hypothesis suggested above—it furthers, to repeat, the values of the State as a group-person. The growing recognition of a population problem, a phenomenon that got powerful impetus with the work of Commission on Population Growth and the American Future,[54] has now been translated into constitutional law. The United States no longer requires an expanding population, as it did during the 19th century to fill an almost empty continent. There is a need to limit population size and rate of growth, else the dreary prognoses of the prophets of ecological doom may well come to realization. Manpower in the mass has become a handicap, the Second Industrial Revolution having not only supplanted much of the need for manual labor but also much of the requirement for

---

[53]There is a footnote in Justice Blackmun's opinion in Roe v. Wade, 93 Sup. Ct. at 733, that mentions the question, but indicates that "no paternal right has been asserted in either of the cases, and the Texas and Georgia statutes on their face take no cognizance of the father."

[54]The Report of the Commission, entitled "Population and the American Future," was published in 1972.

humans to perform menial mental tasks. It took the anonymous Jane Roe and Mary Doe to translate their very personal and very human desires not to be mothers into a national policy against unwanted children, embedded now in the fundamental law, and thus to allow the Supreme Court to articulate a policy of voluntary population limitation in the name of privacy. If one ponders for a moment just what is private about two people copulating and then a woman consulting her doctor and going to a hospital for an abortion, attended by the usual contingent of medical personnel, he comes away in some bewilderment. The Supreme Court moves in mysterious ways its wonders to perform. Let me not carp at a long overdue decision; but do let me shake my head in bewilderment as to how one can make such a decision jibe with orthodox jurisprudence or judicial methodology. And let me note, finally, how the private decisions of a woman can thus be translated into the common good; that is Adam Smith's laissez-faire economics translated into the most intimate of interpersonal relations, for, if Justice Blackmun is to be taken at face value, it is implicit in his decision that by some sort of Smithian "invisible hand" the public good is furthered. It is that notion of the "public good"—not articulated in the abortion opinions—that seems to me to have importance for the notion of privacy in the corporate state.

Wyman v. James is completely different, both in result and rationale. It is consistent only in that it, too, can be said to further the interests of the State as a group-person. There, even in the face of an express constitutional provision on the necessity of warrants before "unreasonable" searches can be made, the Court—again speaking through Justice Blackmun—determined that a welfare recipient could not lawfully bar her home to a social worker who wanted to inspect it. Those who receive the State's treasure must pay for it by not being allowed privacy safe from a search without a valid warrant. The reasoning, if that it is, is again suspect; Blackmun airily jumps from facts to conclusion without touching the ground of structured reasoning, a feat of mental agility which, again, is the habit of judges. The interests of the State in protecting its resources override—in terms of the abortion cases, they constitute a "compelling state interest"—the interests of a woman who merely wants to adhere to the ancient notion of the sacrosanct character of one's home. That Ms. James lost and Ms. Roe and Ms. Doe won is reconcilable to my mind only by the fact that each decision furthers societal interests. And the fact that the Court had to invent a right of privacy for the latter, and to ignore an express constitutional provision for privacy for the former, only adds to the wryly amusing nature of studying the flow of judicial decisions.

Laird v. *Tatum* can be similarly characterized. There, a protester against the Vietnam engagement brought a class action seeking relief against the Army's alleged surveillance of lawful civilian political activity, maintaining that the spying had a chilling effect on their rights of free expression guaranteed by the First Amendment. Not a pure privacy case, to be sure, but surely analogous, as Senator Sam J. Ervin said in 1971:[55] "this claim of an inherent executive branch power of investigation and surveillance on the basis of people's beliefs and attitudes may be more a threat to our internal security than any enemies beyond our borders." But Chief Justice Burger, writing for a bare majority, thought otherwise: The 5–man majority could not perceive that the issue was "justiciable" in a constitutional sense. In other words, no position was taken on the merits; Burger's opinion appears to suggest, however, that the remedy, if any, was legislative rather than judicial: "Carried to its logical end, this approach would have the federal courts as virtually continuing monitors of the wisdom and soundness of Executive action; such a role is appropriate for the Congress acting through its committees and the 'power of the purse'; it is not the role of the judiciary, absent actual present or immediately threatened injury resulting from unlawful governmental action." The meaning of *Laird* becomes clear when it was relied upon in a Court of Appeals decision in August 1972, *Donohoe* v. *Duling*,[56] in which police surveillance and photographing of demonstrators was said not to be justiciable.

Note, particularly, the technique of the Court in *Laird* as compared with the *Abortion Cases*. In the latter, there was no real difficulty in finding that standards of justiciability had been satisfied, not only for Jane Roe and Mary Doe but also for divers other females, completely unknown, who might at some time want to terminate a pregnancy. In *Laird*, because (so it was said in a footnote) Tatum himself was not chilled in his First Amendment rights, he could not assert that others were. Here, as elsewhere, it is manifest that the Justices choose their methodology, and their criteria for justiciability, to suit the case at hand. This is not a new technique, to be sure, for the revered Chief Justice John Marshall early set the tone for such obvious examples of judicial casuistry. What is important, furthermore, is that absent a

---

55Ervin, *Privacy and Government Investigation*, 1971 U. ILL. L. FORUM 137, 153.

56465 F.2d 196 (4th Cir. 1972). As Judge Winter pointed out in dissent, 465 F.2d at 202, this decision goes beyond the holding in Laird v. Tatum.

judicial ruling on the merits there can be no assurance that spying by the Army has ceased. For my purpose, I find Burger's opinion— joined, by the way, by Justice Rehnquist, who should have recused himself[57] (and if he had, would have meant a ruling on the merits for the Court of Appeals had found justiciability) —to fit neatly within the needs of the State as group-person.

But if that be so, what is one to think of the wire-tapping case, *United States* v. *United States District Court for the Eastern District of Michigan?*[58] There, three defendants charged with conspiracy to destroy government property filed a motion for disclosure of elec- tronic surveillance information. The government responded by stating that the Attorney General had indeed approved wiretaps to gather in- telligence information of allegedly subversive domestic organizations. No search warrant had been issued. The argument was that this was a reasonable exercise of presidential power to protect the national security, and that prior judicial approval of the search need not be obtained. (An earlier argument that the President had "inherent" power to wiretap was jettisoned, wisely it appears, when the case got to the Supreme Court). Not so, said the Court in a unanimous (8–0) decision. Warrants must be obtained before wiretaps can be placed in domestic security surveillance.

A victory for privacy, one might say, and certainly it is on first blush. But is it really so? Even if one looks upon it as a privacy de- cision and not, as Justice Douglas said in concurring, that "also at stake is the reach of the government's power to intimidate its critics," one would have to know more about how warrants for wiretaps are in fact granted before reaching a conclusion that domestic security wire- taps are a thing of the past. It is usually possible, and even easy, to find a complaisant judge who can easily be persuaded to issue a war- rant. If so, then the wiretapping case may be a surface victory only, hollow indeed unless followed by the bureaucracy generally. For to paraphrase Justice Douglas, concurring in *Gelbard* v. *United States*,[59] another wiretapping case decided a week after the 8–0 decision, judges could well "become the handmaidens of intentional police lawless- ness." Justice Abe Fortas said it well in *Alderman* v. *United States*:[60]

---

[57]In a petition for rehearing, Justice Rehnquist's failure to recuse himself was challenged, only to be denied in a unique memorandum from the Justice. *See* 41 U.S. L. WEEK 3208 (Oct. 17, 1972).

[58]92 Sup. Co. 2125 (1972).

[59]92 Sup. Ct. 2357 (1972).

[60]394 U.S. 165 (1968).

Wiretapping "is usually the product of calculated, official decision rather than the error of an individual agent of the state." This is not to denigrate the judiciary but merely to point out that judges, too, are human, and oft-times easily persuaded that taps should be imposed. As Senator Edward Kennedy said in 1971,[61] "warrantless devices counted for an average of 78 to 209 days of listening per device, as compared with a 13-day per device average for those devices installed under court order." He concluded that the government's revelations posed "the frightening possibility that the conversations of untold thousands of citizens of this country are being monitored on secret devices which no judge has authorized and which may remain in operation for months and perhaps years at a time." I go one step further: it may be impossible to validate, but I believe it valid to say that all too often judges authorize searches and wiretaps without any real inquiry into the reasonableness of the request or any subsequent monitoring of the manner in which the wiretaps are conducted. The all-too-well-known propensity of bureaucrats to lie or otherwise distort the truth leads me, furthermore, to the reluctant conclusion that even an assertion that wiretaps or army surveillance have been ceased should not be taken as the truth.[62] Professor Carl Friedrich has recently argued that "secrecy is eminently functional in many government operations";[63] if that be so, where better than in the scrutiny of activities considered to be dangerous to the security of the State?

The Supreme Court, in its treatment of the right of groups to remain private, lends some inferential support for that view. By applying a "balanced test" of First Amendment rights, it has found in *NAACP* v. *Alabama* a protected right of association that meant that the NAACP did not have to divulge its membership lists to state authorities, but in cases involving the Communist Party it found no constitutional barrier to disclosure. Such disparate treatment of groups might be rationalized on the notion that when a group is considered dangerous to the peace and order of the nation it loses its right of associational privacy, but if the group is pursuing other goals then its privacy is protected. This, to be sure, did not keep the FBI from wiretapping the telephones of the late Martin Luther King, but that was never litigated.

---

[61]The Kennedy statement is contained in a letter quoted in the concurring opinion of Justice Douglas in the wiretapping case, 92 Sup. Ct. at 2140.

[62]*See, e.g.,* LADD, CRISIS IN CREDIBILITY (1968).

[63]FRIEDRICH, THE PATHOLOGY OF POLITICS 179 (1972).

When the State *really* needs information, then, it can lawfully get it, despite the Constitution and despite any legal or moral notions of personal or associational privacy. As Friedrich put it, "In recent years, the destruction of privacy and the expansion of official secrecy, indeed the whole apparatus of the secret police state, have forced other states to adapt to the world of totalitarianism, to meet their competition with analogous weapons and thus to increase official secrecy and reduce privacy by the institution of police and investigatory methods."[64] In this connection, consider the *Reynolds* and the *Walling* cases. *Reynolds* embeds in the law the notion that investigatory reports of government agencies are not to be used in a tort action against the government, a principle that enshrines "executive privilege" into some sort of constitutional doctrine. That view got added impetus in January 1973 when the Supreme Court in *Environmental Protection Agency* v. *Mink*,[65] in which 33 members of the House of Representatives sought disclosure under the Freedom of Information Act of Executive documents concerning the Amchitka bomb test. No, said the Court, speaking through Justice White, in an opinion that upheld the Executive's claim of institutional privacy. It was, as Justice Stewart said in a concurring opinion, purely a matter of interpretation of a statute and does not involve the so-called doctrine of executive privilege. But surely it has constitutional overtones; and surely it permits the Executive to assert, through the statute, a broad-gauged right to keep its internal documents from the public and even from members of Congress. "Congress chose," says Stewart, "to decree blind acceptance of Executive fiat." Presumably this means that Congress could, if it wished, change the thrust of the Act; but the likelihood of that is too remote to be worth discussion.

Justice Douglas, who seems to be making a record in dissenting this term, maintained that *Mink* means that "the much advertised Freedom of Information Act is on its way to becoming a shambles.... The Executive Branch now has *carte blanche* to insulate information from public scrutiny whether or not that information bears any relation to the interests sought to be protected by subsection (b) (1) of the Act [concerning national defense and foreign policy]." That point of view is stoutly opposed by the majority, particularly Justice Stewart. Douglas ended his opinion with some pertinent language of Madison:

---

[64]*Id.*, at 190.
[65]93 Sup. Ct. 827 (1973).

"A popular government without popular information or the means of acquiring it, is but a prologue to a farce or a tragedy or perhaps both. Knowledge will forever govern ignorance: And a people who mean to be their own Governors, must arm themselves with the power knowledge gives."

Reynolds and *Mink* concern judicial proceedings. "Executive privilege," however, is at its height when data are denied to Congress, as often they are by the Executive, who asserts a right of institutional privacy. There are no definitive Supreme Court cases recognizing such a privilege. Many Presidents, however, have asserted it—and gotten away with it. The Justice Department's position, formulated in 1958, is that withholding information from Congress is a political matter. Said the Attorney General:[66]

> The President is invested with certain political powers. He may use his own discretion in executing those powers. He is accountable only to his country in his political character, and to his own conscience.... Questions which the Constitution and laws leave to the Executive, or which are in their nature political, are not for the courts to decide, and there is no power in the courts to control the President's discretion or decision, with respect to such questions. Because of the intimate relation between the President and the heads of departments, the same rule applies to them.

That bold and bald assertion of Executive power sets the problem. The Executive, as we have seen, considers that the people may be subjected to invasions of their privacy when deemed by the Executive to necessitate it, and even members of Congress may be subject to surveillance, according to the former Assistant Attorney General, now Mr. Justice, William Rehnquist.[67]

We need not tarry to debate the proposition. It is noted to provide the penultimate side of our privacy picture. The last is the *Walling* case, now a quarter-century old but still viable, in which the Supreme Court said that the Federal Trade Commission could conduct extensive investigations into corporate affairs to determine if a law had been violated; there need not be a showing of probable cause. In other words, the power of government to learn about internal corporate

---

[66]The Attorney General's statement was by William Rogers, now Secretary of State. It is quoted in "Executive Privilege: The Withholding of Information by the Executive," Hearings before the Subcommittee on Separation of Powers of the Senate Committee on the Judiciary, 92nd Cong., 1st Sess. p. 24 (1971). Rogers also said: "Congress cannot, under the Constitution, compel heads of departments by law to give up papers and information, regardless of the public interest involved; and the President is the judge of that interest." *Ibid.*

[67]In testimony before the Subcommittee on Constitutional Rights, Senate Committee on the Judiciary.

matters is not limited by the Fourth Amendment's proscription against warrantless searches. Well and good, one might say, and high time too. If government is going to regulate, it must have data. To get it, investigations must be conducted. It's a variation, in some respects, on *Wyman* v. *James*: The interests of the State predominate over the interests of the corporation (in law, a person normally entitled to constitutional protections). That's the point being made—although I might note that a strong case can be built, in my judgment, for the public's right to know about internal corporate matters as well (as Professor Willard Mueller has forcefully argued).[68] But the public is not entitled to "trade secrets" and "financial information" and other corporate data that may come into the hands of government, there being an exception to the Freedom of Information Act to that effect. That means that the State can know but the public cannot—an interesting proposition when one ponders its implications cast against notions of popular sovereignty and popular government.

Those are the cases. There are others, of course, that could have been selected. With some variations, I see in them evidence that tends to validate the hypothesis that I have advanced: Privacy receives protection in the main when the State's interests are at stake and protection of privacy will further those interests. Not always, of course, but enough. Such a statement cuts across the grain of an individualistic conception of privacy. Just as an individualistic conception of law is inadequate, so, too, is that of privacy.

IV. THE SHAPE OF THINGS TO COME

It is at least an *a priori* assumption—in all probability, even more so—that privacy is a value of the middle and upper classes[69] and also that it receives protection in the law when the interests of the State are considered to be furthered. Exceptions, of course, can be cited, but they are mainly in the area of the administration of the criminal law. Privacy, then, seems to be of the same order of legal esteem as the

---

[68]See Mueller, *Corporate Disclosure: The Public's Right to Know* (mimeographed; paper presented at Northwestern University, Oct. 1971).

[69]"Conceivably such sentiments [about privacy] are stronger than ever. This could be in part a product of affluence, privacy being one of the conspicuously-defended values of the middle-class way of life." Thompson, *Real Threat to Privacy*, The Sunday Telegraph, July 16, 1972, p. 20. (N.B.: I am not suggesting that quoting Thompson proves my point.) *See* Roiphe, *Things Are Keen But Could Be Keener*, N.Y. TIMES MAGAZINE, Feb. 18, 1973, p. 8, discussing a television series about a "typical" American family.

law of defamation, a law which in recent years has been torn asunder
by the Supreme Court. Since *New York Times* v. *Sullivan*[70] was decided in 1964, more and more people have been brought under the
umbrella of "public figures" who have a wellnigh insurmountable
task of proving actual malice to recover in tort from those who have
allegedly defamed them (as in *Rosenbloom* v. *Metromedia*)[71] or have
invaded their privacy (as in *Time, Inc.* v. *Hill*).[72]

One should not consider that the *Abortion Cases* greatly expanded
a constitutional right of privacy. By no means is it clear that those
decisions will be employed in other areas. The privacy, too, of groups
such as the NAACP, should be viewed against the lack of protection of
groups such as the Communist Party or the Ku Klux Klan. And the
Wyman v. *James* situation, which permits intrusion without a warrant
into the home of a welfare recipient does not find a correlative protection for the recipient to, say, correct errors in a social worker's file.
Take *Tarver* v. *Smith*[73] as an example. There, Mrs. Tarver was receiving welfare support; her caseworker prepared a highly critical report, which included derogatory comments about Mrs. Tarver, and
recommended that her children be taken from her permanently. After
being told by another caseworker that the file contained false information about her, Mrs. Tarver asked for a hearing to be able to correct the file. This was denied her on the basis that it was a confidential
and privileged document, internal to the state of Washington's Public
Assistant Program. The courts in Washington rejected her case and
the United States Supreme Court denied *certiorari*. Justice Douglas
dissented from that denial, stating that "The ability of the government and private agencies to gather, retain, and catalogue information on anyone for their unfettered use raises problems concerning
the privacy and dignity of individuals." So it does. But the question,
be it noted, was resolved *against* the individual. What is particularly
interesting about this obscure case is that the Court previously (in
1970) had decided in *Goldberg* v. *Kelly*[74] that a welfare recipient was
entitled to "procedural due process" before payments were terminated.
Although the denial of *certiorari*, in technical law, is not a ruling on
the merits, the net result is a person is entitled to a full-dress hearing

---

[70]376 U.S. 254 (1964).

[71]91 Sup. Ct. 1811 (1971).

[72]385 U.S. 374 (1967).

[73]329 L. Ed. 1966 (1971). *See* WESTIN & BAKER, DATABANKS IN A FREE SOCIETY 357–60
(1972) for discussion.

[74]397 U.S. 254 (1970).

before being cut off welfare but that the person cannot get such a hearing merely to try to correct a caseworker's file. That may make sense in the minds of the learned Justices of the Supreme Court, but surely there is something Kafkaesque about a situation in which as Douglas put it, "the petitioner has no rights under state law to a hearing to correct the reports even if they are total lies."

Enough has been said thus far to indicate at least two aspects of privacy: (a) it is a far more complex problem than merely the privacy (however defined) of the individual; and (b) that it is a fragile concept at best, one that will require nurturing in the law as well as a friendly soil in which to grow and expand. Will that growth and expansion occur?

To answer such a question is to attempt to peer into the dark future. One who does not hesitate to take such mental leaps is the supreme technocrat, Mr. Herman Kahn. In an interview published in 1972, Kahn spun out a "scenario" for the future in which he took issue with the "Club of Rome" theorists.[75] He thinks that world population will peak at about 10 billion in the 21st century—roughly triple the present number—although he suggests the figure might go as high as 20 billion. But, he says, "we will lose some privacy, some comfort, but we can get through. 'I was brought up in California. We were very poor, but we had an old car and we'd go off at weekends and get some privacy in the country. You won't be able to do that, and I'm sorry. But we can get by.' "

Agree with Kahn or not, and I for one am far from as sanguine as he is, what he does indicate is that privacy is a resultant of the social milieu—the cultural context—in which any given generation of people live. In order, then, to project the place of privacy in the future, one must be able to envisage that future in a social sense. My view may be briefly outlined: An urbanized, industrialized, crowded world, dominated by technology, and run by a technocratic elite. Already the contours of that "brave new world" may be seen in the United States.

For this discussion of the (possible) shape of thing to come, a useful point of departure is the "garrison-state" hypothesis of Harold D. Lasswell. First enunciated in 1941, Lasswell updated his judgment in 1965 by restating his view that we are entering into a world of garrison-states, a "world of ruling castes (or a single caste) learning how to maintain ascendancy against internal challenge by the ruthless ex-

---

[75]Kahn is quoted in Hebert, *Happily Into Oblivion?*, The Guardian (London), June 24, 1972, p. 10.

374 THE SUPREME COURT

ploitation of hitherto unapplied instruments of modern science and technology.".[76] That, it seems to me, is a model for a type of latter-day fascism—a term I use deliberately and consciously, fully cognizant of its implications—a model that ever increasingly seems to fit the U.S.A. When the means for repression are available, as in the technology of control, and there is less than a burning desire to further freedom (and privacy) as ends in themselves—as ever increasingly seems to be the norm—then perhaps at least tentative agreement may be reached with such sober observers as Claus Offe and Bertram Gross[77] that an indigenous form of "friendly fascism" is in process of creation. Said Gross in 1970: "We must accept the possibility that in this decade our America—despite all that we may love or admire in it—may have a rendezvous with fascism. And we must be aware that if fascism comes to the United States, as Huey Long suggested back in the 1930s, it will come under the slogans of democracy and 100 percent American-ism; it will come in the form of an advanced technological society, supported by its techniques—a techno-urban fascism, American style." (It is worth at least passing mention that Huey Long's son, Senator Russell Long (Democrat, Louisiana) was quoted in October of 1972 that he thought the time had come for a "benevolent dictatorship, if only temporarily.") Gross concludes:

> *In toto*, the warfare-welfare-industrial-communication-police complex would be the supramodern fascist form of what has hitherto been described as "oligopolistic state capitalism." Its products would be: (1) increasingly differentiated armaments (including more outer-space and under-sea in-struments of destruction) that in the name of defense and security would contribute to world insecurity; (2) increasingly specialized medical, edu-cation, housing, and welfare programs that would have a declining relation to health, learning, community, or social justice; (3) industrial products to serve warfare-welfare purposes and provide consumer incentives for ac-ceptance of the system; (4) communication services that would serve as instruments for the manipulation, surveillance, and suppression—or pret-tifying—of information on domestic and foreign terrorism; and (5) police activities designed to cope with the new "crime" of opposing the system, probably enlisting organized crime in the effort.

One need not subscribe to all aspects of Gross' formulation to be able to perceive in current governmental programs, some of which (as we

---

[76]Lasswell, *The Garrison-State Hypothesis Today*, in Huntington (ed.), CHANG-ING PATTERNS OF MILITARY POLITICS (1965).

[77]Offe, *Advanced Capitalism and the Welfare State*, 2 POLITICS AND SOCIETY 479 (1972); Gross, *Friendly Fascism: A Model for America*, SOCIAL POLICY, Nov.–Dec. 1970, p. 44.

have seen) have received judicial approval, to note that he has touched upon a raw, quivering nerve in the body politic of the United States of America. The essence of this new form of fascism—"friendly," as Gross terms it—is the rational, calculated use of irrational means and techniques so as to control or manipulate the populace. Historical fascim, as with Hitler and Mussolini, distrusted "reason"; it was, as William Ebenstein has said, "frankly antirationalist, distrusting reason in human affairs and stressing the irrational, sentimental, uncontrollable elements in man."[78] The modern version is narrowly instrumental and technocratic, operating within the interstices of the established constitutional system broadly construed and conceived. Society itself would be "managed," not merely the economy. In this development, the net result is that people will be "programmed" to want to "escape from freedom" or to fear freedom, to look upon the desire and need for privacy as an aberration. The prophet for the new (and possibly, final) age is B. F. Skinner.[79] In this connection, it is relevant to quote from the recent study by Alan Westin and Michael Baker, *Databanks in a Free Society*:[80]

> If our empirical findings showed anything, they indicate that man is still in charge of the machines. What is collected, for what purposes, with whom information is shared, and what opportunities individuals have to see and contest records are all matters of policy choice, not technological determinism. Man cannot escape his social or moral responsibilities by murmuring feebly that "the Machine made me do it."

> There is also a powerful tendency to romanticize the precomputer era as a time of robust privacy, respect for individuality in organizations, and "face-to-face" relations in decision making. Such Arcadian notions delude us. In every age, limiting the arbitrary use of power, applying broad principles of civil liberties to the troubles and challenges of that time, and using technology to advance the social well-being of the nation represent terribly hard questions of public policy, and always will. We do not help resolve our current dilemma by thinking that earlier ages had magic answers.

> Computers are here to stay. So are large organizations and the need for data. So is the American commitment to civil liberties. Equally real are the social cleavages and cultural reassessments that mark our era. Our task is to see that appropriate safeguards for individual's right to privacy, confidentiality, and due process are embedded in every major record system in

---

[78]EBENSTEIN, TODAY'S ISMS 105 (1954). *See also* EBENSTEIN, TOTALITARIANISM: NEW PERSPECTIVES (1962).

[79]SKINNER, BEYOND FREEDOM AND DIGNITY (1972). *See* Kinkade, *A Walden-Two Experiment*, PSYCHOLOGY TODAY, Jan. 1973, p. 35.

[80]WESTIN & BAKER, *supra* note 73, at 405.

the nation, particularly the computerizing systems that promise to be the setting for most important organizational uses of information affecting individuals in the coming decades.

That is the statement of pious faith, as well as a review of some of the policy problems of the age. What I question about it—and what Westin and Baker do not grapple with—is the "American commitment to civil liberties." If we are now in a positon, as has been suggested above, that that commitment is more formal than actual, more ostensible than real, then the technological means for the manipulated society is terrifyingly present. Present also, or at least apparently so, is something less than a burning desire to further individual liberties, including privacy.

What Gross and Offe are saying, with Alvin Gouldner, is that there is "a rapid growth and interpenetration of the welfare and police bureaucracies."[81] That sentiment has been expressed in economic terms by John Kenneth Galbraith, who in *The New Industrial State* spoke of a "principle of convergence" of industrialized societies (*i.e.,* the U.S.A. and the U.S.S.R.). Galbraith did not meet the problem of individual freedom, but, to repeat, Carl Friedrich has in these terms: "In recent years the destruction of privacy and the expansion of official secrecy, indeed the whole apparatus of the secret police state, have forced other states to adapt to the world of totalitarianism, to meet their competition with analogous weapons and thus to increase official secrecy and reduce privacy by the institution of police and investigatory methods." As nations, within themselves, lose their diversity and grow more unified and homogeneous, so it may be said that nations tend to resemble each other. Of necessity, those called democratic are forced to take on the characteristics of totalitarian nations, so as to be able to compete in the world arena. To the extent that such a formulation is valid, then freedom (and privacy, perhaps) tends to be a sometime thing, limited in time (to a recent few hundred years at most) and in space (to some of the nations of the West).

The planned society is, in sum, the state of things to come. Planning requires uniform, even unified, policies throughout the nation; and that, in turn, means, control techniques and devices must be imposed so as to achieve desired ends. It means, furthermore, that the State will require increasingly large amounts of data of all types and from all sources. That these two requirements will mean a diminution of freedom and privacy should go without saying. Some will think the price is too high and choose to opt out, insofar as that is possible in a shrinking planet. But most will tend to go along.

V. IN SUMMATION

We have travelled a long road, only to come to a dismal end. But it is dismal only for those, to use T. S. Eliot out of context, "with a set of obsolete reponses." For most people, the lessening of freedom and privacy will not be perceived as a loss, either because they never valued it in the first place or because they have been subtly programmed by societal and cultural pressures. As the Grand Inquisitor well knew,[82] man cannot stand the intolerable burden of freedom. Man is conformist, not individualist (as the American myth would have it). "The fear of freedom," as Lionel Rubinoff has said, "is greater than the desire for it."[83] The Inquisitor said that man requires three things —miracle, mystery, and authority. If it is these, rather than atomistic individualism, that drive man, and particularly man in a mass society, then freedom—and privacy, too—are of little or at least of lessening consequence. Skinner has Fraziov say in *Walden Two*: "Most people live from day-to-day.... They look forward to having children, to seeing their children grow up, and so on. The majority of people don't want to plan. They want to be free from the responsibility of planning. What they ask is merely some assurance that they will be decently provided for. The rest is day-to-day enjoyment of life. That's the explanation of your Father Divines: people naturally flock to anyone they can trust for the necessities of life."

By ending on that note of gloom and seeming despair, let me suggest merely that it would be wrong indeed to attempt to equate my set of personal values with those of people generally. If that is what people want—*really* want, as the Grand Inquisitor said—then it ill behooves anyone to say that they should be forced to be free—or private. "Individualism finds its roots," Philip Slater tells us, "in the attempt to deny the reality and importance of human interdependence."[84] We are still the prisoners of an obsolete ideology, that of individual-

---

[82]The Grand Inquisitor appears in DOSTOEVSKY, THE BROTHERS KARAMAZOV, Bk. V, ch. V. It is discussed in RUBINOFF, THE PORNOGRAPHY OF POWER (1968).

[83]*Ibid.*, at 124 (pagination from 1969 paperback edition).

[84]SLATER, THE PURSUIT OF LONELINESS 26 (1970) (pagination from 1971 paperback edition).

ism; we are in a transition period to some variation of *Walden Two*. In this transition, "we seek more and more privacy, and feel more and more alienated and lonely when we get it."[85] One need not accept that statement of Slater. I would cast it another way: Still intellectual prisoners of the ideology of individualism, we are alienated and lonely; a search for privacy will not alleviate that condition. In this age of collective action, we are beginning to perceive the need for community, for interdependence, for engagement and close interpersonal relationships. And the law is reflecting that development.

---

[85]*Id.*, at 7.

SELECT BIBLIOGRAPHY

The literature on the Supreme Court of the United States is enormous; the Court is probably the most studied governmental institution in the entire world, not excepting the presidency. Most of the writings, however, are technical, being of interest mainly to lawyers, and are not concerned with the High Bench as an institution and its role in American society. The bibliography that follows is selective, giving a representative sampling of the more important studies published on the Court in its institutional setting. Only books are included.

In addition to the works listed here, many of the footnotes in the text to this volume give pertinent references. Each of the following books has either a bibliography or extensive footnotes or both. For relevant articles, consult the *Index to Legal Periodicals,* the *Readers Guide to Periodical Literature,* and the *Social Sciences Index.*

Abraham, Henry J. *The Judiciary: The Supreme Court in the Governmental Process.* 3d ed. Boston: Allyn & Bacon, 1973.

Acheson, Patricia C. *The Supreme Court: America's Judicial Heritage.* New York: Dodd, Mead, 1961.

Alfange, Dean. *The Supreme Court and the National Will.* Port Washington, N.Y.: Kennikat Press, 1967.

Beard, Charles A. *The Supreme Court and the Constitution.* Englewood Cliffs, N.J.: Prentice-Hall, 1962. (Paperback reprint with an introduction by Alan F. Westin.)

Becker, Theodore L., ed. (with Malcolm F. Feeley). *The Impact of Supreme Court Decisions.* Rev. ed. New York: Oxford University Press, 1973.

Berger, Raoul. *Congress v. The Supreme Court.* Cambridge, Mass.: Harvard University Press, 1969.

— — —. *Government by Judiciary.* Cambridge, Mass.: Harvard University Press, 1977.

Beth, Loren P. *Politics, the Constitution, and the Supreme Court.* Evanston, Ill.: Row, Peterson, 1962.

Bickel, Alexander M. *The Least Dangerous Branch: The Supreme Court at the Bar of Politics.* Indianapolis, Bobbs-Merrill, 1962.

— — —. *Politics and the Warren Court.* New York: Harper & Row, 1965.

— — —. *The Supreme Court and the Idea of Progress.* New York: Harper & Row, 1970.

Black, Charles L. *The People and the Court: Judicial Review in a Democracy.* New York: Macmillan Co., 1960.

Boudin, Louis. *Government by Judiciary.* New York: W. Godwin, Inc., 1932.

Bozell, Brent. *The Warren Revolution: Reflections on the Consensus Society.* New Rochelle, N.Y.: Arlington House, 1966.

Carr, Robert K. *The Supreme Court and Judicial Review.* Westport, Conn.: Greenwood Press, 1970. (Reprint of 1942 edition.)

Casper, Jonathan D. *Lawyers Before the Warren Court: Civil Liberties and Civil Rights, 1957-66.* Urbana: University of Illinois Press, 1972.

Clayton, James E. *The Making of Justice: The Supreme Court in Action.* New York: E.P. Dutton, 1964.

Corwin, Edward S. *A Constitution of Powers in a Secular State.* Charlottesville, Va.: Michie Co., 1951.

Cox, Archibald. *The Warren Court: Constitutional Decision as an Instrument of Reform.* Cambridge, Mass.: Harvard University Press, 1968.

— — —. *The Role of the Supreme Court in American Government.* New York: Oxford University Press, 1976.

Crosskey, William W. *Politics and the Constitution in the History of the United States.* Chicago: University of Chicago Press, 1953.

Curtis, Charles P. *Law as Large as Life: A Natural Law for Today and the Supreme Court as Its Prophet.* New York: Simon & Schuster, 1959.

Elliott, Ward E. *The Rise of Guardian Democracy: The Supreme Court's Role in Voting Rights Disputes, 1945-1969.* Cambridge, Mass.: Harvard University Press, 1974.

Ervin, Sam J., Jr. (with Ramsey Clark). *Role of the Supreme Court: Policymaker or Adjudicator?* Washington, D.C.: American Enterprise Institute for Public Policy Research, 1970.

Frank, John P. *Marble Palace: The Supreme Court in American Life.* Westport, Conn.: Greenwood Press, 1972. (Reprint of 1958 edition.)

Freund, Paul A. *The Supreme Court of the United States: Its Business, Purposes and Performance.* Cleveland: World Publishing Co., 1961.

Funston, Richard. *Judicial Crises: The Supreme Court in a Changing America.* Cambridge, Mass.: Schenkman Publishing Co., 1974.

— — —. *Constitutional Counterrevolution? The Warren Court and the Burger Court: Judicial Policy Making in Modern America.* Cambridge, Mass.: Schenkman Publishing Co., 1977.

Haines, Charles G. *The Role of the Supreme Court in American Government and Politics.* 2 vols. Berkeley: University of California Press, 1944-1957.

Hirschfield, Robert S. *The Constitution and the Court: The Development'of Basic*

Law Through Judicial Interpretation. New York: Random House, 1962.

Hyneman, Charles S. *The Supreme Court on Trial.* New York: Atherton Press, 1963.

Jackson, Robert H. *The Supreme Court in the American System of Government.* Cambridge, Mass.: Harvard University Press, 1955.

James, Leonard F. *The Supreme Court in American Life.* Glenview, Ill.: Scott, Foresman, 1971.

Johnson, Richard M. *The Dynamics of Compliance: Supreme Court Decisionmaking from a New Perspective.* Evanston, Ill.: Northwestern University Press, 1967.

Kohlmeier, Louis. *God Save This Honorable Court.* New York: Scribner, 1972.

Krislov, Samuel. *The Supreme Court in the Political Process.* New York: Macmillan Co., 1965.

— — —. *The Supreme Court and Political Freedom.* New York: Free Press, 1968.

Kurland, Philip B. *Politics, the Constitution, and the Warren Court.* Chicago: University of Chicago Press, 1970.

— — —, ed. *The Supreme Court and the Judicial Function.* Chicago: University of Chicago Press, 1975.

Kutler, Stanley I., ed. *The Supreme Court and the Constitution: Readings in American Constitutional History.* Boston: Houghton Mifflin, 1969.

Levy, Leonard W. *Against the Law: The Nixon Court and Criminal Justice.* New York: Harper & Row, 1974.

— — —, ed. *Judicial Review and the Supreme Court: Selected Essays.* New York: Harper & Row, 1967.

Lusky, Louis. *By What Right? A Commentary on the Supreme Court's Power to Revise the Constitution.* Charlottesville, Va.: Michie Co., 1975.

McCloskey, Robert G. *The American Supreme Court.* Chicago: University of Chicago Press, 1960.

— — —. *The Modern Supreme Court.* Cambridge, Mass.: Harvard University Press, 1972.

Mason, Alpheus T. *The Supreme Court from Taft to Warren.* Rev. ed. Baton Rouge: Louisiana State University Press, 1968.

Mendelson, Wallace. *Capitalism, Democracy, and the Supreme Court.* New York: Appleton-Century-Crofts, 1960.

Miller, Arthur Selwyn. *The Supreme Court and American Capitalism.* New York: Free Press, 1968.

Miller, Charles A. *The Supreme Court and the Uses of History.* Cambridge, Mass.: Belknap Press of Harvard University Press, 1969.

Murphy, Walter F. *Congress and the Court: A Case Study in the American Political Process.* Chicago: University of Chicago Press, 1962.

— — —. *Elements of Judicial Strategy.* Chicago: University of Chicago Press, 1964.

Paul, Arnold M. *Conservative Crisis and the Rule of Law.* Rev. ed. New York: Harper & Row, 1969.

Rohde, David W. (with Harold J. Spaeth). *Supreme Court Decision-Making.* San Francisco: W. H. Freeman, 1976.

Rosen, Paul L. *The Supreme Court and Social Science.* Urbana: University of Illinois Press, 1972.

Rosenblum, Victor G. *Law as a Political Instrument.* Garden City, N.Y.: Doubleday, 1955.

Rostow, Eugene V. *The Sovereign Prerogative: The Supreme Court and the Quest* for Law. New Haven, Conn.: Yale University Press, 1962.

Schubert, Glendon A. *The Judicial Mind Revisited: Psychometric Analysis of Supreme Court Ideology*. New York: Oxford University Press, 1974.

Scigliano, Robert G. *The Supreme Court and the Presidency*. New York: Free Press, 1971.

Steamer, Robert J. *The Supreme Court: Constitutional Revision and the New "Strict Constructionism."* Minneapolis: Burgess Publishing Co., 1973.

Swisher, Carl B. *The Supreme Court in Modern Role*. Rev. ed. New York: New York University Press, 1965.

Tresolini, Rocco J. *Justice and the Supreme Court*. Philadelphia: J. B. Lippincott, 1963.

Twiss, Benjamin R. *Lawyers and the Constitution: How Laissez Faire Came to the Supreme Court*. Westport, Conn.: Greenwood Press, 1973. (Reprint of 1942 edition.)

Wasby, Stephen L. *The Impact of the United States Supreme Court*. Homewood, Ill.: Dorsey Press, 1970.

Westin, Alan F., ed. *The Supreme Court: Views from Inside*. New York: W. W. Norton, 1961.

———, ed. *An Autobiography of the Supreme Court: Off-the-bench Commentary by the Justices*. New York: Macmillan Co., 1963.

Of special note is a multi-volume history of the Supreme Court, published under the terms of the will of Justice Oliver Wendell Holmes. To date, three volumes have been published:

Fairman, Charles. *Reconstruction and Reunion, 1864-88*. New York: Macmillan Co., 1971.

Goebel, Julius. *Antecedents and Beginnings to 1801*. New York: Macmillan Co., 1971.

Swisher, Carl B. *The Taney Period, 1836-64*. New York: Macmillan Co., 1974.

More extended bibliographic references may be found in the following books:

Klein, Fannie J. *The Administration of Justice in the Courts*. 2 vols. Dobbs Ferry, N.Y.: Oceana Publications, 1976.

Tompkins, Dorothy Campbell. *The Supreme Court of the United States: A Bibliography*. Berkeley: Bureau of Public Administration, University of California, 1959.

INDEX

ABOUT THE AUTHOR

Arthur Selwyn Miller is the author of *Racial Discrimination and Private Education, The Modern Corporate State* (Greenwood Press, 1976), and *Presidential Power.*